EARLY MODERN MARITIME RECIPES

McGill-Queen's Studies in Early Canada / Avant le Canada

Series Editors / Directeurs de la collection :
Allan Greer and Carolyn Podruchny

This series features studies of the history of the northern half of North America – a vast expanse that would eventually be known as Canada – in the era before extensive European settlement and extending into the nineteenth century. Long neglected, Canada-before-Canada is a fascinating area of study experiencing an intellectual renaissance as researchers in a range of disciplines, including history, geography, archeology, anthropology, literary studies, and law, contribute to a new and enriched understanding of the distant past. The editors welcome manuscripts in English or French on all aspects of the period, including work on Indigenous history, the Atlantic fisheries, the fur trade, exploration, French or British imperial expansion, colonial life, culture, language, law, science, religion, and the environment.

Cette série de monographies est consacrée à l'histoire de la partie septentrionale du continent de l'Amérique du Nord, autrement dit le grand espace qui deviendra le Canada, dans les siècles qui s'étendent jusqu'au début du 19ᵉ. Longtemps négligé par les chercheurs, ce Canada-avant-le-Canada suscite beaucoup d'intérêt de la part de spécialistes dans plusieurs disciplines, entre autres, l'histoire, la géographie, l'archéologie, l'anthropologie, les études littéraires et le droit. Nous assistons à une renaissance intellectuelle dans ce champ d'étude axé sur l'interaction de Premières Nations, d'empires européens et de colonies. Les directeurs de cette série sollicitent des manuscrits, en français ou en anglais, qui portent sur tout aspect de cette période, y compris l'histoire des Autochtones, celle des pêcheries de l'Atlantique, de la traite des fourrures, de l'exploration, de l'expansion de l'empire français ou britannique, de la vie coloniale (la Nouvelle-France, l'Acadie, Terre-Neuve, les provinces maritimes, etc.), de la culture, de la langue, du droit, des sciences, de la religion ou de l'environnement.

EARLY MODERN MARITIME RECIPES

Circulating Knowledge in the Atlantic World

Lyn Bennett and Edith Snook

McGill-Queen's University Press
Montreal & Kingston • London • Chicago

ISBN 978-0-2280-2887-1 (paper)
ISBN 978-0-2280-2960-1 (ePDF)
ISBN 978-0-2280-2961-8 (ePUB)

Legal deposit third quarter 2026
Bibliothèque et Archives nationales du Québec

Printed in Canada on acid-free paper that is 100% ancient-forest-free, containing 100% sustainable, recycled fibre, and processed chlorine-free.

This book has been published with the help of a grant from the Federation for the Humanities and Social Sciences, through the Scholarly Book Awards, using funds provided by the Social Sciences and Humanities Research Council of Canada. Funding was also received from the Harrison McCain Foundation Grant in Aid of Scholarly Book Publishing, Office of the Vice-President (Research), University of New Brunswick.

Funded by the Government of Canada | Financé par le gouvernement du Canada | Canada | Canada Council for the Arts | Conseil des arts du Canada

We acknowledge the support of the Canada Council for the Arts.
Nous remercions le Conseil des arts du Canada de son soutien.

McGill-Queen's University Press in Montreal is on land which long served as a site of meeting and exchange amongst Indigenous Peoples, including the Haudenosaunee and Anishinabeg nations. In Kingston it is situated on the territory of the Haudenosaunee and Anishinaabek. We acknowledge and thank the diverse Indigenous Peoples whose footsteps have marked these territories on which peoples of the world now gather.

Library and Archives Canada Cataloguing in Publication

Title: Early modern Maritime recipes : circulating knowledge in the Atlantic world / Lyn Bennett and Edith Snook.
Names: Bennett, Lyn, author | Snook, Edith, author
Series: McGill-Queen's studies in early Canada ; 13.
Description: Series statement: McGill-Queen's studies in early Canada / Avant le Canada ; 13 | Includes bibliographical references and index.
Identifiers: Canadiana (print) 2026015072X | Canadiana (ebook) 20260150789 | ISBN 9780228028871 (paper) | ISBN 9780228029618 (ePUB) | ISBN 9780228029601 (ePDF)
Subjects: LCSH: Formulas, recipes, etc.—Maritime Provinces—History—18th century.
Classification: LCC TX162.3 .B46 2026 | DDC 640.971509/033—dc23

This book was designed and typeset by studio oneonone in Bembo 11/14.
Copyediting by Céline Parent.

McGill-Queen's University Press
Suite 1720, 1010 Sherbrooke St West, Montreal, QC, H3A 2R7

Authorized safety representative in the EU: Mare Nostrum Group BV, Doelen 72, 4831 GR Breda, the Netherlands, gpsr@mare-nostrum.co.uk

Contents

Figures

Acknowledgments

This project wouldn't have been possible without the hard work of the research assistants for the *Early Modern Maritime Recipes* project. Their labour combing through the catalogues, finding aids, and boxes of papers in archives around the region are the foundations of the project. They were also instrumental in creating the *Early Modern Maritime Recipes* database, photographing recipes, transcribing them, and uploading them to the database. So a big thank you to Danielle Arseneau, Annabelle Babineau, Karim Baccouche, Siobhan Carlson, Svetlana Ehtee, Shawna Guenther, Kala Hirtle, Bethany Langmaid, Laura Little, and Nicole Marcoux. Their work was funded by a Social Sciences and Research Council of Canada Insight Development Grant, with additional RA funding coming from the UNB Department of English, the Centre for Digital Scholarship at the Harriet Irving Library, and the Faculty of Arts and Social Sciences at Dalhousie. The Harriet Irving Library also provided the technical expertise for the online database and trained the research assistants in building it. Thank you to Jeff Carter, Camillo Villamizar, and Monica Fitzpatrick, with a special note of appreciation to Jamie MacKenzie (then the director scholarly technologies at the Harriet Irving Library) who organized the library's work on the project and helped us envision how the database could look. The database has continued to be useful to us in writing this book.

An equally heartfelt thank you goes to the librarians and archivists around the Maritimes who helped us search for or locate recipes in their collections. Their assistance in acquiring and licensing recipe images and their frequent willingness to provide them at no cost are much appreciated. Without the knowledge, patience, and generosity of archivists at the University of New Brunswick, the New Brunswick Archives, l'Université de Moncton, Mount Allison University, the University of Prince Edward Island, the Provincial Archives of Prince Edward Island, Cape Breton University, Dalhousie University, Acadia University, and the Nova Scotia Archives, this book wouldn't have been possible. We appreciate the funding we received to support the publication of this book. This includes financing from the dean's office and the Busteed Fund (Arts, UNB Fredericton) and the Harrison McCain Foundation Grant in Aid of Scholarly Book Publishing (UNB).

Many thanks as well to CBC Radio and to the many listeners at conferences and other venues who have shown so much interest in our work. Edith Snook would also like to thank, last but not least, Jeff Lilburn, whose continued support has included excellent cookery skills that have kept her well fed through the long process of writing the book.

EARLY MODERN MARITIME RECIPES

Introduction

Much more than simple sets of instructions, recipes are fascinating historical documents. This book aims to draw attention to some of the recipes that were created, copied, and printed in the eighteenth century in what national maps now identify as Canada's Maritime provinces. This place is the northern part of Wabanakik (the Dawnland), inhabited by the people of the Wabanaki Confederacy, and remains the unceded territories of the Mi'kmaq, Wolastoqiyik, and Passamaquoddy peoples. The recipes discussed in this book are from the mid- to late eighteenth century, when Europeans and North American settlers were shifting away from the French name for the space, Acadia, to using the names of today: Nova Scotia, New Brunswick, and Prince Edward Island. Thus the recipes that survive from this period created, circulated, and preserved knowledge in a space that was deeply informed by the ideas of settler colonialism, an ideology that Europeans used to justify coming to stay in Indigenous lands. For Lorenzo Veracini, the goals of settler colonialism around the world have been to "'tame' a variety of wildernesses, end up establishing independent nations, effectively repress, co-opt, and extinguish indigenous alterities, and productively manage ethnic diversity" – all while covering its tracks.[1] Because of early modern European colonialism, people, both enslaved and free, as well as plants, animals, diseases, and material goods moved around the world – a process that has been called the Columbian Exchange.[2] Eighteenth-century Maritime recipes tell the story of this movement and of settlement in Wabanakik, of settlers' need for food, medicine, and shelter, and for knowledge about them in order to be able to stay. The story of that search for knowledge – sometimes evident in recipes and sometimes hidden – connects the region to Great Britain, western Europe, Africa, the Caribbean, and the eastern seaboard of what would become the United States.

Historical recipes are of growing interest to historians and literary scholars, who have explored the many ways pre-1800 recipes in the United States and Europe (and especially Great Britain) have provided an archive for understanding processes of making and sharing knowledge.[3] While today we tend to think of recipes as providing instructions for food and drink, historically they were used to record and exchange knowledge that encompassed a wide variety of fields, including food but also medicine, animal care, cosmetics and perfumes, agriculture, crafts (like leather tannery or metallurgy), and household products. Recipes were used in domestic spaces, as they are now, but they also provided instructions for practices undertaken in professional contexts – for making medicines used by physicians, for example – and were used to share innovative knowledge within scientific societies. This breadth of usage makes recipes an inclusive literary form that was accessible to and created and used by people with a range of literacy skills, educational statuses, and occupations.

Recipes can provide insight into multiple aspects of history. They can be grounded in historical understandings of the natural world. Plant ingredients appeared in recipes undergirded by botanical studies of plants' properties by people in different cultures around the world, while animal ingredients belied cultural beliefs about what could be consumed (and what could not). Recipes can draw on historical knowledge of chemistry and thinking about substances and how they can be expected to react with each other and heat, while also relying on historically specific technologies. Medical recipes provide a window into ideas of anatomy and physiology that can be quite different from our own. In the period covered in this book, a recipe's ingredients are the end result of commercial exchanges, things being bought, sold, and transported, locally and across oceans and continents. The cost of ingredients used in historical recipes can document not just the socio-economic status of users, but also a person's or a culture's sense of taste – what was regarded as delicious, as well as what was tasteful or proper. Even beyond taste, the products that recipes produce can be a testament to the desires and fears of individuals and societies, including religious, cultural, and national values. Not always records of processes that were actually used, recipes can be fictions that articulate aspirations for what could be: what could be useful, tasteful, or innovative and a new way of doing things. Read as a form of life-writing, individuals' recipes can also document intellectual lives informed by experiment (attempts to make recipes or improve them), reading (efforts to collect recipes from a range of sources), sociability (the sharing of recipes among family, friends, and communities), and labour and caregiving (the use of recipes, including to tend to the self and others). Though today caution is merited in making them, with their sometimes-dangerous ingredients, historical recipes are interesting because they tell a story about knowledge, about what counts as knowledge, about who can make it and how.

Recipes are highly collaborative and portable texts. The processes and ingredients they recommended can reflect the opinions of experts, but they can also record the practices of family members and acquaintances. Hence recipes exist within networks of knowledge and can bridge the space between institutionalized learning and domestic spaces, linking universities, academic societies, and professional organizations, such as the Royal College of Physicians and the Royal Society, with kitchens, sickrooms, gardens, and shops. Pamela H. Smith argues, for instance, that craft knowledge, such as that used by the metalsmith, overlapped with and contributed to early modern science in using precision instruments, in relying on careful observation, trial and experiment, and in having a theoretical framework; craftspeople, she points out, thus developed a form of "'vernacular science' in which 'making' does constitute 'knowing.'"[4] Vernacular science is not confined to the work of craftsman. Looking at the recipe culture of early modern domestic medicine, Elaine Leong similarly argues that there are "deep connections in epistemic practices among various early modern knowledge communities," that the household shared with the laboratory an interest in the natural world and in valuing "experience and observation" in making knowledge.[5] Ranging through food, medicine, agricultural, and household practices, the recipes in this book are grounded in a similarly expansive approach to knowledge-making, displaying a commitment to experiment, to the exchange of knowledge about materials and processes across disciplines, and to the production of knowledge at diverse cultural sites, both within the household and outside of it.

Very few recipes discussed in this book are original. Frequently they are copied or reprinted from other sources, and that reproduction moves recipes across time, space, and culture. Even those recipes for which we have not found an exact source are probably not entirely unique; similar recipes nearly always circulated in print, the variations sometimes indicating innovations on the part of a user within a generally accepted practice. With their ingredients, sources, techniques, and proposed results, the recipes discussed in this book reveal aspects of what Maritime settlers thought about what to eat and drink, how to cure the maladies of human bodies, how to grow food, how to care for (some) domesticated animals, how to kill other creatures designated as pests, and how to build and care for a home, among other things. Some recipes strive for innovation and the future, while others look to the past. With sources in England and the United States, Africa, Asia, and the Caribbean, Maritime recipes document the movement of this knowledge around the world. Every recipe has a complicated story, and *Early Modern Maritime Recipes: Circulating Knowledge in the Atlantic World* tells some of these stories.

This book is an extension of the *Early Modern Maritime Recipes* (EMMR) project, which produced a publicly available, searchable database that collects all of the recipes that we have so far located in Maritime archives.[6] Although our search was wider, we found recipes in provincial archives in Charlottetown, Halifax, and Fredericton, in university archives at Acadia, Dalhousie, Mount Allison, and the University of New Brunswick, and in the New Brunswick Museum Archives and Research Library. The database, which remains a work in progress, is searchable by type of recipe, contributor (the collector or named source), the source type (print or manuscript), locations, and year, as well as by keywords, which can turn up ingredients, tools, actions, and the names of people and newspapers, among other things. Each recipe is presented with an image of the recipe (whether handwritten or printed in a newspaper or almanac), a transcription of the original version, notes on unfamiliar terms, and source identification. At time of writing, the database includes 585 recipes categorized according to several types – Agriculture, Construction, Cosmetic, Drink, Food, Household, Medicine, Miscellaneous, and Veterinary Medicine (a slightly more expansive set of categories than we use in this book) – with some recipes falling into two categories. "To Preserve the Face from Being Deformed by the Small-Pox," for instance, is categorized as both a medical and a cosmetic recipe.[7] As in many early modern recipe collections, medical recipes represent the largest category in the database, encompassing more than 50 per cent of the total number of entries, exceeding in number the sum of all other recipe categories combined, including those for food and drink. The preponderance of medical remedies may be because two of the most extensive early modern recipe collections preserved in Maritime archives were created by Loyalist physicians: William James Almon, who relocated to Halifax in 1780, and William Paine, who lived for a time in both Halifax and New Brunswick before returning in 1787 to Massachusetts.[8] For this book, we have selected a few of the most representative, original, complicated, or singular recipes to draw out their stories in considerably more detail than the database can. Every recipe is its own research project, and this book investigates the sources and circulation history, the ingredients, measurements, and techniques, and the uses and logics of the recipe to tell a particular story about eighteenth-century knowledge culture in the British Atlantic world.

As a companion to this book, the EMMR database can provide a sense of the range of recipes that come from a single source or location, the multiple ways in which recipes use a single ingredient, or the variety of methods used for creating a particular medicine or food. The EMMR database builds on work done by the Nova Scotia Archives' online collection, *What's Cooking: Food, Drink and the Pleasure of Eating in Old-Time Nova Scotia*, which collects images of food and drink recipes spanning a longer time period.[9] Moving beyond the culinary, the EMMR database offers more recipes from before 1800, is searchable in different ways, and draws attention to the full range of fields in which recipes were used; it also connects Nova Scotia recipes to the pre-1800 recipes that survive in Prince Edward Island and New Brunswick, whose histories are deeply intertwined.

The recipes studied in this book were circulating well before the first recipe books were printed in what is now called Canada.[10] The first printed recipe book was *La cuisinière bourgeoise*, an edition printed in Quebec City in 1825 of a well-known French cookbook. Printed in Kingston in 1831, *A Cook Not Mad* is the first known English-language recipe book, an Upper Canadian edition of an American cookbook. The first locally compiled recipe books, respectively published in Montreal and Toronto, were *La cuisinière canadienne* and *The Frugal Housewife*, both appearing in 1840.[11] In the Maritimes, the first locally printed recipe book was published in New Brunswick, where the 1871 volume titled *Secret Knowledge Disclosed; or, A Plain Way to Wealth* by Richard Moore, was printed in "Bonnie Braes" (an unknown place) and included recipes for farmers, druggists, mechanics, cooks, and others.[12] The first culinary recipe book to appear in the region was *Cuisine; A Compilation of Valuable Recipes* by the "ladies of St. John" (*sic*), which appeared in 1878.[13] In Nova Scotia, the first locally created recipe book was the 1888 *Church of England Institute Receipt Book* published in Halifax, and in Prince Edward Island, the first published compilation was another community church cookbook, the *Jubilee Cookbook* (1897) produced by the Ladies' Aid Society of a Charlottetown Methodist church.[14] Many of the recipes considered here also date earlier than the first American cookbook, Amelia Simmons's 1796 *American Cookery* published in Hartford. Well before these recipe books appeared in North America, however, newspaper printers in British North America and the United States frequently included recipes in their pages. From when newspapers first began appearing in Nova

Scotia in 1751, in New Brunswick in 1783, and in Île Saint Jean/Prince Edward Island in 1787, many of them printed recipes.[15] Eighteenth-century printers also included recipes in a variety of published almanacs, which provided on a yearly basis useful information for citizens, such as dates, astronomical calendars, economic data, and the names of notable people in government, military, or legal professions, amongst other things. The printed recipes discussed here are drawn from these newspapers and almanacs.

Alongside these unique early print documents, recipes also survive in Maritime archives in manuscript form, in the handwritten recipes preserved among recipe books, notebooks, letters, and loose papers in family fonds. The archive of Maritime manuscript recipes is, however, distinct from the better-known and more commonly studied British and American manuscript recipe collections. In archives in Britain, Europe, and the United States, many handwritten domestic recipe collections from before 1800 survive as books – with a substantial number of these being compiled by women.[16] While there are a few recipe collections like these in Maritime archives, most notably the recipe collections of Dr William James Almon (1755–1817), Dr William Paine (1750–1833), and Sarah Creighton Wilkins (1774–c.1849), much more common are handwritten recipes saved not in recipe books but alongside other types of writing, such as account books, letters, diaries, a memoir, a planting journal, notebooks, military order books, church records, and other personal papers. Also different from archives elsewhere, which include many recipe collections belonging to women and families, the handwritten recipes in Maritime archives from before 1800 predominantly come from English-speaking settler men. In these and other ways, the recipes studied in *Early Modern Maritime Recipes: Circulating Knowledge in the Atlantic World* are unique documents that provide insight not only into the daily intellectual lives of eighteenth-century settlers in the northern British Atlantic world, their interests in medicine, food, and building a home, but also into the circulation of knowledge in the context of colonialism. Even though the recipes do mostly come from the papers of settler men, they occasionally afford glimpses of the knowledge practices of more marginalized groups. In contextualizing a unique collection of recipes, this introduction first discusses the genre as a literary form to connect recipes to how eighteenth-century settlers considered the work of making knowledge. It then lays out the attributes of the surviving archive of Maritime recipes, which is deeply rooted in the region's political history, before finally examining the relationship between recipes and home.

WHAT IS A RECIPE?

The word *recipe* comes from Latin, the second singular, imperative verb for *recipere*, receive. It was, until the nineteenth century, frequently synonymous with the word *receipt*.[17] A practical, instructional genre, recipes have long shared some features (although not all of them appear in every recipe): a title, notations on ingredients, remarks on preparation, guidance on application and/or storage, statements of evaluation or efficacy, and sources.[18] With these characteristics as a guide, the definition of a recipe that we used in our research was an expansive one, encompassing both the short process descriptions that are most typical of the form and longer texts that take the process description into related genres. Thus included in the *EMMR* database and examined in this book are recipes proper, as well as prose instructions laid out in diaries and letters, which are distinct from recipes primarily in their more personal forms of address, and some longer experimental essays that use aspects of the recipe genre to argue for and explain a new or innovative process.

Recipes have a long history in Europe. In England, printers began putting out recipe collections in the decades after the invention of the printing press, starting with *The Boke of Cookery* (London, 1500). Because recipe books were popular throughout Europe, English-language recipe culture frequently included recipe books and individual recipes translated from other European languages; as Elaine Leong puts it, "Early modern Europe was awash with recipes."[19] Alongside recipe collections for a range of products and processes, early modern "books of secrets" also engaged with a wide-ranging set of topics but distinguished themselves from recipe books by promising esoteric and hitherto well-kept "secrets." The popular *The Secretes of the Reverende Maister Alexis of Piemount* (first published in Venice in 1555 and London in 1558), for example, included recipes for remedies to treat diseases and cure wounds, while also including instructions for making perfumes, confitures, cosmetics, skin care products, hair dyes, teeth cleaners, dyes, inks, and varnishes, as well as describing more arcane processes like sublimating mercury and staying young.[20] Working more in the genre of domestic recipes, Hugh Plat compiled *The Jewel House of Art and Nature* (first printed in 1594) to offer agricultural instructions, recipes for distillations, and useful tips on things like how to make timber last long in water, how to secretly carry gold, or how to make bad paper bear ink.[21] Medical recipes were an extremely popular genre and were used professionally by physicians, surgeons, and apothecaries, and by irregular practitioners in domestic contexts; medical recipes were printed in a variety of forms, often but not only in Latin, including in "herbals, formularies, didactic pharmaceutical manuals, *consilia* offering medical diagnosis and advice, and general medical compendia" – an approach that, Alisha Rankin explains, was influenced by "ancient and Arabic medical texts."[22] As a popular form of vernacular medical text, medical recipes were also printed for use by lay practitioners, as well as professionals.[23] Our book shows the use of medical recipes in professional contexts, for both Paine and Almon recorded numerous medical treatments and remedies from English and American sources alongside those they devised themselves. The single collection of French remedies may also come from a more professional medical context while Sarah Creighton Wilkins's medical recipes emerge from a more domestic practice (although some of her recipes come from physicians).[24]

In the early modern period, recipes were not exclusively written for and used by women, but some popular recipe books were directed specifically at female audiences, which made it an especially important genre for female readers in an era with low female literacy rates. One early work, John Partridge's *The Treasurie of Commodious Conceits, & Hidden Secrets* (first printed in 1573), included in its "huswives closet" culinary recipes, as well as recipes for medical remedies, fumigations (pesticides for rooms and clothes), sweet waters (perfumes), dyes, soaps, and sealing wax, among other things.[25] Plat's very popular *Delightes for Ladies* (first printed in 1600) included sections on preserves, distillation, cookery, and perfumes and cosmetics. Hannah Woolley became one of the first women to forge a career as a recipe writer, printing multiple recipe books, starting with *The Ladies Directory* (1661), a well-known collection of culinary, medical, and perfume recipes. The interest in recipes in all their forms transferred to North America, where British North American newspapers printed recipes well before recipe books began to be printed on the western side of the Atlantic.

Some of these European cookery books were available in the Maritimes (as they were in other parts of what is now Canada and the United States).[26] An unnamed book of cookery was listed for sale by an auctioneer in *The Halifax Gazette* in 1754, while notices of sale for British cookbooks – *The Art of Cookery* by Hannah Glasse (1708–1770) and *The British Housewife* by Martha Bradley (fl. 1740s–1755) respectively – appeared in *The Nova Scotia Chronicle* in 1770 and in *The Nova Scotia Gazette and the Weekly Chronicle* in 1772.[27] The estate inventory of Marie Marguerite Rose (Madame Jean-Baptist Laurent) (c. 1736), an enslaved woman in Île Royale (now called Cape Breton), indicates that she owned a French cookbook, *Le cuisinier royale et bourgeois* (1691) by François Massialot (1660?–1733), a cook in French aristocratic houses.[28] Marie Marguerite Rose had been brought to Louisbourg from Africa by a French army officer. In her late thirties, she was emancipated and subsequently married Jean Baptiste Laurent, a Mi'kmaw man, with whom she ran an inn – the recipe book in their possession.[29] It is important to note that neither our book nor the *Early Modern Maritime Recipes* database attempts to account for the thousands of recipes like these that were printed elsewhere and read in the Maritimes, except, crucially, in so far as the recipes were reprinted in the newspapers of Nova Scotia, New Brunswick, and Prince Edward Island, or were copied by hand and preserved in personal papers. With printed recipes, our focus is on recipes printed in the region, but these had often already appeared in print in Britain, the American colonies, or, after the American Revolution, in the United States in books or newspapers – sometimes with attributions, sometimes without. This kind of copying, some of which we might call plagiarism today, is a longstanding feature of European recipe culture that continued in the Americas (to offer just one example, *Tiffany's Upper-Canada Almanac for the Year 1802* reproduced a number of recipes from *The Frugal Housewife* by Susannah Carter, which had first been printed in London in 1742).[30]

The features of the recipe genre – the title, the ingredients, and process descriptions – are grounded in the knowledge creation processes with which the form is engaged. Most recipes in this book have titles that explain what the recipe is for. This might include a process ("To Pickle Berwick Salmon," "To Brew"), a product ("Receipt to make HESSIAN SOUP," "Ginger Wine"), or a problem ("A Receipt for the Bite of a Mad Dog" or "Methods of Treatment to be used for the Recovery of Persons apparently dead by drowning"). Some recipe titles offer evaluative statements to recommend them, as in "An Admirable Receipt for a Consumption," or with the words like *proved* or *approved*, as in "An approved Remedy for Nephritic Disorders." The language of proof can also appear at the end of a recipe, as in statements like "I find from experience …," which can assess the experiment and endorse the recipe's efficaciousness from experience.[31] Recipe titles also frequently document names, which creates a concept of recipe authorship that, as Michelle DiMeo explains, should encompass the recipe originator (the inventor of the technique) or donor (the one who gave it to the collector).[32] Thus recipes can have names like "Mr. Cook's Remedy for a Cough" or "Mrs. Clarks Receipt For strengthening," where Cook and Clark might have invented the technique or they may just have shared it with the collector. Occasionally recipes may be published anonymously, as with the Hessian Soup recipe sent to a newspaper by "A Friend to the Poor." Where recipes name an author in these ways, whether as originator or donor, the name supports the recipe's authority, helping to establish that it is offering effective, trustworthy knowledge. Names in recipes might thus be seen as a form of witnessing, a practice that Steven Shapin points to as important in early modern science in turning belief into "proper knowledge" shared by a collective; in science, the individual philosopher could not make knowledge in isolation but had to be witnessed and spoken to by trustworthy observers.[33] Elaine Leong and Sara Pennell bring Shapin's emphasis on trustworthiness to bear on recipe culture when they argue that, with early modern recipes, "their realizable value was tied up with the trustworthiness of the relationship on which the exchange [of recipes] was based"; this trustworthiness was assessed through the donor's "social, economical, and political" position, by family and social relationships, and by profession (ministers and apothecaries could be trustworthy on medicine, as could physicians, while farriers could be trusted sources of veterinary medical information).[34] Thus, when recipe names document kinship relations, supporting a recipe's value in a note like "from Aunt Margaret's American Cooking Book," the aunt's name enhances trust in the recipe. So, too, the "Friend to the Poor," who is, it is suggested, driven by altruism and community care. The names in recipe titles also gesture to expertise, as in "By M. Parmentier, Member of the College of Pharmacy at Paris" or the "Bath Society for the Encouragement of Agriculture, Arts, Manufactures, and Commerce." Another route to securing a recipe's authority is class status, which can also be marked in recipe titles, as in "Count Rumford, Hasty-Pudding" and "Lady Eleanora Dundas's Recipe." "S^{r}. W^{m}. Pepperels Housekeeper Indian Pudding" likewise identifies Pepperrell's status as a baronet, without naming the non-elite housekeeper, but her household role, that she is a housekeeper and thus has experience in cookery, adds to the recipe's trustworthiness, alongside Pepperrell's elite identity. The authority of the recipe – supported with gestures to proof and with names – was important because recipes were a product of a culture of experiment, where trial, observation, and outcomes were important, in food, as in medicine and other matters. This culture of experiment is on full display in the "Cure for Death by Drowning," which ends with promises to pay rewards to those who attempt the methods and write in to the Society proposing the techniques with evidence of effectiveness.

Further to the way that recipes offer a highly collaborative form for creating and conveying knowledge are the ways that recipes document the multiple relationships people can have with a recipe. Alongside recipe authors (those named who could be the inventor, the donor, or even the collector), recipes can offer traces of the thoughts and practices of recipe makers. Makers can become commentators when they record their responses, perhaps indicating approval or making changes, sometimes in the process of copying.[35] Scribes or copyists write recipes down, while collectors or compilers gather recipes together, collecting them from their social networks or their reading. Collectors may also have been the copyists actually doing the writing, but collector and copyist could also be different people if the compiler happened to work with a scribe or if the compiler collected recipes from multiple copyists. Although the manuscript recipes discussed in this book carry few direct traces of such practices, pre-1800 recipes were also exchanged as gifts bestowed on the occasion of marriage or in pursuit of patronage or as bequests made in wills.[36] A recipe, then, was rarely the production or possession of a single individual; rather, recipes put on display complex networks of social relationships used in knowledge creation. It may be true, as Henry Notaker says of some early modern recipes, that "Originality was not an aim in itself; it was more important to imitate and transmit the work of one's predecessors."[37] But the story told by the recipes compiled here is somewhat more complicated, first because the transmission of knowledge seldom meant perfect reproduction. Not only could the names attached to a recipe be lost or changed through reproduction, but even the recipe itself could also change in a kind of early modern "telephone game" that is common in recipe culture. As Michelle DiMeo explains, "when comparing recipes of a similar or the same name across early modern recipe books, the variations between quantities, ingredients, and syntax are diverse, and it is rare to find two or three recipes that are exactly the same across multiple books."[38] Even more, some recipes do present themselves as innovations, in part to capture changing fashions, but also to engage with a conceptions of scientific and social progress.[39] As "Remarks on the Manufacturing of Maple Sugar" puts it, "He who enables another to obtain any necessary of life, either cheaper or more independently than heretofore, adds a new source of happiness to man." In this way, eighteenth-century settler culture imagined new recipes contributing to the progress of knowledge.

Alongside positioning recipes within communities, the key components of a recipe were and are process descriptions intended to turn readers into makers. Unlike the modern recipe with its established conventions, however, few of the eighteenth-century recipes considered here set out the list of ingredients at the beginning and then follow up with fulsome, exact directions. Rather, recipes tend to start with the process description itself, which is typically chronological (often starting with the verb *take*), and rely on action verbs that explain what to do with the ingredients. Process descriptions also often left out important information, like quantities, relying instead on readers' tacit knowledge of what to do.[40] Sara Pennell and Michelle DiMeo suggest that these omissions occur because an historical recipe is more of an *aide-mémoire*, less a guide to replication than an assistance to the maker in using or remembering his or her own existing knowledge in the field.[41] In a colonial context, this tacit knowledge is frequently rooted in European practices.

The trickiest components of historical recipes for modern readers to understand are likely eighteenth-century measurements of volume and weight, which were not yet standardized even though some of the names of measures are familiar, like ounces, pounds, and gallons. Many European units of weight were rooted in units named during the period of the Roman Empire, but by the eighteenth century, the value of these weights varied across Europe: the weight of a pound, for instance, ranged from 0.4079 kilograms for the *livre* in Marseilles to 0.4960 kilograms for the *pund* in Denmark.[42] Liquid measures could vary even more than weights.[43] Even within Britain, the values of weights and measures differed across counties.[44] Different commodities used different measures, as well, so that a wine gallon used for oil and honey and other liquids (measuring 231 cubic inches or 4 quarts), standardized in 1707, differed from the corn or grain gallon (268.8 cubic inches) and from the beer or ale gallon (282 cubic inches).[45] Although a pint was then, as now, ⅛ of a gallon, and a quart 2 pints, the eighteenth century also had other measures of volume for liquids, likely less familiar today: a gill (¼ pint), a hogshead (48 ale gallons, 63 wine gallons), a pipe (2 hogsheads), a barrel (31.5 wine gallons), and a tun (252 wine gallons). These values, too, changed with different commodities, so, for instance, a barrel of beer was 34 gallons; of butter or soap, 32 gallons; and of herring or eels, 30 gallons; while a barrel of salmon was 42 gallons.[46] Pounds and ounces were used to measure dry goods, primarily with the avoirdupois system, although the Troy system was used for measuring gold and the apothecary system for medicines.[47] The avoirdupois ounce was 437½ grains (the smallest unit of weight) or 1/16 of an avoirdupois pound, while a hundred weight (a larger unit of weight) was 112 pounds. In the apothecary system, used in some medical recipes, an ounce was instead the equivalent of 1/12 of an apothecary's pound, 8 drachms or 24 scruples, with a drachm (or dram) being 3 scruples and a scruple being 20 grains.[48]

Colonies tended to use the same measures as the capital of the colonizing state, so the colonies of British North America generally patterned themselves after measurements used in London.[49] What is now the Maritimes was subject to two colonial powers, both France and England, with the result that when the British moved to establish control of the formerly French colony they also changed the measuring systems. Bruce Curtis describes the history of weights and measures in

Canada as a "messy coexistence of English and French metrological practices," although after 1759, the governors of British North America sought to introduce British standards. Britain regularized its weights and measures further in 1824, when it moved to the imperial system, which established the gallon at 277.5 cubic inches and the bushel at 8 gallons and remains in use today. After Confederation, Canada adopted the imperial system with its first Weights and Measures Act in 1873.[50] Evidence of this variability appears in one of the French medical recipes in the book that calls for five quarts of white wine, "Mesure d'angleterre." The United States took a different direction. Although the thirteen colonies had also started out using British measures, in 1789 the Constitution gave Congress the power to set standards for weights and measures, a power it would finally use in 1832 when legislation established the gallon at 231 cubic inches (a return to the wine gallon, a rejection of Britain's imperial gallon).

Recipes also use many unofficial measurements to convey their instructions. Temperature is measured informally, not with references to degrees, as now, but to fires that are slow, low, or smart. Some instructions for measurement of volume rely entirely on tacit knowledge, prescribing amounts like "some" or "a little" or "a large piece." One recipe discussed in this book indicates that one should "Mix as much water as you think it will require," an explicit reference to the maker's understanding of the process. Some instructions become more specific through turning to household objects – a spoon, a glass, a kettle, or a pail – for measures, but again, the maker must, from experience, cope with the variety in sizes of glasses and pails. Measurements could be made in more practical ways as well, as with a recipe for pickle that suggests adding enough salt to water that the pickle will be "strong enough to bear an Egg." Cost could also become a measurement – a "pennyworth" – as could comparisons to other well-known materials, like the size of a walnut or a piece of money or the thickness of pudding or of buttermilk. Culinary and medical recipes also specify amounts of ingredients with reference to the taste of the maker, using language like "season it to your taste," or that of the patient, as in the instruction to add wine and sugar "to the palate & strength of the patient." Especially when the recipe is directed towards feeding the poor, recipes can also include costs, for ingredients and for the energy required to cook them. That one recipe for making potato bread acknowledges that the "abstract" "cannot wholly give an idea of the process" and that those who want to make the bread "must be obliged to have recourse to their own experience" is generally characteristic of recipes. In the practical instructions of recipes and their explanations of processes for making or doing, recipes are also systems of knowledge, social relationships, personal experiences, experiments, aspirations, and the knowledge of recipe makers, donors, and inventors.

THE ARCHIVE

The archive of recipes in the region we now call the Maritimes is corralled by its history of settler colonialism, as Europeans came to claim Indigenous territories, and by imperialist conflicts between the French and British. The region was first and remains the territory of the Mi'kmaq, Wolastoqiyik, and Passamaquoddy peoples. Mi'kma'ki comprises seven regions: Kespe'k ("last water or land"), Siknikt ("a drainage place"), Epekwitk aq Piktuk ("lying in the water place" and the "explosive place"), Kespukwitk ("last flow"), Sipekne'katik ("wild potato area"), Eskikewa'kik ("skin dresser's territory"), and Unama'ki aq Ktaqmkuk ("foggy lands" and "lands across the water").[51] Wolastokuk, the traditional territory of the Wolastoqiyik, stretches along the Wolastoq River (now on maps as the Saint John River).[52] And to the west of Wolastokuk, along the St Croix River, is Passamaquoddy territory. When they arrived, the French called much of this space Acadia, which the British renamed Nova Scotia. New Brunswick became a separate colony from Nova Scotia in 1784, while Île Saint Jean/St John's Island was renamed Prince Edward Island in 1799. Île Royale/Cape Breton finally became part of Nova Scotia in 1820. It is not our wish here to give a complete history of the region, a job more ably done by historians like David Bell, Margaret Conrad, Naomi Griffiths, John Hiller, Elizabeth Mancke, Daniel Paul, John Reid, Harvey Amani Whitfield, and many others.[53] The brief history provided here aims only to explain the grounds on which the recipe archive was created. Exploring the connections between New England and the Maritime provinces, Elizabeth Mancke sees in the region in the eighteenth century "intersecting and competing, 'spaces of power,'" where "economic, political, cultural, or military" systems were multiple and contested.[54] With no clear centres of colonial power exerting control over the region, there were instead claimants whose spheres of interest could overlap.[55] This diverse and shifting social, cultural, and political context is evident in the pre-1800 recipe archive.

Indigenous peoples of the Wabanaki Confederacy, like Indigenous peoples across the Americas, have their own knowledge systems, their own approach to food, medicine, and shelter, and to sharing that knowledge with others. As Daniel Paul explains, "Prior to European settlement the Mi'kmaq lived in countries that had developed a culture founded upon three principles: the supremacy of the Great Spirit, respect for Mother Earth, and people power ... As a result they enjoyed the benefits of living in a harmonious, healthy, prosperous and peaceful social environment."[56] European explorers, traders, and fisherman first made contact with Indigenous peoples of the region in the sixteenth century, trading goods, especially furs, and fishing, and learning from Indigenous peoples about the geography, food, medicines, and transportation routes – but also spreading diseases. Smallpox killed many Indigenous people throughout the Americas and weakened Indigenous communities even before Europeans attempted to establish settlements in the seventeenth century.[57] Although the Mi'kmaq were still in control of their own territories, the French claimed the territory called Mi'kma'ki and Wolastokuk – and more – as a colony, La Cadie/Acadia, in 1603 and established a fort, Port Royal, in 1605. The colony did not thrive, but the region did persist as French territory in European law for over a century. Marking the weak hold of the French in the 1620s, King James I of Great Britain granted a Scotsman, Sir William Alexander, much of Mi'kma'ki, and he attempted to establish another colony at Port Royal, although it was returned to the French again in 1632. Migration from France would increase through the seventeenth century, and Acadian communities developed with economies rooted in the fur trade, fishing, and agriculture.[58]

By the beginning of the eighteenth century, there were Acadian communities on Île Royale, along the Bay of Fundy, and the Petitcodiac and Memramcook rivers, and after 1711 on Île Saint Jean.[59] When the Treaty of Utrecht was signed in 1713 to end a European war – a war that had also seen fighting in North America, with the Wabanaki Confederacy aligned with the French against the British – the French conceded much of Acadia to the British, except Île Royale and Île Saint Jean. The peoples of the Wabanaki Confederacy were not signatories to this treaty despite its supposed reassignment of their land, their continued control of much of it, and their position as the majority population.[60] Ending a three-year war between people of the Wabanaki Confederacy and the British, the first treaties were signed in 1725. They included articles of peace and promises from the British that "Said Chiefs & their Respective Tribes all marks of Favour, Protection & Friendship" and that "Indians shall not be Molested in their Persons, Hunting Fishing and Shooting & planting on their planting Ground nor in any other Lawfull occasions."[61] The change in colonial power left Acadians in a difficult position, with the British demanding an oath of allegiance. While some attempted to move to French-held territories, such as Louisbourg, others remained where they were.[62] By the 1740s, the Acadian population had increased to about nine thousand people, with about two hundred British soldiers also living in the region; the population of Indigenous people was probably around four thousand. A key port and settler population centre, Louisbourg was both a military fort and a hub for trade in cod and other goods moving between France, the Caribbean, and Acadia.[63] Alongside the French inhabitants, the population of Louisbourg included as Conrad and Hiller explain, "Basque fishermen, German and Swiss soldiers, a few Irish, Scots, and Spanish sojourners, and both Native and black servants and slaves."[64] Marie Marguerite Rose, the recipe book owner, was at first among the enslaved Black residents.

In the years before the Treaty of Paris in 1763, conflicts between the English and French continued in Europe and North America, discord that profoundly affected Acadians and Indigenous people. This was also the period of the first recipes being printed in Nova Scotia. The fighting between the English and French included battles at Louisbourg, where an army of New Englanders took Fortress Louisbourg for the British in 1745, only to have it returned to France in 1748 (the English would take over again in 1758). The French also built a new fortress, Fort Beauséjour, on the Isthmus of Chignecto to stake a claim to the areas outside of peninsular Nova Scotia for France and create a space into which Acadians living under British control could move. The British, for their part, established new forts, first in Halifax in 1749 and then in Windsor and, near Fort Beauséjour, at Fort Lawrence.[65] In 1755, the British seized Fort Beauséjour, after which the French also surrendered other forts in the region. Also in 1755, the British commenced the *Grand dérangement*, which saw the removal of Acadians from Grand Pré, the Minas-Cobequid area, Annapolis, and in the next several years from the Petitcodiac-Memramcook region, Île Saint Jean, and Île Royale, and attempts to disperse them to the American colonies. By 1762, from a population of about 14,000 Acadians, about 11,000 had been expelled, many of whom died as a result. Families were also broken up.[66] The Mi'kmaq also suffered from British moves to enhance their control of the region, for the establishment of Halifax in their territories in 1749 under the guidance of Governor Edward Cornwallis was a "new and unacceptable form of encroachment."[67] The British response to Mi'kmaw resistance was to order British subjects in the region to kill Mi'kmaw people "wherever they are found" and to encourage settlement between 1750 and 1753 by nearly 2,500 "Foreign Protestants," German and Swiss settlers who were meant to enhance the population loyal to Britain (they were important in the founding of Lunenberg).[68] The Mi'kmaq, Wolastoqiyik, and Passamaquoddy all signed treaties of peace and friendship with the British in 1760–61, although "the British continued to treat the Mi'kmaq in a most contemptuous and outrageous manner," as Daniel Paul explains.[69] The 1763 Treaty of Paris would officially end French colonial claims in North America, apart from the islands of Saint Pierre and Miquelon, which allowed them to maintain access to the North Atlantic fishery. The Acadians who had been able evade expulsion and those who were able to make their way back resettled in less populated areas like western Nova Scotia, Cheticamp in Cape Breton, Malpeque on Île Saint Jean, and what is now northern and southeastern New Brunswick and in the upper Saint John River Valley.[70] The Treaty of Paris also changed the lives of Indigenous people, ending Mi'kmaq cooperation with the French and changing how they could live their lives.[71] It is in these early years of Halifax's existence, in 1752, that John Bushell, who had moved to Nova Scotia from Boston, commenced printing the first English-language newspaper to be printed in what is now Canada, *The Halifax Gazette*;[72] the paper printed "A Receipt for the Bite of a Mad Dog" in that same year.

The earliest manuscript recipes in our book come from the migration that occurred as the British sought more settlers to take over land dispossessed from the Acadians. From New England, England, Germany, Scotland, and Ireland, these settlers established communities on the south shore of Nova Scotia, in the Annapolis Valley, in the Saint John River Valley, and the Isthmus of Chignecto.[73] The largest group arrived between 1760 and 1763 from New England (the seven to eight thousand so-called Planters), and it is in the papers of men from this group and from individuals part of the one thousand Yorkshire Settlers who came between 1772 and 1776 that the earliest handwritten recipes survive.[74] Although there were some settlers in Nova Scotia who sympathized with the Patriots, Nova Scotia and St John's Island, which had become a separate colony in 1769, did not generally join in with attempts to remove British power when the American Revolutionary War broke out in 1775.[75] Although the Mi'kmaq and Wolastoqiyik also contemplated joining the effort against the British, and some individuals did fight alongside the Patriots, there were more who did not want to participate in another European war.[76]

Most of the recipes surviving in Maritime archives from before 1800 are from the period after 1783, which marked the end of the American Revolutionary War and the establishment of the United States. The war's end brought the largest significant influx of English-speaking settlers to the region in the Loyalists, who were Americans that had remained loyal to the British Crown. The 35,000 Loyalists were a large and diverse group that included some elite members (ministers, military officers, lawyers, and merchants) and many more regular soldiers, farmers, craftsmen, and fisherman. Also among the Loyalists were a substantial number of African-descended people, including enslaved people brought by white Loyalist enslavers and Black Loyalists, who had fought for the British in exchange for freedom from their American enslavers.[77] Loyalists settled in Saint John and the Island of Saint John, but the largest number went to Nova Scotia.[78] While white Loyalists received substantial land grants, Black Loyalists did not and were treated harshly in the law and faced violence from white settlers – circumstances of impoverishment, hunger, and injustice that led to the departure in 1792 of 1,100 to 1,200 free Black Loyalists, led by Thomas Peters, to Freetown in Sierra Leone.[79] Slavery did not end in the Maritimes until 1833–1834 when British law abolished it in all its colonies.[80] The new English-speaking population of Loyalists strengthened settler colonial structures in the region, prompting the growth of the cities of Halifax and Saint John, the establishment of legal, government, church, and educational institutions and more printing shops and newspapers, the development of trade in fish, timber, and ships, and increased importation of consumer products, including some luxury goods.[81] For the Indigenous peoples in the region, this large influx of new settlers taking more and more land and food resources was an existential threat. They were able to obtain "licenses of occupation" – which Paul calls "the ultimate blow to Mi'kmaq dignity" – but still no land was reserved for Indigenous inhabitants.[82] "The newcomers," says John Reid, "had no concept of the Mi'kmaq as treaty partners," and settlers took locations on the ocean and along rivers and cleared fields in ways that both blocked Indigenous access and degraded the environment.[83] Mi'kmaw resistance to the neglect of the treaty relationship is evident in a 1794 Mi'kmaw petition that "lamented the failure of the British to act as their 'Brothers,' even though 'when they made peace with the English, there was Country enough in Nova Scotia for all the English, French, and Indians then in the Province.'"[84] By 1800, which marks the terminal point for this book's primary focus, Halifax and Saint John were cities of 8,000 and 2,400 inhabitants, while Fredericton, Charlottetown, and Sydney had populations of 750, 500, and 200; a small elite of government officials and merchants commanded wealth and power but the rest of the settler population led more difficult lives, many making a living through fishing, farming, and trade.[85] About eight thousand Acadians also survived, as did a population of Indigenous people that numbered in the thousands.[86] Although a third of the free Black Nova Scotians had left in 1792, the two-thirds who remained represented another two thousand people.[87] The year 1800 sees the Maritimes as a place inhabited by diverse peoples experiencing the consolidation of British colonial power – some benefiting from it while others experienced it as violence and theft. In that year, for instance, a Nova Scotia legislative committee would "[call] attention to the 'distresses of … the aboriginal proprietors of this country.'"[88] The year 1800 also dates before the arrival of Scottish Highlanders, a group who would make another distinct mark in the territory. Eighteenth-century Maritime recipes, then, were created and used by people seeking to make a home in a new place within a context of war and colonial violence, and recipes survive mostly from those who benefited from British colonial power.

That the surviving recipe archive leaves out many people and knowledges rooted in the Maritime region and has mainly preserved English-speaking settler papers is characteristic of colonial archives generally. Crystal Fraser and Zoe Todd write of the "inherent colonial realities of the archives as institutions," a reality that means that archives across what is now called Canada have historically collected documents belonging to "white men who dominated exploration, political and other 'great men' tropes of Canadian history"; this is the case for state archives, especially, which they argue were originally intended "to create national narratives that seek to legitimise the nation state by excluding Indigenous voices, bodies, economies, histories, and socio-political structures realities that raise questions about who controls archives."[89] Harvey Amani Whitfield similarly highlights the silencing of Black lives in Maritime archives. The documents that preserve traces of Black people – such as "runaway advertisements, slave for sale notices, the *Book of Negroes*, court records, wills, government documents, church records, petitions, letters, and other sources" – were often created by people with "incredibly demeaning views of people with African descent."[90] Not only were archival materials not created by Black people, but the archive also preserves and "privileges the accounts, words, and opinions of slaveholders and other powerful people in society."[91] Ian McKay's study of the history of the Nova Scotia Archives explores the impact of colonialism more broadly on its historical collection practices. He argues that "the Public Archives of Nova Scotia had been centrally concerned with upholding the honour of the British Crown. Much of the mission of such a colonial archive was the documentation and defence of the empire's policies, especially with respect to the racialized minorities it had felt obliged to dispossess (Mi'kmaq), deport (Acadians), or marginalize (African Nova Scotians)."[92] Recipes in archives are not immune to this deeply political history.

We have not found many recipes that overtly and explicitly preserve in writing eighteenth-century knowledge practices of Indigenous people, people of African origins, or Acadians. Neither have others. Studying food history at Louisbourg, for instance, Anne Marie Lane Jonah and Chantal Véchambre's 2012 book *French Taste in Atlantic Canada, 1604–1758* uses recipes not from the Louisbourg archives – we couldn't find any and evidently neither could they – but draws instead on French cookbooks and other historical documentation of food to reconstruct cooking and eating in Île Royale's Fortress Louisbourg; they found just one recipe, preserved in a French legal record, for a cake created at the fortress.[93] The Nova Scotia Archives does have one collection of French-language recipes, a 1755 booklet of medical remedies preserved among the "Pernette Papers."[94] We have included these in the EMMR database and a selection in this book. Given its provenance, however, the booklet may not have been compiled by Acadians but by one of the "Foreign Protestants" who arrived in the region between 1750 and 1752. The Pernette Papers also preserves nearly sixty medical remedies in German with Latin titles.[95] These recipes likely also originated with the Foreign Protestants, many of whom came to Nova Scotia from the Duchy of Württemberg in what is now the southwest corner of Germany. Colonial archives did not include the papers of eighteenth-century Acadians. George Rawlyk calls Acadians a "people of the spoken rather than the written word," which would affect recipe culture.[96] Early modern France certainly had an extensive written recipe culture, but the radical disruption and displacement of the *Grand dérangement* was certainly not conducive to the preservation of written recipes in any case. Melvin Gallant and Marielle Boudreau in *A Taste of Acadie* create their account of Acadian food history by linking travel narratives and memoirs that describe food to more recent oral accounts of Acadian recipes.[97] Laurie Lacey's *Micmac* [sic] *Medicines: Remedies and Recollections* similarly turns to interviews that recount an oral history of plant-based remedies used by the Mi'kmaq.[98]

The traditional exclusion of oral knowledge from archival collections certainly impacts our recipe research. As Greg Bak argues, archives are only "one form of social memory" and "may be less reliable, and archival records less authentic, than other forms of social memory, including Indigenous oral traditions."[99] Indeed, Lacey's book is prefaced by a foreword from Rose Knockwood-Morris from the Gold River Reserve reminding readers that herbal medicine continues to be passed down from elders, and that the knowledge has needed to be protected from the impacts of colonialism: "The use of plants, roots and herbs for medicinal purposes had to be practiced in an underground fashion because of fear that the outside world and Reserve institutions would arrest this age-old basic need."[100] If the absence of a written archive of eighteenth-century recipes that foreground Indigenous knowledge practices is an outcome of colonial ideas about whose lives it was important to preserve, the absence of records in colonial archives could also be a result of persistent Indigenous sovereignty and some ability to protect knowledge from colonial extraction.

The use and possession – but not always the content – of oral knowledge can, however, be discerned in some written archival records. For instance, the knowledge of enslaved Black people in what is now the Maritimes is evident in the notices of sale that document the enslaved person's skills and knowledge. *The Halifax Gazette* in 1752, for example, included a notice offering for sale by Joshua Mauger an unnamed female slave, "Creole born, [who] has been brought up in a Gentleman's family, and capable of doing all sorts of Work belonging thereto, as Needle-Work of all sorts, and in the best Manner; also Washing, Ironing, Cookery, and every other Thing that can be expected from Such a Slave."[101] The phrase "in the best Manner" suggests a high level of skill and knowledge of contemporary processes. Another unnamed woman, when she was offered for sale in Halifax in 1779, was identified as an "exceedingly good cook" – surely suggesting a strong knowledge of culinary recipes that were popular among settlers in Nova Scotia – while a woman offered for sale in New Brunswick in *The Royal Gazette* in 1787 similarly was described as "well acquainted with all kinds of household business, and particular is an excellent COOK."[102]

These records of deep practical knowledge extend also to work outside the house. An unnamed boy offered for sale in *The Royal American Gazette* in Shelburne in 1786 was said to be "very handy at Farming, House-Work, or attending Table," and an unnamed man, offered for sale in 1799 by newspaper publisher John Ryan, was described as able to "do all sorts of Farming work and is a handy House Servant."[103] There is little doubt that these highly skilled, unfree people were using recipe knowledge, even as their knowledge has not been recorded and their labour and personhood were not respected. Even if they did not own recipe books like Marie Marguerite Rose did, these enslaved people were surely using recipe knowledge. It is important to remember that the recipes collected here represent only a portion of then-available knowledge concerning the ways that people ate, cured diseases, and made homes more comfortable for themselves and others. Recipes also may not represent the practices of people doing the labour, but instead account for the ideas of those with access to print or the ability to read and write and keep records.

Our approach to marginalized knowledge throughout this book is to document its presence by bringing to bear scholarship of the circulation of Indigenous and African knowledge of medicinal plants, remedies, and foods in the Atlantic world. As Londa Schiebinger argues in *Secret Cures of Slaves: People, Plants, and Medicine in the Eighteenth-Century Atlantic World*, "Europe dominated the medical complex as it did the plantation complex economically, politically, and militarily, yet people, goods, labor, food, timber – and, we will add, disease, knowledge, and medical remedies – moved promiscuously between continents, masters and slaves, and imperial monopolies."[104] Recipes track this circulation of knowledge, both in their use of ingredients first understood and used by marginalized people and in the way that recipes remember the techniques they used. Because recipes can remember, by drawing on these memories, recipes can become a testament to marginalized knowledges of Black, Indigenous, and Acadian people and to the adoption or taking of that knowledge into Anglo-American and European recipe cultures.

Across its chapters, this book explores aspects of the transfer of knowledge from Indigenous, African, and other non-European cultures into settler cultures and the circulation of knowledge within and across the colonial and national borders of England, France, Africa, India, South America, the Caribbean, and the colonies of the northeast that are the focus here. Importantly, however, recipes tend to overtly cite only European and American sources, leaving settler indebtedness to other sources unacknowledged. We did locate one printed recipe explicitly referencing the knowledge of Black people. "Effectual Cure for the Stone" describes the work of an enslaved man in Virginia who devised an effective remedy for treating kidney and bladder stones. The article was published in numerous American newspapers, and it appeared in *The Halifax Gazette* in 1794. References to "Indian Corn" and "Indian Pudding" offer the only explicit references to Indigenous food resources, even though settler and European adoption of Indigenous foods and medicines extends well beyond the use of corn. More commonly, non-European knowledge is simply used without credit. For example, while a recipe on potato bread published in *The Nova Scotia Magazine* credits a French agronomist, there is no recognition of the potato's origins in Indigenous agriculture and diets (beyond its newness to European plates). Similarly, a recipe for making maple sugar gestures to a settler experimenter of "established character for candour and integrity" as a source for knowledge of sugar making and, though it acknowledges that the practice "has been known many years," does not make visible how Europeans first learned about sweeteners made from maple sap from Indigenous peoples, including the Mi'kmaq. We work to draw out these uncredited sources in the stories we tell about recipes.

Archives' historical collection practices may also underpin the predominance of recipes belonging to men in this book, with men's papers having been historically considered more worthy of preservation by families and institutional archives from the eighteenth century. Although archives in England and the US hold many recipe books compiled by women, sometimes over several generations, we were able to locate in Maritime archives only one substantial collection by a woman from the period in question (a few recipes likely recorded by or attributed to women are scattered among other papers). The collection of Sarah Creighton Wilkins (1774–c.1849) is extensive and informative and, though most of its entries are dated well into the nineteenth century, some could have been devised if not recorded before her 1799 marriage to politician and judge Lewis Morris Wilkins; the notebook's first dated entry is a book catalogue dated 1779.[105] Perhaps the most comprehensive collection considered here, Wilkins's notebook includes recipes for numerous food items, beverages, household products, and an array of medicines. With this exception, the vast majority of the recipes published on the *EMMR* database and explored in more detail in this book were recorded or printed by men of British descent, and many of these name other English and American men as sources.

Despite the genre's strong historical association with women's knowledge, the absence of recipes by women in the archives might also be rooted in women's literacy levels and how they could use their time. Even though Anglo-American women in the eighteenth century enjoyed higher levels of literacy than their forebears, more women than men were unable to write. Reading in England and America was taught before writing, with the consequence that some British and settler women may have learned to read without learning to write, and thus to use written recipes without being able to record them; in New England, whence many Loyalist women originated, literacy was valued and writing was increasingly taught even to poor girls after the 1740s, although low social status and poverty, as well as rural geography, often correlated with illiteracy among women.[106] In eighteenth-century Nova Scotia, too, educational opportunities for poor children were limited – a factor that also informed low literacy rates among the Black population.[107] One study of female litigants in Nova Scotia courts between 1749 and 1801 – women who were all Anglo-American – suggests that about 59 per cent of the litigants could write, with higher literacy rates among populations who were arriving from the United States than from Britain.[108] A written recipe culture could have arisen among privately educated women in late-eighteenth-century Nova Scotia who, like their American compatriots, had better educational opportunities; recipes would not be unfamiliar in an education system that emphasized "domestic and drawing room values" that included needlework alongside grammar, writing, accounting, painting, and geography.[109] If these women did produce more recipes, however, they did not survive to be preserved in the region's archives before the nineteenth century. It is also possible that settler women in the eighteenth-century Maritimes were simply too busy working in a sometimes harsh and unfamiliar environment to spare time for writing things down. The latter explanation becomes even more compelling when we consider that recipes were often recorded for descendants rather than the use of an author who may have already been intimately familiar with their methods and ingredients. Nevertheless, the strong representation of male recipe writers, collectors, and sources in the circulation of recipe knowledge should disrupt any lingering sense that recipes have been exclusively the work of women.

THE HOUSEHOLD AS PLACE OF EXPERIMENT

Studies of recipes have played an important role in drawing attention to the critical place of the household in the history of science – and of knowledge-making more generally. Steven Shapin showed that for members of the Royal Society in early modern Britain, "by far the most significant venues were the private residences of gentlemen or, at any rate, sites where places of scientific work were co-extensive with places of residence, whether owned or rented."[110] Alongside these gentlemen scientists were the Sisters of the Royal Society studied by Lynette Hunter, women like Katherine Jones, Lady Ranelagh (1615–1691) – sister of Robert Boyle (1627–1691), founding member of the Royal Society – who, as her recipes make clear, also engaged in scientific investigations at home. As Hunter explains, the "kitchen or still room of any substantial estate" had "virtually everything" needed to conduct experiments. Indeed, this similarity between kitchen and laboratory would contribute to efforts by scientific gentlemen to distinguish their labour from that of the kitchen in order to increase its prestige.[111] In the history of medicine, too, these elite British country houses are for Elaine Leong a "site of science," where not only the kitchen and stillroom have the same equipment as a laboratory or apothecary shop, but there might also be libraries for reading and outdoor spaces that permit the observation of plants and animals; the household is a space where knowledge-making belongs not only to the gentlemen scientists but also to other members of the household, such as wives, daughters, and servants.[112] It is only in the nineteenth century that scientific work came to take place primarily outside the home; before this, as Alix Cooper explains, "[n]atural inquiry in early modern Europe … often constituted a family project to which a variety of household members would contribute."[113] Cooper tracks natural inquiry further down the social scale to include the households of physicians, artisans, apothecaries and other professionals, and the households of peasants, as well as high-ranking aristocrats.[114] The recipes in this book demonstrate that this history of domestic knowledge-making continued on the other side of the Atlantic Ocean.

Scientific exploration certainly continued in the northeast colonies that are now identified as the Maritimes. Scholars like Susan Scott Parrish and Anya Zilberstein have looked at how the study of natural philosophy continued amongst settlers of British North America more generally. Parrish argues that Britain's North American colonies were "a meeting place or battleground for once distant peoples, microbes, plants, and animals that produced a strange new world for all"; they were, even more, "a place for the fabrication of facts that traveled eastward to avid consumers" back in Europe.[115] Zilberstein, adopting a slightly different stance, argues that the northeast (including Nova Scotia) was not seen as especially strange or exotic by the British, with the result that naturalists in the region used the study of the natural world to make it "a more domesticated, familiar and European place," to place it in "the mainstream."[116] The recipes considered here – from food to medicine to agriculture to any of a range of other household products – show how natural knowledge was moved, implemented, supplemented, and altered, sometimes turning to local products but even more often to ingredients that could only have been procured from abroad and were being used in Europe.

If Maritime households were places for making knowledge as they were in Europe, the houses themselves were not necessarily the grand country houses that have been core repositories of domestic recipe collections and scientific study. The elite amongst early European settlers did attempt to build houses that reflected their claims to status, wealth, and dignity, reproducing a social hierarchy in a hierarchy of spaciousness.[117] But most of the Loyalists were not from privileged backgrounds, and this population built more humble homes, first with logs and later with hewn timber and boards in styles influenced by New England architecture, which for its part drew on folk styles from the southeast of England.[118] Colonial kitchens were the central space in a home, sometimes serving as the home's main communal space, as was characteristic of French settler homes, and sometimes construed as a separate but still large space, a model more typical in English settler homes.[119] The kitchens of eighteenth-century colonial homes focused on the fireplace, its heat used not just for cooking, but also for preserving, laundry, cleaning, smoking, and light; the fireplace's technologies, as Fiona Lucas notes, typically enabled cooking by "boiling, broiling, frying, roasting, and baking" with pots, spits, pans, and ovens.[120] These are the same tools needed to produce most recipes – culinary or not. The recipes considered here suggest that, like British kitchens, settler kitchens in eighteenth-century British North America were not just spaces for cookery but served also as spaces for creating experimental knowledge, work that could require the fireplace, pots and pans, bowls and spoons. The recipe for maple sugar stands out as an exception in naming all the distinct tools and fires it requires outside. That male recipe collectors and creators would be part of the knowledge exchange in domestic spaces is perhaps less surprising than might first appear. Sara Pennell explains that British kitchens were less gendered spaces than sometimes thought, not only because of the importance of male cooks in elite households, but also because they were inhabited by "servants, lodgers, children, and visitors" and, for many, were spaces of artisanal labour, as well as cooking; kitchens are, she adds, an "experimental zone."[121] Recipes highlight how domestic knowledge-making work was wide-ranging and included cooking, medicine, agriculture, and other forms of household knowledge.

The experimental place of the home also offered a means of claiming land. Colonial housing was driven by the need to survive and "a wish to colonize territory and settle population as part of an expansion of European society into the New World."[122] Thinking about homes in Atlantic Canada in particular, Rachel Bryant's *The Homing Place: Indigenous and Settler Literary Legacies of the Atlantic* argues that "the shifting idea of the home place" represents one of the ways "non-Indigenous Maritime writers and readers have articulated, revised, and ultimately controlled their relationships to the places they inhabit, effectively and continuously claiming and imagining this region, to which they are relative newcomers, as their own intellectual property."[123] If Bryant is describing talk of home in the literature of the region, her words could also be describing eighteenth-century recipes, which document ways of knowing the place that settlers had come to inhabit. As they think about food, drink, medicine, pests, cleaning, agriculture, and construction, recipes claim space, in effect mapping their intellectual property, their ways of knowing onto the land. Recipes are a component of colonial domesticity and can, Kathryn Kish Sklar argues,

> weave together subjective needs and larger social norms in an intimate regimen that shapes household material culture and the reproduction of daily life. Domesticity is about intimate space, but it is also about the location of that space in a wider world. Domesticity is about women, but it is also about men and children. It defines and limits behavior, but it also creates space for innovation. Above all, because it seeks to reproduce daily life, it is a malleable

> process, a set of relationships that are ever-changing – along with the life course of those in its domain and their intersection with larger social forces.[124]

Recipes are part of daily life, but they are also the product of wider social forces and political power. They carry ideas about the natural world, about plants, animals, and human bodies, and they represent particular ways of knowing. The authors of "Becoming Undisciplined" observe that the "take" that so often begins a recipe is an extractive directive that supports a natural hierarchy, one in which humans assume priority over plants and animals (the human may take and use materials and lives, inherently accorded less value); recipes, they argue, use "language that replicates the masterful logic of colonial sciences."[125] In supporting this hierarchy, in their reliance on tacit knowledge, which is often rooted in European history and practices, and in taking knowledge from colonized subjects, recipes play a role in furthering the extractive logic of settler colonialism. In the eighteenth-century Maritimes, the history of settler domesticity is never far from the history of colonialism. As Kish Sklar notes, "The history of settler societies takes us backstage in imperial projects, revealing complexity and conflict not always visible in official documents. And the history of 'domesticity,' the intimate patterns of daily life, helps frame the study of that complexity and conflict."[126] Documents of intellectual lives lived around material things, eighteenth-century Maritime recipes tell complicated stories about daily life, stories linked to the history of recipes, to knowledge-making practices, to political history, and to the lives of individuals and their families.

TEXTUAL INTRODUCTION

In transcribing recipes from their print or manuscript sources, we have endeavoured to preserve the original line breaks, capitalization, punctuation, and spelling. In printed texts that employ common eighteenth-century letter substitutions – such as u/v, i/j, vv/w – we have selected the modern spelling. Some abbreviations have been expanded for clarity.

CHAPTER ONE

Food

For culinary historians, food is an important aspect of identity: "You are what you eat." The recipes included in this chapter are thus particularly striking in how they do not represent what we think of as Maritime foods. There are no recipes involving blueberries or maple syrup. No moose. No lobster. No oysters. No fish cakes. No *pâte à la râpure* (rappie pie), fricot, or any other Acadian dish. Lady Ashburn pickles have not emerged, and neither has hodge-podge. Not only do the recipes collected here not represent the diversity of food cultures in the region, they also do not even represent what English-speaking settlers ate regularly in the eighteenth century. There is little record of common foods, like bread, for instance.[1] Rather than evincing commonly held food knowledge in the region, these pre-1800 recipes seem more likely to track the exceptional. Many are speculative (recipes about what people could eat), interventionist (about things people should eat), informative (about how people eat elsewhere), and occasional (how to feed a crowd or what to eat when ill). The food recipes are also economical and commercial, often interested as much in food's cost and transportation as in its taste. They are sometimes interested in deliciousness, but health, cost, and preservation are surely as significant in the recipes that were preserved by being printed, reprinted, or written down.

The picture of food culture presented here is thus quite narrow. Although the region was inhabited by Wabanaki, African, Acadian, and other non-English-speaking European people, the culinary recipes recorded and preserved in the region's archives or printed in the region's newspapers are all in English. Hence the Maritime archive profoundly limits the picture of food culture that recipes can provide because, of course, all of the people who inhabited the region were eating. Dorothy Duncan's *Canadians at Table: A Culinary History of Canada* turns to archaeological scholarship, European travel narratives, letters, and diaries to sketch a history of what Indigenous, French, and English-speaking people ate before 1800 in what would later become Canada.[2] Anne Marie Lane Jonah and Chantal Véchambre's *French Taste in Atlantic Canada, 1604–1758* uses trade and legal records, personal accounts, inventories, travel narratives, and French recipes to create a detailed picture of the food culture at Louisbourg.[3] What they identify as the first Acadian recipe is "*un gâteau rond*" made of a quarter bushel of flour, six eggs, and a half pound of butter, to be made at the "fête des Rois"; the ingredients – which are not attached to any instructions – survive as part of a 1649 French rental agreement at Port Royal, where the rent is to be paid in this cake.[4] With a real dearth of non-English recipes surviving, those preserved in Maritime archives represent the food culture of English-speaking settlers and tell a story about their search for food knowledge.

Settler food culture does, however, reach out to other cultures and food practices. "Foodways research," Eric D. Tourigny shows, "does not simply look at what people ate, but represents a critical examination of the ways people thought about and interacted with food: how and why they obtained it, distributed it, prepared it, preserved it, and consumed it."[5] In colonial British North America, these influences include, as Tourigny summarizes, "tradition, the history of colonialism, and industrial and technological developments."[6] Recipes track foodways. They show how recipe creators and collectors thought about food and how they considered preparing it and preserving it. A testament to influences, the English-language settler recipes are not as narrow as they first appear. With copying and reprinting, they make visible the presence of British and American food cultures and, usually less obviously, how colonialism informed how people thought about food and what they could eat. The recipes include foods such as sugar, molasses, and rice that were produced by enslaved people in the Caribbean and South Carolina as well as a recipe for mango that may include a fruit from the Caribbean in an Indian-style chutney. A few recipes here document how what were less familiar Indigenous foods, like corn, potatoes, and tomatoes, became part of European and American diets (see also the discussion of maple sugar in the agriculture chapter). The recipes also present arguments for change and innovation, for adopting new foods, such as the hasty pudding from New England and a healthful couscous from Africa, and new food preparation techniques, such as a new method for leavening bread and a milk preservation technique from Asia. Catsup recipes come to Nova Scotia via England, the United States, and China, while haricot, long a part of English cookery, also comes from France, whose cuisine had a long-standing influence on English food. There are many more examples of this kind.

Food played an especially important role in driving European colonialism in Wabanaki territory. Europeans took animals, plants, seeds, and fruits from the Americas back to Europe, while also importing European plants and animals to the region. When Jacques Cartier voyaged through the Gulf of St Lawrence in 1534, he noted many familiar plants; in what is now Prince Edward Island, he recorded seeing peas, gooseberry bushes, strawberries, raspberries, and wild oats, and around the Baie des Chaleurs, he saw wheat, oats, currant bushes, plums, nuts, apples, beans, and a fruit he described as "figs."[7] Victoria Dickenson writes that the "impression" conveyed by Cartier's and Samuel de Champlain's accounts of their travels "is one of vegetable abundance, a natural garden yielding produce sweeter and larger than that of Europe, and without effort."[8] Plants resembling those already grown in European gardens that could be transported as seeds or rootstocks, which included corn, beans, squashes, and Jerusalem artichokes, readily became part of sixteenth- and seventeenth-century European gardens.[9] By 1700, Acadians were growing European vegetables such as cabbages, turnips, beets, onions, carrots, shallots, parsnips, peas, and salad greens, as well as grains including corn, rye, and oats; they had orchards with pear and cherry trees, and they kept pigs, sheep, and cows, using the wool for clothing and the milk for food. Their diet also included game, such as partridge and hare, and fish, such as cod, gaspereau, shad, and sardines.[10] Brandy, molasses, oil, pepper, rum, sugar, and vinegar were imported.[11] The *Grand dérangement* disrupted these food traditions, however, as Acadians were removed from their lands. Those who were able to return came back to land less conducive to agriculture, and diets narrowed to hardier vegetables such as turnips, cabbage, and potatoes, grains, and wild berries; fish also became much more important than it had been.[12]

Fish functioned as an especially important contact zone in Wabanakik. A major European cod fishery in Newfoundland and the Gulf of St Lawrence had existed since the sixteenth century.[13] From that time, cod was transported back to Europe in salted or dried forms; though salt fish could be made on board ships, drying required access to land and temporary French settlements where the fish were cleaned, salted, and dried. These settlements also led to trading relationships between the French and Indigenous peoples in the northeast.[14] Salmon were especially abundant in the region in the eighteenth century and had been for centuries, with most rivers flowing into the Atlantic Ocean without natural barriers serving as salmon runs.[15] Marc Lescarbot (c. 1570–1641), who visited Port Royal in 1606 and

1607, included a chapter on fishing practices in his *Histoire de la Nouvelle France*, where he reports that when the French at Port Royal in what is now Nova Scotia caught salmon, the fish were so abundant that only their collective strength could carry away the nets.[16] The earliest French travellers, including Lescarbot and Nicolas Denys (1603–1688), also observed an abundance of lobster and other shellfish in places like Cape Breton and Port Royal.

Lobster had been harvested in the Mediterranean with nets and baskets and in France with traps, and European travellers and settlers continued to employ these methods in the Americas while also adopting the Mi'kmaw method of using spears and harpoons to catch lobster.[17] Lescarbot also documents the Mi'kmaw skill in catching fish with weirs, spears, and nets, indicating as well the cultural significance of fish for the Mi'kmaq and for the Wolastoqiyik peoples.[18] According to his account, the Indigenous fishers

> do make a hurdle, or weir, that crosseth the brook, which they hold almost up straight, propped against wooden bars, arch-wise, and leave there a space for the fishes to pass, which space they stop when the tide doth retire, and all the fish is found stayed in such a multitude that they suffer it to be lost. And as for the dolphins, sturgeons, and salmons, they take them after that manner, or do strike them with harping-irons, so that these people are happy. For there is nothing in the world so good as these fresh meats.[19]

The fish recipes included in this book document how the abundance of fish translated into value as an export commodity for settlers. After the Treaty of Paris in 1763 ceded European claims to the northwest Atlantic to Britain, the British expanded on the extensive salmon fisheries established in New England in the seventeenth century. William Davidson, a Scotsman experienced in the salmon fishery, played an important role in Maritime salmon fishing. Davidson received a large land grant from the Nova Scotia governor that allowed him to fish the Miramichi River, with the stipulation that he also had to settle on and clear the land. By the mid-1770s, he was exporting yearly 660,000 to 850,000 pounds of the river's salmon that had been preserved by pickling. Davidson's fishing methods were criticized by another Loyalist, Benjamin Marston, who complained that the salmon nets stretched across the river from shore to shore, "at every proper place to stop fish." The "cross nets, while they are set," he noted, "absolutely stop the whole body of them from getting up to their spawning places and must eventually, much lessen, if not destroy the breed."[20] Davidson was not alone in extracting large numbers of salmon. Across the region between 1760 and 1784, settlers shipped three to eight million pounds of fish (with about 35 to 40 per cent of that weight comprised of the pickle) each year to Europe, the American colonies, and the West Indies. By the second quarter of the nineteenth-century, river barriers and the vast numbers of fish removed from the ecosystem meant that the Maritime salmon population was in danger.[21] The recipes for pickling salmon included here are as much a testament to support of the trade as they are about good eating.

The period before 1800 was also defined by hunger, and some recipes reflect this deprivation. The disappearance of populations of sea birds as well as many kinds of fish because of European fishing and settlement especially impacted the Mi'kmaq and Wolastoqiyik, who relied on the oceans and rivers for their food. The region's Indigenous peoples moved with the seasonal migrations of fish, birds, and mammals and did not consider themselves to be separate from the natural world in the ways Europeans tended to do.[22] The Mi'kmaq divided the regions of Mi'kmaki into *netukulowómi* (hunting territories) for different families to have stewardship or custodianship of and to practise *netuklulimk* ("the process of supplying oneself," of "avoiding not having enough," and the instruction to "take only what you need").[23] Although the eighteenth-century Treaties of Peace and Friendship did not cede Mi'kmaw rights to fish and hunt, colonial authorities proceeded as if they had and made resources available to British subjects without consideration for those treaty rights.[24] As a result, the Mi'kmaq faced severe food shortages by the 1820s and, as Daniel Paul states, "Over the period 1760 to 1867, indirect genocide by starvation took a great toll."[25] The effects of colonialization on Indigenous diets have been long lasting.

The Mi'kmaq were not alone in facing hunger in the period covered by this book. While a concern in Nathalie Cooke's *What's to Eat? Entrées in Canadian Culinary History* is "the shaping of culinary taste in Canada,"[26] what may be as striking in the recipes considered here is the extent to which recipes are not primarily interested in taste, whether taste refers to sensations of the flavours of sweet, salty, sour, bitter, or umami or to aesthetic judgments about what is tasteful, fashionable, or desirable to present at the table. Instead, a number of recipes confront hunger. Printed recipes for dishes like Hessian soup and potato soup seem to be responding to a context of deprivation, and the recipe is meant to be used to create foods that can be offered as charity for the poor. Such printed recipes often include their cost as evidence for their cost-effectiveness, an addition that defines their purpose as much as their taste. Although the recipients of charity are not defined, poverty was rife in the region during the 1780s when the English-speaking population rose dramatically (and the printing of recipes increased concomitantly). Among the thousands of Loyalists who came to Nova Scotia after 1783, only the wealthiest were able to avoid hunger and the need to spend years living in tents or huts. Some Loyalists ended up with allotments that could not be readily used for food production, with Black Loyalists in particular being offered smaller portions of even less cultivable land than their white counterparts. The Acadians who chose to return to 1780s and 1790s Nova Scotia after being expelled during the 1755 *Grand dérangement* were made to settle in less fertile and more remote areas than they had previously inhabited. When there was economic development, the benefits were felt more by English-speaking Loyalists than others. This severity of the political and economic hardship contributed to the departure of many free Black Loyalists in 1792 for Sierra Leone, while some white Loyalists opted to return to the United States.[27]

A long-standing component of European food culture, hierarchy and hunger persisted in the ways European settlers interacted with food in Wabanaki territory. Lescarbot's account of life in Port Royal in the winter of 1606 includes a story of the invention by Samuel de Champlain (1574?–1635) of *L'ordre de bon temps*, created "to keep us merry and cleanly concerning victuals."[28] Lescarbot describes a great banquet where the steward of the feast marched, with his napkin on his shoulder and staff of office in hand, into the banquet with a train of people bearing dishes for the feast. Lescarbot reports that

> we had abundance of fowl, as mallards, outards, geese, grey and white, partridges and other birds: item, of elans (or stag-flesh), of caribous (or deer), beavers, otters, bears, rabbits, wild-cats (or leopards), nibachès, and such like, which the savages did take, wherwith we made good dishes of meat as in the cook's-shops that be in La rue aux Ours (Bear Street) and greater store; for of all meats none is so tender as elan's flesh.[29]

Lescarbot's is a tale of abundance, but it is also a representation of the colonial and class hierarchies of seventeenth-century European food culture. Lescarbot records that the French relied on Mi'kmaw hunting skills for many of these dishes, even as his language and naming of the Mi'kmaq dismisses and dehumanizes them. Social status also mattered at the table among the French, as he records that the governor of the feast, bearing a staff of office, marches at the head of a train carrying all the dishes that Lescarbot documents with pride as being equal to those in Paris. As in many European travel narratives from the period, Lescarbot's representation of food has political dimensions, in this case selling the colonial project to his fellow Europeans with his tale of bounty. Food could also be aimed at reinforcing order. In 1752, a celebration of the birth of the Duc de Bourgoyne, a son to the heir to the French throne, at Île Royale provided "an opportunity to reinforce the social fabric by including all, while making the stature of each [class] completely clear," with celebrations around food and drink especially marked by hierarchy: the governor hosted a dinner attended only by military officials and ladies, while the community attended a religious service, observed a parade of officials and the lighting of a bonfire, and were given wine from several of the governor's barrels, with cautions going out to soldiers to ensure that no disorder erupted as a result.[30]

European hierarchies at the table are neither uniquely French nor concluded by the nineteenth century. Bonnie Huskins's study of Saint John and Halifax public feasts considers how settler food and its rituals "expressed hierarchy and defined the boundaries of inclusion and exclusion."[31] The balls and banquets – which restricted attendance to civic and provincial officials, military officers, and mercantile elites – were an "opportunity for the display of respectability, breeding, and refinement": the presentation of food was governed by rules of precedence, the food itself was French, and toasts were made only by men.[32] Non-elites in Nova Scotia, as in England, were invited only to outdoor public feasts that "functioned as instruments of paternalism" and were "based on the premise that a full stomach ensured favourable and loyal sentiments."[33] The use of food in charity, a component of the public feasts, is also evident in the work of the Charitable Irish Society of Halifax founded in 1786 by Irish members of the colonial elite and others.[34] The group worked to provide food, especially bread, to the needy, while also regularly holding banquets on Saint Patrick's Day and occasions that "involved the expression of national feeling for Ireland."[35] The recipes for foods to be provided as charity emerge from this sociable context to address a literate audience with resources – the ability to fund charitable dishes – rather than the impoverished and hungry themselves, replicating the paternalistic processes that in part define food charity in the period. The recipes with very large quantities, such as the plum cake considered in this chapter, may also have been intended for public feasts or occasions.

The importance of food preservation as an aspect of cookery is evident also in the recipes studied here. Eighteenth-century Europeans preserved food by transforming it through pickling, salting, smoking, and curing, all technologies that were much older.[36] Indeed, the Roman poet Martial (c. 38–103) wrote about ham, while the second-century physician Galen (129–c. 216) admired salted pork. In the seventeenth century, hams from various regions of Europe were regarded as culinary delicacies, although fresh beef was of higher status than salted.[37] Salted meat was particularly important between the fifteenth and nineteenth centuries as an essential component of victualling long ocean voyages and feeding armies and navies; British navy rations included salted meat (beef and pork), beer, and biscuit, while salted meat was also the foundation of the diet of soldiers in the British army. Still subject to occasional spoilage from faulty preservation techniques, salted meat always needed to be desalinated by boiling to render it palatable.[38] Found in the recipe collections of men, recipes for food preservation included here are part of this military, colonial context as much as they are part of women's work in the kitchen-life. The gendering of some aspects of food preparation is also a component of the cheese recipe included here.

Pre-1800 Maritime culinary recipes are part of a less studied moment in Canadian food history. In *What's to Eat?*, Nathalie Cooke suggests that the lens of Canadian cookbooks divides Canada's culinary history into five periods, the first of which is contact and settlement, defined in her work by nineteenth-century cookbook publications.[39] The recipes selected for our book all appeared in print or were collected before this era. Their message about contact and settlement is often less organized, offers little in the way of narrative argument, and is less reflective of the local context. As with other categories of recipes considered here, the culinary recipes are by-and-large not original but were taken from British and American newspapers, almanacs, and recipe books printed on both sides of the Atlantic. Perhaps what stands out most about eighteenth-century recipes from what are now the Maritime provinces is their difference from later Canadian recipe cultures in the way that they manufacture identity. Alison Norman argues that in Upper Canada in the nineteenth century, British settlers' adoption of Anishinaabeg and Haudenosaunee foods such as wild rice, maple syrup, and game "was part of their transformation from Britons to Canadians."[40] The recipes discussed in this book offer very little sense of the local (the recipe for pickling salmon, for instance, turns not to the Miramichi but to Scotland). Neither do they do the work that Katharina Vester sees happening in the recipes of late-eighteenth- and early nineteenth-century America: the creation of "practices, dishes, and rituals expressing a specific American character" because "inventing a national cuisine is indeed an important part of imagining community, history, and tradition."[41] Americans in the late eighteenth century, Vester goes on, "came up with recipes that would produce the right kind of citizens and embody superior national values."[42] The recipes printed and circulating in the Maritimes before 1800 did not come attached to these kinds of nationalist discourses. What we do see is a cosmopolitanism – a global scope – that is perhaps at odds with (problematic) notions of Maritime culture that emphasize the homogeneity of the region. Still, some recipes, like the one for gingerbread, do connect to foods like molasses that would later become part of Maritime identity. The recipes that follow also highlight the use of food in commerce, which persists in a region that is now home to frozen food giant McCain's as well as Cavendish Farms (owned by J.D. Irving Ltd), and where food continues to be a significant export.

MEAT AND FISH

To Make Beef or Pork Pickle

We found this recipe in two places: it was copied into a notebook compiled by Garrett Clopper (1753–1823) between 1790 and 1799 (see figure 1.1 and the transcription further in this section), and it is also preserved on a sheet of paper pasted into the diary and order book kept by Anthony Allaire (1755–1838) for the year 1780 (see figure 1.2).[43] Both men served as lieutenants in the King's New Brunswick Regiment under the command of Thomas Carleton.[44] This regiment was formed in 1793 when France declared war against England, and it disbanded in 1802.[45] Of Dutch descent, Clopper served in the British army and arrived in Fredericton from New York in 1783, where he married Penelope Miller and was a recorder of deeds and wills and coroner for York County.[46] Allaire was born in New Rochelle, New York, but had Huguenot (French Protestant) ancestry. He came to Nova Scotia and eventually to Fredericton in 1783, where he wed Mary Simonds (1755–1838). Though Allaire served in South Carolina at the siege of Charleston and the Battle at King's Mountain, which proved to be a significant victory for the American forces, his published diary provides a record of his time as a lieutenant in the British forces between March and November 1780.[47] Allaire died in 1838 in Fredericton. We have not found another print source for the recipe and, given that the two men likely knew one another, it does seem possible that one shared the recipe with the other. The following recipe is not unlike others for pickled beef or pork from the period.

To make Beef or Pork Pickle

To 4 Gallons of Water add
6 pounds of Salt ¼ lb Sal
Prunella[48] & ½ lb Coarse brown
Sugar ~ boil it well and
strain it ~ when cold put
in the meat & keep it well
covered ~ boil up the pickle
again as often as you find it
necessary

The sal prunella used in this recipe is made by melting saltpetre (the name for potassium nitrate, also used as an ingredient in gunpowder) in a crucible to produce nitrites, which would preserve a red colour in the meat; it was first used in the meat curing process in the mid-seventeenth century in England and was often accompanied by sugar because saltpetre on its own made meat tougher.[49] Given the suggestion made by one contemporary author that ¼–½ ounce of sal prunella is enough for one hundred pounds of meat, it seems likely that the recipe was meant to preserve a large quantity of meat, although the recipe doesn't specify. Or, the recipe may – like others from the eighteenth century – use dangerous amounts of sal prunella.[50]

Clopper and Allaire were not the only military men who kept recipes for salted meat. The frequently reprinted "Admiral Pocock's Receipt for pickling Beef, Pork, Mutton, &c. and keeping the Meat good and sweet" likewise describes a pickling technique that has military origins.[51] George Pocock (1706–1792) had entered the British navy in 1718 and reached the rank of admiral by 1762, commanding ships in European and Indian waters and in the Caribbean.[52] This recipe calls for putting the meat in four gallons of water with a pound and a half of sugar, six pounds of salt, and two ounces of saltpetre, boiling it, and storing it to produce a meat claimed to be as "tender as a chick."[53] Though salted meat lasted a long time, it needed to be treated to become palatable again. A recipe for "restoring" salted pork or beef that appears in the orderbook of Brigadier General George Townsend (1723–1807) – the commander of British troops in Quebec in the 1760s – suggests something of this restoration process. Townsend's recipe calls for steeping the salted meat for twenty-four hours in water, changing the water three times, scraping the salt off

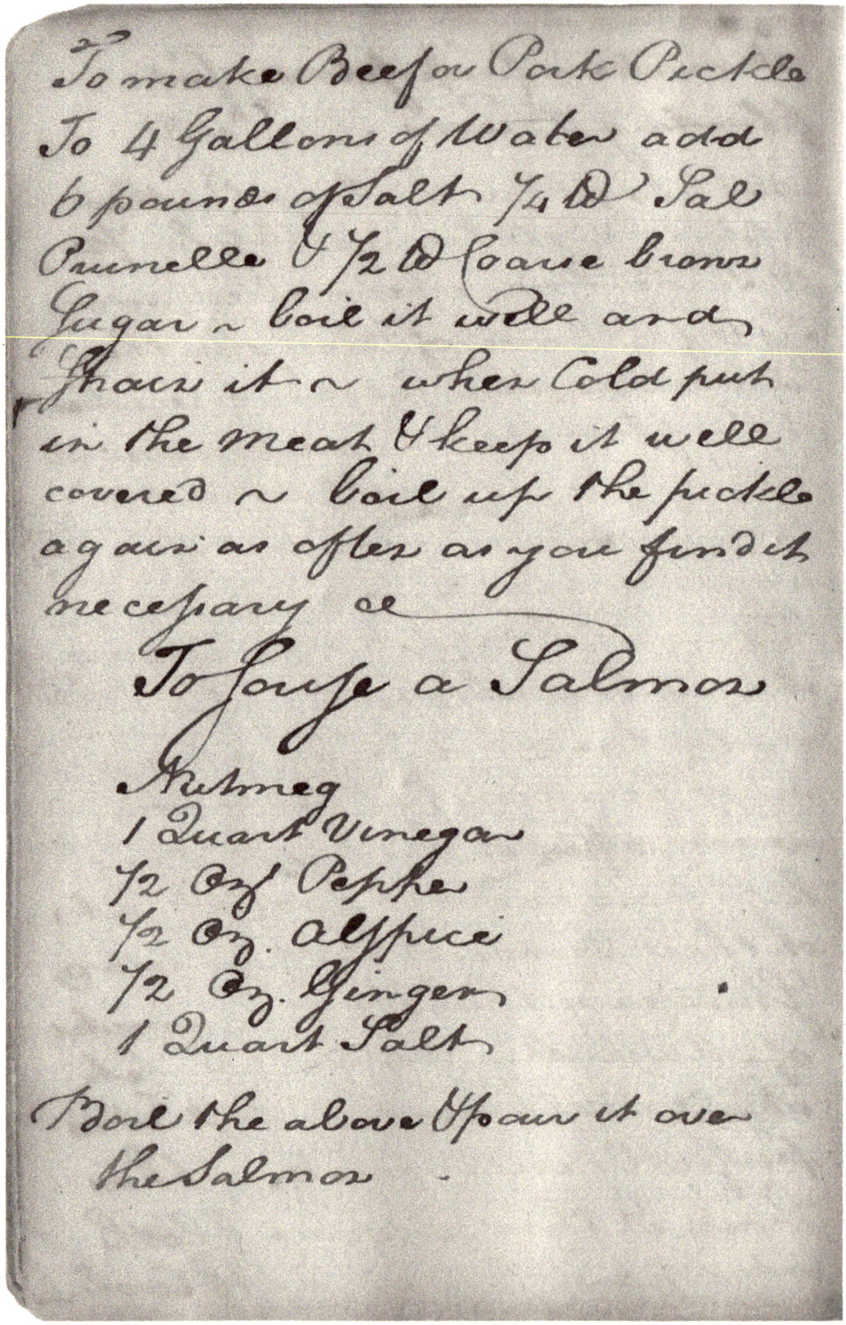

To make Beef or Pork Pickle
To 4 Gallons of Water add
6 pounds of Salt 1/4 lb Sal
Prunelle & 1/2 lb Coarse brown
Sugar ~ boil it well and
Strain it ~ when Cold put
in the meat & keep it well
covered ~ boil up the pickle
again as often as you find it
necessary

To Souse a Salmon

Nutmeg
1 Quart Vinegar
1/2 Oz Pepper
1/2 Oz. allspice
1/2 Oz. Ginger
1 Quart Salt

Boil the above & pour it over
the Salmon -

Figure 1.1 Above
To make Beef or Pork Pickle. Garrett Clopper, Journal.

Figure 1.2 Opposite
To Make Beef or Pork Pickle. Anthony Allaire, Diary and Order Book.

Fredericton Monday June 15th 1795 –

The inhabitants of this Parish have at length had the consolation of attending

To Make Beef or Pork Pickle – 55

To 4 Gal.ns of Water add 6 lb Salt, 1/4 lb Sal. Prunella, and 1/2 lb Coarse brown Sugar. boil it well, and Strain it, when cold put on the Meat, and keep it well covered. boil up the Pickle again as often as you find it Necessary –

Receipt for Pickling Salmon

First boil in fresh Water, then put in warm Wine, and when cold kept in the broth it was boil'd in for 8, 12 or 14 Days afterwards one or more pieces are taken out and put in Vinegar

Soft Waffles –	Dough Nuts	Wigs –
3 lb Flour.	4 lb Flour.	3 lb Flour.
1/2 lb Butter.	1/2 lb Butter.	3/4 lb Butter.
12 Eggs –	1 lb Sugar.	1 lb Sugar
3 Quarts Milk.	3 Eggs.	12 Eggs.
	1 Quart Milk	1 Quart Milk.
	1/2 pint good Yeast. –	

the meat with each change, and then boiling it "with their Pease as usual."[54] Like Townsend's and Pocock's, Clopper's and Allaire's recipes highlight a masculine military recipe culture that is perhaps not well known in the twenty-first century, although the recipe for the bread baked today in the living-history museum at Fortress Louisbourg is based on a recipe found in *Détails militaires* (1750), a manual that recorded instructions for the French army.[55]

Receipt for Pickling Beef

This recipe is part of a collection of papers that belonged to William Trueman (1720–1797), a Methodist farmer from Yorkshire who migrated with his wife Ann to what is now Point de Bute, Westmorland County, New Brunswick, in 1775.[56] This undated recipe is from the Trueman family scrapbook held in the Mount Allison University Archives and seems to be in William Trueman's handwriting.

Receipt for Pickling Beef

Take four Gallons of water
tow Pound of Muscovado Sugar[57]
four Ounces of salt peter[58] tow
Quarts of common salt. Boil
all well and scim well until
the pickle bears an egg and
when cold put in your Beeff.

Although some amounts differ, this recipe is similar to "Admiral Pocock's Receipt" discussed earlier. More fulsome in its explanation of the process than Trueman's recipe, the version of Admiral Pocock's recipe in *The Burlington Almanack* calls for adding one and a half – rather than two – pounds of muscovado sugar, two ounces – rather than four – of saltpetre, and six pounds – rather than two quarts – of bay or common salt to four gallons of water. The Pocock recipe adds, "let it boil, being careful to take all the scum off, as it comes up."[59] Suggesting that Pocock's recipe may have been regularly adapted, another recipe with the same ingredients that appeared in *New England Farmer, and Gardener's Journal* in 1837, recommended and tested by one "H.C.," calls for a peck of salt, four ounces of saltpetre, one and a half pounds of brown sugar, and four gallons of water.[60] Trueman's recipe for pickling meat highlights how effective food preservation was essential both to colonial military endeavours and to colonial settlement.

That these recipes for salted meat are all associated with men may confirm that, in the eighteenth-century Maritimes, men were involved in this element of food production. According to Sarah F. McMahon, food preservation was "the least gendered phase in the foodways process."[61] Her study of eighteenth- and nineteenth-century daybooks and diaries concludes that while salting and pickling pork did resemble cooking, which was most often done by women, men may have held particular responsibility for meat, taking it singly or collectively from slaughtering and butchering through the preservation process.[62]

Lady Eleanora Dundas's Recipe

Preserving meat was not exclusively the province of men, however. In a 5 June 1798 letter to his wife Mary, Jonathan Bliss (1742–1822) offers Lady Eleanora Dundas's recipe for salted beef.[63] A Massachusetts-born Loyalist and lawyer who was in England during the American Revolutionary War, Bliss had returned to British North America to take up the post of New Brunswick's attorney general in 1785. Though he found colonial life difficult, he seems to have achieved some comfort in domestic life after his 1790 marriage to the much younger Mary Worthington of Springfield, Massachusetts, Bliss's former home. Writing to his friend Benedict Arnold, who had once owned his Saint John house, Bliss expressed the wish to "make my Fire side happy even in this wretched country." Mary would die the year after Bliss's letter to her, on 17 April 1799.[64]

The recipe's original source, as the title suggests, is Lady Eleanora Dundas. The daughter of the ninth Earl of Home, Eleanora (née Home, 1759–1837) married Thomas Dundas in 1784. Thomas Dundas (1750–1794) was a Scottish MP and army officer who had served in the British army in the American Revolutionary War and was stationed in Halifax between 1785 and 1788.[65] A nearly identical recipe to the one Bliss sent his wife, "A Receipt for Pickling Beef," can be found in the 1785 manuscript recipe collection titled *Collection of Lady Eleanora* held at the Wellcome Library in London.[66] Appearing first among her receipts for medicine and cookery, Lady Eleanora's pickled beef recipe instructs the user to take

> Four English gallons of water six lb
> salt dryed, two pounds coarse Sugar two ounces
> salt Peter, boil it altogether and skim it,
> When no skim rises & it is perfectly clear
> then take it off and when cold pour it over
> your Beef.

Lady Eleanora's instructions do not appear to have been published elsewhere. Bliss's letter does not make clear how he had acquired the recipe, but the date of the letter does suggest that it remained in circulation more than a decade after Lady Eleanora had left Nova Scotia. She had arrived in Halifax in September 1786 and was in Saint John by October 1786, before continuing on to Quebec in April 1787, where she gave birth to a child in July 1787. After travelling to Montreal and Niagara, Lady Eleanora returned home to Scotland in 1788.[67]

Lady Eleanora Dundas's Recipe

4 Gallons of Water, 6 Pounds of Salt Dried, 2 Pounds of Coarse Sugar, 2 Ounces of Salt Peter, boil all together and skim it; when no scum rises, and it is perfectly clear, then take it off; and when cold pour it over your Beef – Your friend Col. Elligood says, Pack the Beef 2 Days in Salt to take out the Blood – This may be more necessary in a warm Climate. He puts 6 Gal. water.

A significant element of this recipe – beyond the way it further highlights the importance of salted meat in the culinary history of the Maritimes – is that the only important difference between Bliss's epistolary receipt and that recorded in Lady Eleanora's notebook is the original's specification of "English gallons." Although it was only in 1832 that the American gallon of 231 cubic inches was legally adopted – after this recipe was shared – the sizes of gallons still varied internationally. The specification of English gallons may gesture to the recipe's use in a colonial context since the distinction would have been less necessary in Britain itself. Bliss's further report on Ellegood's recommendation to pack the beef in salt for two days suggests the colonel's use and attempt to improve the original method.

To Cure Hams

The following instructions "To Cure Hams" are another of Garrett Clopper's recipes.[68] Another form of preserved meat, ham differs from pickled pork in the technique used to make it. Methods for curing ham or bacon also include drying and sometimes smoking, whereas pickled pork is merely stored in the wet brine.[69] Like the instructions for pickling meat, this recipe prescribes salting the meat with saltpetre, but further directs the user to hang the meat to smoke after it is removed from the brine. We have not found another source for the recipe.

To Cure Hams

To each Ham of 10 lbs take 1 Oz
Salt Petre ~ 2 Oz of Sugar and 2
handfull of Salt, mix them toge-
ther and Rub the Hams well there:
-with, and Pack them in a tight
Vessel there to lay two weeks.
then take them out, and with
the Pickle they make, the Salt &c.
that Remains in the Vessel undis:
solv'd (adding a sufficiency of
other Salt) make as much pickle
strong enough to bear an Egg as
will cover the Hams after they
are again Pack'd in the Vessel, boil
the Pickle till no scum rises, let
it cool and pour it on the Hams,
let them lie another fortnight,
then hang them up to smoak

Made in Europe since the Roman period, ham was produced in a variety of ways across eighteenth-century Europe. In England, some regional ham-making techniques relied primarily on salt, while in other areas, molasses, spices, or herbs might be added.[70] For example, the recipe "To cure Hams" in *The Complete Family Cook*, published in London in 1796, while not linked to a particular English county, adds to a salt and saltpetre rub a mixture of herbs (thyme, laurel, marjoram, savoury, and juniper) and specifies that after the ham has been smoked in the chimney, it should be rubbed with wine and vinegar and covered with ashes.[71] A comparison between this recipe and Clopper's, which includes none of the herbs or the wine, may suggest that Clopper's recipe was more invested in the preservative aspects of ham-making than the flavour profile.

To Pickle Berwick Salmon

This recipe was published on 13 August 1767 in *The Nova Scotia Gazette*, a newspaper printed in Halifax by Robert Fletcher (fl. 1766–1785) between 1766 and 1770.[72] Fletcher had moved to Halifax from London in 1766 when he was appointed government printer. He held this position until 1770, when he closed down his printing business to focus on his bookstore. The paper was then taken over by Anthony Henry (1734–1800), who merged Fletcher's paper with his *Nova Scotia Chronicle* to create *The Nova Scotia Gazette and the Weekly Chronicle.*[73]

This recipe for Berwick salmon is followed by another for pickling salmon "to keep in hot countries" and both were also printed, along with the preface referring to America, in *The Virginia Gazette* on 2 July 1767, a little less than six weeks before they appeared in the Halifax newspaper.[74]

The following Receipts, which are excellent, may possibly afford some hints for improving the pickling of Sturgeon and other fish in America.

To pickle BERWICK SALMON.

FILL your copper full of water, to every ten gallons of water put seven pounds of common salt, let it boil half an hour for pickle, then take out of the copper as much of this pickle as you will have occasion for; put your Salmon (first split and cut into five pieces) into the remainder of the boiling pickle, and let it boil between thirty and forty minutes, then take the Salmon out carefully to prevent its breaking, and lay it on wooden gratings in a cold place to cool quickly; if you have more Salmon to boil, you may boil it in the same liquor before you throw it away; after the Salmon is quite cold and the pickle likewise, pack the Salmon in small kits,[75] and let it be covered with the following liquor, viz. One quart of the pickle you took out of the copper before the Salmon was put in to boil, and five quarts of vinegar, and head up the kit close. *N.B.* Salmon will not do for pickling, unless it be twelve or eighteen hours out of the water in warm weather, and two days in cold, and what is pickled the latter end of the season, will keep three or four months if the kit is not opened, and

> gets no air; but will not be good above ten days
> or a fortnight after opening.

Berwick is a town that lies on the English part of the River Tweed that flows primarily through Scotland near the North Sea coast. It had for centuries served as an important site for the British salmon fishery, and the method of pickling and drying the salmon described in the recipe allowed the movement of the fish within the UK (it was only after 1788 that it became possible to ship fresh Scottish fish by packing it in ice, but only in the colder months and only as far as London).[76] The use of the term *kitt* (or kit) suggests a commercial context as well.[77] The recipe's purpose, then, is to bring this European and specifically commercial way of transporting salmon to the Americas. This is not the only method available. Indigenous peoples in northeastern North America preserved salmon by drying or cooking it, freezing it in winter, and curing it with salt.[78] The most common European method in the Atlantic fishery had been salt curing, which entailed packing the fish in layers in barrels with salt, thus pickling the fish in the juice from its own flesh. After two weeks of being pressed in this way, the fish would be cleaned and repacked into barrels with clean salt.[79] The Berwick salmon recipe likely aims to establish another economical way of preserving salmon for commercial purposes.

That the recipe is more interested in preserving salmon for sale than in ensuring good taste is evident in its difference from English recipes for pickled salmon created for home use. These specified the addition of more flavours that included spices as well as vinegar and salt. A recipe titled "To Pickle Salmon to keep all the Year," printed in an eighteenth-century book on angling, calls for putting pieces of fish into a mixture of three parts vinegar and one part water and adding a handful of salt as well as pepper, mace, cloves, and nutmeg. More spices are added after the liquid is removed, when the salmon is put into a barrel between layers of mace, cloves, pepper, and nutmeg, and the barrel filled with the pickling liquid as well as more vinegar that had been boiled with bay leaves.[80] Not just the work of anglers, salmon pickling was also done at home, as the popular recipe collection *The Compleat Housewife* by Eliza Smith (d. 1732?), first published in 1727, suggests. Putting into further relief the pared-down flavour profile of the Berwick salmon recipe, and drawing attention to how the commercial Berwick salmon recipe drew on methods used at home, Smith's recipe similarly recommends first boiling the salmon and then packing it in closed barrels. Her recipe pays more attention to taste at each stage, however. The recipe calls for cooking cut-up salmon in a boiling pickle of "good" vinegar (another signifier of a concern with taste) and not just salt but also spices (black pepper, Jamaican pepper, cloves, and mace). When the fish has been removed and cooled, it should be put into a "Barrel or Stein" with bay leaves and spice added between the layers. The recipe stresses the importance of method to preserving, specifying that the fat needs to be scummed off the cold pickle before it is poured over the fish a second time and that the barrel needs to be covered "very close."[81] The recipe for Berwick salmon focuses more narrowly than these other fish pickling recipes on the preservative practices.[82]

To Carry Fish Alive to a Great Distance

This recipe appeared in *The Weekly Chronicle* on 26 March 1791.[83] Published on Saturdays and offering local news as well as news from America and Europe, the newspaper was established in Halifax in 1786 and ran until the death of its founder, William Minns (1763–1827).[84] Minns was the son of a physician who had emigrated from England to Massachusetts around 1735. A Loyalist, he left Boston in 1776, departing with his sister Martha first to Rhode Island and then to Nova Scotia. Minns found his way into printing through Martha, who married John Howe, the Halifax printer who published *The Halifax Journal* (1780?–1800) and *The Nova Scotia Magazine*; after working as a printer in Howe's shop, Minns began publishing *The Weekly Chronicle* on his own.[85]

Despite its oddness, this recipe appears to have had a long publication life. It appeared as a note from "P.C." in *The Gentleman's Magazine* in London and the Dublin edition of *The London Magazine* in July 1752 – almost forty years before its publication in Nova Scotia.[86] It also appeared again in 1812 in the New York newspaper *Shamrock*.[87]

To carry FISH alive to a great Distance.

TAKE an ounce of white sugar-candy,[88] and as much salt-petre as is about the size of walnut, and as much wheat flour; mix them together, and put the mixture in a little bottle in your pocket.

This quantity is sufficient for a pail of water Having provided a convenient vessel to carry the fish, and put in it some white bread crumbled when the water begins to grow warm, and the fish put up their heads to the top, then add a small quantity of this powder into the water, which

> cools it and preserves the fish.
> The water, if possible, should be changed
> every four or five miles, and the powdered salt
> petre, &c. added as often as you see occasion.
> By these means trout may be brought above 40
> miles, alive and well.

Given that these instructions recommend a pail for the fish, they appear to come from a land-based fishing practice rather than one associated with the boatload quantities of fish that Europeans had been taking from the North Atlantic in salted and dried form. The smaller-scale fishery underpinning these instructions earned its most literary veneration in Izaak Walton's *The Complete Angler, or Contemplative Man's Recreation*, which was published repeatedly between its initial appearance in 1653 and 1800, including in 1791. The work's narrator, Piscator, says fishing is an "excellent" and "ancient" art not unlike poetry, given that the angler "must not only bring an enquiring, searching, observing wit, but he must bring a large measure of hope and patience, and a love and propensity to the art itself."[89] This recipe shares with *The Complete Angler* an interest in inquiring and searching. Although the instructions do not explain why the fish must be kept alive, the method may offer a way of ensuring the opportunity to eat fresh catch, a challenge in the absence of refrigeration.

The method proposed in this recipe seems to seek specifically to enable the consumption or processing of fresh fish nearer home, specifically within forty miles of the catch. A note in the 1791 edition of *The Complete Angler* more explicitly articulates this desire for live fish: carp, it says, lives the longest once removed from the water, and in Holland "it is a common practice" to keep the fish alive for up to a month "by hanging them in a cool place, with wet moss in a net, and feeding them with bread and milk." Bread appears repeatedly in *The Complete Angler* as a fish food as well as bait, so its use in the recipe in *The Weekly Chronicle* may be meant to function in this way.[90] The saltpetre specified in the recipe may be intended to make the water cooler. *The Ladies Best Companion* (1775), for instance, offers a recipe to "make Ice to cool Wines in Summer" that suggests putting two ounces of saltpetre into three quarts of water, putting the mixture into a bottle, and lowering the bottle into a well for six hours; when it is pulled up, the bottle will, the recipe claims, be filled with ice.[91]

A heightened interest in angling developed in British North America between 1760 and 1840, especially among British military officers, and several gentlemanly trout anglers note the excellence of the River Philip in Nova Scotia for trout and salmon fishing.[92] While both the Mi'kmaq and Europeans had long dealt with the problem of preserving fish by drying it,[93] this recipe seems concerned with enabling the consumption of fresh fish. Like the recipe for pickling Berwick salmon, the recipe is still interested in food preservation – in this case, keeping the fish alive until they can be eaten or preserved.

SOUP AND STEW

Receipt to Make Hessian Soup

Submitted by "A Friend to the Poor," this recipe for a hearty and economical soup was published in a 1768 letter to *The Nova Scotia Gazette*, a weekly publication that began in August 1766.[94] The *Gazette*'s final issue would appear on 30 August 1770, after which it merged with *The Nova Scotia Chronicle and Weekly Advertiser* to become *The Nova Scotia Gazette and the Weekly Chronicle*.[95] The recipe was later printed in the *Pennsylvania Packet* on 21 April 1789, without the final sentence but as a part of a letter from Nayland, Suffolk, in England recommending the recipe as "a cheap and wholesome dinner for six persons"; suggesting that this recipe might have come from Nova Scotia, the recipe is preceded by a report that a gentleman from Nova Scotia had written to tell his friends in England of an impending hard winter, a warning he had received from Indigenous people who "had been down with them" and "who pass for prophets in the country." The soup is recommended for those who might want to assist their "poor and industrious neighbours in this very severe weather."[96]

To the PRINTER,

SIR,

By inserting the following you will oblige a constant Reader.

Receipt to make HESSIAN[97] SOUP.

TAKE seven Pints of Water, one Pint of split Pease, one pound of lean Beef cut into small pieces, three quarters of a pound of potatoes, three ounces of ground rice, two heads of cellery, three leeks; season it to your taste with pepper, salt, and dried mint; let them all boil

> together till reduced to five pints: Then strain it through a cullender. This will dine six people, and the expence is very small, and it is extremely nourishing.
>
> a friend to the poor.

The name *Hessian* points to German origins for the soup. Relatively few recipes for Hessian soup are extant, and those that do survive appeared after the recipe in *The Nova Scotia Gazette*. A recipe for Hessian soup is included in the well-known English cookbook *A New System of Domestic Cookery* (1810) by Maria Rundell (1745–1828).[98] Rundell's recipe also incorporates split peas, potatoes, celery, and carrots, but more specifically calls for "a neat's tongue" and "half an ox's head" rather than the "pound of lean Beef" indicated in the *Gazette*'s version.[99] Directions for making Hessian soup can also be found in a collection titled *The Cook's Complete Guide on the Principles of Frugality* (1810).[100] Written "By a Lady," the book's author is identifiable as Esther Copley (1786–1851) by her attribution also as the "Authoress of *Cottage Comforts*," a book aiming to improve the "welfare and happiness" of "the labouring classes" that appeared in at least twelve editions by 1834.[101] Like *Cottage Comforts*, the aim of *The Cook's Complete Guide* is to promote good health, as it recognizes "that many diseases have been aggravated, if not caused, by an indulgence in improper food" and that "many maladies have been prevented and removed by a proper regard to diet."[102] Though Copley's recipe, which uses similar ingredients to the *Gazette* and Rundell recipes, was published more than four decades after the version that appeared in *The Nova Scotia Gazette*, its inclusion in a book whose subtitle claims to offer guidance "On the Principles of Frugality, Comfort, and Elegance" also implies that, like the recipe submitted to the *Gazette*, "the expence is very small" but the reward "nourishing." In all cases, the cooked soup is strained through a sieve or colander and is well seasoned; the use of "rice flour," or what "A Friend to the Poor" calls ground rice, is specified in Copley's and Rundell's recipes only if needed to thicken the soup.

Less than a decade after this recipe appeared in *The Nova Scotia Gazette*, about 30,000 Hessian mercenaries would cross the Atlantic to fight with British forces in the American Revolutionary War. Revolutionaries like Thomas Jefferson not only criticized the British for the move but also sought to recruit the German soldiers to their side with promises of land and liberty. Although these efforts were not immediately successful, as the war went on some Hessians did join the Revolutionary cause or desert the British military altogether. Hessian soldiers, whose diaries suggest a concern with food, complained that potatoes were not as readily available in America as they were in Germany; this recipe, however, specifies a rather large quantity and thus provides an early notation in the history of the potato in what is now the Maritimes.[103]

Potato Soup

The following recipe was printed in *The Nova Scotia Packet and General Advertiser*, the third newspaper established and printed in Shelburne, Nova Scotia.[104] The newspaper was published between 1785 and 1789 by James Humphreys (1748/9–1810), a Philadelphia Loyalist who continued in the printing trade after his 1784 arrival in Nova Scotia. During his time in Shelburne, Humphreys was active as a printer and a merchant, and he served also in local government. He had returned to Philadelphia by 1797 and died in 1810.[105]

The recipe is excerpted and slightly altered from "On the Culture of Potatoes," an essay by a Reverend H.J. Close of Trimley, Suffolk, printed in *Letters and Papers on Agriculture, Planting, &c. Selected from the Correspondence-book of the Society Instituted at Bath, for the Encouragement of Agriculture, Arts, Manufactures, and Commerce* (1786).[106] The essay offers a wide-ranging report on the five years of experiments Close claims to have conducted with potatoes; his experiments focused on fertilizers, planting and harvesting methods, yields, costs of agricultural production, and the uses of potatoes.[107] The essay cites a Mr Hanway as the recipe's original author.[108] Close's essay, "On the Culture of Potatoes," is excerpted again in two related encyclopedias: *Encyclopaedia Britannica; or, A Dictionary of Arts, Sciences, and Miscellaneous Literature*, printed in Dublin in 1790, and *Encyclopaedia; or, A Dictionary of Arts, Sciences, and Miscellaneous Literature*, printed in Philadelphia in 1798.[109]

Extract of a letter sent to the Bath Society by the Rev. H.J. Close, on the cultivation of potatoes, and their great value as a food for the poor.

"Potatoes are a cheap and an excellent substitute for peas in soups and broths, allowing double the quantity. The following is a receipt for making potatoe soup, which I have weekly distributed among the poor in my neighbourhood, to their great relief.

	s.	d.
An ox cheek, - - -	2	6
Two pecks potatoes, - - -		6
Quarter peck of onions, -		3
An ounce of pepper, - -		2
Three quarters of a pound of salt,		1
One peck of coals to boil it, -		3
Total,	3	9

"Boil the above ingredients in ninety pints of water, over a slow fire, till reduced to sixty. I have added the expence of every article according to their prices with us, that gentlemen may perceive at how very cheap and easy a rate they may feed sixty of their poor neighbours. I find from experience, that a pint of this rich soup, with a small piece of the meat, is sufficient to satisfy a working man with a good, pleasant, hearty meal."

The recipe in *The Nova Scotia Packet* is slightly different from the one found in Close's 1788 essay. It calls for an ox's cheek rather than a head, to the same cost, and for an ounce of pepper, for two pence, rather than an ounce and a half of pepper, for three pence, as in the original. The cost of the coals, likewise three pence, is also included in the total cost of the recipe, which is not done in the original version. The persistence of costing with the recipe's ingredients – even including the cost of the heat – suggests that frugality rather than flavour is at the core of the recipe's purpose. The recipe's gesture to gentlemen who feed their poor neighbours, however, directs the instructions to more privileged English-speaking Nova Scotians who could provide charity to their neighbours rather than to those who were themselves hungry.

This recipe's advocacy for potatoes suggests they were not yet widely or eagerly consumed by Europeans. Close writes that he wants the potato to be "admitted in the constant course of crops," which would entail a change to the customs of British agriculture.[110] To prove the vegetable's benefits, Close reports that he has been cultivating potatoes and feeding them to cattle and pigs, as well as his children, and his poorer neighbours have followed his example and are now growing the vegetable in their gardens.[111] It was only in the nineteenth century, after this recipe's publication, that the potato became widely grown and eaten in Europe as a staple crop and inexpensive food. The eventual success of the potato came about in part because of widespread warfare, which frequently destroyed grain crops, as well as grain harvest failures that resulted in widespread hunger among the European population.[112] The chapter on agriculture in this book documents more of the history of potato growing in what is now the Maritimes.

Harrico of Mutton

This handwritten recipe is pasted into a page of the *Almon Scrapbook* (1780–1800) held at the Nova Scotia Archives.[113] Though added to the scrapbook at a later date, the recipes were likely recorded sometime between 1780 and 1800 by women in Halifax's well-known Almon family.[114] As we know from extant letters, the hand does not correspond with that of Rebecca Byles Almon (1762–1853), the wife Dr William James Almon and one of the first of the Almon women to reside in Halifax. Rebecca was also one of thirteen children to well-known Loyalist clergyman Mather Byles (1734/5–1814), and a clue to the identity of the scribe might be found in another mutton recipe in the same hand, titled "Receipt of our dear Mary Byles of Granada."[115] Mary Byles was likely the wife of Mather Byles III, who lived in Granada from at least 1792 to 1797, and thus was the sister-in-law of Rebecca Byles Almon.[116] If not Rebecca Byles Almon, the recipe seems to have been recorded by someone who also knew Mary Byles well.

Harrico of Mutton.

A Neck or Loin of mutton cut it into Six peices Flour it
& Fry it brown on both Sides in a Stew Pan then pour
out all the Fat put in some Turnips & Carrots cut like
Dice, Two dozen of Chesnuts blanched two or three lettices's cut
small six little round onnions a bundle of sweet Herbs
Some Pepper & salt, Two or three blades of mace, Cover
it close & let it Stew an Hour then take off the Fat &
Dish it up.
Eat it to be sure

In the eighteenth century, the French word *haricot* was used to describe a stew or ragout made of mutton and vegetables.[117] What may be the first English recipe

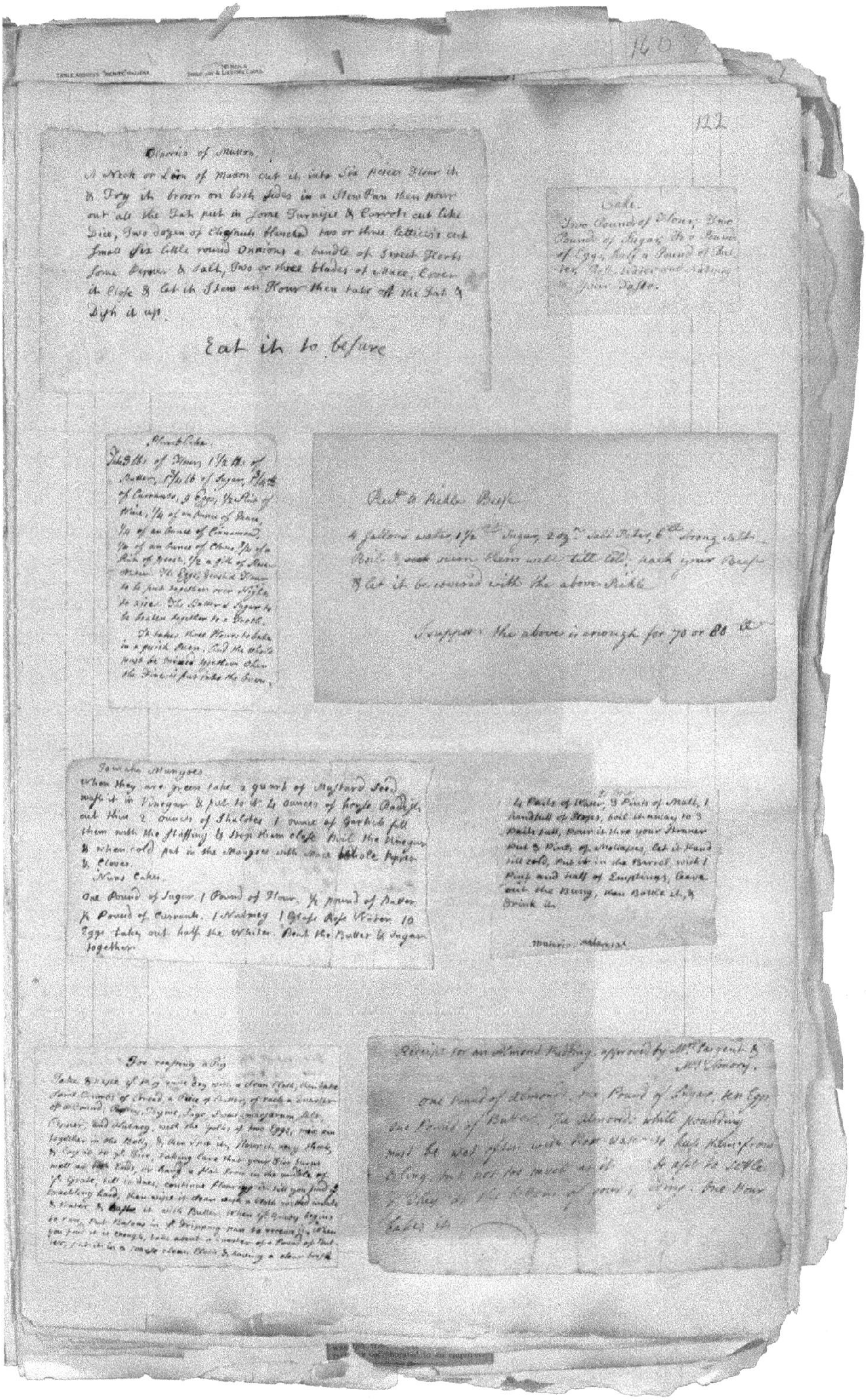

Figure 1.3
Harrico of Mutton. *Almon Scrapbook*.

for haricot, titled "Harrico of a Neck of Mutton" and included in a popular collection by Elizabeth Raffald (bap. 1733–1781), uses the same method as the Almon recipe, which entails frying the pieces of meat and then stewing with vegetables; Raffald recommends cutting the mutton into chops, browning them, and then putting them into a pot with water, carrots, turnips, celery, asparagus, cabbage, and "chyan" (cayenne).[118] The recipe draws on French cookery. *The Court and Country Cook*, a 1702 translation of the famous late-seventeenth-century French cookbook *Le cuisinier royal et bourgeois* by François Massialot, includes a recipe for "Cutlets in Haricot and otherwise" that recommends putting mutton cutlets "in Haricot," or in a stew, with turnips, "well-season'd Liquour" and chestnuts, also used in the Almon recipe.[119] The recipe was not used only by the chefs of dukes, as Massialot was. A 1780 English translation of an account of life at the Bastille by Joseph Marie Brossais du Perray (1731–18?) describes Sunday suppers in the notorious Paris prison as including "a small dish of *haricot* in which bones and turnip abound"; the *haricot* was evidently not the finest, for du Perray also notes that "the oil they give turns the stomack: it is only fit for lamps."[120] The prison's cooks, it seems, did not do as the Almon recipe recommends at the browning stage and "pour out all the Fat" and again "take off the Fat" before serving, perhaps because the Bastille kitchen, du Perray also notes, served as the source of "immense profits" and "the governor's gold mine," with an income "augmented in proportion to the bad fare of the prisoner."[121]

In English, the term *haricot* seems to have been more popular in Scotland, where it appears in several eighteenth-century Edinburgh publications. Mrs Frazer's *The Practice of Cookery*, for example, includes a recipe "To make a Haricot of Mutton" stewed with onions, carrot, and turnip,[122] while Susanna MacIver's *Cookery and Pastry* offers instructions for making a dish by the same title.[123] Not reserved for lamb and mutton, *haricot* also appears in George Dalrymple's *The Practice of Modern Cookery*, which offers instructions for making "Haricot of Hare" in a book claiming in its subtitle that its contents have been *Adapted to Families of Distinction, As Well as to Those of the Middling Ranks of Life*.[124] Elizabeth Cleland's *A New and Easy Method of Cookery* substitutes deer meat, noting in a recipe "To stew Venison" that it "may be haricot after the same Manner as Mutton is"; the book also offers a recipe "To Make a Mutton Haricot."[125]

Like the Almon recipe, which calls for "sweet Herbs" and "three blades of mace" as well as salt and pepper, the *haricot* recipes found in the Edinburgh cookbooks are well seasoned, with Frazer's and MacIver's specifying salt and spices and Cleland's more specifically indicating the addition of cloves and nutmeg as well as claret.[126] Explicitly intended for a genteel consumer, Dalrymple's recipe is the most elaborate, calling for shallots, garlic, cloves, salt, and whole pepper as well as "a faggot [a bundle or bunch] of parsley and sweet herbs," and "half a Pint of white-wine."[127] Among these recipes, however, the addition of chestnuts is unique to the *Almon Scrapbook*'s "Harrico of Mutton," though they are added to some English stews. The English cookbook *The London Art of Cookery* (1789) by John Farley (1755/6–1827), for instance, specifies the addition of "some chestnuts roasted and blanched" in a recipe for stewing pheasants.[128]

It is unclear whether the chestnuts used in the Almon recipe were of the European or American variety, both of which bear edible fruit. According to the Canadian Chestnut Council, "people familiar with the American chestnut in the northeastern USA migrated to Nova Scotia and brought seeds of American chestnut with them"; hence "The presence of these trees is often associated with the migration of the United Empire Loyalists following the War of Independence in the USA." Though widely destroyed by an early twentieth-century blight that decimated the once chestnut-abundant forests of the eastern United States, American chestnuts can yet be found in "several chestnut trees distributed throughout Nova Scotia," including one in Ashdale, Hants County, that is now one of the largest in North America.[129] Though it seems unlikely that the Loyalists' American trees would have matured to the point of bearing fruit when the Almon recipe was recorded sometime in the late eighteenth century, chestnuts could have been imported to Nova Scotia from England or the eastern seaboard.

Other ingredients, like the Almon recipe's "lettice's," would have been locally available. Though it may seem odd to modern tastes to use lettuce in a cooked dish, eighteenth-century English cookbooks frequently include its leaves in recipes for gravies, soups, and stews, and sometimes also refer to "cabbage-lettuce." Along with the Almon recipe's other vegetable ingredients, carrots and turnip, lettuce and cabbage are cool-season crops that would have been easily grown in Nova Scotia, as would many of the "sweet herbs" that may have included varieties of readily cultivated basil, mint, and sage. The indicated mace, a spice derived from the husk of the nutmeg fruit indigenous to Indonesia and used in English cookery since about 1600, would most likely have been imported from the West Indies. Extensive and well-established trade routes among the British colonies and the Caribbean islands would have made mace and nutmeg readily available in colonial Halifax.

BREAD

A Method to Make Potato Bread

This recipe appeared in the 4 April 1794 issue of the monthly periodical *The Nova Scotia Magazine*.[130] The magazine was published in Halifax between 1789 and 1792 by William Cochran (1757–1833), the president of King's College in Windsor, and after 1790 by John Howe (1754–1835). Directions for "Maple Sugar" and a "Method of Making Mortar," which are included elsewhere in this book, were also printed in *The Nova Scotia Magazine*.[131] Howe was a Loyalist born in Massachusetts who arrived in Halifax with his wife Martha in 1780. Soon after, he began working as a printer, a profession he had previously held in New England. The publication was the earliest magazine to appear in Canada, publishing (or republishing) literary, philosophical, historical, and anthropological essays, biographical notes and memoirs, poetry, directions for living, news, and many sets of instructions. *The Nova Scotia Magazine* failed in 1792 due to a lack of subscribers, but Howe nevertheless served as the king's printer in Nova Scotia, postmaster of Halifax, justice of the peace, and spy. He was also the father of Joseph Howe, who would become premier of Nova Scotia, a member of Sir John A. Macdonald's cabinet, and eventually the lieutenant governor of Nova Scotia.[132]

"A Method to Make Potato Bread" had previously appeared in *The Annual Register, Or a View of the History, Politics, and Literature, for the Year 1779*, published in London in 1780 and 1786.[133] The English instructions appear to be a condensed and loose translation of *Manière de faire le pain de pommes de terre, sans mélange de farine* by Antoine Augustin Parmentier (1737–1813), which had been printed in Paris in 1779 and then included in Parmentier's *Recherches sur les végétaux nourissans* in 1781.[134]

A METHOD TO MAKE POTATOE-BREAD WITHOUT THE ADMIXTURE OF FLOUR.

[By M. Parmentier, Member of the College of Pharmacy at Paris.]

Of the STARCH.

the potatoes must be well washed;
they must be ground fine with the
assistance of a tin rasp; they are thereby
converted into a liquid paste, which must
be diluted in water, and well agitated, in

order to empty it into a sieve placed over a proper vessel. The water passes with the starch of the potatoes; this starch must be well washed in several waters; it is to be divided into small pieces, and exposed to the air, in order to dry it: it is of a most exquisite whiteness. The substance which remains in the sieve is the most fibrous part; it must be dried after all the moisture is pressed out of it; it may be used in the composition of brown bread, or may be given in that state to poultry.

Remarks. – One pound of potatoes contains three ounces of starch, two ounces of fibrous substance and extractive matter, and eleven ounces of vegetative water. These substances vary according to the nature of the soil and the species of the potatoe. It is to clear this root from the super abundance of water which it contains, and to separate the starch from the other substances which constitute the potatoe, that the foregoing process is put in practice. You may, in lieu of a rasp, which renders the operation tedious, substitute a broad wheel with double parallel spokes, upon the same axis or axletree, shod with plate iron, stamped with holes, instead of hands of iron, or any other instrument; besides, necessity and practice will soon clear up that point.

The starch extracted from potatoes has this advantage; that it may be kept for many years without the least alteration, and will still subsist without corruption, or untouched in a frozen potatoe, even when animals will not eat it.

Of the PULP. – Put the potatoes in boiling water; when they are boiled enough, cast away the water, and peel them; and, with the assistance of a wooden roller, reduce them into a paste, which, by grinding grows stiff and elastic. When there are no more clots or lumps in the whole mass, then the pulp is in perfection.

Remarks, – The parts which constitute the potatoe are in its natural state divided; after boiling, these parts are so united as to be but one homogenous mass. The starch, the fibrous substance which floated, as one may say, in the vegetative water, are in it dissolved.

It is from this very simple operation that the whole fabrication of potatoe bread depends; without it, no panification:[135] moreover, the potatoe must necessarily be in that state when we intend to mix it with any other grain, such as buck wheat, barley, or oats: under any other form, its union with these sorts of grain will make, at best, but a coarse bread.

Of the BREAD. – Take five pounds of dried starch, and five pounds of the pulp; dissolve a suitable quantity of leaven on yeast in warm water the eve or night before. The mixture being exactly made, let it lie all night in the kneading-trough, well covered and kept warm until the next day; this is the second leaven; then add five pounds more of starch, and the same quantity of pulp, and knead it well. The water must be in proportion as a fifth part, that is to say, that upon twenty pounds of

> paste there must be five pounds of the water. You must observe that the water be used as hot as possible.
>
> The paste being completely kneaded, it must be divided into small loaves: this bread requires slow preparation, and the oven must be equally and moderately heated: it will require two hours baking.
>
> The salt with which they season the bread in some provinces is also necessary for this: the quantity depends on the taste; but half a drachm[136] seems to be sufficient.
>
> Any one may easily conceive that this abstract cannot wholly give an idea of the process, and that those who have the fabrication of this bread at heart must be obliged to have recourse to their own experience, because no exact account is to be expected when a new preparation is to be performed.

Antoine Augustin Parmentier, here identified as "M. Parmentier, Member of the College of Pharmacy at Paris," was a pharmacist who served in the French army in Europe during the Seven Years War (1757–1763). He was taken prisoner by the Prussians and, after his release at the war's end, began to conduct research on potatoes, which he had been fed while imprisoned. His interest was piqued by their positive effects on his health. In 1773, he published the results of his study in *Examen chimiqe des pommes de terre* in Paris. In 1785, Parmentier received a royal seal of approval for the potato from Louis XVI, whose court began serving the tuber, but the king also praised Parmentier for finding bread for the poor. Although Louis XVI was executed during the French Revolution in 1793, Parmentier survived the upheaval and was in 1802 made a member of the Légion d'Honneur by Napoleon.[137]

Parmentier's work on potatoes was known in England beyond the excerpt in *The Annual Register. Recherches sur les végétaux nourissans, qui, dans le temps de disette, peuvent remplacer les aliments ordinaires* (1781) was translated and printed in London in 1783 as *Observation on such Nutritive Vegetables as May be Substituted in the Place of Ordinary Food, in Times of Scarcity*. The first vegetable considered in the *Observation* is the potato, which is said to be eaten in Germany and Ireland but regarded with some suspicion elsewhere. "The vegetable kingdom," the *Observation* maintains, "affords no food more wholesome, more easily procured, or less expensive, than the Potatoe."[138]

Efforts to popularize the potato as a viable food option came during a time when hunger was common in Europe. Shifting political and social relationships, climate effects, high food prices, stagnant wages, and wars disrupted markets and labour and determined who had access to food and who did not. Structural changes in nascent capitalist systems that saw the emergence of large-scale markets also left some people without access to food.[139] Pre-Revolutionary France had its own particular food supply problems. Food shortages sparked food protests, such as the Flour War of 1775 that erupted in Paris and its environs in response to poor grain harvests, increased grain prices, and the emergence of national free markets for grain under Louis XIV. Because bread was at the centre of the diet for many, grain flour was a crucial commodity.[140] Potatoes provided an alternative to grain in a time of scarcity.

The recipe for potato bread was part of an eighteenth-century move to make the diet of working people in Europe a political and national concern. Ensuring that workers could eat a hearty diet gained the attention of governments, which drew connections among food, working bodies, and nationalism. Although European colonialism had brought the potato to Europe in the sixteenth century, even by the mid-eighteenth century it had not become a popular food across the continent.[141] Parmentier's studies of the benefits of the potato, as well as recipes showing how the potato could be used in making a staple food, are significant both in attempting to address European hunger and in spreading knowledge of the vegetable around the European Atlantic world. Using the potato in bread is meant to transform a staple food. Nevertheless, knowledge of potatoes in eighteenth-century Nova Scotia did not depend entirely on Parmentier and *The Nova Scotia Magazine*'s English-speaking readers. Although potatoes were not commonly grown by Acadians before 1755, they were grown – and eaten – in small quantities around Acadia before the *Grand dérangement* and became an important food crop among Acadians who returned.[142]

A Method of Making Leaven / Another Way of Making Leaven

The following methods for making bread leaven were published in the 4 April 1791 issue of *The Nova Scotia Magazine.*[143] Though no original source has been found, an entry titled "Receipt for Making Bread without Barm, by the Help of a Leaven" credited to "the Dublin Society" and published in Hannah Glasse's *The Art of Cookery* (published from 1747 onwards) suggests broader contemporary interest in finding ways to raise bread without the use of barm, the yeast harvested from the froth on fermenting ale.[144]

A METHOD of making LEAVEN, without any to begin with, which may some-times be of Service to Country People who bake their own Bread.

WARM a quart or three pints of
flour in a skillet or some other
vessel, stirring it while warming to prevent
its burning; then with more flour and
warm water make as much dough as you

—

want for Leaven,[145] bury it in the midst of
the warm flour, sit it where it will keep
warm, and in a few hours the Leaven will
be good and fit for use.

ANOTHER WAY OF MAKING LEAVEN.

TAKE two pounds of potatoes; boil
them and bruise them fine, add to
them half a pound of brown sugar, half a
pint of emptings[146] and a pint of warm water,

—

mix them well together, and set them by
the fire, but not too near until they rise,
then put them by in a crock or stone jug.
Half a pint will make a batch of bread.

The first of the above recipes, "A Method of Making Leaven," is akin to sourdough starter. That the recipe offers instructions not for bread but for a bread ingredient may in part explain why the recipe for potato bread discussed above constitutes the only bread recipe we've so far located. As a staple in the early modern diet made so often that the ingredients and method were known by heart, household bread recipes likely did not need to be written down. The proposal in "A Method of Making Leaven" that the recipe "may some-times be of Service to Country People who bake their own Bread" does, however, suggest that town and city dwellers not only had more ready access to the ale yeast most often acquired from local brewers, but they may also have been more likely to purchase bread from a local baker (and therefore had no need to make bread or leaven). Alongside the previous recipe, "A Method to Make Potatoe-Bread without the Admixture of Flour," which was published in part to promote the not-yet ubiquitous potato, the second method here, "Another Way of Making Leaven," also uses potatoes and sugar. Innovation, it seems, made these *Nova Scotia Magazine* recipes worthy of publication.

CONDIMENTS

Catsup

The first recipe here, for catsup, is one of several recorded by an unknown source and pasted into a book titled *The Militia Laws of the Province of Nova Scotia* and held in the Nova Scotia Archives.[147] Although the archive dates the book to 1828, it is possible that the recipes were recorded earlier and then put into the book for safe-keeping. Catsup (or ketchup) was a very popular condiment in the eighteenth century. A likely source of this "Catsup" recipe is "To make CATCHUP" in Hannah Glasse's *The Art of Cookery*; Glasse's version ends specifying that the preserve will keep for two years and the recommendation, "This gives the best Flavour of the Mushrooms to any Sauce. If you put to a Pint of this Catchup, a Pint of M[R]um, it will taste like foreign Catchup."[148]

Catsup

take the large flaps of mushrooms pick nothing but the straws
and dirt from them then lay them in a broad earthen pan strewn wth
a good deal of salt over them Let them be till the next morning
then with your hand break them put them into a stew-pan
Let them boil a minute or two then strain them through a
coarse cloth and wring it hard. Take out all the juice Let it

stand to settle then pour it of[f] clear run it through a flannel
bag then boil it to a quart of the Liquor put a qua[r]ter of an
ounce of whole ginger and half a quarter of ounce of whole
pepper. boil it briskly a quarter of an hour then strain
it and when it is cold put it into pint bottles In each
bottle put some mace [- -] cloves cork it tight.

To Make Ketchup

The second recipe, "To Make Ketchup," is held in the Nova Scotia Archives' Miller Family Fonds, whose earliest items date from 1755, although it seems likely this recipe dates to the nineteenth century.[149] This recipe is an abbreviated version of one for "Mushroom-Ketchup" published in *The Female Economist* and attributed to a "Mrs. Smith" that was printed in London in 1810 and 1817. The Nova Scotia copyist has, however, not included Smith's instruction to cover the cork with leather and keep it in a dry place or incorporated the concluding paragraph explaining that if the ketchup is "well-boiled" it will keep for two or three years; the recipe also omits the original's recommendation to add mace, cloves, and nutmeg.[150] Mrs Smith's recipe was also printed in *The Housewife's Guide; or The Economical and Domestic Art of Cookery* by Mrs Deborah Irwin, another recipe book printed in London, likely in 1830.[151]

To Make Ketchup

Take the largest mushrooms you can procure: mash them well
with your hand: throw some salts among them the proper
proportion is six ounces of salt to a peck of mushrooms
let them stand two nights: then strain it & press the Mushroom
as hard as possible put it into an Iron sauce pan with
Jam[a]ica & black peper corns bruised a few shalots
some ginger sliced & a little horse raddish boil it an hour
strain it. and when cold bottle & corke it close.

Mushroom catsup (or ketchup) was inspired by a fermented Chinese fish sauce and bears little resemblance to today's ubiquitous tomato version. Neither sweet nor fruity, mushroom catsup was a highly seasoned brown sauce used primarily in fish and meat dishes that, according to the *Smithsonian Magazine*, first appeared as a recipe for "katchup" in Eliza Smith's *The Compleat Housewife* (1727).[152] Recipes for the condiment differ, but all describe extracting liquid from the mushrooms by first salting and then simmering, squeezing the simmered mushrooms through cheesecloth, and adding spices such as pepper and ginger to the extracted liquid. It takes a large quantity of mushrooms to make even a small bottle of sauce and, given that the above recipe "To Make Ketchup" specifies a proportion of "six ounces of salt to a peck of mushrooms," it seems likely that the making of it often included even more than a peck of the fungus. In *The Country Housewife* (1728), Richard Bradley (1688–1732), the English author of many works on gardening, notes that September is the month "that produces great numbers of Mushrooms in the Fields," and is when "chiefly that we ought to provide ourselves with them for making of Ketchup."[153]

The Nova Scotia Archives' *What's Cooking* online collection includes additional recipes for mushroom ketchup. "To Make Catchup" is one of eleven recipes that begin the 1786 "a memorandum of cash expended for the use of Mrs. Wentworths house," a document preserved among records compiled by Nova Scotia's first commissioner of public records, Thomas Beamish Akins (1809–1891).[154] Similar in method and ingredients to other catsup recipes discussed here, this one instructs the maker to

> Take the mushrooms wipe them Clean pound them in a
> mortar then strew some Salt over them and let them stand
> all night then put them in a Stone jugg and boil them
> in a Kettle of Water then Straine it & boil the Liquor
> in a Skillet with some Cloves & whole Peper
> when it is Cold put it in Bottles for your use put
> wax on the Corks to Keep Air out.

Another recipe was copied into a Miss Elizabeth Aitken's commonplace book (also in the Miller Family Fonds), dated 1809. Simply titled "Catchup," the recipe is mushroom-based and well-seasoned and seems to acknowledge the condiment's Chinese origins in suggesting, as Hannah Glasse's recipe does, that "if you put a Pint of Rum to this Catchup, it will taste like foreign Catchup": this recipe is, however, attributed to a Mrs Osmer and not Glasse.[155] The size of the indicated proportions in these Nova Scotia recipes points to a correspondence with those found in English cookbooks: that large quantities of mushroom ketchup were made partly because it kept well in corked bottles that were, the Commissioner of

Public Records recipe suggests, sometimes also sealed with wax to help keep the sauce even longer. In *The Country Housewife*, Bradley includes in his recipe "To make Mushroom Ketchup" the assertion that "I have had a Bottle of this sort of Ketchup, that has been open'd and set by for above a Year, that has not received the least Damage," and claims to know others who "have kept it in Quart Bottles to use as Occasion required, and have kept it good much longer than I have done."[156] It is telling of the condiment's hardiness that a later edition of Bradley's book adds a recipe "To make KETCHUP to keep ten Years" whose ingredients include beer and pickled anchovies,[157] while a recipe in a later edition of Penelope Bradshaw's (d.1753/4) book goes even further in offering a recipe for "An Excellent Ketchup, that will keep Fifty Years."[158] Enduring and hardy, mushroom ketchup seems to have been well-equipped to survive the rigours of transport in an age when cargo travelled virtually unprotected from often-dramatic changes in temperature and humidity. Richard Bradley's recipe for a ketchup that will keep ten years comes with the promise that "You may carry it to the Indies,"[159] though whether he means the East or West Indies is unclear. The remedy for "Ringworms" included in the Medicine section of this book also suggests that the condiment travelled at least as far as India.

Used not only as a condiment (and sometimes medicine), mushroom ketchup also frequently appeared as an ingredient in English cookbooks. *The Country Housewife* specifies mushroom ketchup in offering directions for serving fish during the month of March, which include combining "mushroom ketchup" with butter, white wine, and beef gravy, and in a "Sauce for boil'd Fish," the ketchup is mixed with beef gravy, onion, white wine, horseradish, lemon peel, and herbs.[160] Elizabeth Raffald's *The Experienced English Housekeeper* puts mushroom ketchup to wide use, where it appears in "To Dress a Turtle" as well as the recipe to prepare a "Mock Turtle" made from "the largest calf's head you can get."[161] In Raffald's book, ketchup is also poured on broiled mutton steaks, specified among the ingredients for a roux used in making "hash Mutton," combined with lemon in preparing a poultry dish described as "hash Fowls," and included in directions for how "to raggoo Pigs Feet and Ears."[162] Applied also to game, mushroom ketchup is combined with anchovy in fricasseeing rabbits and mixed with red wine and walnuts in preparing Raffald's "Ducks *a-la-mode*."[163] Sarah Harrison's 1733 *The House-Keeper's Pocket-Book*, a volume claiming to offer "Above Three Hundred Curious and Uncommon Receipts," includes ketchup as an ingredient in a savoury sauce to be served as an accompaniment to "Beef Steaks with Oysters."[164] The recipe specifies that the "Oyster Liquor" poured off precooked oysters be mixed with "a little Mace or Nutmeg, some whole Pepper, a Clove or two," finished with "a little white Wine, and a piece of Butter roll'd in Flour to thicken it," and that it will benefit from the addition of "an Anchovy or Mushroom-ketchup" that is optional but "will make it very rich."[165] That mushroom ketchup was widely used by many cooks is further suggested in Richard Briggs's 1794 *The English Art of Cookery*, where the ingredient is specified no fewer than sixty-four times.[166]

Popular in England, mushroom ketchup appeared also in North American cookbooks that include the 1845 Montreal publication *Modern Practical Cookery*, which offers directions "To Make Mushroom Ketchup,"[167] and the 1841 edition of *The American Housewife*, which specifies a process for making "Mushroom Catsup" that begins with layering salt and mushrooms to "remain several days."[168] Mushrooms would have been plentiful in the long Maritime autumns, and foraged fungi would need to be made into a sauce or dried for preservation over the winter and into the following year. Although mushroom ketchup has not persisted in contemporary North American diets, it appeared as an ingredient in Canadian and American cookbooks well into the twentieth century, where it is sometimes used as an alternative to Worcestershire sauce. A Maritime example appeared in *The Surprise Cookbook* by Anne Clarke, which was made for the St Croix Soap Company, in St Stephen, NB, in 1899, and includes a recipe for mushroom ketchup as well as specifying its addition in several recipes, including a "Savory Beef Tea" in the "Sick Room Cookery" section, thus highlighting a persistent belief in the condiment's medicinal value.[169]

Tomatoes

Along with the directions for preparing "Catsup," the following instructions titled only "Tomatoes" are essentially a recipe for tomato ketchup that was also pasted into *The Militia Laws of the Province of Nova Scotia*.[170] Acknowledged as coming from "Aunt Margaret's American Cooking Book," the original source for the recipe appears to be *The Improved Housewife, or Book of Receipts* by Mrs A.L. Webster, first published in 1843, likely in Hartford.[171] Aunt Margaret thus appears to be a relative of the copyist. The published recipe is included in a section on pickles and, although this recipe is dated later than the others in this book, we include it here to draw in something of the story of the now-familiar and ubiquitous tomato ketchup that would eventually supersede the mushroom version.

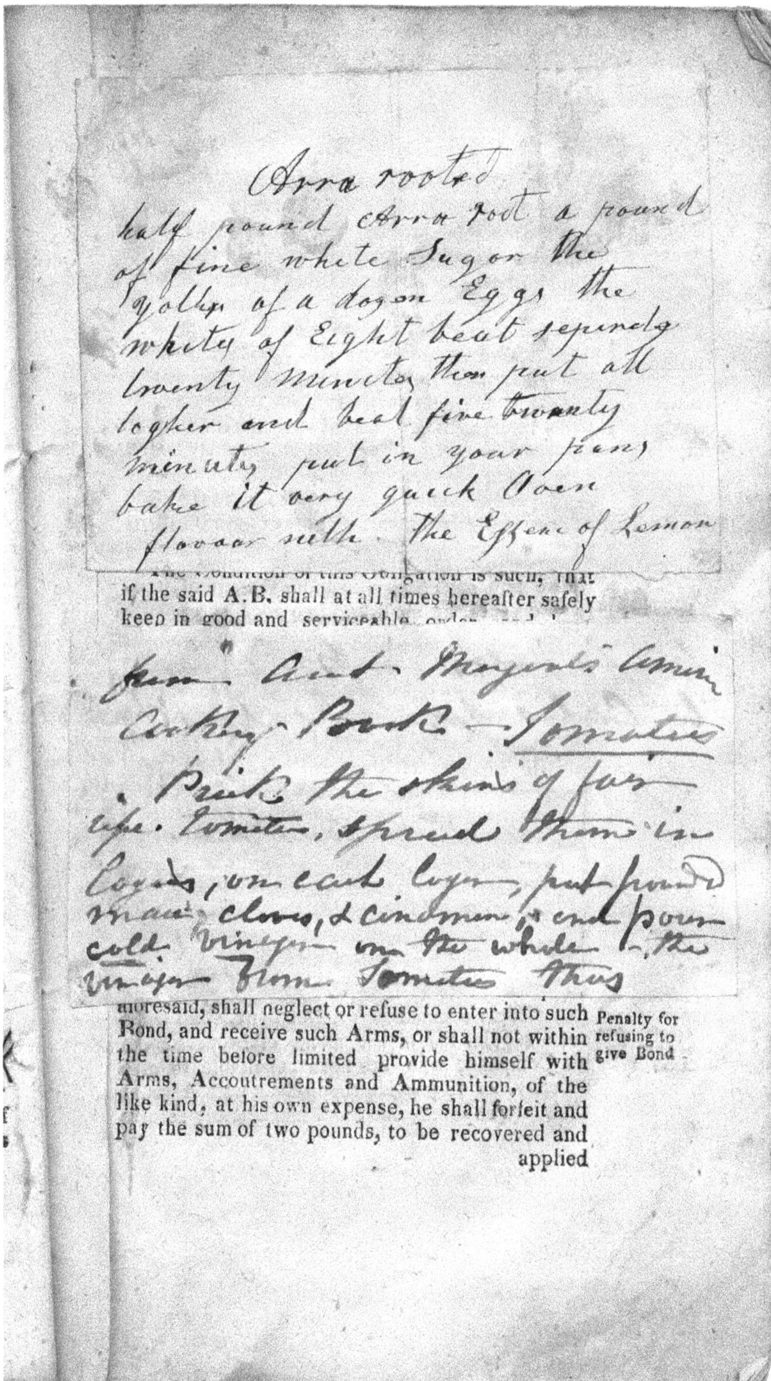
Arra rooted
half pound Arra root a pound of fine white Sugar the yolks of a dozen Eggs the whites of Eight beat seperately twenty minutes then put all togher and beat fine twenty minutes put in your pans bake it very quick Oven flavour with the Essence of Lemon

if the said A.B. shall at all times hereafter safely keep in good and serviceable

From Aunt Margaret's Cooking Book — Tomatoes
Prick the skins of fair ripe Tomatoes, spread them in layers, on each layer put pounded mace, cloves, & cinnamon, and pour cold vinegar on the whole — the vinegar from Tomatoes thus

aforesaid, shall neglect or refuse to enter into such Bond, and receive such Arms, or shall not within the time before limited provide himself with Arms, Accoutrements and Ammunition, of the like kind, at his own expense, he shall forfeit and pay the sum of two pounds, to be recovered and applied

Penalty for refusing to give Bond

Figure 1.4
Tomatoes. Militia Regulations Book.

from Aunt Margaret's American Cooking Book – Tomatoes

Prick the skins of fair
ripe tomatoes, spread them in
layers, on each layer, put pounded
mace, cloves, & cinnamon, and pour
cold vinegar on the whole - the
vinegar from Tomatoes thus …

Though the *Militia* book version ends with "thus," suggesting that part of the recorded recipe is missing, the version published in *The Improved Housewife* reads, "The vinegar from tomatoes thus prepared, is preferable to *catsup*," thus noting a cultural shift away from the mushroom version and marking at least one author's preference for the tomato ketchup that would eventually replace it.

The later date of the tomato version likely has much to do with the fact that the tomatoes called for in the recipe, along with potatoes and corn, are native to the Americas. As a wild plant – the *Lycopersicon* within the Solanaceae family – tomatoes are native to northwestern South America; they were domesticated in Mexico by Indigenous peoples who cultivated and ate them as salsas with chilli peppers. Sixteenth-century Spaniards encountered many types of tomatoes in Aztec markets in Tenochtitlan, as well as salsas and stews made of tomatoes, chilli peppers, and squash seeds. Francisco Hernandez, compiler of an early Spanish herbal of American plants, noted that the tomato had medicinal uses, and was used to treat sore throats, headaches, earaches, stomach aches, and mumps. The Spanish took tomato seeds to Europe in the sixteenth century, but they were not regularly cultivated and eaten in the region until the eighteenth century; the first seventeenth-century Italian recipes for tomato sauce "in the Spanish style" do suggest, however, that the Spanish had adopted the Aztec method of preparing tomatoes in a sauce.[172] Philip Miller's *The Gardener's Dictionary* (1733) says of love apples: "The *Italians* and *Spaniards* eat these Apples, as we do Cucumbers, with Pepper, Oil, and Salt, and some eat them stew'd in Sauces &c., but considering their great Moisture and Coldness, the Nourishment they afford must be bad." By 1737, Miller had added that "they are called by the Portugese and Spaniards Tomato's."[173]

Tomatoes were adopted into European diets relatively slowly because of the plant's resemblance to those from the toxic *Solanum* genus, a group that includes belladonna and mandrake, and the plant was at first used more for ornamental purposes.[174] Even as late as 1797, however, the "Love Apple" was yet "supposed to be more or less poisonous."[175] The tomato's popularity prevailed nevertheless. Now eaten throughout the world, tomatoes arrived in North America with European settlers in the eighteenth century.[176] This "Tomatoes" recipe documents one route of transmitting knowledge about tomatoes via family members and an American recipe book.

To Make Mangoes

This recipe for preserving mangoes dates from between about 1780 and 1800 and, like several of the recipes from the Almon family, was recorded on a sheet of paper glued into the *Almon Scrapbook*.[177] Written in the same hand as multiple other recipes, it was likely recorded by someone other than Rebecca Byles Almon, whose assumed handwriting differs.[178]

To make Mangoes

When they are green take a quart of Mustard Seed
wash it in Vinegar & put to it 4 ounces of horse Raddish
cut thin 2 ounces of Shalotes 1 ounce of Garlick fill
them with the stuffing & stop them close Boil the vinegar
& when cold put in the Mangoes with Mace Whole Pepper
& Cloves.

Mangoes may seem an odd ingredient to find in eighteenth-century Halifax, but the *Oxford English Dictionary* (OED) notes that "mangoes" can refer to "A pickle resembling that made of green mangoes" or a pickle many of any whole fruits.[179] Sarah Harrison's "To Mango Cucumbers" is an example of the former type, as her recipe provides instructions on creating cucumber pickles by pressing garlic or shallot into the cucumbers and then covering them with long pepper, mustard seeds, mace, ginger, and cloves, as well as vinegar; this mixture, the recipe notes, should be thrice boiled, the last time with alum to give the cucumbers a "fine green Colour."[180] The Almon recipe's noting that the mangoes are to be used "When they are green" suggests that alternative fruits were likely used. Although the Almon version does not indicate how much produce the recipe can pickle, the quart of mustard seed does suggest a mixture intended to preserve a significant amount; however, the quantity of finished product this recipe aims to produce remains uncertain without indicating how much vinegar should be used.

Given the long-established British trade routes with the Caribbean, it is possible that mangoes were available in colonial Halifax, though we have found no evidence to indicate as much. Cultivated for some four thousand years in India, and introduced "to East Africa in the 9th or 10th centuries," the mango tree was brought to the Caribbean, South America, and Mexico by the Spanish and Portuguese as early as the sixteenth century, "reaching Barbados in 1742 and Jamaica by 1782."[181] Mango is, however, a rather perishable fruit that was often pickled before transport, and it is unclear whether the recipe was meant to pickle actual mangoes or whether it was to be used in Halifax or in the Caribbean. The Almon family did have Caribbean connections, and it is possible that other family members were the recipe's source given that the *Scrapbook* also includes instructions for preparing mutton stew credited to "Our dear Mary Byles of Grenada."[182]

SWEETS

Plumb Cake and Drop Cake

Both of the following recipes for "Plumb Cake" come from the *Almon Scrapbook* held at the Nova Scotia Archives.[183] The first manuscript also features a recipe for "Drop Cake" recorded on the same sheet of paper. The recipes were, however, likely recorded sometime between 1780 and 1800 by the women of Halifax's well-known Almon family, and all three cake recipes appear to be in the same hand as the recipes for "Harrico of Mutton" and "To Make Mangoes" discussed in earlier chapters. We have not found a printed source for these recipes.

Plumb Cake.

7 lb Flour, 4 lb Sugar, 3 lb Butter, 2 dozn. Eggs, ½ oz Cloves, ½ oz of Mace, ½ oz Cinnamon ½ oz Nutmegs, 4 lb Currants, 1 Bottle of Wine, ½ lb Citro[n].

Plumb Cake.

Take 3 lbs of Flour, 1½ lbs of Butter, 1¾ lb of Sugar, 1¾ lb of Currants, 9 Eggs, ½ Pint of Wine, ¼ of an Ounce of Mace, ¼ of an Ounce of Cinnamon, ¼ of an Ounce of Cloves, ¾ of a Pint of yeast, ½ a gill of Rose-

Water. The Eggs, Yeast & Flour
to be put together over Night
to rise. The Butter & Sugar to
be beaten together to a Froth.
It takes three Hours to bake
in a quick Oven. And the whole
must be mixed together when
the Fire is put into the Oven.

Drop Cake.

1 lb Flour, ¾ lb of Loaf Sugar, ½ lb Butter, 4 Eggs,
some rose water, a little spice, grated lemon
Peel.

According to the OED, plum cake is "A cake containing raisins, currants, and often orange peel and other candied fruits."[184] Like the Almon plum cakes, the English versions were most often made not from what we know as plums but with currants or other dried fruits. The quantities in the first "Plumb Cake" recipe (featured in this section) are very large: four pounds of currants as well as seven pounds of flour, four pounds of sugar, three pounds of butter, a bottle of wine, and two dozen eggs. Though eighteenth-century eggs were smaller than today's supermarket variety, twenty-four is a large but necessary number of eggs that served as the cake's sole means of rising in the absence of another leavening agent such as yeast or pearl ash, the precursor of baking soda and baking powder.[185] Given that no directions for the method of making are included with the ingredients, it is unclear whether the very large cake was to be baked in one or two or several pans, though one of such impressive size was surely meant to be preserved, shared, or served at a large gathering.

Though fruitcakes like this one did not become popular for weddings until Queen Victoria started the trend with her 1840 marriage to Prince Albert, William Ellis's recipe for "A Herfordshire Plumb-cake for Harvest" does suggest that plum cakes were sometimes meant to feed a hungry crowd in eighteenth-century England. "Such a cake," Ellis notes, "some Farmers Wives bake twice a Week, to have one of them constantly by them during the Harvest; not only to give the Harvest-men now and then a Slice, but is also a Sort of Entertainment for a neighbouring Visiter."[186] In any case, the amount of sugar, dried fruit, and wine ensured that the cake would keep for quite some time, and most plum cake recipes in published eighteenth-century British cookbooks are equally large. As with Ellis's directions for the harvest plum cake, one of Catharine Brooks's recipes "For Making a Plumb Cake" specifies "half a Peck of Flour,"[187] while Elizabeth Cleland's "A Plumb-cake or Bun" calls for six pounds of currants and twenty eggs,[188] and Mary Kettilby's "An extraordinary Plumb-Cake" specifies seven pounds of flour and seven of currants along with sixteen eggs.[189]

The *Almon Scrapbook*'s second "Plumb Cake" recipe is about half the size, calling for only 1 ¾ pound of currants as well as three pounds of flour, nine eggs, and half a pint of wine. The large amount of yeast specified does not, however, refer to the dry packaged yeast we most often use today. Like the recipes found in English cookbooks, this one refers to the yeast-filled liquid derived from homebrewing or purchased from a local brewer, which generally acted more slowly and was inconsistent in potency. Mary Kettilby's recipe, for example, calls for "a full pint and half of Ale yeast,"[190] while Penelope Bradshaw's instructions "To make a Plumb Cake," specify using an entire "Quart of Ale-yeast."[191] This second, more detailed "Plumb Cake" recipe in the *Almon Scrapbook* differs from the first also in including directions, instructing the baker that the eggs, yeast, and flour are "to be put together over Night to rise" and that the butter and sugar are "to be beaten together to a Froth." Like Bradshaw's direction to lay the cake "before the Fire to rise,"[192] the Almon recipe notes that "the whole must be mixed together when the Fire is put into the Oven," presumably also to allow the yeast more time to do its work while the oven heats. Though half the size of the more concise "Plumb Cake" recipe, this cake nevertheless "takes three Hours to bake in a quick Oven," which by today's standards seems an unusually long cooking time for an oven-baked confection.

The recipe for "Drop Cake" is much more modest than either "Plumb Cake" recipe, indicating quantities that more closely approximate those familiar to home bakers today: a mere pound of flour, a little less sugar, half a pound of butter, and only four eggs. Like the plum cake recipes, this one also requires imported ingredients, specified in this case merely as "a little spice" and "grated lemon peel" for the drop cake, versus approximately four tablespoons each of cloves, mace, cinnamon, and nutmeg as well as citron required for the larger "Plumb Cake." Though the "Drop Cake" recipe does not describe a specific method, the baker would have understood that the batter was to be dropped on a tin or sheet and baked like cookies.

Thick Ginger Bread

The recipe for "Thick Ginger Bread" was printed in *The Halifax Gazette* in November 1765 under the heading "Approved Receipts."[193] The first edition of *The Halifax Gazette*, identified as Canada's first newspaper, had been printed by John Bushell (1715–1761), a printer from Boston, in March 1752. Bushell had begun his career as an apprentice in Boston; he moved to Halifax in 1751 and started *The Halifax Gazette* the next year.[194] The paper was published between 1752 and 1766 and was edited by Richard Bulkeley (1717–1800) after 1758. Bushell died in 1761, and his former assistant, Anthony Henry, worked with Bulkeley and continued to print *The Halifax Gazette* until 1766, when government patronage was transferred to Robert Fletcher's *Nova Scotia Gazette*; Henry would go on to launch *The Nova Scotia Chronicle* in 1769.[195] *The Halifax Gazette* printed news from Europe, the British colonies in America and the Caribbean, and from Nova Scotia.[196]

Like many recipes that appeared in Nova Scotia newspapers, this recipe does not credit a source. Nearly identical instructions by the same title had, however, been published in Mary Kettilby's 1714 *A Collection of Above Three Hundred Receipts in Cookery, Physic and Surgery*; printed in London. Kettilby's recipe differed only in spelling, using the unmodernized "Flower," "Carraway-seeds," and "Candy'd," and in requiring "beat" rather than "beaten" ginger.[197] That the recipe appeared also in Lady Charlotte Campbell Bury's significantly later 1844 collection, *The Lady's Own Cookery Book*, suggests that the recipe was both successful and popular.[198] Though Bury lays subtitular claim to a "Large Collection of Original Receipts," the recipe was not actually original, having appeared in Kettilby's earlier book, which had been published in five editions by 1734 and has a title page that characterizes the work as a collection "By several hands." Given gingerbread's long-standing popularity, it may be that the recipe was acquired from more than one source.

Thick ginger bread

A Pound and a half of flour takes up one pound
of treacle, almost as much sugar, an ounce
of beaten ginger, two ounces of caraway seeds,
four ounces of citron, and lemon peel candied,
the yolks of four eggs; cut your sweet meats,
mix all, and bake it in large cakes, on tin plates.

As is typical for eighteenth-century recipes, the instructions for making "Thick Ginger Bread" do not offer consistently precise measurements, instead leaving the exact amount of sugar for the baker to determine. Though the recipe does indicate that one is to "cut," "mix," and "bake," it does not specify whether the gingerbread should be baked in a "quick" (or hot) oven or at a more moderate temperature. Missing also is any indication of what size other than "large" tins should be used to bake the gingerbread or whether the tins should be greased. Like many published recipes, this one relies on the baker's experience to fill in gaps that may seem odd to a modern reader, implying in doing so that most home cooks would have been familiar with various methods of making the enduringly popular dessert.

Ginger had been available in England since at least the eleventh century, and gingerbread itself may have been brought to Western Europe in that period by knights returning from crusades against Muslims in the eastern Mediterranean. Gingerbread was commonly eaten at festivals and fairs in medieval Europe.[199] Europeans started growing ginger using enslaved labourers in the Caribbean in the sixteenth century, exporting the plant to northern Europe. Its popularity in northern European diets partly depended on a Galenic understanding of the plant as hot and moist, which made it useful as an aphrodisiac and as medicine specific to the humours of cold, moist bodies living in more northern climates.[200] In English recipes from the fifteenth century onward, ginger was used in medicines as well as in gingerbread and other foods.[201] Eighteenth-century English cookbooks thus offered an abundance of recipes for making gingerbread that, like *The Halifax Gazette*'s receipt for "Thick Ginger Bread," assume a degree of familiarity on the user's part. Richard Bradley's *The Country Housewife*, for example, specifies the inclusion of "half a Pound of Sugar" in one recipe for gingerbread, but indicates no precise amount for an additional sweetener, advising the maker only to "wet it pretty stiff with nothing but Treacle," a sugar syrup like molasses.[202] Like Bradley's, most English recipes for gingerbread also call for large amounts of sweetener. *The Family Jewel*, a popular compilation of recipes by Penelope Bradshaw, specifies "two Pounds of Treacle" and "Half a Pound of Sugar" to "three Pounds of Flour" in its instructions for making gingerbread,[203] while the recipe "To make fine Gingerbread" in *The Lady's Best Companion* by Charlotte Cartwright calls for "half a pound of sugar" and "a pound and a half of treacle" to "as much flour as is necessary to make it into a paste."[204] The large amounts of sugar and treacle used in its making may have helped to preserve the gingerbread for extended periods of time, as Bradley's second recipe, "To make a good GINGERBREAD without Butter," suggests in noting that the finished product "will be good some Months."[205]

The treacle used in this recipe is historically important in the Maritimes. Entering into the English language in the late seventeenth-century, the term *treacle* refers to "an uncrystallized syrup produced in the process of refining sugar," the British name for what in North America is more commonly called *molasses*.[206] Also used in the Indian pudding recipe featured in this section, molasses "has become," Diane Tye argues, "a kind of commemorative food for Atlantic Canadians," the sort of food that is important to "personal food systems" and invokes nostalgia for an idealized past.[207] The importance of molasses to the region is rooted in its economic history. From the seventeenth century onwards, European planters traded the sugar produced in the Caribbean colonies by enslaved labourers, as well as sugar's by-products – molasses and rum – for lumber, salt fish, and salt beef from the colonies in North America; molasses was also refined in other American colonies and shipped to Nova Scotia and Europe before the American Revolution.[208] If not for the first time, the recipe for "Thick Ginger Bread" brings a long English tradition of gingerbread making to Nova Scotia, where the treacle specified as one of its core ingredients was an important commodity.

Hasty Pudding / Indian Pudding

The following pudding recipes (along with a further set of instructions on how to boil potatoes) appear on a page of the *Almon Scrapbook*.[209] For the pudding recipes, as the title suggests, the copyist seems to have concisely summarized recipes that appear in the chapter on "Indian Corn" in the essay "Of Food" included in an anthology titled *Essays, Political, Economical, and Philosophical* that was first published in 1796 by Sir Benjamin Thompson, Count Rumford (1753–1814).[210]

Count Rumford, Hasty-Pudding

2 Pints of water, [td.] g^{r}. of salt^disolved~~boiled~~ in the
Water, ½ lb of Indian meal. Stirred in by little &
little till it is enough, which may be known by
a wooden spoon standing on end in it.

From the same S^{r}. W^{m}. Pepperels Housekeeper Indian Pudding

3lb of Indian Meal (sifted) put into a large bowl, pour 5 pints of
boiling water & stir well-together, add 3 q^{ts}. of lb mollasses
& 1 oz of salt, there being all well mixed, pour into a bag thoroughly
cover in boiling water, leaving an empty space about the 6th.

Part of its contents, for room to swell: Put
it into boiling water, a boil without in-
-termission 6 hours. 1lb of suet may be
added. Or 1 lb. of dried apples. or huckle-
berries.

The source of these recipes, Benjamin Thompson, was born in Massachusetts and started out in life as an apprentice to a storekeeper in Salem. He became a schoolteacher with an interest in scientific experiments, then fled to England in 1776 because of the American Revolution. After serving in the British military, Thompson was created Count Rumford in 1792 for his services to Karl Theodor of Bavaria, which included improving stoves and fireplaces, promoting potatoes for the Bavarian diet, and advocating coffee as a substitute for alcohol.[211] Representing himself as a scientist interested in practical improvements, he approaches corn in "Of Food" in *Essays, Political, Economical, and Philosophical* with an eye to its nutritional and economic benefits as a component of the British diet, especially for the poor; the essay includes not just recipes but a cost breakdown for corn dishes, sauces, and heat to do the cookery. He describes "Indian Corn" as "the most nourishing, cheapest, and most wholesome that can be procured for feeding the Poor."[212] Corn is, he adds, a common food in Northern Italy, where it is most often served as polenta, and throughout the Americas, where it is used as food for animals and for humans in bread and pudding. He cites the putative testimony of enslaved people in the West Indies who supposedly prefer corn to rice pudding because it presumably made them stronger, in doing so drawing a line of evidence between their alleged experience and the diet of British workers.[213] The recipes for pudding, then, are part of Rumford's efforts to persuade the British of corn's economic advantages.

The first recipe in the Almon notebook for Count Rumford's "Hasty-Pudding" appears in narrative form in Rumford's essay, with the copyist extracting only the ingredients. Rumford explains that "Hasty Pudding" offers "the most advantageous method of using Indian corn as Food," describing it as "a dish that is in the highest estimation throughout America, and which is really very good, and very nourishing."[214] Its further advantages encompass its capacity to be made in large quantities, preserved for several days, and then prepared in other ways, such as being toasted, eaten instead of bread, served with sauce or milk, and as an addition to soup; he includes ingredients for a dish of boiled cabbage, boiled beef, and slices of hasty

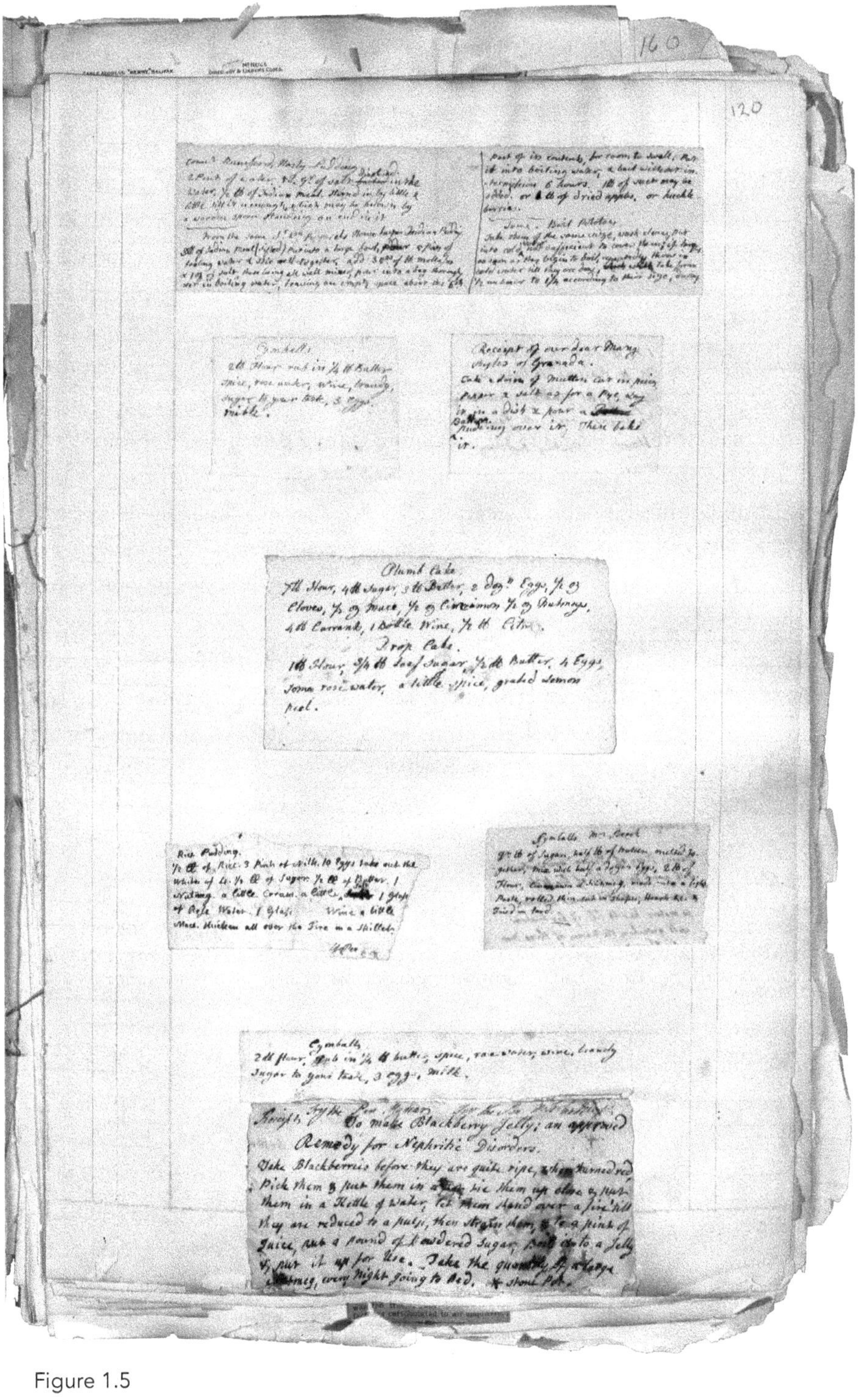

Figure 1.5
Count Rumford, Hasty Pudding. *Almon Scrapbook*.

pudding fried in butter or lard – a "favourite dish in America."[215] The precise quantities in the Almon notebook recipe of two pints of water, 58 grains or 1⁄20 lb. of salt, ½ lb. of Indian meal are from Rumford's account of his own "experiment" in England with making a pudding to feed the poor, a dish he costs at one and one sixtieth of a penny.[216] Rumford has also explained the method of stirring in small quantities of corn at a time, the cooking time, and a means to know when the consistency is right: when "the wooden spoon used for stirring it being placed upright in the middle of the kettle, if it falls down, more meal must be added," which the notebook recipe gestures to but does not fully replicate with its instruction that the consistency "may be known by a wooden spoon standing on end in it."[217]

The second "Indian pudding" recipe comes from a passage in "Of Food" where Rumford goes on to recommend the "Indian (bag) pudding" for those just beginning with such puddings – an indication that the dish may be relatively new. This recipe is set apart from his essay in more typical recipe format, "Approved Receipt for making a plain Indian Pudding." Like the first pudding recipe, this second Indian pudding is, according to Rumford, also very cheap to make, costing nine pence and half a farthing.[218] In including the Indian pudding recipe, Rumford continues to represent himself as an experimenter. He explains that he caused the Indian pudding to be made under his direction by a "person born and brought up in North America, and who understands perfectly the American art of cookery in all its branches." A footnote identifies this person as "the housekeeper of my friend and countrymen, Sir William Pepperel" of Portland Square in London.[219] William [Sparhawk] Pepperrell (d. 1816) was the grandson of Sir William Pepperrell (1696–1759), the son of a wealthy merchant who had emigrated from Britain to what is now Maine. The elder Sir William Pepperrell made his name commanding an expedition against Fortress Louisbourg in 1745, which ended with the French surrender. Shortly thereafter, he was made a colonel in the British army, eventually achieving the rank of lieutenant general in 1759. For his services, he had in 1746 been created a baronet (hence the title Sir), the first such title for someone born in America. Upon his death in 1759, Sir William left his large Maine estate to his grandson, Willam Sparhawk, who was required to take the name Pepperrell with his inheritance.[220] Having succeeded to the title of Baronet in 1774, this Sir William Pepperrell is the recipe's source and the one named in the Nova Scotia copy of recipe. A Loyalist, Sir William Sparhawk Pepperrell sailed for England in 1775, his estate having been confiscated; his wife died en route and was buried in Halifax. He received five hundred pounds a year from the British government and was regarded as a leader among Loyalist exiles before his death in London in 1816.[221]

The name "Hasty Pudding" precedes the corn pudding that Rumford describes, but the dish itself has North American origins, as Rumford acknowledges. Hasty pudding seems as first to have referred to a pudding made in haste; the first reference to a hasty pudding may be in *A Short Inventory of Certayne Idle Inventions* (1581), where "hasty pudding" is mentioned as the only good result of haste (no indication of its ingredients is given).[222] Another earlier recipe for hasty pudding in a bag in *The Art of Cookery* (1654) by Joseph Cooper – "chiefe Cook to the Late King," Charles I – is for a recipe of cream, flour, nutmeg, salt, and sugar boiled in a bag; when it is done, it is to be buttered "as a hasty Pudding," which may suggest that while the boil-in-bag technique is not the usual one, the hasty, quickly made pudding itself is well-known.[223] By the late eighteenth century, the hasty pudding had assumed some renown in America as a pudding made from corn, as it is in the recipes discussed here. Katharina Vester places corn and the hasty pudding at the centre of the earliest American efforts to create a republican, democratic cuisine, albeit one that omits any consideration of "unequal access to resources" because of gender or race.[224] Harvard's Hasty Pudding Club adopted its name in 1795 in recognition of the pudding's popularity in Massachusetts.[225] Connecticut-born Patriot poet and diplomat Joel Barlow (1754–1812) published a long mock-heroic poem, "The Hasty Pudding," in praise of the dish in *New York Magazine* in 1793, republishing it in Fairhaven, Vermont, as a book in 1796.[226] A long apostrophe to "Dear Hasty Pudding" describes and praises the pudding as one of many dishes of corn eaten in America that is "to every Yankee dear";[227] as Barlow traces the poem's "lineage and […] race," he situates the pudding's history in America, specifically in the labour of an Indigenous woman (described with a racist epithet) who, before Columbus arrived,

> First gave thee to the world – her works of fame
> Have liv'd, indeed, but liv'd without a name.
> Some tawny Ceres, goddess of her days,
> First learnt with stones to crack the well-dry'd maize,
> Through the rough sieve to shake the golden show'r,
> In boiling water stir the yellow flour:
> The yellow flour, bestrew'd and stirr'd with haste,
> Swell in the flood and thickens to a paste,
> Then puffs and wallops, rises to the brim,
> Drinks the dry lumps that on the surface swim;
> The lumps at last the busy ladle breaks

> And the whole mass its true consistence takes.
> Could but her sacred name, unknown so long,
> Rise, like her labours, to the son of song,
> To her, to them, I'd consecrate my lays,
> And blow her Pudding with the breath of praise.[228]

Thus, although the name *hasty pudding* is English, Barlow situates the pudding's roots in the Americas, specifically in the work of the anonymous Indigenous woman who first made pudding of corn, who shook the corn into the boiling water and stirred and thickened it. He promises to write poetry to her to claim and celebrate the corn pudding as a Yankee food within a poem that, as one of its critics says, "emphasizes the Americanness and provincialism of Indian corn" and celebrates "the common man and of commonplace folk themes and folk culture."[229] In so doing, the poem self-consciously appropriates Indigenous knowledge in the service of settler identity, in the name of distinguishing Americans and the English. The hasty puddy becomes, as Vester says, a way for Barlow to "[depict] the settlers as the legitimate heirs to the land rather than as colonizers, a role now projected upon the defeated British."[230]

The recipes for hasty pudding repeat some of the moves of Barlow's poem. The people named as sources of these recipes are men – Rumford and Pepperrell – while the female housekeeper is not named. Omitted as well are the Indigenous people from whom the use of corn has been learned, just as Barlow's poem says the "sacred name" of the pudding's inventor is "unknown so long," thereby relegating Indigenous peoples to a mythical past. Neither does the recipe invoke the enslaved people from whom corn's merits had, according to Rumford's own account, also been proved, in effect erasing that history by circulating the recipe without reference to its historical context. Yet its inclusion in the Almon recipe collection does attest to how a method of cooking corn seems to have made its way from North America to England and back to North America, to Nova Scotia rather than New England. Further, despite the pudding's strong Patriot attachments evinced in Barlow's poem, the recipe in the *Almon Scrapbook* has its explicitly Loyalists origins rooted in the knowledge of Rumford and that of Pepperrell's housekeeper. Hence hasty pudding was not confined to republican eaters but also made its way to England and to Nova Scotia with Loyalists, where it yet incorporated Indigenous knowledge into the settler diet.

To Make a Rice Pudding / Rice Pudding

"To make a Rice Pudding" was published in a 1765 issue of *The Halifax Gazette*.[231] The second recipe for rice pudding in this section, dating from about 1780 to 1800, was recorded on a sheet of paper and glued into the *Almon Scrapbook*.[232] Written in the same hand as several other recipes, it was most likely recorded by a female member of Halifax's Almon family.[233] The first recipe from *The Halifax Gazette* can be found in several eighteenth-century recipe books from the 1730s and '40s, among them *The Complete Family-piece: and, Country Gentleman, and Farmer's Best Guide*, a work "collected by several very eminent and ingenious Gentlemen" and *The Lady's Companion*.[234] It was also included in Mary Kettilby's *A Collection of Above Three Hundred Receipts in Cookery, Physick and Surgery*, first printed in 1714.[235] We have not found a source for the second recipe.

To make a RICE PUDDING.

Grind, or beat half a pound of rice to flour;
mix it by degrees with three pints of milk, and
thicken it over the fire with care, for fear of
burning, till it is like a hasty pudding; when it
is so thick, pour it out, and let is stand to cool:
put to it nine eggs, (but half the whites) three
or four spoonfuls of orange flower water: melt
almost a pound of good butter, and sweeten it to
your taste. Add sweetmeats, if you please.

Rice Pudding.

½ lb of Rice. 3 Pints of Milk. 10 Eggs take out the
whites of 4. ½ lb of Sugar ½ lb of Butter. 1
Nutmeg. a little Cream. a little‸salt 1 glass
of Rose Water. 1 Glass Wine a little
Mace. Thicken all over the Fire in a skillet.

Rice pudding and hasty pudding are comparable English puddings. Indeed, the first rice pudding recipe uses a comparison to the thickness of a hasty pudding to explain the consistency wanted here, and it thus seems likely that hasty pudding was the better known of the two. The comparison is not unique to this recipe. For example, a rice pudding recipe that calls for thin cream, cinnamon, rosewater, sugar, and rice in *The Ladies Cabinet Enlarged and Opened* (1654) uses the same comparison to a hasty pudding to provide an understanding of its desired thickness.[236]

These recipes are for rich desserts. The *Halifax Gazette* recipe offers a version that incorporates nine eggs along with "almost a pound of good butter" and specifies the addition of "orange flower water" for flavour, as well as sweetener and sweetmeats to taste. Dating also from the late eighteenth century, the *Almon Scrapbook* recipe seems equally rich with its ten eggs, three pints of milk, and quarter pound of butter, but differs from "To Make a Rice Pudding" in also calling for "a Little Cream," specifying "Rose Water" rather than orange flower water, and incorporating wine as well as mace for flavouring. Both Nova Scotia recipes list ingredients that would have originated elsewhere, including mace from Indonesia and sugar from the Caribbean. A limited part of the European diet before the early modern period, rice became commonly traded in the eighteenth century, and it was grown in Africa, Southeast Asia, and the Carolinas, as well as in Italy.[237] Rice in Nova Scotia may have come from South Carolina or Georgia. In the eighteenth century, rice grown by enslaved people was a major export from these two states, its value standing after only tobacco, wheat flour, and fish in British North America; rice was shipped from the more southern regions of the western Atlantic coast to the more northern British colonies as well as to the Caribbean, Britain, and Europe.[238]

In early modern kitchens, rice seems to have been primarily used to make puddings, cakes, soups, and rice milk, but was occasionally included in meat-based recipes. Rice appears in only two additional recipes in the EMMR online database: one for Hessian soup that was published in a 1768 letter to *The Nova Scotia Gazette* and appears here under "Soup and Stew," and the other recommending a "cooling and slender" diet in a 1782 letter written by the surgeon John Marshall from Halifax to an ailing "Miss McDonald," Nelly (Helen) Macdonald (1750–1803), of St John's Island; the health regimen includes "Barley or rice boiled, with milk."[239] In England, a 1725 book on the management of workhouses recommends "Boil'd Rice Pudding, or Rice Milk" in its "Bill of Fare" for the week, while the weekly bill of fare itemized in "A Table of Diet for Patients in the Infirmary for the County of York" suggests "Rice-Pudding" for Monday's noontime dinner in its specifications for a "Full Diet," as well as its guidelines for a "Low Diet," "Milk Diet," and "Dry Diet," the latter alluding to Galenic medicine in proposing to counter the negative effects of an overly wet humoral imbalance.[240] These uses of rice pudding suggest something of rice's culinary versatility and its status as a grain suited to both the prosperous and poor and the hearty and ailing. Unmediated by ingredients of affluence such as the eggs, cream, butter, and wine specified in the pudding recipes, rice also served as food for the indigent and invalid.

FOOD FOR HEALTH

Recipes for foods that would restore the unwell to health had long been a part of medical culture. Food and diet served as a cornerstone of early modern regimens for health.[241] Within the Galenic medical tradition, which focused on the qualities of hot / cold and wet / dry in bodies and the natural world, the humoral qualities of food were used specifically to counter constitutional imbalances and return the body to physical equilibrium, but food could also treat the convalescent with more humorally neutral foods, such as gruel and meat broths.[242] Even as medical theory moved away from the Galenic paradigm, recommendations that the sick consume foods thought to be both fortifying and easy to digest persisted. Entire cookbooks aimed specifically at preparing nourishment for the sick appeared in England and North America after the 1880s. First published in 1904 in Boston, *Food and Cookery for the Sick and Convalescent* by famed American cookery writer Fannie Farmer (1857–1915) continued this tradition into the twentieth century.[243] According to Ken Albala, historically, cooking for the convalescent often focused on foods that were "nourishing, restorative, easy to digest, and interestingly 'light' in both consistency and color so as not to tax the system excessively"; this diet for the ill could include white foods, like bread, foods that were bland or humorally neutral, like meat broths, and foods that were boiled or poached, rather than roasted or fried, with boiling serving as something akin to pre-digestion.[244] The "Receipt to Make Blackberry Jelly" and the description of how to eat baobob document the interest in medicinal foods not only with cooks but also among physicians and colonial botanists.

Mrs. Clarks Receipt for Strengthening

The first three recipes for health discussed here were recorded by Sarah Creighton Wilkins (1774–c.1849) in her manuscript notebook, the only extensive collection we have found that is clearly credited to a woman.[245] Wilkins was the daughter of Lucy Clapp and John Creighton, an English militia officer who settled in Lunenburg in 1753, where he was a judge and politician. In 1799 in Lunenburg, Sarah

Creighton married Lewis Morris Wilkins (1768–1848), a lawyer who was the same year elected to the Nova Scotia House of Assembly from Lunenburg Township. In 1816, he was made a judge and resigned his political position. The family, which included seven children, later moved to Windsor, Nova Scotia, where they were known for their hospitality. Wilkins likely died in 1849, a year after her husband.

Wilkins's first recipe for strengthening is credited to a Mrs Clark and presented as her creation; though Mrs Clark's identity is unknown, the recipe records both her existence and her medical authority.

Mrs. Clarks Receipt
For strengthening

Cut a neats foot in pieces
put it into a deep Pan.
grate over it a Nutmeg, &
half a lb of Sugar – two quarts
of Milk. let it be baked till
quite tender – strain it off
before it is cold – when cold take
off the Fat. take two or three
cups full a day warm –

The strengthening quality of this dish hangs on its ingredients. In the early modern period, beef held particular importance in forming the English constitution, with the ox used in this recipe seen as especially strengthening because of the animal's well-known strength and size.[246] Nutmeg, which is indicated in this as well as in the panada recipe, was likewise thought to be strengthening; *The Useful Family Herbal* – an eighteenth-century herbal by John Hill (1714?–1775) that was printed into the nineteenth century – notes that nutmeg "is an excellent Spice, it strengthens the Stomach, and assists Digestion."[247] Sugar was commonly found in early modern medicines, used to "'stir up,' soothe, loosen, or moisturize elements in labile humoral bodies; and to isolate and intensify the properties of a given foodstuff."[248]

Salep and Panada

Sarah Creighton Wilkins's panada (or panado) and salep recipes are found on the same page of John Farley's *The London Art of Cookery* in a section called "Proper Nourishment for the Sick."[249] It seems likely that this is Wilkins's source. Farley himself, however, seems to have taken the recipes from Hannah Glasse's *The Art of Cookery* (1747), another popular eighteenth-century recipe book with a chapter on "Directions for the Sick," which includes (like Farley's chapter) recipes for meat, fish, and poultry broths, bread- and grain-based soups, and milk drinks. Farley's and Glasse's recipes for panada/o and salep call for the same ingredients, but Farley's language is slightly different from Glasses's (but like Wilkins's). For instance, Glasse's recipe "To boil Salup" begins with a definition of salep – "a hard Stone ground to Powder, and generally sold for one Shilling and ounce" – and ends with the recommendation of another ingredient – "Lemon if it will agree."[250] Glasse's recipe "To make Panado" ends by confirming that "This is hearty good Diet for sick People."[251] These touches are found in neither Farley's recipe nor Wilkins's, and where Glasse's recipe calls for a "nice clean pan," Farley's and Wilkins's a "clean saucepan."[252] Still, Glasse's recipe for panada was a popular one, appearing in multiple other recipe books with small variations.[253]

Sick Kitchen Cookerry -
Salop

Take a large tea spoonful of the
powder of Salop, & put it into a
pint of boiling water. Keep stirring
it till it becomes a fine Jelly & then
put in wine & sugar to the palate
& strength of the patient

Salep was newer to English medicinal recipes than beef. *The Useful Family Herbal* describes the salep plant, *Orchis orientalis*, as being like the common orchis (orchid) native to England, but with larger roots that were sent dried from Turkey. It is, Hill says, "an excellent Restorative, to be given to persons wasted with long illnesses." This herbal also recommends the method of use indicated in Creighton's recipe.[254]

Panada

Put a blade of Mace & a large piece
of crumb of bread & a quart of water in
to a clean saucepan. Let it boil 2
minutes then take out the bread &
bruise it very fine in a basin
Mix as much water as you think it

will require, put away the rest &
sweeten it to Palate - put a bit of
butter not bigger than a walnut but
do not put in any wine, it will spoil
it - Grate in a little Nutmeg.

The word *panada* (or sometimes *panado*) likely finds its origins in the French *panade* (a bread soup) and was first used in England in the late sixteenth century. Mary Kettilby's recipe collection suggests this food's health functions. Its title "Panada, for a Sick or Weak Stomach" highlights its function as food for the sick, while the recipe itself explains, "This is very Nourishing, and never offends the Stomach. Some season with Butter and Sugar, adding Currants, which on some Occasions are proper; but the first is the most grateful and innocent."[255] The quality of "innocence" in food seems to refer to its gentleness on the stomach.

Receipt to Make Blackberry Jelly

Subtitled "an approved Remedy for Nephritic Disorders," this blackberry jelly recipe was recorded on a loose sheet of paper pasted into the *Almon Scrapbook*.[256] The copyist may have taken this recipe from a Nova Scotia newspaper. The recipe was published as part of an article entitled "Efficacy of the Black-Berry Jelly, in Curing the Stone and Gravel" in *The Nova Scotia Packet and General Advertiser* (7 September 1786) and *The Nova Scotia Magazine* (3 December 1790). The earlier appearance credits the *New-York Journal* as its source.[257] An untitled article was indeed published in *New-York Journal, or the Weekly Register* in New York on 3 August 1786, providing an account, which persists in the versions printed in Nova Scotia, of a gentleman afflicted with gravel and stone who took this medicine every night before going to bed and was cured of his kidney stones, which the article claims were broken up and discharged easily.[258] The title used here, referring to nephritic disorders, does not change the remedy's purpose but uses more technical medical language (*nephritic* refers to the kidney).

**To make Blackberry Jelly: an approved
Remedy for Nephritic Disorders.**

Take Blackberries before they are quite ripe, when turned red,
Pick them & put them in a [pot] tie them up close & put
them in a Kettle of water, let them stand over a fire till

> they are reduced to a pulp, then strain them to a pint of Juice, rub a pound of powdered sugar, Boil it to a Jelly, & put it up for Use. Take the quantity of a large nutmeg, every night going to Bed. *stone pot.

Native to England and naturalized in North America, blackberries had long been used to treat bladder and kidney stones. In eighteenth-century Halifax, well-known Loyalist and clergyman Rev. Dr Mather Byles, the father of Rebecca Byles Almon, wrote to his Boston sisters that he had experienced no symptoms of his "nephritic Complaints" since he had begun "constantly taking Blackberry Jelly."[259] In England, *The Compleat Herbal* recommends a blackberry "decoction or powder of the root" as "good to break or drive for the gravel and the stone in the reins and kidneys," echoing almost verbatim Nicholas Culpeper (1616–1654), whose well-known herbal was published in revised editions throughout the seventeenth century.[260] Among Indigenous populations across the globe, the Rubus plants that include blackberry were also used for "strengthening pregnant women, relieving morning sickness, aiding in childbirth, stimulating the uterus at the beginning of labor, and relieving menstrual cramps."[261]

Of the Bark or Leaves of a Tree Called Baobab

This largely transcribed discussion of the baobab's benefits was recorded on page 120 of a notebook kept by Handley Chipman (1714–1799) and dated 1776.[262] The miscellaneous collection of over two volumes also includes essays, poetry, and notes on news and history.[263] A magistrate and deputy of the Rhode Island General Assembly, Chipman was one of several thousand Planters whose "arrival after 1760 is wedged between the deportation of the Acadian French (1755–59) and the coming of the American Loyalists (1783–84)."[264] Descendants of seventeenth-century English settlers in New England, the Planters originated in Connecticut and Massachusetts as well as Rhode Island, and were recruited to Nova Scotia with the promise of land left empty after the Acadians were expelled in the 1755 *Grand dérangement*. In 1761, Chipman took up a land grant of one thousand acres in Cornwallis, Kings County, now the town of Kentville, where he later became justice of the peace and judge of probate.[265]

The notebook entry replicates almost verbatim an account published in a 1764 medical miscellany, *The Medical Museum*, a collection attributed only to "Gentlemen of the Faculty."[266] Knowledge of the baobab and its uses in both entries is credited to French explorer and botanist Michel Adanson (1727–1806), after whom the tree was named *Adansonia digitata*.

Of the bark or Leaves of a Tree called Baobab

Mr. Adanson,[267] Saith the principal food
of the Negros at Senegal is called couscous,
it is a kind of paste made of the flour of
Millet, into which some meat or fish is in:
:fused, Into this they always put two or three
pinches of Lalo.[268] This is the bark or Leaves
of a tree called Baobab, dried in the Shade
and reduced to a Powder, which they keep
dry in Little Cotton Bags, without any other
care, they add this to their food, not to give
it a Relish, but to keep up a free perspiration
in their body's, which is health to them, and
to Allay the too great heat of the blood, &c
Experience he saith hath taught him this
ptisan[269] alone is ^not only^ sufficient to remedy
against ardent fevers, but also against th[e]
heat of Urine, which is frequent there from
July to Nov[embe]r: the fruite of said tree he saith
is not Less useful, then its Leaves, the pulp
has an agreable taste, but he saith wine
ought to be abstained from &c.

Chipman's account of the Senegalese use of baobab recognizes the value of a plant whose leaves are now known to be rich in vitamins A and C, essential amino acids, iron, and calcium, and are yet eaten as a cooked vegetable in West African and Sudanese cuisine.[270] Baobab remains widely used in Senegalese cooking, particularly in the preparation of couscous, as here, and in medicine.[271] Like foods such as mushroom ketchup and blackberry jelly, the baobab served as both food and medicine, in this case one that was used to treat respiratory and digestive problems, high blood pressure, tumours, wounds, and even malaria.

Though it seems unlikely that the tropical tree and its products were available in eighteenth-century Nova Scotia, many African plants, such as cotton, flax, the castor oil plant, and coffee, were part of eighteenth-century European and American cultures.[272] Neither was couscous commonly used in eighteenth-century Anglo-American recipes, although according to the OED, the first recorded mention of couscous in an English text can be found in the *Medical & Chemical Receipts* (1593) by the inventor and recipe book author Sir Hugh Plat (1552–1608), which makes marginal mention of the "cuscusow in barbary."[273] Even so, the medicinal benefits of baobab may have been intriguing for its allegedly cooling properties. Chipman recorded his entry in a context where achieving optimal health still depended on the humoral theory that originated in ancient Greece and, in its Galenic version, endured well into the eighteenth century and beyond. In aiming to achieve the ideal balance of hot, cold, dry, and moist, Chipman's entry notes, lalo could "Allay the too great heat of the blood," "remedy against ardent fevers," and protect against "th[e] heat of Urine." The baobab's extolled benefits against excessive heat evidently encouraged its use beyond Africa and into present-day India, where "the fishermen of Gujarat eat baobab leaves with their food and consider them 'cooling.'"[274]

MISCELLANEOUS

Rennet for Cheese

This 1793 recipe for making rennet, an enzyme that facilitates coagulation in the cheese-making process, was recorded by Dr James Dinwiddie (1746–1815) in one of his lecture notebooks.[275] Dinwiddie was a Scottish scientist who lectured widely throughout the United Kingdom. The renown of his experiments earned him an invitation to accompany the British embassy to China, after which he lectured in India and was appointed to the College of Fort William in Calcutta (now Kolkata). In 1997, his notebooks were discovered in a Halifax basement and subsequently donated to the Dalhousie University Archives. It is unclear how Dinwiddie's papers ended up in Nova Scotia or whether anyone in the eighteenth-century Maritimes had access to them.[276]

Rennet for Cheese is made
as follows. A calf's stomach
emptied of its contents but not
washed, laid in Salt for one
month, turned every morning

at the end of the month take
it out of the salt and extend
it in cross sticks, hang up 'till
dry – The size of a Crown piece
put into half a pint of boiling
water the preceding evening is
sufficient for 20 Gallons of Milk
– Temperature about 90° - -
– Stomach of a pidgeon and
– Flowers of Artichokes macerated
in warm water will produce the
same effect.

Though most often rendered from a calf's stomach, the term *rennet* is applied to any substance used to curdle milk in the cheese-making process. Dinwiddie's recipe specifies macerated artichoke flowers, which were often used in Italian cheese-making, particularly in Florence, though rennet was sometimes made with nettles and other types of thistle. Dinwiddie also offers pigeon stomach as a substitution, even though only ruminant stomachs produce the chymosin that is the primary active ingredient in rennet derived from calves. Instructions for making bovine rennet and for making cheese can also be found in numerous English publications that include books on husbandry, recipe collections, and guidebooks for managing house and farm. Richard Bradley's *The Country Housewife*, for example, details rennet and cheese-making over several pages, while in *The Compleat Farmer*, Robert Brown notes that he "shall not mention any thing about the making of butter and cheese, because most good house-wives are acquainted with the way of doing it."[277]

As Brown's comment implies, British women had long been responsible for making both rennet and cheese, "an exacting and arduous trade" that, according to Sally McMurry, "was used to protect and even to enhance women's position" on farms where caring for livestock was most often relegated to men.[278] That women were reluctant to share their expertise may account for why English cheese recipes "seem sketchy," as Sandra Sherman puts it.[279] In America, however, the knowledge and corresponding status enjoyed by English dairy women did not persist in a context where "men participated in cheesemaking to a greater extent."[280]

Given that it is the most effective means of preserving milk, cheese had likely been made in the Maritime region since Samuel de Champlain accompanied the expedition of Pierre Dugua de Monts (1558–1628). In May 1604, the settlers arrived at what they called Acadia with vessels bearing "provisions, tools, building materials, livestock, and other things needed to carry the men through the winter."[281] The noted livestock most certainly included cattle, and by the beginning of the eighteenth century the average Acadian household at Port Royal had just over nine head of cattle.[282] After the expulsion of the Acadians, settlers from Germany were provided cows by the colonial government, while New Englanders brought cows with them and were also encouraged to round up and care for livestock the Acadians had been forced to leave behind.[283] By 1789, livestock raised in the Chignecto region that joins Nova Scotia to New Brunswick were plentiful enough to be driven to Saint John along with "considerable quantities" of cheese sent also to Halifax.[284] Nevertheless, cheese-making knowledge seems to have struggled somewhat in British North America. While English cheese by the early nineteenth century had become characterized by region, large volume production, the shipping of cheese over long distances, and the regulatory regimes that are all features of an industrial market system, the same was not true of North American cheese.[285] Although colonists brought English cheese-making methods with them, McMurry argues that "specialized cheesemaking knowledge atrophied because markets were scarce, cows seldom milked year-round, and cheese [was] but an insignificant element in the diversified Northern farming enterprise."[286] An industrial cheese manufacturing industry in what is now Canada emerged first in Ontario only in the 1860s, but there were also cheddar cheese factories established in Sussex, New Brunswick, in the same decade, in the Annapolis Valley in 1870, and in Prince Edward Island in 1882.[287]

We have yet found no other instructions for making cheese among personal papers in Maritime archives, but instructions for cheese-making were published in *The Nova Scotia Magazine* in 1791, suggesting some local interest in the late eighteenth century. "Directions for Making Cheese" (1 March 1791) and "Receipt for Making Parmesan Cheese" (5 November 1791) call for the addition of rennet in the process of heating the milk to encourage coagulation.[288] That these instructions from *The Nova Scotia Magazine* appear to have been published widely may suggest an interest in improving the craft in the Americas. The directions appeared through the summer of 1791 in newspapers in Philadelphia, Hartford, Newport, Bennington (VT), Litchfield (CT), Charleston, Boston, Worcester, New Haven, Newburyport (MA); they were published again in 1793 in Walpole (NH) and in 1795 in Salem (NY), in 1798 in Chambersburg (PA), and in 1799 in Peacham (VT).[289] Several of these publications cite the *Quebec Herald* as their source, while one, the newspaper from Salem, cites *The Nova Scotia Magazine*. The state of cheese-making in the region may be implied by the suggestion in "Directions for Making Cheese" that cheese-making is not as well-developed a skill as some would like:

"dairy-women are often as much pains to spoil their milk by making it into very bad cheese, as they would then be to make that which was very good," and invokes Britain, where cheese is made well with different methods in different regions, recommending the recipe's method as "perhaps inferior to none that are made in England."[290] That Dinwiddie's recipe covers only a part of the cheese-making process in detailing the manufacture of rennet suggests some wider knowledge of the overall process.

On the Sugar of Milk

These instructions were copied into the manuscript notebook of Dr William James Almon (1755–1817), very likely from a printed source.[291] Husband to Rebecca Byles Almon, Dr Almon was born in Providence, Rhode Island, and learned medicine as an apprentice to a physician in New York and in the British army, the context for his arrival in Halifax as a surgeon to a garrison stationed there. By 1783, Almon had established himself in private medical practice, and by 1785 he had received the valuable appointment physician to the poor house.[292] Almon was likely interested in this recipe because of the substance's purported medicinal benefits.

This text had appeared under the title "On the Sugar of Milk. By Mr. Jahrig, of Petersburgh. Translated from the French" in *The Literary Magazine and British Review* in May 1792.[293] It was also printed in *New Encyclopaedia: Or, Modern Universal*, under a similar title and with a further note that it had also previously appeared in the *Bath Register* on 30 June 1792.[294] The French source referenced in *The Literary Magazine* may be "Sur le sucre de lait naturel, par M. Jahrig, à Pétersbourg," which appeared in the November 1791 edition of *Observations sur la physique, sur l'histoire naturelle et sur les arts*, a journal edited by three members of French scientific academies.[295]

On the Sugar of Milk

By Mr. Jahrig of Petersburgh
During the travels which I undertook by order of
the Academy of Petersburgh, among the Mogul tribes
who inhabit the frontiers of the government of Irkutz
beyond the lake Baikal,[296] on the banks of the river
Salenga,[297] I was particularly stuck with the ingenious
manner in which these people preserve during their

long winters, a very great quantity of Milk, which they suffer to freeze, in iron kettles, which serve the[m] likewise for other purposes. When the milk contained in These kettles is perfectly congealed, they place them over a gentle fire, and take out the milk, reduced to a cake of ice, by means of a wooden spatula. This operation is begun on the commencement of the first cold for the milk is then found in greatest abundance, and the cakes of ice obtained by these means assume, as may be readily supposed the form of the kettle in which they freeze, and may be preserved all the winter. What, however excited my curiosity most was to see all these cakes of frozen milk, covered to a conside-rable depth with a white and apparently farinaceous powder – I observed the same thing in my small dairy which I was obliged to establish on the same plan with those of, of these wandering people, and the children of my shepherds often brought me plate-fuls of that powder which they ate, and which they used also to sweeten various articles of their food. After this discovery I caused a number of cakes of frozen milk to be conveyed from a lower apartment to the top of a wooden House which I occupied, and which was a part of a temple consecrated to the idols of these pagan People. These cakes in that place were exposed to the immediate contacts of the dry cold air, which prevails in that country almost the whole year. These cakes were placed perpendicularly, and by these means were more expo-sed to the effects of the air. I visited them very often and I perceived that this exposure contributed daily to increase the farinaceous substance, with which their surface was covered. Every week I took it away by scraping the cakes, to the depth of two inches, and afterwards spread it out upon a broad dish, in order that the cold might destroy any remains of moisture, which would have prevented it from keeping for a length of time. This flour when thus exposed to a great degree of cold, and consequently freed from all its moisture, had a remark -able sweet and sugary taste. If dissolved in warm water, and when strongly stirred by means of a chocolate stick,[298] one may procure from it, at all times and in all places excellent and well tasted milk. This discovery I consider as of great utility, since it may enable navigators to supply themselves with milk during long sea-voyages. Nothing will be requisite but to make the necessary preparations with care.

As I here speak of an experiment which I repeated seve -ral times, I can safely assure those who may be disposed to try it, that it will always succeed, but at the same time, I am inclined to think that all countries will not be equally favorable to the formation of this singular substance. The country in which I then resided, is one of the most elevated in the northern part of Asia, an alpine country, where the rivers are covered with ice, almost six months in the year, though it lies under the fiftieth degree of latitude.

Another peculiarity of this country, is the dry cold air, which prevails in it for a great part of the year. Dry winds as well as rain and snow, seldom come from the west: they come almost always from the North, and are generally preceded by a very mild South wind which blows for some time. The dry rarified air which continues here all winter increases the evaporation of all moisture contained in these ice cakes, and leaves nothing but the milk, the essential and so constituent part, under the form of a white powder.

To obtain, in a little time, a large quantity of this powder it will be necessary to employ raw, in preference to, boiled milk. By making use of the latter, or that from which the cream has been taken, little or none will be obtained. Care also must be taken not to expose new milk, while it retains its natural

> heat, to the cold; for the sudden contact of the cold
> carries all its fat and caseous parts, towards the
> middle of the mass, so that the parts purely
> aqueous alone occupy the external surface. The
> interior part, which then appears rough, is often chang-
> -ed into a buttery substance, and produces no suga-
> -ry powder. That all the fat and sugary parts
> might be more equally distributed throughout
> the whole mass of milk, I suffered that newly
> taken from the cows to cool, and then pouring it
> into broad shallow kettles.

As the sources for this recipe suggest, it is part of a series of studies of milk by eighteenth-century European scientists. The recipe's context is explained in *A Dissertation on the Sugar of Milk* by J.L. Dyvernois, identified as a physician to the king of Prussia. Translated from French and published in London in 1753, this work cites other physicians and professors, including a professor of medicine in Saxony who studied milk and a physician in Venice who claimed to have invented the sugar of milk; an appendix by the translator (likely David D'Escherny, a Scottish physician who was admitted as a licentiate to the College of Physicians in 1759) surveys milk research in Leyden and Italy. The sugar of milk, says the translator, has been used successfully abroad and is well made in Switzerland, where milk is particularly healthful, but is less well-known in England. The title page outlines the substance's multiple medical effects: "its great Efficacy in Consumptions, hectic Fevers, the Scurvy, Vapours or Hysterics, and hypocondriacal Complaints, the Asthma and Gout."[299] Like many foods, milk was imagined to have particular effects on health.

Sugar of milk was made from whey. Milk, the dissertation explains, is made of three substances that have different natures and virtues: cream, which mollifies and relaxes and works against acid or corrosive substances; "the cheesy part," which thickens the blood and obstructs small vessels and is the only harmful part; and the serous part, or whey, that can be made into a mild salt or sugar that can add moisture to the body and "cool and sweeten a thick, acrid, and black Blood" and is generally medically useful.[300] Whey gives its qualities to the sugar of milk, a "mixt Salt."[301] The sugar of milk thus functions as a medicine because many diseases, the treatise explains, are caused by thick blood that contains particles too big for the blood vessels and thus slow blood circulation and cause stoppages, especially in the bowels and glands, leading to illness. The sugar of milk helps to restore circulation and purify the blood and is particularly helpful for old people and for women suffering from the vapours, a swelling in the stomach that causes a feeling of suffocation and vertigo or light-headedness. Sugar of milk could also be prescribed when whey itself was thought too dangerous, such as when the stomach is too weak and acidic or the body too phlegmatic.[302]

The instructions from Jahrig reproduced in the Almon notebook are not explicitly engaged with the medical uses propounded in contemporary milk research but instead appear to represent a method for storing milk and for a pleasant drink. Recounting Jahrig's experiments on his roof, however, the recipe also takes a scientific approach. In describing a method for creating a form of powdered milk that could be carried on sea voyages, it also gives the product commercial and political importance in its potential to support English colonialism and the nation's war efforts. Although the health impacts of the drink are unmentioned, the name for the powder is nevertheless retained, and the entry demonstrates the migration of food knowledge from Mongolia to Nova Scotia by way of France and England.

Cheap Substitute for Sugar

This entry, which also appears in the notebook of Dr William James Almon, records instructions from two separate sources describing how to make sugar substitutes from honey and treacle.[303] The first part of Almon's entry appeared in London in a July 1793 issue of *The Phoenix; Or, Weekly Miscellany Improved* under the title "Means of lessening the Consumption of Sugar," and was likely derived from a second unnamed source.[304] The entry's second part, titled "Cheap Substitute for Sugar," is credited to "The celebrated Mr. Lowitz of Petersbourg." Lowitz was likely the German-born Johann Tobias Lowitz (1757–1804) noted in *Crell's Chemical Journal* as discovering the effectiveness of charcoal "in preventing the putrefaction of water" and the means of "concentrating vinegar" to produce "the highest degree of strength"; Lowitz was a member of the Imperial Academy at St Petersburg, Russia.[305]

> A pastry-cook at Hamburgh named Holzen, amas-
> -sed a considerable fortune by using white honey, in-
> -stead of sugar, in syrups, cordials, stewed fruit
> and confectionary. He procured his Honey from
> Hungary, Walachia,[306] and Spain; and the method
> he employed to purify it was as follows:

> After having melted, scummed, and clarified it, he dipped into it five or six times successively, a large nail, made each time, red hot in the fire. He also mixed with every half pound of honey a spoon--ful of spirituous liquor, which destroyed its melleous taste. Tarts, especially those composed of cherries or gooseberries, stewed fruit, prunes [etc.] made with this Honey, were much finer, and wholesomer than those made with Sugar, and cost only half the expence, as the price of honey is much less, than that of Sugar, and as twelve ounces of the former will go as far as sixteen ounces of the latter.
>
> **Cheap Substitute for Sugar**
>
> The celebrated Mr. Lowitz of Petersbourg has invented the following process for obtaining a suc--cedaneum to sugar equally pleasant and salutary Viz. Take twelve pounds weight of treacle wth the same weight of water; then grossly bruising three pounds of charcoal thoroughly burnt, mix the whole in a caldron, and let the mixture boil gently; for half an hour; on a clear wood fire. – After pouring the liquor through a strain--ing bag, replace it on the fire, that the super--fluous water may evaporate, and the treacle attain its original consistence.[307]

Why Almon decided to record not one but two recipes for a sugar substitute is unclear. Once reserved only for the wealthy, sugar was widely available and affordable in Britain and its colonies by the eighteenth century; as Elizabeth Abbott notes in her wide-ranging history of sugar, "especially in England, sugar sweetened even the poor man's palate" to the point that Britain "had its sugar colonies and its peoples' voracious sweet tooth to thank for its expanding empire."[308] Along with pepper, nutmeg, cloves, cinnamon, and other spices, sugar made its way to the early modern Maritimes from the West Indies, where it was made by enslaved labourers. It sometimes came directly from the Caribbean and sometimes made its way first to the United Kingdom and then to Maritime ports. A 1785 issue of *The Royal*

American Gazette, for example, included an advertisement from Sullivan and Mills promoting goods, including loaf sugar, available at their store on the "Corner of King and Water Streets" in Shelburne, about two hundred kilometres from Halifax, that had "lately arrived from London."[309]

As a physician, Almon was perhaps intrigued by the promise of a "wholesomer" product made from honey that could be produced locally. Although in 1782 Virginia politician, oenophile, agriculturalist, and future president Thomas Jefferson (1743–1826) noted that "bees have generally expanded themselves into the country," by which he meant Virginia and proximate regions, he also notes that "the honey-bee cannot live through the winter in Canada" (by which he means the region that now comprises part of the province of Quebec) and questions the bee's ability to "bear the cold" in northern climes.[310] Yet the inclusion of three articles that encompass "Essay on Bees, Honey, and Honey-Dews," "Observations on the Origin of Honey," and "Useful Method of Preserving Bees, Lately Adopted in America" in *The Nova Scotia Magazine* suggests that there was some interest in producing honey in eighteenth-century Nova Scotia.[311] Honey is also specified as an ingredient in numerous medical remedies we located in Maritime archives, but appears in only one that is not medical, "A Receipt to make a Rich Pleasant Wine."[312] Though honey does behave differently than sugar when used in cooking, that it does not appear elsewhere as a substitute for sugar may also suggest that honey was prized more for its "wholesomer" medicinal benefits than it was valued for food.

Almon's interest in charcoal as a means of clarifying is evident also in a separate entry describing the usefulness of charcoal in cleaning utensils, improving oral hygiene, and purifying water, a discovery credited to "a gentleman at Petersburg" who is undoubtedly also "The celebrated Mr. Lowitz."[313] Using charcoal to transform treacle, a thick liquid rendered from sugar cane that is similar to molasses, promises to produce a sweetener "equally pleasant and salutary" to refined sugar.[314] The process of refining sugar also includes filtering to remove impurities and whiten, usually with bone char. Though the method described here does not evaporate "superfluous water" to the point of producing sugar crystals, the thirty minutes of boiling does imply some degree of concentration in a result that may be of the "original consistence" of treacle but is likely to become more clear with the help of charcoal filtering and a "straining bag."

CHAPTER TWO

Drink

Settlers in the colonial Maritimes consumed a variety of beverages, many of which were imported. Along with tea and coffee, ships brought various kinds of wine and brandy from Europe as well as the Caribbean rum often associated with seafarers but ubiquitous in the early modern Atlantic World. The inventories of goods from Fortress Louisbourg suggest that people across social ranks, from the governor, to officers, to merchants and fishermen, had a variety of forms of alcohol in their possession, including wine from France, Spain, and Madeira, as well as chartreuse from France and rum from the Caribbean; beer was produced in Louisbourg at home and in a local brewery.[1] The full range of drink recipes in the *Early Modern Maritime Recipes* database suggests that British settlers in the region fabricated a variety of drinks, many of which were alcohol based. These include recipes for drinks made by steeping almonds, lemons, and other ingredients in spirits, or, as in "An Approved Method of Making Cider," making a beverage from apples.[2] There are also recipes for non-alcoholic drinks, such as the recipes in Sarah Creighton Wilkins's collection for "A Good Nourishing Drink" made from milk, soda water, and a "Diet Drink."[3] Many common drinks, like coffee and tea, are not represented in recipes, except teas made from plants or trees to be used medicinally, as in the recommendation to take a tea of garden tansy found in Dr Almon's recipes.[4] Given the popularity of both beer and wine in Britain and its colonies – and the relatively recent resurgence of making both in Maritime Canada – the recipes that follow focus on beer and wine making.

The eighteenth-century recipe culture represented here stands alongside significant alcohol imports to the region in the eighteenth century. James Moreira argues that "rum has been a persistent force in shaping the political, economic, and social environments of the Atlantic Provinces"; rum was a trade good produced by enslaved people in the Caribbean that became the source of great wealth for some, like Joshua Mauger (1725–1788), who made his fortune trading in rum and founded a distillery in Halifax in 1751 before leaving to become an MP in England.[5] Rum was also a "factor in rebellion," "a source of loyalty," and an aspect of daily life that brought pleasure, but was also blamed for social problems inspiring a temperance movement that began to emerge in the 1790s and gave rise to the temperance societies that would become plentiful in the nineteenth century.[6] With just one distillery in Halifax, most wine and spirits were produced elsewhere. A major port of entry for alcohol in the eighteenth century, Saint John had merchants selling sherry, brandy, rum (from the Caribbean and New England), port, and wine from Lisbon, Madeira, and Tenerife, as well as coffee and tea.[7] As for Nova Scotia, Emily Burton writes that "Early Halifax had no shortage of places in which alcohol was consumed, from the illegal 'grog shops' of Barrack Street to licensed establishments that were little more than a private home with a sign, to the finer inns, taverns and coffee shops of the small town."[8] Grog shops and taverns were frequented by soldiers and sailors for whom they served as sites of sociability; military and naval elites and those who saw themselves as gentlemen sought out more respectable taverns, such as the Golden Ball in Halifax that served as a venue for "exclusive sociability" where "decent drunkness" could be accepted, as a gathering place for members of the Nova Scotia Supreme Court, and as a location for meetings of charitable societies.[9]

Alcoholic beverages were not imbibed solely for pleasure. They can also be seen "As commodities serving physiological and medicinal functions" that, notes Robert James Merritt, have "aided Canada in several ways: as water purifiers, beverages, painkillers, palliative drugs, and in customary festivities."[10] Moreover, such beverages worked also to support the British imperialist enterprise, not only through the importation of cultural practices that served as markers of taste, refinement, and "Britishness," but also in the way that the British used alcohol in attempts to undermine Indigenous cultures and communities.[11] Merritt writes that by the late nineteenth century, Hariot Dufferin (1843–1946), wife to the governor general who served from 1872 to 1878 and a teetotaller herself, suggests that her own practice of serving wine as well as the traditional "Yorkshire wassail-bowl" to her guests confirms that "traditional drinking values entered the domestic sphere, even if royal and imperial rituals lost symbolic power from routinized public consumption."[12] The "politics of taste" associated with the consumption of wine and spirits had become, in other words, firmly entrenched within the home.[13]

BEER

The following recipes for beer come from the papers of prominent Loyalists. Long made by North American settlers, beer was a staple beverage preferred over water in Britain and its colonies. Indeed, Derrek Eberts writes that "Beer has been brewed in Canada for at least 450 years, and most likely much longer," given that the Indigenous peoples were already brewing spruce beer, "likely for generations." Among settler populations, "Louis Hébet, Canada's first farmer, is claimed to have brewed beer in 1627 to celebrate a birth."[14] Among the British settlers, New Englanders were as early as the 1630s advised to bring the "barley, hop-roots and copper kettles" necessary to brewing a beverage too cumbersome and therefore too costly to import.[15] In the early modern Maritimes, beer was brewed at home and also sold at the numerous "taverns, alehouses, inns, houses of entertainment, and public houses" licensed in Nova Scotia from 1749. Because brewing was a natural extension of their work in the kitchen, many of those "common Tipling Houses" were "owned and operated by women."[16] Though it is unlikely that either William Paine or the Almon family brewed beer for public consumption, the recipes below suggest that even the most prosperous settlers sometimes made their own.

A Receipt to Make Spruce Beer from the Essence of Spruce

This recipe for spruce beer is preserved in the 1769 *First Notebook of Medical Memoranda* of physician William Paine (1750–1833), made while he yet resided in his native Massachusetts.[17] Paine graduated from Harvard in 1768 and began to practise medicine in Massachusetts before pursuing a medical degree in Scotland. He subsequently served as an apothecary and then physician in the British Army. Paine and his family were among the many Loyalists who migrated to Nova Scotia at the end of the American Revolutionary War. Although he received substantial land grants and became an alderman in Saint John, he stayed in what would become New Brunswick only until 1787, when he returned to Massachusetts and re-settled

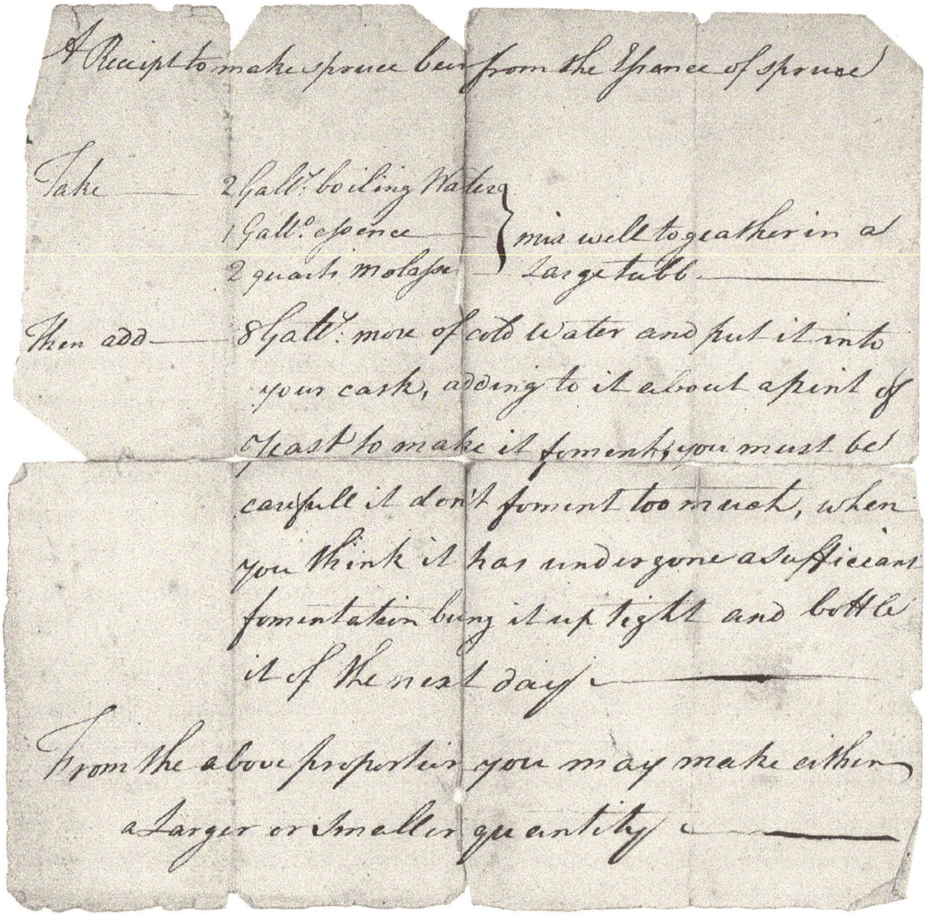

A Receipt to make spruce beer from the Essance of spruce

Take ——— 2 Galls: boiling Water
1 Gall: essence } mix well togeather in a
2 quarts molasses } Large tubb ———

Then add ——— 8 Galls: more of cold Water and put it into your cask, adding to it about a pint of yeast to make it foment; you must be carefull it don't foment too much, when you think it has undergone a sufficient fomentation bung it up tight and bottle it of the next day ———

From the above proportion you may make either a Larger or Smaller quantity ———

Figure 2.1
A Receipt to make spruce beer from the Essence of Spruce. Paine Family Papers.

his family in Worcester. As a thinker and physician, Paine was associated with the Massachusetts Medical Society, the American Academy of Arts and Sciences, and the American Antiquarian Society; he was also recognized with an honorary MD from Harvard.[18] We have not found another source for this particular recipe.

A Receipt to make spruce beer from the Essence of spruce

Take ______ 2 Galls: boiling Water

1 Gall: essence } mix well together in a

2 quarts molasses } large tubb_____

Then add __ 8 Galls: more of cold water and put it into
your cask, adding to it about a pint of
Yeast to make it foment you must be
carefull it don't foment too much, when
you think it has undergone a sufficiant
fomentation bung it up tight and bottle
it of the next day.
From the above proportion you may make either
a Larger or Smaller quantity.

Paine's recipe calls for a gallon of essence of spruce, long used by Indigenous peoples and, given that it is rich in vitamin C, famously consumed by Jacques Cartier and his crew to treat and prevent scurvy in what has become "one of the best-known stories in Canadian medical history."[19] Already popular in Germany, spruce beer was "taking off in Britain" around the time Paine recorded his recipe,[20] and records of forest products exported from Massachusetts in 1791–92 suggest that it was available in that locale.[21] Like other spruce beer recipes, Paine's specifies using molasses as the sweetener necessary to feed the yeast that converts sugar to alcohol. The recipe produces about ten to twelve gallons of beer but indicates that it can also be scaled to make larger amounts. Paine likely made the beer for household consumption, but in an age when physicians often made their own medicines, it is possible that he also prescribed it to his patients. Sometimes recommended to treat venereal disease and other complaints, spruce beer was in 1756 noted in *The Gentleman's Magazine* as "esteemed good in the scurvy and the like foulness of the blood and its juices" as well as "a good restorative in all inward bruises."[22] Spruce beer is also recommended as a "Prophylaxis, or Method of Preventing Infection" in a newspaper clipping preserved in the notebook of Halifax physician William James Almon.[23]

Native to North America, the spruce tree was used by Indigenous peoples across the Americas for medicinal purposes, and "spruce beer probably originated from spruce needle tea drunk as a health beverage."[24] One illustration of the adoption of Indigenous knowledge by New England settlers, John Josselyn (1608–1675) includes his accounting of the plants of New England, *New Englands Rarities* (1672), that "The tops of Green Spruce Boughs boiled in Bear [beer], and drunk, is assuredly one of the best Remedies for the Scurvy, restoring the infected party in short time; they also make a Lotion of some of the decoction"; by *they*, he surely means one of the Algonquin peoples inhabiting what is now called New England.

His book couples "physical and chyrgical remedies wherewith the natives constantly use to cure their distempers, wounds, and sores" to description of plants and animals that aims to illustrate the value of New England as a colony.[25] Consumed by the Acadians as well as British and American soldiers, spruce beer was most often used by Europeans to counteract and prevent scurvy.[26] According to Philip Miller (1691–1771), author of the 1733 guide *The Gardeners Dictionary*, the trees "used to make Spruce Beer" were "brought from *America*, and planted in *Devonshire* and *Cornwall*," where they were presumably used to make the beer that appears in English recipe books most often as an ingredient in other beverages.[27] *An Authentic Narrative of the Success of Tar-Water* (1746) by Thomas Prior (1682?–1751) describes "The way of making spruce beer in Newfoundland" using black spruce branches,[28] an ingredient confirmed by English botanist John Claudius Loudon (1783–1843) in his explication of spruce beer brewing earlier recorded by Henri-Louis Duhamel du Monceau (1700–1782); Loudon explains that du Monceau confirms "white spruce is never used" to make the beer "in the country about Halifax and the Maine."[29]

In the American colonies, a recipe for beer made from spruce boughs appeared in *The New-England Farmer* of 1790,[30] while "For Brewing Spruce Beer" stands out as the final entry in Amelia Simmons's 1796 *American Cookery*, the first cookbook written by an American to be published in the United States.[31] In a time when "most of the alcohol consumed in northeastern British America was imported," most often as rum and wine, "spruce beer was an exception."[32]

To Brew

The following handwritten recipe for beer from the Almon family scrapbook was recorded sometime between 1780 and 1800.[33]

To Brew

: 4 Pails of Water, 3 Pints of Malt, 1 Handfull of Hops, boil it away to 3 pails full, pour it thro your Straner put 3 Pints of Mollasses, let it stand till cold, put it in the Barrel, with I pint and half of Emptings,[34] leave out the Bung, then Bottle it, & Drink it.

Comprising a more conventional beer recipe than Paine's, the directions offered here are also noteworthy for their brevity. By contrast, a popular manual titled *The Lady's Companion* – with rules for conduct through all ages of life and every part of housewifery (published 1737 and after) – devotes the equivalent of three full pages to describing the process for brewing "strong October Beer," while other eighteenth-century publications such as George Watkins's *The Complete English Brewer* (1770) and E. Hughes's *A Treatise on the Brewing of Beer* (1796) devote entire books to the topic.[35] More focused on ingredients than method, the Almon recipe suggests users familiar with a practice that was as much a part of everyday life as preserving and pickling. The relatively small quantity produced also suggests frequent brewing. Like most beer recipes, this one calls for hops and malt, a familiar ingredient made by "malting" germinated grain, most often barley. It is unclear, however, where the Almon family would have acquired the ingredients needed for making beer. Records indicate that malt and hops were imported from England to Newfoundland in the eighteenth century,[36] though the Maritime climate would have been more hospitable than the north Atlantic island to the necessary hops vines and grain that may have been grown locally. Molasses, of course, would have been imported from the Caribbean, and the specified emptings would likely have been reused from a previous batch or acquired from another local brewer. That the recipe ends with the imperative "Drink it" further confirms that the beer was meant to be consumed soon and often.

Like their American counterparts, not all settler families in the eighteenth-century Maritimes would have enjoyed the means to purchase equipment that remained largely unavailable in rural areas.[37] But home brewing would have nevertheless provided a reliable beer supply to many households before Alexander Keith (1795–1873) founded Halifax's first commercial brewery in 1820.

WINE

Winemaking knowledge in the eighteenth-century Maritimes would have arrived via Britain and the American colonies. Though domestic winemaking in England really began with the 1066 Norman conquest, grapes were first introduced to the British Isles by the Romans. With the fourteenth-century onset of the "Little Ice Age," the growing season became too short to allow for adequate ripening. Undeterred by the weather, Britons continued to make wine from ingredients other than grapes. Instructions for winemaking can thus be found in countless English manuscript and print collections, and scores of extant recipes in hundreds of recipe books attest to British resourcefulness in producing wine from all kinds of native vegetation. Even the title of William Graham's 1770 winemaking guide, *The Art of Making Wines from Fruits, Flowers, and Herbs, All the Native Growth of Great Britain*, confirms the diversity of plants used to produce wine. Though Graham's book does include recipes for wines made from grapes that were dried and likely imported, it offers many more recipes using fruits such as apples, pears, cherries, peaches, plums, apricots, and a variety of berries, as well as turnip, birch, roses, and mint – all unusual ingredients for today's winemakers.[38] Though far less substantial than the wine recipes offered in Graham's book, the EMMR online collection nevertheless includes over a dozen receipts for making wine from herbs and berries as well as from dried grapes. Though it is clear that large quantities of wine were imported to the colonies, extant Maritime wine recipes attest that settlers also made their own and did so using ingredients that reflect both British influence and colonial resourcefulness in domestic winemaking.

A Receipt: To Make Sage Wine Not Inferior to Hermitage Claret

The following recipe for making wine from red sage was published in the 1789 edition of *The Nova Scotia Calender*, an almanac published on a yearly basis by Halifax printer Anthony Henry.[39] The author is Metonicus, a pseudonym derived from the word *metonic*, the name given to the nineteen-year cycle that it takes for the moon to return to the same position relative to the sun. The recipe appears to be a paraphrased version of instructions "To Make Sage Wine," credited to an unknown "Mrs. E.B.," that appeared in the sixth edition of *The Country Housewife and Lady's Director* (1732) by Richard Bradley.[40] Nearly identical instructions were printed also in the anonymous 1744 collection *Adam's Luxury, and Eve's Cookery* whose subtitle lays claim to "the best and most approved Methods of raising and bringing to the greatest Perfection, all the Products of the Kitchen-Garden."[41] Still another nearly identical recipe was published in the 1753 fifteenth edition of Eliza Smith's *The Compleat Housewife*,[42] where it appears between "To Cure Blindness" and "Ways of Eating Pickled Herrings." Despite their similarities to the version that appeared in *The Nova Scotia Calender*, however, the English recipes do not also claim a result "not inferior to Hermettage Claret," the wine originating in the hermitage appellation of France's Rhône Valley.

A RECEIPT

To make Sage Wine not inferior to Hermettage Claret.

TO three Gallons of Water put six Pounds of Sugar; boil and scum till you think it boiled enough; then pour into a Tub, in which are half a Peck of *Sage Leaves*; *Red Sage* is the properest, well picked and washed; when the Liquor is cool, put in the Juice of four Lemons beaten well with some good Yeast; mix well, and cover and let them stand forty-eight Hours, then strain through a fine Hair Seive, and put into a Vessel not too big, and, when it has done working, stop it close. In three Weeks Time it will be fit to bottle, when add to each Bottle a Lump of Loaf-Sugar. When ripe drink; which it will be in three Months Time.

Native to the Mediterranean region but naturalized in England and North America, sage (*Salvia officinalis*) is a member of the mint family long grown in countless kitchen gardens throughout Britain, and the herb had been used in winemaking since at least the Middle Ages, albeit with the addition of honey before sugar became widely available. Given that many kinds of seeds were imported to the colonies, garden variety sage was likely readily available in eighteenth-century Nova Scotia. A list of garden seeds published in the 9 May 1785 edition of Shelburne's *The Royal American Gazette*, for example, lists several herbs that include "Sage and catnip" to be sold by John Creighton in his Halifax shop.[43] This recipe specifies red sage as "the properest" kind, and half a peck of its leaves are called for along with three gallons of water and six pounds of sugar. Like other recipes for making wine held in Maritime archives, this one specifies the addition of lemon juice and "good yeast," though not the more specific "ale yeast" indicated in the English recipes. Given that the availability of imported fruit was unpredictable and inconsistent, securing an appropriate number of lemons would have been hit-or-miss in colonial Nova Scotia. As Captain William Moorsom would later write in his 1830 *Letters from Nova Scotia*, "sometimes pine apples are almost rolling about the streets of Halifax; at other times, a lemon cannot be procured at any price."[44] Sugar, however, was a non-perishable ingredient produced by enslaved people in the Caribbean – which was closer to the Maritime region than to Europe – and was readily available, and many other wine recipes specify the addition of lump sugar at the time of bottling.[45] Perhaps consumed for its resemblance to "Hermettage claret" as well as its alcohol content, wine made from a plant long valued for its medicinal properties may also have been taken as medicine.

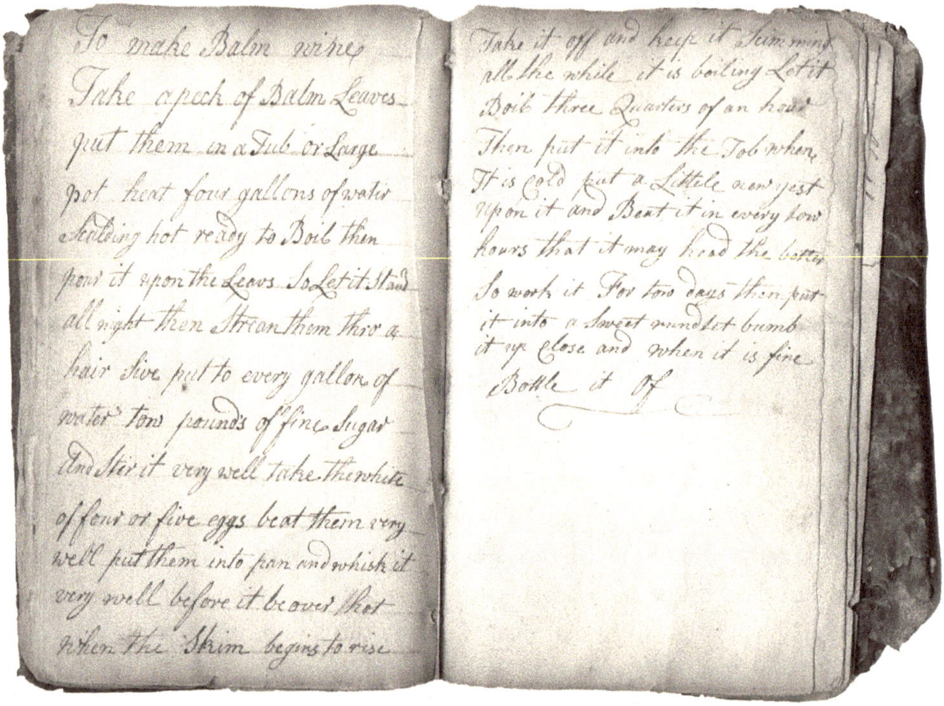
To make Balm wine
Take a peck of Balm Leaves
put them in a Tub or Large
pot heat four gallons of water
Scalding hot ready to Boil then
pour it upon the Leavs So Let it Stand
all night then Strain them thro a
hair Sive put to every gallon of
water tow pounds of fine Sugar
And Stir it very well take the white
of four or five eggs beat them very
well put them into pan and whisk it
very well before it be over hot
when the Skim begins to rise

Take it off and keep it Skimming
all the while it is boiling Let it
Boil three Quarters of an hour
Then put it into the Tub when
It is cold put a Little new yest
upon it and Beat it in every tow
hours that it may head the better
So work it For tow days then put
it into a Sweet runlet bung
it up close and when it is fine
Bottle it of

Figure 2.2
To make Balm wine. Trueman Family Fonds.

To Make Balm Wine

Recorded in the mid-eighteenth century, the following recipe for balm wine comes from a notebook attributed to John and William Trueman.[46] The manuscript, which includes Bible verses and hymns as well as recipes, is dated to before the family left Yorkshire. The book did, however, travel with the family to New Brunswick, where William Trueman established his 134-acre Westmoreland County farm in 1777.[47] Though the book includes notes referencing the years 1750 and 1771–72, dates that precede the family's migration, it includes later entries as well; the manuscript text is also written in several different hands, confirming that multiple people compiled and used the notebook. The notebook's recipe for balm wine is also found in the 1769 edition of *English Housewifery* by Elizabeth Moxon (fl. 1740–1754).[48] Originally printed in 1741 in Leeds, a West Yorkshire city not far from Trueman's native Bilsdale, Moxon's collection of "four hundred and fifty receipts" appeared in sixteen editions that culminated with the London publication of 1808.

To make Balm wine

Take a peck of Balm Leaves
put them in a Tub or Large
pot heat four gallons of water
Scalding hot ready to Boil then
pour it upon the Leavs So Let it Stand
all night then Strian them thro' a
hair Sive put to every gallon of
water tow pounds of fine Sugar
And Stir it very well take the white
of four or five eggs beat them very
well put them into pan and whisk it
very well before it be over hot
when the Skim begins to rise
Take it off and keep it Scimming
all the while it is boiling Let it
Boil three Quarters of an hour
Then put it into the Tob when
It is cold put a Little new yest
Upon it and Beat it in every tow
hours that it may head the better
So work it For tow days then put
it into a Sweet rundlet bumb
it up close and when it is fine
Bottle it of.

Originating in southern Europe and long grown in England, the lemon balm to which the recipe presumably refers is related to mint and has also become naturalized in North America. Balm also appears in James Creighton's list of seeds for sale, suggesting that the herb was grown domestically in the colonial Maritimes and would have been readily available.[49] What is unusual about this recipe is not that it uses balm to make wine, but that it calls for the addition of egg whites, which are not included in other eighteenth-century recipes for balm wine. Richard Bradley's *The Country Housewife*, for example, does not specify eggs in "To Make Balm Wine."[50] Neither do the instructions "To Make Wine of Mint, Balm, and Other Herbs, &c." in William Graham's *The Art of Making Wines* make mention of eggs.[51] Though raw egg whites have been used by winemakers as a fining agent used to draw out undesirable particles and qualities, the recipe indicates that the four or five egg whites are to be heated along with the balm, sugar, and water mixture. Made from only four gallons of water, the recipe specifies that the final product be put into a rundlet, a term first used in the fourteenth century to describe a vessel whose smaller size has a maximum capacity of about six gallons, and then closed up with a bung, a stopper Trueman mistakenly transcribes as "bumb." The wine is to be kept "close" in the vessel and bottled only once it is "fine" and therefore free of floating particles. Given that lemon balm has long been used to treat a variety of ailments, the wine may also have been taken for medicinal purposes.[52]

Ginger Wine

From the papers of New Brunswick physician William Paine, this recipe has no known other source and may be original to him.[53]

Ginger Wine

Boil 20wt of Sugar & 1 qr lb of
Raw ginger in 20 Gallons of Water
when nearly cool, add 1 quart
of Lemon juice & 1 gallon
of Brandy; pint of yeast
let it stand in a cask a
fortnight, when it will be fit
to Bottle

Although we have not found another source for this recipe, instructions for making fortified ginger wine do appear in several eighteenth-century English publications. Bradley's *The Country Housewife*[54] skips the brandy used in this recipe but adds liquorice and is identical to a recipe titled "To Make Ginger Wine" that was published in the 1739 second edition of *The House-Keeper's Pocket-Book* by Sarah Harrison (1733–1777).[55] Ginger wine had originated in England and was commercially manufactured in London beginning in 1740; this English influence may also have included recognized medicinal benefit, ginger having long been used to counteract nausea and later thought also to protect against cholera.

Paine's recipe is for a large quantity of wine, specifying boiling twenty weight of sugar (roughly twenty pounds or nine kilograms) with a quarter pound of raw ginger in twenty gallons (approximately seventy-six litres) of water. In contrast, Bradley's recipe calls for twenty quarts (or five gallons) of water, while Moxon's *English Housewifery* calls for fourteen quarts.[56] Once transferred to a cask, the wine "will be fit to bottle" in a fortnight, its readiness expedited by the addition of brandy.

A warm-climate plant from Southeast Asia that migrated to the Mediterranean region via India, ginger was imported to England as early as the eleventh century.[57] Many other eighteenth-century Maritime recipes call for ginger, which transports well, suggesting that it was readily available in the colonial Maritimes. With the addition of a large quantity of sugar, a quart of lemon juice, and an entire gallon of brandy, Paine's ginger wine is composed almost exclusively of imported ingredients. The exception is the yeast. Without the yeast that naturally grows on grapes and berries, Paine's recipe also calls for a pint of yeast that would have been obtained from a local brewer or from his own beer making.

Receipt for Ginger Wine

Dating from the late eighteenth or early nineteenth century, this recipe is one of several pasted into *The Militia Laws of the Province of Nova Scotia.*[58] Its source seems likely to be Mrs Smith's *The Female Economist, or, a Plain System of Cookery for the Use of Families*, where the recipe appears in an almost identical form. The recipe pasted into *The Militia Laws* leaves out, after the word *ginger* in line two, "bruised and boiled in a muslin bag," an omission that has all the ingredients simply mixed together.[59] The final line in the printed version – another option, "N.B. Put raisins in the barrel, if you like it" – is also omitted, perhaps because the copyist didn't like raisins. This source dates the recipe to the early nineteenth century.

receipt for Ginger Wine

To twenty pounds of Moist Sugar[60] add ten
Gallons of Water ten Ounces of Ginger
the‸Rimes of ten Seville Oranges and ‸Ten lemons
do not put the peel in till you have done Scumming it
Let it boil ten minutes After the Peel is in
put it in tub til quite Cold put the juice of the
Lemons and Oranges into the Barrel
And to ten Gallon's add a quart of Brandy
Let it stand 4 months – it is the best to make
it Early in the Spring put two spoonfuls of Yeast
into the Cask

Using only ten gallons of water, this recipe makes about half the amount of ginger wine as Paine's. The recipe does, however, call for the same amount of sugar, which at twenty pounds to ten gallons of wine makes for a significantly higher ratio that corresponds with the proportionately larger ten ounces of ginger. This ginger wine also includes orange juice as well as lemon, and adds the rind as well as the juice. Despite the higher proportions of sugar and ginger, however, this "Receipt for Ginger Wine" calls for about half the proportion of brandy at one quart per ten gallons of wine, where Paine's recipe would reduce to two quarts per ten gallons. The recipe also specifies what is likely a much smaller proportion of yeast at two spoonfuls versus one pint, a lesser amount that may account for the significantly longer "4 months" in the cask.

Green Gooseberry Wine

The following recipe for gooseberry wine comes from Sarah Creighton Wilkins's notebook.[61] Along with a recipe for "Mrs. Philips of the Heath House Staffordshire Approvd & Good Ginger Wine," this is one of only two wine recipes that appear in Wilkins's collection. It bears some similarity to a recipe for "English Champagne Wine" printed in *The Gardener's Magazine* in 1832 that when made well, the author claims, "has deceived some of the knowing ones."[62] Pointing to the fruit's importance, *The Gardener's Magazine* also includes details for building a machine to crush gooseberries.[63] The printed version is longer but begins like Wilkins's recipe by calling for adding to every pound of gooseberries, in print specified as "full grown but not changed colour for ripening," a pint of cold water, then pressing out the fluid and adding to every quart of the rendered liquid a pound of sugar. The recipes' methods then diverge, with the printed version recommending putting the liquid directly into a cask and adding isinglass, a clarifying agent derived from the swim bladders of fish, after the fermentation period; Wilkins instead puts the liquid first into a tub and adds brandy and sugar only after fermentation.

Green Gooseberry wine

To every pound of Gooseberries a pint
of cold water to every quart of water that
Liquor when strained a pound of sugar
mash the fruit well & put them in a
Tub with the water & let them stand
until next day - then strain it disolve

> The Sugar in the water or Liquor & put it
> in the Cask stir it every day till done
> fermenting a pint of very best Brandy
> is a sufficient quantity for 5 Gallons
> put half of it in when you turn the
> wine & the other half when you stop the
> Cask some sugar Candy in Lumps is a
> good thing ¼ of a pound
> this wine should stand till Goose berries
> Blossom next year.

As with several other recipes included in this chapter, Wilkins's instructions for "Green Gooseberry Wine" point to the necessity of using what was locally available in the absence of wine grapes that had yet to become well established in Nova Scotia. Wilkins does not, however, specify whether she used gooseberries indigenous to the northeastern United States and Canada or whether she had access to the European kind. Both answers seem equally plausible. A European "gooseberry craze" caught on in the northeastern United States in the early 1800s,[64] and Nova Scotia's close ties with New England and the eastern seaboard suggest that the popularity of gooseberries likely extended also to the Maritime provinces. Gooseberry clubs or societies were first formed in England beginning in the mid-eighteenth century,[65] and it is possible that imported bushes were planted in the Maritime region even earlier than 1800. Given that gooseberries had been employed in British cooking since at least the Tudors, it seems likely that Wilkins used an introduced European variety rather than a native North American kind, especially since European gooseberries are still considered very good for winemaking, with some varieties "often similar in size and flavor to grapes."[66] Wilkins specifies green gooseberries not yet ripe enough to produce sugar sufficient to ferment on their own, and the recipe thus calls for a pound of sugar to be added to every quart of gooseberry juice, or what she calls the "Liquor" derived from mashing the gooseberries and mixing each pound with a quart of water. Though it is unclear whether Wilkins used native gooseberries, which are smaller and have less flavour, her recipe nonetheless relies heavily on imported ingredients that include a relatively large amount of sugar added at the beginning of the fermentation process, followed by a quarter pound of "sugar Candy in Lumps when you stop the Cask" as well as "a pint of the very best Brandy" per five gallons of wine, half to be added when the wine is "turned" and the remainder when it is "casked."

The comparative dearth of wine recipes in Wilkins's collection may suggest the prosperous Wilkins family not only enjoyed the means to purchase and consume the imported kind, but also preferred it. Yet there is much to suggest that gooseberry wine was sometimes valued as highly as that made from grapes. Printed English collections offer scores of recipes for gooseberry wine. Like the recipe in *The Gardener's Magazine*, one by Mary Cole describes the finished product as "a very rich wine, [that] when it has been kept in bottles two or three years, will drink like champagne."[67] Echoing Cole's assessment, a gooseberry wine recipe published in *The Farmer's Magazine* and credited to "a Gentleman in Forfarshire," now the county of Argyle in Scotland, claims that the finished product "has often been mistaken for Foreign Wine of a fine quality," noting also that "the sooner it is bottled, the more it will sparkle and resemble champaign."[68]

To Make Green Current Wine

Sometime in 1794, this recipe was recorded in the Trueman family scrapbook in an unknown hand (it is not the same hand that entered "To Make Balm Wine" in the John and William Trueman notebook).[69] No other source has been identified.

To Make green Current wine

... let your currents be clean from the
stems, to every Pound of fruit ad one
quart of water, bruise your currents well,
and put them with the water in a tub
to stand for 3 days stiring them 3
times a day, strain of the fruit and
to every Gallon of this juice ad 3½ lb
of sugar, and to every 5 Gallons
ad . quart spirits ____

Indigenous to Europe and North America, currants are of the genus *Ribes* that includes gooseberries. Though it is unclear whether the Trueman recipe used currants from native or imported bushes, most cultivated varieties are of European origin and ripen to white, red, or black, and instructions for making currant wine that appear in numerous English collections most often call for ripe red or white currants. A "Receipt for Making Currant Wine" published in *The Nova Scotia Magazine* in 1791 calls for the "full ripe" fruit.[70] Regardless of variety or extent of ripeness, however, all wine made from naturally tart currants requires large amounts of sugar to facilitate fermentation and sweeten the wine. The Trueman recipe thus calls for three and a half pounds of sugar to be added to every gallon of juice made by adding a quart of water to every pound of bruised fruit. The source of the currants may be uncertain, but the colonial winemaker's reliance on imported ingredients is nevertheless evident in the addition of spirits that not only fortified the wine but were also used to kill off yeast and thereby stop fermentation.

Currant Wine

Sometime between 1780 and 1795, Anthony Allaire recorded this recipe for currant wine in his diary and order book.[71] The section of the recipe on fining (from "To fine it down" to the end) is found under the entry for wine in *Cyclopædia: or, An Universal Dictionary of Arts and Sciences* (1738 and after), but we have not found a source for the first five lines, which describe the use of currants.[72]

Currant Wine

To ten Gallons, thirty pints Juice
thirty lb Sugar, as much water
as will fill the Vessel after the
Juice and Sugar is in to Ten
Gal One quart of Brandy.
To fine it down-
Take shavings of green beech having
first taken of all the rind, boil it
an hour in water, to extract their
rankness, afterwards drie them in
the Sun, or in an oven, A bushel of
these serve for a tun[73] of Wine.
These put the liquor in a gentle
working, and purify it in twenty
four Hours, they also give it an
agreeable flavour.

Specifying only "ten Gallons" of fruit, Allaire is unclear about the kind of currants used to make his wine. Like Trueman's recipe, Allaire's also calls for a large amount of sugar, but only half the proportion of spirits at one quart of brandy to ten gallons of juice and sugar. Most other currant wine recipes did not use a fining process that was most often left to unfold naturally but was sometimes expedited with the addition of isinglass specified also in the recipe for "Green Gooseberry Wine." Applying a winemaking technique gleaned from print culture more specifically to currants, Allaire calls for shavings of green beech added "To fine it down," which would result in a wine more quickly removed of harsh tannins and impurities than Trueman's green currant wine. The recipe specifies a rather large amount of shavings that were likely gleaned from the American beech native also to the Maritime provinces.

Receipt to Make Raisin Wine

The following receipt from New Brunswick physician Willaim Paine is one of two recipes for raisin wine in his papers and one of only three grape-based wine recipes so far uncovered in Maritime archives.[74] We have not found another source for this recipe.

Recipt to make Raison Wine

In Oct. fill a Pipe[75] half full of Raisons
fill it up with water lett it stand
till the Spring then draw it off & after
a year Bottle it; if you want it sweet
sooner & vice versa.

Recommending half filling a pipe – which is a very large container – the recipe would produce a generous quantity of wine from grapes that may or may not have been dried given that, in the eighteenth century, "raisin" was sometimes used to describe "A cluster or bunch of grapes" even though the term was used also to describe the dried kind.[76] Unlike recipes for wine made from other kinds of ingredients, this one does not call for the addition of sugar, yeast, or brandy, which does suggest that the raisins were dried fully ripe and that the grapes bore enough natural yeast to generate fermentation. The wine was to stand for several months "till the Spring," at which time it would be drawn off the sunken sediment known as lees and bottled only after aging for an additional year in the pipe.

That a recipe titled "Receipt to Make Raisin Wine" was also published in *The Nova Scotia Gazette* on 31 December 1767 suggests a broader interest in making wine from grapes.[77] Taken together, however, these recipes make for a limited selection that point to both a lack of available ingredients and a greater interest in consuming imported wine. The singularity of Paine's recipes thus raises not only the question of where he obtained the fruit, but also how he managed to procure such large quantities. Though it is well-known that wine grapes were first cultivated in Nova Scotia's Bear River in 1611, it is unclear whether the vines produced viable fruit. Success in Bear River does, however, seem unlikely: even the avid horticulturalist and well-known oenophile Thomas Jefferson failed to produce wine from vines he planted in the much more temperate climate of Monticello, his estate in central Virginia. Though Paine's recipes predate his 1783 acquisition of granted lands in Passamaquoddy, New Brunswick, it seems no more likely that he would earlier have successfully produced wine grapes in his native Worcester, Massachusetts; if that is the case, the recipe's specification of filling the pipe in October may have had more to do with the cooler temperatures advantageous to winemaking than the timing of an uncertain or non-existent harvest.

That the grapes used in Paine's recipes may have been dried and imported is further implied by receipts for raisin wine that appeared in English publications. The recipe "To Make Raisin Wine" credited to one Mrs Harpur and posthumously published in the second edition of a collection by Anne Battam (?–1755) specifies using "one hundred weight of Smyrna" and "ditto of Malaga raisins,"[78] while the collection of Mary Kettilby specifies using "five pounds of *Malaga*-Raisins shred small" in her recipe "to Make Raisin Elder-Wine."[79] According to Peter Latta's account of eighteenth-century Nova Scotia immigrant life, raisins were indeed readily "available at the traders."[80] Likely also sold by merchants in New Brunswick, raisins in the 1770s were imported to Paine's native Massachusetts along with wine, figs, lemons, and oranges that travelled from England to Marblehead.[81] Most tellingly, raisins were advertised for sale by John Spooner in the 16 November 1767 edition of the *Boston Evening-Post* immediately following a "Receipt to Make Raisin Wine."[82]

To Make a Hogshead of Good Raisin Wine

Recorded in 1768 or later, Paine's second grape-based recipe offers more detailed instructions than the previous one.[83] The original source is unknown, but the recipe does share a number of resemblances to the 1767 "Receipt to Make Raisin Wine" published in *The Nova Scotia Gazette*, including the use of 420 pounds of raisins, a hogshead, and "a gallon of French brandy."[84]

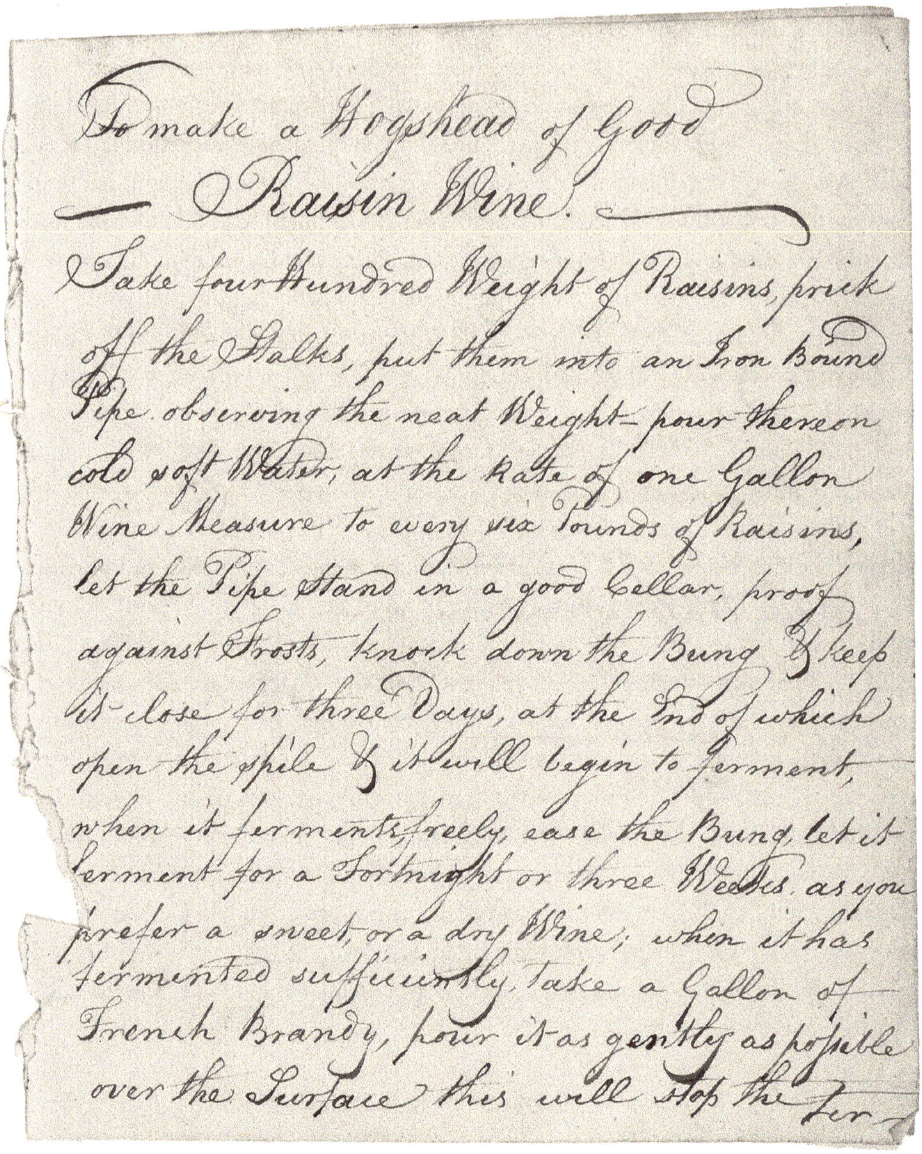
To make a Hogshead of Good
Raisin Wine.

Take four Hundred Weight of Raisins, prick off the Stalks, put them into an Iron Bound Pipe observing the neat Weight – pour thereon cold soft Water, at the Rate of one Gallon Wine Measure to every six Pounds of Raisins, let the Pipe Stand in a good Cellar, proof against Frosts, knock down the Bung & keep it close for three Days, at the End of which open the spile & it will begin to ferment, when it ferments freely, ease the Bung, let it ferment for a Fortnight or three Weeks, as you prefer a sweet, or a dry Wine; when it has fermented sufficiently, take a Gallon of French Brandy, pour it as gently as possible over the Surface this will stop the Fer-

Figure 2.3a and b
To make a Hogshead of Good Raisin Wine. Paine Family Papers.

fermentation & make it subside, then bung it close & knock in the Spile.

N.B. The above is best done in the Month of October, let it stand about six Months or from October to April, then put in a Cask & you will draw off a Hogshead of Clear Wine (what remains may be made excellent Vinegar by the Addition of brown Sugar) To have it in Perfection let the Wine stand one Year, then draw it off into a Quarter Cask, & keep it a year longer.

To make a Hogshead[85] of Good
- Raisin Wine -

Take four Hundred Weight[86] of Raisins, prick off the Stalks, put them into an Iron Bound Pipe observing the neat Weight[87] – pour thereon cold soft Water, at the Rate of one Gallon Wine Measure to every six Pounds of Raisins, let the Pipe stand in a good Cellar, proof against Frosts, knock down the Bung[88] & keep it close for three Days, at the End of which open the spile & it will begin to ferment, when it ferments, freely, ease the Bung, let it ferment for a Fortnight or three Weeks, as you prefer a sweet, or a dry Wine; when it has fermented sufficiently, take a Gallon of French Brandy, pour it as gently as possible over the Surface this will stop the fermentation & make it subside, then bury it close & knock in the Spile.
N.B. The above is best done in the Month of October, let it stand about six Months or from October to April, then put in a Cock & you will draw off a Hogshead of Clear Wine (what remains may be made excellent Vinegar by the Addition of brown Sugar) To have it in Perfection let the Wine stand one year, then draw it off into a Quarter Cask, & keep it a year longer.

Like Paine's "Recipt to Make Raison Wine," this recipe also suggests that starting the wine is "best done in the Month of October." The maker is first instructed to "prick off the Stalks" of the requisite "four Hundred Weight of Raisins" before soaking them in water. The mixture is then left for "a Fortnight or three Weeks" to produce "as you prefer a sweet, or a dry Wine." The longer wine is left to ferment, the more the sugar will be consumed by the yeast, and the longer period of time will produce a drier wine. This second recipe also specifies that the wine is to be made in an "Iron Bound Pipe," its large capacity confirmed by the requisite "four Hundred Weight of Raisins" and the later addition of "a Gallon of French Brandy" to "stop the Fermentation and make it subside." After drawing off the wine into a hogshead, the wine is to be aged for one year "To have it in Perfection" before being drawn off the lees, the remnants that can be used to make "excellent Vinegar by the Addition of brown Sugar" and by being put into "a Quarter Cask" to be aged "a year longer."

CHAPTER THREE

Medicine

The eighteenth century was something of a watershed moment in the history of English medicine. As with much else, medical practice in Britain's colonies reflected what was happening in the British Isles. At the time, European medicine remained tied to long-standing tradition while also accommodating changes that anticipated the emergence of a more modern medicine associated with the nineteenth-century discovery of effective anaesthetics and the acceptance of germ theory. Marked by continuity as well as change, eighteenth-century medical practice yet remained deeply rooted in the work of Roman physician Galen, whose theories of the humours were at the forefront of English medicine in the sixteenth and seventeenth centuries. Galenic medicine was predicated on the belief that physical and emotional health depended on achieving and maintaining the proper balance of hot, cold, moist, and dry humours that, in various combinations of black bile, yellow bile, blood, and phlegm, were respectively thought to make up the choleric, melancholic, phlegmatic, and sanguine dispositions. While medical thinking was still informed by abstract theories of the humours, it was also inflected by a growing emphasis on empirical observation and practical experiment. Influenced not only by the work of French philosopher René Descartes (1596–1650), who advocated the use of concrete evidence based on empirical observation, medical practice leading up to the eighteenth century was shaped also by the work of the chemical physicians following the lead of Swiss physician Paracelsus (1493–1541), who pioneered the use of medicines concocted from ingredients such as mercury, sulphur, and iron. Physicians of the eighteenth century by and large saw no contradiction in continuing to bleed patients – a practice we now know to be more often harmful than helpful – while also employing medicines made wholly or partly from sometimes poisonous chemical compounds and experimenting with new medical discoveries such as inoculation and obstetrical forceps.

Eighteenth-century medical culture included a strong contingent of domestic medical practitioners. Domestic healers, often women, used their knowledge of medicinal herbs – and sometimes also surgery and chemical medicine – in treating family, friends, servants, and neighbours with tried-and-true remedies that often proved more efficacious than those prescribed by physicians. For centuries, literate British women would record these remedies in household recipe collections, many of which survive in British (and American) archives. Those recipe books were often dominated by medical "receipts," which could be passed down for generations, recorded alongside directions for making various comestibles, beverages, and other household products. This practice continued among settlers in the Americas (and domestic recipe collections from the Americas do survive, if not from the eighteenth-century Maritimes). As in England, the practices of physicians and of domestic healers in the British colonies were not entirely distinct from each other. Typically for physicians of their day, Dr William James Almon of Halifax and Dr William Paine (for a time, of New Brunswick) also relied on medicines that likely originated in the household and use homegrown ingredients, such as the garden tansy prescribed by Almon to treat "painful Menses" or the extracted beet juice Paine recommends for use as a nasal spray. Though we found in Maritime archives only one complete collection attesting to the domestic healing practices of settler women, that manuscript, the notebook that belonged to Sarah Creighton Wilkins, is comprised of about two thirds medical remedies – and many of these draw on the knowledge and practice of physicians in an ongoing give-and-take of medical knowledge. As well as recording recipes attributed to Dr Charles Blick, Dr Potter, and [Herman] Boerhave (1668–1738), a Dutch physician, Wilkins's notebook records two remedies in Latin, specifies ingredients that include chemical concoctions such as "spirit of minderus" and calomel, and offers a list of the "Component Parts of Popular Patent Medicines," suggesting in a number of ways an exchange of medical knowledge that moved also from the professional or learned to the domestic. As Holly Dickinson's thesis on Wilkins's medical recipes suggests, she sought to align her remedies with professional medical practices, while also drawing on the practices of female social network.[1]

The importance of medical remedies to Maritime settlers is evident not only in the many recipes preserved in the notebooks of Almon, Paine, and Wilkins, but also in the remedies found in other manuscript sources that include diaries and loose papers as well as other documents seemingly unrelated to recipe culture, such as church records and even an accounting ledger. Medical recipes were also printed in newspapers, magazines, and almanacs, with print materials sometimes preserved by pasting clippings into notebooks. As with those for food and drink, medical recipes recorded in the region reflect the colonial context in which they were preserved. One of the French recipes we discuss, for example, cites a French source a few decades old but specifies English measurements in recognition of its colonial context. Medical remedies also confirm allegiance to both older European medical practices and the acceptance of newer ones. Some recipes had circulated more than a century before they were published or compiled in the region, while others cite British or American publications and advocate newer techniques. Making an implicit argument for the new, one printed recipe even satirizes older practices. Only rarely do the medical recipes discussed here not rely on printed sources from elsewhere: the absence of an evident source is telling and might suggest a technique that was developed in the region (such as in "safest and best Method" for being inoculated against smallpox that was printed in *The Nova Scotia Gazette and the Weekly Chronicle* in 1775). The sources of medical recipes we've discovered include authoritative publications like those of the Royal College of Physicians of London, the published works of European physicians, and the many domestic recipe collections published in Britain for a variety of audiences; they also include recipes from American newspaper as well as other British and European publications and sometimes refer to more local practices.

Differing widely in form and content, consistent among these many and varied sources is the absence of any acknowledgment of colonial and British medicine's indebtedness to Indigenous and African sources. The recipes included here by and large address diseases of particular concern in eighteenth-century Europe, such as rabies, gout, stone, scurvy, and smallpox. Addressing the latter are "To Preserve the Face from Being Deformed by the Smallpox" and "Hints on the Method of Inoculating against Smallpox," which credits the discovery to English physician Edward Jenner (1749–1823) with no mention of the practice's African origins or its subsequent adoption in Turkey, whence it was famously brought to England by Lady Mary Wortley Montagu (1689–1762). Other medicinal remedies were brought to the colonies by the enslaved Africans who populated the Caribbean and the eastern seaboard, bringing their healing practices with them. West African *materia medica* also mingled with Indigenous medical knowledge on plantations, although as Schiebinger notes: "there were important asymmetries. In all instances, reports of West Indian cures – whether those developed by slaves, Indigenous peoples from the region, or Europeans – were authored by Europeans."[2] In the recipes discussed here, the only mention of African medicine comes in the account titled "Effectual Cure for the Stone," which describes how an enslaved man traded his remedy for his freedom; tellingly, however, the man remains unnamed, and the authority of the medicine rests in his named white patient and those around him.

Various recipes in this chapter also imply that Europeans learned about the medicinal uses of native plants from Indigenous populations. Historically, guaiacum (*Lignum vitae*), senna, sassafras, sarsaparilla, and tobacco – all from the Americas – as well as opium from India played an important role in eighteenth-century European medicine.[3] Thus some knowledge of American plants such as cinchona, the Peruvian bark that appears in countless remedies, and tolu, a South American balsam used in a variety of medical applications, moved from the Americas to Spain to the English-speaking world to be specified in Maritime print and manuscript recipes that include "An Admirable Receipt for a Consumption" and "Turlington's Balsam." Remedies also arrived in the region from British colonies further afield, as with the described cure for ringworm that is explicitly sourced from India. Settlers in eastern North America also learned from Indigenous peoples about more local plants, such as American pokeweed, which Paine specifies as a cancer treatment, and the medical use of tobacco, which had been part of European medicine since the sixteenth century. Indigenous sources of knowledge about ingredients like these, however, always go unmentioned.

Within a medical culture deeply invested in the citation of sources, the occlusion of Indigenous knowledge was not simply an oversight. Printed colonial travel narratives, which often document some of the circumstances behind the transfer of Indigenous medical knowledge throughout Europe, document how European perspectives were rooted in their own sense of superiority. Travellers often adopted a derogatory stance towards Indigenous peoples, naming them "savages," for instance, even as they recorded their medical knowledge in ways that could be reproduced in Europe. Drew Lopenzina identifies this contradictory process – broadly evident in colonial texts – as "unwitnessing," a form of refusal to acknowledge Indigenous cultures even as early modern Europeans were noticing and recording many aspects of those cultures. As Lopenzina explains, Europeans developed a dichotomy between savage and civilized and maintained that dichotomy by "categorically refusing to acknowledge the cultural validity, even the essential humanity, of that which was being culturally eliminated."[4] Refusing to cite Indigenous peoples as sources of medical knowledge in a colonial context thus serves as a means of undermining Indigenous sovereignty, thereby asserting colonial authority over knowledge as well as lands. Resistance to such extractive approaches might be evident in the comment made by the anthropologist W.H. Mechling who was attempting to record Mi'kmaw and Wolastoqiyik medical practices in the early twentieth century and noted that the old people at St Mary's First Nation are "difficult to deal with."[5]

European and settler recipes also stripped Indigenous ingredients of a rich and complex cultural context, turning them into commodities to be exploited. That North American plants appear in eighteenth-century settler and European recipes simply as scientific objects to be utilized thus represents a kind of refusal to acknowledge Indigenous ways of knowing and being. As Potawatomi biologist Robin Kimmerer writes in *Braiding Sweetgrass: Indigenous Wisdom, Scientific Knowledge and the Teachings of Plants*, "To be native to a place we must learn to speak its language," a process that can only happen by listening and learning from nature; while Kimmerer values science, she also argues that "Science can be a language of distance which reduces a being to its working parts; it is a language of objects. The language scientists speak, however precise, is based on a profound error in grammar, an omission, a grave loss in translation from the native languages of these shores."[6] Eighteenth-century settler recipes often speak the language of objects. The consequences of this way of thinking were significant. Laurelyn Whitt writes in *Science, Colonialism, and Indigenous Peoples: The Cultural Politics of Law and Knowledge* that *biocolonialism* (a term that could define the kind of commodification of knowledge and resources that we especially see in medical recipes) "is sharply at odds with the web of prescriptions and proscriptions that guide the process of knowing within indigenous contexts. It also clashes directly with the role responsibilities toward the natural world that many indigenous peoples have historically assumed."[7] Only very rarely evoking a relationship to Indigenous peoples, settler recipes never convey any sense of responsibility to ensure that medicinal plants would continue to thrive; they are instead appropriated from their Indigenous context, renamed in Latin, and claimed by European systems that had little relationship to the land from which the knowledge arose.

RABIES

A Receipt for the Bite of a Mad Dog

This recipe was printed in *The Halifax Gazette* on 9 December 1752.[8] According to a preface that appears with it, *The Halifax Gazette* reprinted the recipe from *The Dublin Journal*. Perhaps another recipe is being referenced, but "A Receipt for the Bite of a Mad Dog" that appeared in the September 1747 edition of *The Dublin Journal* actually offers a somewhat different remedy that specifies putting in milk overnight the leaves of scabies or devil's bitt, an ounce of powdered tormentile roots, castor, and asafoetida, to make a drink to be taken three mornings in a row at the full moon or at the change of the moon.[9] *The Halifax Gazette*'s recipe did, however, appear in the 30 September–14 October 1752 edition of *The Ladies Magazine* in London, just before it was printed in Halifax.[10] Recipes for treating the bites of mad – or what we now call *rabid* – dogs were common in seventeenth- and eighteenth-century recipe collections.

A Receipt for the Bite of a mad Dog.

Take the youngest Shoots of the Elder Tree, strip it of the outside Bark, then take of the grind Rhind[11] two large Handfuls, put it into Five Pints of strong Ale, let it simmer together about Fifteen Minutes, drain off the Liquor, squeezing the Rhind dry, when cold, put in into Bottles, and drink Half a Pint Morning and Evening made warm, washing the Place affected with some of the Liquor. The Patient should be kept warm, and the Medicine to be repeated every New and Full of the Moon for two of three Times.

The same as the above may be observed in Regard to large Cattle, only given them a Pint to drink instead of Half a Pint.

For centuries, treatments for bites from mad dogs had been a frequent concern in European recipes. The bites of mad dogs were addressed in classical medicine by well-known figures that include Pliny (23 CE–79), Celsus (fl. 1st century CE), Dioscorides (40–c.90), and Galen, by Arab and Jewish writers, and by medieval and early modern physicians and in popular books of remedies.[12] For example, a book of secrets by the Italian alchemist Girolamo Ruscelli (1518–1566), published in English as *A Verye Excellent and Profitable Booke Conteining Sixe Hundred Foure Score and Odde Experienced Medicines* (1569), recommends "Against the bitings of mad

Dogges" boiling in wine gentian roots, myrrh, and the eyes of burnt crabs, and then straining the resulting liquid, which should then be drunk by the cupful three mornings in a row.[13] The problem with such bites, according to one eighteenth-century medical text, is that the wound heals but symptoms persist, including a delirium that could include barking and hydrophobia. The cause, it was believed, was that the saliva of the mad dog altered the blood of the bite victim.[14]

In a context where purported remedies could include mercurial ointments, multi-stage treatments, proprietary medicines, and bleeding, this recipe seems relatively simple.[15] But its method is not unique. The situation of the treatment against the phases of the moon is part of the long-standing practice of medical astrology, a practice that related disease to the influence of planets, stars, and lunar phases. Although now considered a pseudo-science, and beliefs about the relationship between the heavenly bodies and the human body were not consistent over the years, astrology remained a component of institutionalized medicine until at least the nineteenth century.[16] The use of tree bark in a veterinary treatment for bitten animals, as is the case with this recipe, is found also in the 1660 recipe "A very good Medicine for the Biting of a Mad dog," where sweet-briar tree bark, betony, bay-salt, and water are boiled together and the bitten animal given the water to drink, while the wound is washed with it.[17] The methods used to treat humans are akin to that used on animals. Similarly, the recipe in *The Halifax Gazette* is prefaced by a note from "Philanthropos," who suggests that the remedy has been used for years by a family and that publishing it "may be of great Benefit to Mankind in general, as well as the Animal Creation."[18]

RINGWORM

This unusual method of treating ringworm was published in *The Royal Gazette and the Nova Scotia Advertiser* on 8 December 1789.[19] Begun the same year, this newspaper was the fourth to be printed in Halifax by Anthony Henry (1734–1800), who had been appointed king's printer; his previous papers were *The Halifax Gazette*, *The Nova Scotia Gazette and Weekly Advertiser*, and *The Nova Scotia Chronicle and Weekly Advertiser*. Politically careful, *The Royal Gazette and the Nova Scotia Advertiser* printed foreign news, official government notices, and advertisements for local businesses. Publication ceased when Henry died in 1800.[20]

Credited to "Sir Paul Joddrell," the ringworm remedy purports to be extracted from a letter by an unknown "Gentleman of the Faculty at Fort St. George" that

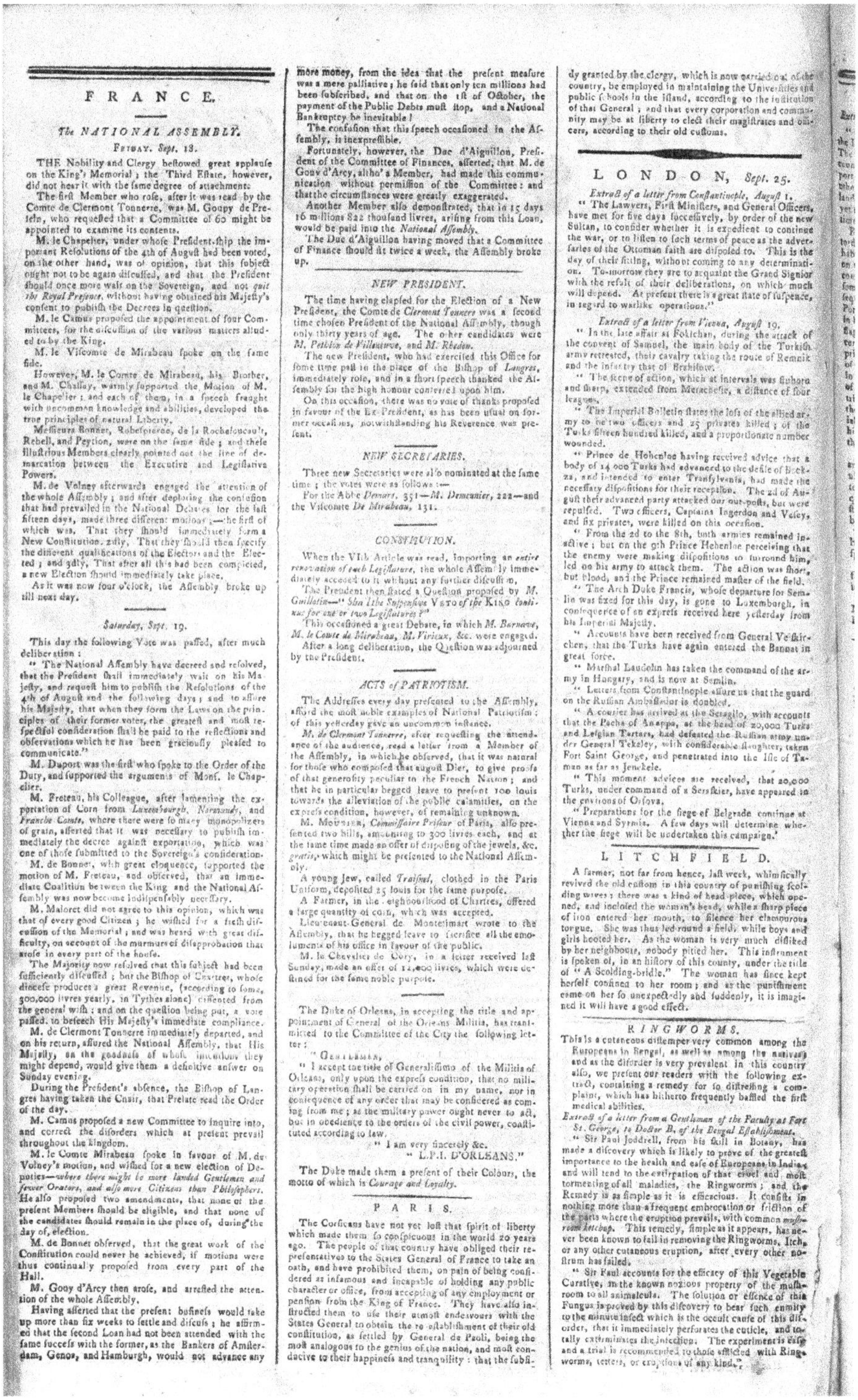

FRANCE.

The NATIONAL ASSEMBLY.

FRIDAY. *Sept.* 18.

THE Nobility and Clergy bestowed great applause on the King's Memorial; the Third Estate, however, did not hear it with the same degree of attachment.

The first Member who rose, after it was read by the Comte de Clermont Tonnerre, was M. Goupy de Prefeln, who requested that a Committee of 60 might be appointed to examine its contents.

M. le Chapelier, under whose President-ship the important Resolutions of the 4th of August had been voted, on the other hand, was of opinion, that this subject ought not to be again discussed, and that the President should once more wait on the Sovereign, and not *quit the Royal Presence*, without having obtained his Majesty's consent to publish the Decrees in question.

M. le Camus proposed the appointment of four Committees, for the discussion of the various matters alluded to by the King.

M. le Viscomte de Mirabeau spoke on the same side.

However, M. le Comte de Mirabeau, his Brother, and M. Chassay, warmly supported the Motion of M. le Chapelier; and each of them, in a speech fraught with uncommon knowledge and abilities, developed the true principles of natural Liberty.

Messieurs Bonnet, Robespierre, de la Rochefoucault, Rebell, and Peytion, were on the same side; and these illustrious Members clearly pointed out the line of demarcation between the Executive and Legislative Powers.

M. de Volney afterwards engaged the attention of the whole Assembly; and after deploring the confusion that had prevailed in the National Debates for the last fifteen days, made three different motions;—the first of which was, That they should immediately form a New Constitution. 2dly, That they should then specify the different qualifications of the Electors and the Elected; and 3dly, That after all this had been completed, a new Election should immediately take place.

As it was now four o'clock, the Assembly broke up till next day.

Saturday, Sept. 19.

This day the following Vote was passed, after much deliberation:

"The National Assembly have decreed and resolved, that the President shall immediately wait on his Majesty, and request him to publish the Resolutions of the 4th of August and the following days; and to assure his Majesty, that when they form the Laws on the principles of their former votes, the greatest and most respectful consideration shall be paid to the reflections and observations which he has been graciously pleased to communicate."

M. Duport was the first who spoke to the Order of the Duty, and supported the arguments of Mons. le Chapelier.

M. Freteau, his Colleague, after lamenting the exportation of Corn from *Luxembourgh*, *Normandy*, and *Franche Comte*, where there were so many monopolizers of grain, asserted that it was necessary to publish immediately the decree against exportation, which was one of those submitted to the Sovereign's consideration.

M. de Bonnet, with great eloquence, supported the motion of M. Freteau, and observed, that an immediate Coalition between the King and the National Assembly was now become indispensibly necessary.

M. Maloret did not agree to this opinion, which was that of every good Citizen; he wished for a fresh discussion of the Memorial; and was heard with great difficulty, on account of the murmurs of disapprobation that arose in every part of the house.

The Majority now resolved that this subject had been sufficiently discussed; but the Bishop of Chartres, whose diocese produces a great Revenue, (according to some, 300,000 livres yearly, in Tythes alone) dissented from the general wish; and on the question being put, a vote passed, to beseech His Majesty's immediate compliance.

M. de Clermont Tonnerre immediately departed, and on his return, assured the National Assembly, that His Majesty, on the goodness of whose intentions they might depend, would give them a definitive answer on Sunday evening.

During the President's absence, the Bishop of Langres having taken the Chair, that Prelate read the Order of the day.

M. Camus proposed a new Committee to inquire into, and correct the disorders which at present prevail throughout the kingdom.

M. le Comte Mirabeau spoke in favour of M. de Volney's motion, and wished for a new election of Deputies—*where there might be more landed Gentlemen and fewer Orators, and also more Citizens than Philosophers.* He also proposed two amendments, that none of the present Members should be eligible, and that none of the candidates should remain in the place of, during the day of, election.

M. de Bonnet observed, that the great work of the Constitution could never be achieved, if motions were thus continually proposed from every part of the Hall.

M. Gouy d'Arcy then arose, and arrested the attention of the whole Assembly.

Having asserted that the present business would take up more than six weeks to settle and discuss; he affirmed that the second Loan had not been attended with the same success with the former, as the Bankers of Amsterdam, Genoa, and Hamburgh, would not advance any more money, from the idea that the present measure was a mere palliative; he said that only ten millions had been subscribed, and that on the 1st of October, the payment of the Public Debts must stop, and a National Bankruptcy be inevitable!

The confusion that this speech occasioned in the Assembly, is inexpressible.

Fortunately, however, the Duc d'Aiguillon, President of the Committee of Finances, asserted, that M. de Gouy d'Arcy, altho' a Member, had made this communication without permission of the Committee: and that the circumstances were greatly exaggerated.

Another Member also demonstrated, that in 15 days 16 millions 822 thousand livres, arising from this Loan, would be paid into the *National Assembly*.

The Duc d'Aiguillon having moved that a Committee of Finance should sit twice a week, the Assembly broke up.

NEW PRESIDENT.

The time having elapsed for the Election of a New President, the Comte de *Clermont Tonnere* was a second time chosen President of the National Assembly, though only thirty years of age. The other candidates were *M. Pethion de Villeneuve*, and *M. Rhedon*.

The new President, who had exercised this Office for some time past in the place of the Bishop of *Langres*, immediately rose, and in a short speech thanked the Assembly for the high honour conferred upon him.

On this occasion, there was no vote of thanks proposed in favour of the Ex-President, as has been usual on former occasions, notwithstanding his Reverence was present.

NEW SECRETARIES.

Three new Secretaries were also nominated at the same time; the votes were as follows:—

For the Abbe *Demars*, 351—*M. Demeunier*, 222—and the Viscomte *De Mirabeau*, 131.

CONSTITUTION.

When the VIth Article was read, importing an *entire renovation of each Legislature*, the whole Assembly immediately acceded to it without any further discussion.

The President then stated a Question proposed by *M. Guillotin*—"*Shall the Suspensive* VETO *of the* KING *continue for one or two Legislatures?*"

This occasioned a great Debate, in which *M. Barnave*, *M. le Comte de Mirabeau*, *M. Virieux*, &c. were engaged.

After a long deliberation, the Question was adjourned by the President.

ACTS of PATRIOTISM.

The Addresses every day presented to the Assembly, afford the most noble examples of National Patriotism; of this yesterday gave an uncommon instance.

M. de Clermont Tonnerre, after requesting the attendance of the audience, read a letter from a Member of the Assembly, in which he observed, that it was natural for those who composed that august Diet, to give proofs of that generosity peculiar to the French Nation; and that he in particular begged leave to present 100 louis towards the alleviation of the public calamities, on the express condition, however, of remaining unknown.

M. MOUNIER, *Commissaire Priseur* of Paris, also presented two bills, amounting to 300 livres each, and at the same time made an offer of disposing of the jewels, &c. *gratis*, which might be presented to the National Assembly.

A young Jew, called *Traisnel*, clothed in the Paris Uniform, deposited 25 louis for the same purpose.

A Farmer, in the neighbourhood of Chartres, offered a large quantity of corn, which was accepted.

Lieutenant-General de Montelimart wrote to the Assembly, that he begged leave to sacrifice all the emoluments of his office in favour of the public.

M. le Chevalier de Cory, in a letter received last Sunday, made an offer of 12,000 livres, which were destined for the same noble purpose.

The Duke of Orleans, in accepting the title and appointment of General of the Orleans Militia, has transmitted to the Committee of the City the following letter:

"GENTLEMEN,

"I accept the title of Generalissimo of the Militia of Orleans, only upon the express condition, that no military operation shall be carried on in my name, nor in consequence of any order that may be considered as coming from me; as the military power ought never to act, but in obedience to the orders of the civil power, constituted according to law.

"I am very sincerely &c.

"L.P.J. D'ORLEANS."

The Duke made them a present of their Colours, the motto of which is *Courage and Loyalty*.

PARIS.

The Corsicans have not yet lost that spirit of liberty which made them so conspicuous in the world 20 years ago. The people of that country have obliged their representatives to the States General of France to take an oath, and have prohibited them, on pain of being considered as infamous and incapable of holding any public character or office, from accepting of any employment or pension from the King of France. They have also instructed them to use their utmost endeavours with the States General to obtain the re-establishment of their old constitution, as settled by General de Paoli, being the most analogous to the genius of the nation, and most conducive to their happiness and tranquility: that the subsidy granted by the clergy, which is now carried out of the country, be employed in maintaining the Universities and public schools in the island, according to the institution of that General; and that every corporation and community may be at liberty to elect their magistrates and officers, according to their old customs.

LONDON, *Sept.* 25.

Extract of a letter from Constantinople, August 1.

"The Lawyers, First Ministers, and General Officers, have met for five days successively, by order of the new Sultan, to consider whether it is expedient to continue the war, or to listen to such terms of peace as the adversaries of the Ottoman faith are disposed to. This is the day of their sitting, without coming to any determination. To-morrow they are to acquaint the Grand Signior with the result of their deliberations, on which much will depend. At present there is a great state of suspence, in regard to warlike operations."

Extract of a letter from Vienna, August 19.

"In the late affair at Fokichan, during the attack of the convent of Samuel, the main body of the Turkish army retreated, their cavalry taking the route of Remnik and the infantry that of Brahilow.

"The scene of action, which at intervals was stubborn and sharp, extended from Meracheste, a distance of four leagues.

"The Imperial Bulletin states the loss of the allied army to be two officers and 25 privates killed; of the Turks fifteen hundred killed, and a proportionate number wounded.

"Prince de Hohenloe having received advice that a body of 14 000 Turks had advanced to the defile of Bockza, and intended to enter Transylvania, had made the necessary dispositions for their reception. The 2d of August their advanced party attacked our out-posts, but were repulsed. Two officers, Captains Ingerdon and Vesey, and six privates, were killed on this occasion.

"From the 2d to the 8th, both armies remained inactive; but on the 9th Prince Hohenloe perceiving that the enemy were making dispositions to surround him, led on his army to attack them. The action was short, but blood, and the Prince remained master of the field.

"The Arch Duke Francis, whose departure for Semlin was fixed for this day, is gone to Luxemborgh, in consequence of an express received here yesterday from his Imperial Majesty.

"Accounts have been received from General Vesskirchen, that the Turks have again entered the Bannat in great force.

"Marshal Laudohn has taken the command of the army in Hungary, and is now at Semlin.

"Letters from Constantinople assure us that the guard on the Russian Ambassador is doubled.

"A courier has arrived at the Seraglio, with accounts that the Pacha of Anappa, at the head of 20,000 Turks and Leigian Tartars, had defeated the Russian army under General Tekeley, with considerable slaughter, taken Fort Saint George, and penetrated into the Isle of Taman as far as Jenekele.

"This moment advices are received, that 20,000 Turks, under command of a Seraskier, have appeared in the environs of Orsova.

"Preparations for the siege of Belgrade continue at Vienna and Syrmia. A few days will determine whether the siege will be undertaken this campaign."

LITCHFIELD.

A farmer, not far from hence, last week, whimsically revived the old custom in this country of punishing scolding wives; there was a kind of head-piece, which opened, and inclosed the woman's head, while a sharp piece of iron entered her mouth, to silence her clamourous tongue. She was thus led round a field, while boys and girls hooted her. As the woman is very much disliked by her neighbours, nobody pitied her. This instrument is spoken of, in an history of this county, under the title of "A Scolding-bridle." The woman has since kept herself confined to her room; and as the punishment came on her so unexpectedly and suddenly, it is imagined it will have a good effect.

RINGWORMS.

This is a cutaneous distemper very common among the Europeans in Bengal, as well as among the natives; and as the disorder is very prevalent in this country also, we present our readers with the following extract, containing a remedy for so distressing a complaint, which has hitherto frequently baffled the first medical abilities.

Extract of a letter from a Gentleman of the Faculty at Fort St. George, to Doctor B. of the Bengal Establishment.

"Sir Paul Joddrell, from his skill in Botany, has made a discovery which is likely to prove of the greatest importance to the health and ease of Europeans in India, and will tend to the extirpation of that cruel and most tormenting of all maladies, the Ringworms; and the Remedy is as simple as it is efficacious. It consists in nothing more than a frequent embrocation or friction of the parts where the eruption prevails, with common *mushroom ketchup*. This remedy, simple as it appears, has never been known to fail in removing the Ringworms, Itch, or any other cutaneous eruption, after every other nostrum has failed.

"Sir Paul accounts for the efficacy of this Vegetable Curative, in the known noxious property of the mushroom to all animalcula. The solution or essence of this Fungus is proved by this discovery to bear such enmity to the minute insect which is the occult cause of this disorder, that it immediately perforates the cuticle, and totally exterminates the infection. The experiment is easy and a trial is recommended to those afflicted with Ringworms, tetters, or eruptions of any kind."

Figure 3.1
Ringworms, *The Royal Gazette and the Nova Scotia Advertiser*, 8 December 1789.

had been sent "to Doctor B. of the Bengal Establishment." Fort St George was established by the East India Company as its headquarters in Madras (now Chennai), a city in the eastern Indian state of Bengal. Sir Paul Joddrell (1746–1803) was an English physician who at the request of King George III in 1797 went to India to serve as physician to the nawab of Arcot, Muhammad Ali Khan Wallajah, an ally of the East India Company.[21] The ringworm treatment described in the excerpt is one of several recipes from Maritime archives that serve as both food and medicine. Blackberry jelly, for example, is clearly a food (and included here in the chapter on food), but it is also specified as a treatment for kidney stones and other nephritic disorders. Extending the truism that food is medicine to its topical application, Joddrell's solution to ringworm is the application of mushroom ketchup (or catsup), a popular condiment in the eighteenth century that is also discussed in our food chapter.

RINGWORMS.

This is a cutaneous distemper very common among the Europeans in Bengal, as well as among the natives; and as the disorder is very prevalent in this country also, we present our readers with the following extract, containing a remedy for so distressing a complaint, which has hitherto frequently baffled the first medical abilities.

Extract of a letter from a Gentleman of the Faculty at Fort St. George, to Doctor B. of the Bengal Establishment.

"Sir Paul Joddrell, from his skill in Botany, has made a discovery which is likely to prove of the greatest importance to the health and ease of Europeans in India, and will tend to the extirpation of that cruel and most tormenting of all maladies, the Ringworms; and the Remedy is as simple as it is efficacious. It consists in nothing more than a frequent embrocation or friction of the parts where the eruption prevails, with common *mushroom ketchup*. This remedy, simple as it appears, has never been known to fail in removing the Ringworms, Itch, or any other cutaneous eruption, after every other nostrum has failed.

"Sir Paul accounts for the efficacy of this Vegetable Curative, in the known noxious property of the mushroom to all animalcula.[22] The solution or essence of this Fungus is proved by this discovery to bear such enmity to the minute insect which is the occult cause of this disorder, that it immediately perforates the cuticle, and totally exterminates the infection: The experiment is easy and a trial is recommended to those afflicted with Ringworms, tetters,[23] or eruptions of any kind."

Known in ancient India and by the Roman physician Galen, "[r]ingworm had attracted attention of the physicians of all ages" by the time Dr Joddrell encountered this remedy.[24] The skin disorder also earned mention in *De Morbis Cutaneis*, "[t]he founding text of British dermatology" by Daniel Turner (1667–1741), an English physician and surgeon who was the first to be awarded an honorary doctor of medicine by Yale University.[25] Numerous topical treatments appear in eighteenth-century medical books. Though most texts devote more attention to describing the disease than suggesting ways to treat it, they do include remedies ranging from herbal applications to ink. A domestic manual titled *The Ladies' Friend* by physician Stephen Freeman (1739–1790) of London and Antigua even recommends a mixture of salt water and urine. Though Freeman avers that "the remedies which Europe affords, are both more certain and more speedy," he nevertheless also acknowledges "an epithem [or topical application] made of the flowers of brimstone, and the juice of the Ring-worm shrub" native to South America as the best of the remedies "used by the West-Indians."[26] If a preface to the remedy published in *The Royal Gazette and the Nova Scotia Advertiser* describes ringworm as "very prevalent in this country also," which likely refers to England, the remedy's appearance in a Nova Scotia newspaper suggests that ringworm may have also made its way to Nova Scotia, with the publication bringing the knowledge of Indian medical practitioners first to England and then to the Americas.

The recipe claims mushroom ketchup to be efficacious against ringworm; in concluding that "this Fungus is proved by this discovery to bear such enmity to the minute insect" that it will "totally exterminate the infection," however, the author misses the fact that the ringworm understood as "animalcula" is not a worm at all but, as we now know, a fungus by another name.

SMALLPOX

A dreaded affliction in the early modern period, smallpox was well-known in Europe from at least the Middle Ages but likely became more virulent in the seventeenth century, when mortality rates had "increased so considerably that it became included as one of the principal causes of death."[27] High infection rates and widespread death persisted through the eighteenth-century until the advent of vaccination in 1798.

European travellers and colonists brought smallpox to North America as early as 1520, where the disease that claimed the lives of 20 to 50 per cent of afflicted

Europeans nearly eliminated previously unexposed Indigenous populations, killing entire tribes.[28] Smallpox was especially deadly among Indigenous populations because mild variants that provided immunity to more deadly strains in Europe had not long or widely circulated, which left Indigenous populations more vulnerable.[29] By 1900, a pre-contact population of over seven million people in North America had declined by some accounts to only 375,000 across the continent.[30] In service to the colonial enterprise, some Europeans also attempted to spread smallpox purposefully. In July 1763, a colonel suggested to General Jeffrey Amherst (1717–1797), the British "Major General in America" between 1758 and 1763, that blankets infected with smallpox could be distributed to spread the disease among the Mi'kmaw population, a proposal to which Amherst responded with approval: "You will do well to try to Innoculate the Indians by means of Blankets, as well as to try Every other Method that can serve to Extirpate this Execrable Race."[31] He is clearly not recommending inoculation for preventative purposes but using the word in its first, literal sense – to engraft or insert – to argue for the disease's potential to kill. Epidemics that affected Indigenous peoples more adversely than European populations in the Americas have persisted beyond the eighteenth century.[32]

Among settler populations, smallpox appeared in a number of Maritime outbreaks. The Louisbourg epidemic of 1732–33 arose from a French ship on its way to Quebec that docked with smallpox-infected settlers on board. The outbreak that "killed at least 150 people" was followed by others in 1745, 1748–49, 1755, and 1758, with the 1755 outbreak deemed to be an epidemic.[33] That outbreak may have begun with Royal Navy ships sent to Halifax, but it also spread to Louisbourg as well as to civilians in Halifax; the disease continued to kill people in 1756 and 1757 and may have influenced a delay to a British attack on Louisbourg.[34] Another outbreak began "in late June or early July 1775,"[35] the same month and year that the following "hints" for inoculation appeared in the 4 July 1775 edition of *The Nova Scotia Gazette and the Weekly Chronicle*. This time, smallpox seems to have played "a major factor in the cancellation by the Americans of an invasion of Halifax."[36]

From the port of Halifax, smallpox spread "rapidly to other parts of Nova Scotia," including Lunenburg and nearby Windsor.[37] Among the Annapolis Valley's Planter community, the disease seems also to have disrupted the peace. In the winter of 1776, an arrest warrant addressed "To Either of the Constables of Horton," a community in King's County, charged that one Andrew Davison and two other men "on the thirteenth D[ay] of February" did "in an Angry and menacing Manner threaten that they would Shoot & be the death of any person or persons who should attempt to remove from the House of Said Andrew Davison his Son Andrew

Davison Junr then & there being Infected with the Small Pox." Signed by Lebbius Harris and Nathan Dewolf and issued on the basis of statements sworn by Duncan Reed and George Halyburton, the document does not indicate why the "Justices assigned to keep the peace in the County" had attempted to remove the afflicted child. The aim in charging Davison and his co-offenders was, however, to ensure future peace in finding "Sureties for their Good Behavior" and for the offenders to "be otherwise Dealt with according [to] Law."[38] In June of the same year, notes Allan Marble, Andrew Davison along with John Bishop were convicted of "Introducing the smallpox to this Town contrary to a law of this Province." Although Marble mentions that "Both Bishop and Davidson 'acknowledged they did inoculate their family, but pleaded they did not understand the law,'" his recounting does not indicate how the two men were thought to have introduced the virus to their community.[39] These eighteenth-century epidemics persisted in the Maritimes and throughout North America until at least 1782, though occasional outbreaks were recorded well into the nineteenth century.[40]

Ideas about inoculation were already percolating in the Americas. In the context of an epidemic that began in Boston in April 1721 and eventually saw more than half of the city's population infected, Boston physician Zabdiel Boylston (1676–1766) in June of that year began a program of inoculation he describes in his *An Historical Account of the Small-Pox Inoculated in New England*, and he is well known for having introduced the practice to the Massachusetts colony.[41] Using a small amount of "variolus Matter" taken from an afflicted person introduced to the recipient through skin punctures, Boylston began his efforts at home where, he writes, "I inoculated my son *Thomas*, of about six, my Negro Man, *Jack*, thirty six, and *Jackey*, two and an half Years old."[42] In first administering to his own child, Boylston followed in the steps of the English aristocrat Lady Wortley Montagu, whose husband served as the British ambassador to Turkey. Writing to a friend that smallpox causes no harm in that country because the disease was prevented by "old women" using a practice of "ingrafting" that entailed introducing a small amount of the live smallpox virus through the skin. In 1718, Wortley Montagu had her young son inoculated against the disease that had already taken the life of her brother and had come very close to taking her own, and she introduced the procedure to England upon her return. In April of the year Boylston began his program in Boston, the inoculation of Wortley Montagu's younger daughter inspired Caroline, Princess of Wales (1683–1737), to treat her own two children. The royal daughters were, however, inoculated only after the practice had first been tested on condemned criminals and abandoned children.[43] Though Boylston does not suggest that he tested the procedure on the servant Jack or the child Jackey before administering it to his own son Thomas, he does not indicate whether the enslaved members of his household were given a choice in the matter. Fortunately, the inoculation seems to have turned out well for all three. According to the *Historical Account*, the recipients did suffer the anticipated after-effects, taking ill for "two or three Days," but, Boylston writes, it was nevertheless "plain and easy to see, with Pleasure, the difference between having the Small-Pox this way, and that of having it in the natural way."[44] The Boston physician went on to inoculate dozens of other Bostonians throughout the summer and fall of 1721, listing the recipients' names in the *Historical Account* along with their dates of inoculation.

In the 1722 treatise *A Narrative of the Method and Success of Inoculating the Small Pox in New England*, Benjamin Colman (1673–1747) and Daniel Neal (1678–1743) confirm that "Dr. *Boylston* one of the Physicians of *Boston* ventur'd to introduce the *Inoculation*, into the Town about *Midsummer* last," but suggest a slightly different timeline. The *Narrative* instead indicates that Boylston did use Jack and Jackey as test subjects, noting that he "first tryed the Experiment on two of his Slaves, and then upon his Son, a child of about five or six Years old, with all the Success He could desire." Despite the experiment's success and the good outcome for Boylston's son, there remained considerable resistance to the practice, attested to by reactions so vehement that the physician sometimes feared for his life. As the *Narrative* goes on to explain, "it is incredible to think what a Storm of Reproach fell upon the Doctor within a few Days for his bold Attempt," a response that included other physicians publicly insisting "That the Inoculation was prejudicial to the Welfare of Mankind."[45] According to Colman and Neal, there was also "publish'd about the same Time, in the *Boston Newsletter*, an indecent Satire, wherein the Author, after having inveighed bitterly against the *Inoculation*, calling it *Wicked* and *Felonious*, and comparing it to the Infusion of the most venomous Poison into the Blood." The author evidently referred "the Case to the *Divines*," who did not respond as the invective writer had hoped, instead offering praise that was met with a similar response. Faring "no better than the Doctor," the *Narrative* explains, the clergy who expressed their support for Boylston were subsequently "insulted in the Streets, and were hardly safe in their own Houses."[46]

Another 1722 work, published anonymously as *An Account of the Method and Success of Inoculating the Small-Pox, in Boston in New-England*, nevertheless praises Boylston's program of inoculation. The *Account* is prefaced by a letter addressed to Hans Sloane (1660–1753), the president of the London College of Physicians, and signed by Jeremiah Dummer (1681–1739), a Harvard graduate and author of *A Defense of the New England Charters.* The *Account* proper is, however, assumed to be the work of Cotton Mather (1663–1728), the clergyman and pamphleteer best known for his key role in the Salem witch trials who took the pro side in what has become known as the Boston inoculation controversy.[47] Most distinctive about the *Account*, however, is not the attribution to Mather, but its recognition of African knowledge conspicuously absent in other versions. Named in reference to an ancient North African tribe Mather used also to describe his man Onesismus (b. before 1706–), it was a "*Garamantee* Servant," the author explains, who first offered the account's unnamed "Gentleman" details of "a Method frequently used in *Africa*, and which has been practis'd on himself, to procure an *easy Small-Pox*, and a perpetual security of neither *dying* by it, nor being again infected with it."[48] To confirm the story, the "Gentleman well known in the City of *Boston*," who is presumably Mather, sought further corroboration. After hearing about inoculation from the "*Garamantee* Servant," the gentleman "successively met with a Number of *Africans*; who all, in *their* plain Way, without any Combination or Correspondence, agreed in *one Story, viz.* that in their Country (where they use to die like *Rotten Sheep*, when the *Small-Pox* gets among them) it is now become a *common thing* to cut a Place or two in their Skin" to "put in a little of the Matter of the *Small-Pox*," after which "no Body every dy'd of doing this, nor ever had the *Small-Pox* after it." The testimony of Boston's African population did not, however, fully convince the unnamed gentleman of the efficacy and safety of smallpox inoculation. Though Mather had been gifted Onesismus in 1706, it was not until 1716, "Some Years after he had receiv'd his first *African* Informations," that the gentleman "found publish'd in our *Philosophical Transactions*" a communication from "That very valuable Person, Dr. *Emanuel Timonius*" writing from Constantinople with first-hand "Proof of the *Practice*, *Safety*, and *Success* of this Operation" that he finally accepted the credibility of the Africans' claims. That the findings from Turkey "agreed with what he had from *Africa*," the author makes a point of noting, came also "to our Surprize."[49]

As happened frequently in eighteenth-century recipe culture, Africans are not credited with knowledge of inoculation. Neither the "Number of *Africans*" nor the "*Garamantee* Servant" is granted sole or lasting credit for bringing first-hand knowledge of the method and its efficacy to Boston. Shifting focus to Boylston, the *Historical Account*'s author instead explains that it was the physician's "enterprising Genius" and "singular Dexterity in his Practice" that won the day. Boylston may have "perform'd Things not attempted by any" of the town's other physicians, but the physician is upheld as especially heroic in that he "thought it most generous to make his first Beginning upon his *own Family*; and here, to make not only two

Slaves, but a beloved *Son* of his own, (about five or six Year of Age) the Subjects of it."[50] Despite Boylston's efforts and the evident success of the inoculations, however, *An Account of the Method and Success of Inoculating the Small-Pox* also notes the many objections, remarking that "It is incredible, what a *Storm* was rais'd, and very much of it principally owing to some of our enrag'd *Physicians*, on this Occasion."[51] Despite the resistance shown by some members of the medical community, it turns out that "the *Opposers* could not hinder the *Proselytes* from increasing." Rather than being put out of business, it seems that "Dr. *Boylstone* has his Patients multiplying" with the happy result that "instead of any one miscarrying, they come off easier" than if they had acquired the disease the "natural" way.[52]

Boylston's inoculation program evidently met with some success, but the reactions of some Bostonians worked also to thwart "the general acceptance of inoculation" to the extent that "in the 1740s, the colonial governments in New York, Connecticut, Maryland, and Virginia issued proclamations prohibiting its use." The London College of Physicians, however, "declared its strong approval of inoculation in 1754," and the procedure continued to be performed in the colonies despite ongoing resistance.[53] Some twenty years later, Loyalist Thomas Robie seems to have "enflamed the patriot majority of Marblehead in 1773 when he had himself and his family inoculated against smallpox" before his 1775 move to Halifax, "a decision many radicals believed was a part of Tory conspiracy to spread the disease among the town's inhabitants."[54] Resistance in Marblehead culminated in January 1774 when a group of men, "armed with tubs of tar, rowed out to the newly built inoculation hospital on Cat Island, set fire to the despised institution, and burned it to the ground."[55] Inoculations nevertheless continued and, some fifty years after Boylston, Dr John Jeffries (1745–1819) recorded in his extant ledger the details of those he administered in Boston in 1775 and in Halifax from 1776 to 1779, where he served as a British naval surgeon after evacuating Boston at the onset of the Revolutionary War.[56] Having inoculated his son at Boston's Rainsford Island Hospital in June 1775, Jeffries also "inoculated children at the hospital on Georges Island" during a "large smallpox outbreak" in Halifax.[57] According to his ledger, Jeffries administered the treatment to adults as well as children as young as a few days old. Inoculations in Nova Scotia were not, however, limited to Halifax. In Liverpool, an inoculation hospital was established in January 1776, but with limited success: at least some of the town's residents met to "generally sign an agreement not to be inoculated" after the procedure was seen to "itself cause the disease in some."[58] In Windsor, a 5 June 1777 letter to Lieutenant Governor Mariot Arbuthnot (1711–1794) from surgeon Michael Head[59] explains "That in the years 1775 and 1776 the small Pox spread itself from Hallifax to the Townships of Windsor, Newport, Horton, & Falmouth." Unlike Liverpool, those communities saw "in consequence thereof, the Inhabitant Generally resolved on Enoculation, to prevent its direfull effects." A number of those who "apprehended the small Pox would make great havock & destruction" Head describes as being "soe extremely poor as to be totally unable to pay for their Enoculation" let alone "any part of the necessary medicines," and the surgeon was thus compelled to write the lieutenant governor petitioning reimbursement for the work done in aid of those among the inoculated fifty-eight "who are totally unable to make him any recompence."[60]

Given the prevalence and seriousness of the disease, it is noteworthy that, compared to remedies for illnesses like gout, consumption, and stone, treatments and preventatives for smallpox appear infrequently among the recipes held in Maritime archives, a gap that might be explained by the inoculation controversy that may also account for why the contributor of "Hints on the Method of Inoculating against Smallpox" chooses to remain anonymous, signing off only as "A Member of the Community." Smallpox does, however, earn mention in an untitled diary entry from Halifax, dated September 1792, noting that "The small-pox which had broken out among some negroes has begun to spread through the Town." In addition to blaming the Black inhabitants of Halifax, the entry lauds "Dr. Jenner" and his "novel cure for it which consists in scratching the arm of a person and daubing in some of the pox."[61] Though Edward Jenner did develop the safer cowpox-based procedure he first used in 1796 and introduced in his 1798 *An Inquiry into the Causes and Effects of Variolae Vaccinae*, the diary writer mentions neither the treatment's African origins nor the contribution of Lady Mary Wortley Montagu, whose efforts continued to be lauded in the colonies more than a century later. A Mrs M. Guyot, for instance, wrote an account of the 1885 Montreal epidemic that praises "Lady Mary Worthy" as "the first English person" to try inoculation, as well as the "great triumph of medicine" that is Jenner's vaccine.[62] Ongoing vaccine hesitancy in the colony is suggested in the diarist's reporting that "The patient is supposed to suffer a very mild case and be permanently cured but most of the people are suspicious and will have nothing to do with it."[63]

Hints on the Method of Inoculating Against Smallpox

These instructions on the "safest and best Method" for being inoculated against smallpox were printed in *The Nova Scotia Gazette and the Weekly Chronicle* in 1775.[64] A merger of *The Nova Scotia Gazette* and *The Nova Scotia Chronicle*, *The Nova Scotia*

Gazette and the Weekly Chronicle was Anthony Henry's third newspaper in Halifax, a weekly paper printed between 1770 and 1800 that published laws, public notices, local news, and reprinted pieces from American newspapers.[65] We have not found another source for these instructions, so they may refer to the Halifax context.

Mr. Printer,

as the Small Pox has made its appearance in
more than one House in Town it is much to
be feared it may spread, particularly as this Distem-
per was not contracted by Contagion[66] which proba-
bly indicates a disposing influence to this Malady
either in the generality of Constitutions or the Air.
From these Considerations I beg leave to offer to
the public a few Hints on the Method of Innoculating,
which may be of use to poor Families who can ill
afford to pay a Practitioner to attend.
Eight or nine Days before Innoculation and dur-
ing the whole illness let the patient abstain from
Meats, Spices, Butter, Wine, and all high seasoned
Food, regard however being had to the Strength and
Constitution of the Patient.
Three Days before Innoculation let the Patient
take a Vomit of Tart Emittick[67] proportioned to the
Age and strength of the Patient.
On the Day of Innoculation let the Patient take
Ten Grains of Calamel[68] in a Pill at Bed time; this
Dose is calculated for a grown Person of a healthy
Habit, and must be proportionally lessened for a
younger or weakly Person.
The next Morning the Patient should take a Purge
of the kind most agreeable, powdered Jalap[69] may pos-
sibly be the best; repeat the Pill and Purge on the
fourth and seventh Days after Innoculation.
On the eighth Day after Innoculation let the Pa-
tient take a Vomit of Tart Emitt.
The Patient shou'd avoid severe Exercise, violent
Passions, or warm Rooms.

> Common Drink should be Barley Water sweetened with Brown Sugar, and one Ounce of powdered Cream Tart in half a Gallon of Decoction.
> The Opinion of the most experienced in this Disorder is that the safest and best Method of conveying the Infection is by small Punctures of a Lancet dipp'd in the variolus[70] Matter.
> A Member of the Community.

Offering how-to instructions for those who could not afford to have inoculations administered by a physician or surgeon, the letter opens by noting that the disease had appeared "in more than one House in Town" but giving no indication of how many households or persons might have been infected. When the opening paragraph insists that the disease "was not attracted by Contagion," the author may be using *Contagion* to mean contracted only by direct physical contact with others, thereby refuting it as a cause of this particular outbreak. Rather, the author speculates that the cause may be "a disposing influence to this Malady either in the generality of Constitutions or the Air," suggesting in doing so that smallpox sufferers are either predisposed to the disease or contract the virus by airborne means, or perhaps both.

Anticipating some ongoing resistance to inoculation, the letter writer self-identified as "A Member of the Community" treads carefully, asking leave to convey information presented not with certainty but with the possibility that it might prove useful. Offering not a hard and fast solution, the author notes that subtlety must be applied also in the execution. Recommending a regimen covering the "Eight or Nine days" preceding the inoculation and the duration of the inevitable after-effects, the patient is to abstain from "Meats, Spices, Butter, Wine, and all high seasoned Food," but that the recommendation be taken with regard "to the Strength and Constitution of the Patient." Likewise, the purgative to be administered three days before the treatment should be "proportioned to the Age and strength of the Patient," and the calomel to be taken on the day the inoculation is administered must also "be proportionally lessened for a younger or weakly Person." Given that tartar emetic and calomel are both extremely toxic and now recognized to be "invariably fatal in sufficient doses,"[71] the writer's advice seems prudent and perhaps self-protective.

The pre-inoculation purging regimen is complemented by another on the day after inoculation, to be followed by another "on the fourth and seventh Days." For this, the writer suggests "powdered Jalap," a medicinal ingredient the *Edinburgh Pharmacopoeia* describes as "esteemed as an excellent purgative in cold phlegmatic constitutions."[72] Most often given as a purgative and laxative, jalap was sometimes mixed with "Alkaline salts, or soaps" thought to "correct its supposed virulence" by preventing it from adhering "to the coats of the intestines."[73] Both jalap and calomel would later be described in the 1793 manual *The Clinical Guide* by Edinburgh surgeon William Nisbet (1759–1822) as "purgatives of a drastic nature" that "frequently operate in both directions."[74] The final stage to the regimen is to give the patient another vomit, which is recommended to be added to the "Barley Water sweetened with Brown Sugar" prescribed as the patient's "Common Drink." Throughout recovery, the patient is also advised to "avoid severe Exercise, violent Passions, or warm Rooms." Though it seems unlikely that anyone undergoing the described regimen would be inclined to take any exercise – let alone the "severe" kind – the patient might understandably be tempted to indulge the strong emotions and warm temperatures the author cautions against.

In the final paragraph, the letter writer strategically moves from what is presented as personal opinion to describing a practice employed by "the most experienced in this Disorder," advising that the "safest and best Method of conveying the Infection is by small Punctures of a Lancet dipp'd in the variolus Matter." Though "inoculation did not penetrate deeply into life before it was introduced from Constantinople early in the 18th century," there is some evidence to suggest that a method of "variolation" used to introduce the smallpox virus with the aim of achieving immunity "appears to have been in use in Wales since at least as early as 1600." Other methods of "buying the pocks" were also described in Scotland, where "wool contaminated with smallpox material was wrapped around a child's wrist," while elsewhere in Europe "smallpox scabs were held for some time in the child's hand" and "others had the child wear smallpox-infected clothes."[75] Purporting to share a method of smallpox inoculation not associated with common or folk practice but instead offering the more trustworthy knowledge of "the most experienced" bolsters the letter's authority, its substance, and its author. At the same time, invoking the authority of "the most experienced" allows the author of the "Hints" to deflect responsibility for devising, or even advising on, the actual procedure of inoculation. Taking up the more tentative stance akin to that evident in the opening paragraphs, the letter closes with a simultaneous gesture of affirmation and denial, perhaps a necessary strategy when promoting inoculation in a time and place where "most of the people are suspicious and will have nothing to do with it."[76]

To Preserve the Face from Being Deformed by the Smallpox

This recipe was included in the 1791 issue of *The Nova Scotia Calender*, published by Anthony Henry.[77] The almanac for 1791 includes charts, diagrams, and lists that detail the astrological influence of constellations on parts of the body, make prognostications about the moon's phases and the weather for each month of the year, and name important figures in Nova Scotia (judges, members of the House of Assembly, army staff, the firefighters for Halifax, and the like). It also includes content not specific to 1791, such as tables of measurement for bushels, pecks, and gallons, money conversion tables for different currencies, and the Jewish calendar. The recipes are found on the last page.

A common type of recipe, this particular one is found in several eighteenth-century recipe collections, including *Dr. Lowers, and Several Other Eminent Physicians, Receipts Containing the Best and Safest Method for Curing most Diseases in Humane Bodies* (1700), a collection of recipes by Richard Lower (1631–1691) and others, *The Good Samaritan* (1761) by Theophilus Lobb (1678–1763), and Peregrine Montague's *The Family Pocket-book* (1762).[78]

To preserve the Face from being deformed by the Small-pox.

Take an ounce and a half of pomatum;[79] of oil of almonds, one ounce; of spermaceti[80] and virgin's wax,[81] of each three drachms;[82] of damask rose water, one ounce; set them all together over the fire, and as soon as they are melted, take them off, let them stand then till they are cold, then make a hole, and drain out the water, and with a feather anoint the patient's face.

The method used in this recipe is long-standing. For instance, Hannah Woolley's *The Queen-Like Closet* (1670) offers a recipe "To get away the Signs of the Small Pox" that similarly uses white rosewater and pomatum made with spermaceti and oil of almonds.[83] The popularity of the treatment documents how smallpox scars were a major concern, second only to potentially dying from the disease. In Lady

Mary Wortley Montagu's poem "Six Town Ecologues," printed in 1758, the section called "Saturday. The Small-Pox" is narrated by a woman called Flavia, who cries that she has become

> A frightful spectre, to myself unknown!
> Where's my complexion? where my radiant bloom,
> That promis'd happiness for years to come?

After lamenting the loss of lovers and loss of power, Flavia adds, "Ye cruel chymists, what with-held your aid! / Could no pomatums save a trembling maid?" before concluding that physicians were of no assistance despite their promises.[84] Montagu's brother William died of smallpox in 1713, and Montagu herself had smallpox in 1715, the disease resulting in the loss of her eyelashes. If the smallpox scars could have value for servants as a testament to their immunity and ability to safely care for children, the resulting disfigurement often diminished marriage prospects – especially for women, as Montagu's poem suggests. With smallpox scars came the perception of a loss of beauty. Encouraged perhaps by the visibly damaging effects of smallpox on women as well as their role as medical caregivers, "The success of the vaccination movement," Michael Bennett notes, "owed a lot in its early years to the support of women," who saw to it that their children were vaccinated.[85] This recipe further suggests that European beauty standards emphasizing unmarked skin – without pimples, freckles, or scars – also made their way across the Atlantic.

GOUT

A "notoriously painful and debilitating" disease, gout became increasingly common through the seventeenth to nineteenth centuries.[86] The high incidence of gout in eighteenth-century England, when the disease "seems to have risen to almost epidemic proportions,"[87] has since been explained by high amounts of lead ingested through paint and liquor and, more recently, by rapidly growing sugar consumption.[88] As Katherine Allen notes, gout was "a chronic disorder associated with the elite who had a rich, meat- and alcohol-heavy diet" that "afflicted mainly men," and was thus associated with prosperity, success, and conspicuous consumption.[89] Sometimes seen as a badge of honour among the affluent, gout was taken as "a sign of superiority, with a penchant for princes, patricians – and even philosophers," as it gained status as "a high-profile condition," "a disease of the

Quality,"[90] and a fashionable disease of "luxury and the upper classes."[91] Gout was, however, a disease of contradictions: it was valued to a degree because it was thought to guard against other "mutually exclusive" diseases.[92] Further, although gout is today associated with a particular kind of arthritis that usually affects the feet and hands, gout in the eighteenth century had a wide variety of symptoms, encompassing stomach disorders and rheumatic fever. In his treatise on scurvy and gout, chemist Francis Spilsbury describes the disease's "proteus nature," observing, "Like as the Pine-apple is considered as containing the taste and flavour of many different fruits, so a great many disorders of the body are, under different appellations, to be found in the Gout."[93] And even as gout was associated with the wealthy, gout sufferers could become the subject of ridicule and disdain, perhaps most notably in the well-known satirical illustrations of William Hogarth (1697–1764).

For the Gout

This recipe signed by "Doctor Rare" was published in the 1 November 1780 issue of *The Nova Scotia Gazette and the Weekly Chronicle.*[94] Though the recipe's method and components – which include a flayed and pulverized kitten – may be shocking to the modern reader, there is a long history of medical recipes specifying ingredients that encompass flayed puppies, bull penises, and frog spawn as well as the "turds" and urine of sundry animals. Attributed to "a very antient Dutch Author," the recipe's original source is likely Lorenz Fries's (1490–1531/2) *Spiegel der Artzny* (1518), a popular German medical guide published in Strasbourg that derives a gout ointment from the fat of a roasted goose stuffed with kittens. Professing the wonders of "this Salve," Doctor Rare makes a more adamant claim to "cureth the gout" than Lorenz Fries, who maintains of his ointment only that it "withdraws the pains in the joints."[95] Though bolder in its promises than the original, the Doctor Rare remedy nevertheless uses a similar method and ingredients. According to W.S.C. Copeman's translation, Fries instructs the user to "Roast a fat old goose and stuff with chopped kittens, lard, incense, wax and flour of rye" to produce "drippings applied to the painful joints."[96]

Mr. PRINTER.

The following receipt for the Gout is exactly transcribed from a very antient Dutch[97] Author, which I wish to be published in your paper, for the benefit of such as are subject to that honourable Malady.

For the gout

TAKE an ould Fat Goose, prepare her as if you would roast her: Then take a Kitline[98] or young cat, flea[99] it, cast away the head and entrails thereof, and contund[100] the flesh thereof in a Mortar, add as then thereto fat bakone[101] One ounce, three quarters of an Ounce of Wax; as much white Rosine,[102] and whyte Frankinsence; beat all these together, and replenish therewith the Goose: broach her, and sow her fast to the spit least any thing fall thereout; roast her, and receive the droppings thereof in a dripping pan: when as now the Goose is dressed and roasted that she droppeth no more, throw her as then away, least any body eat thereof.

And this Salve of Unctione cureth the Gout,

Doctor RARE

Throughout the eighteenth century, the use of such folksy and largely ineffective medicines declined to virtually disappear by the nineteenth. Published in 1780, Doctor Rare's bizarre directions for making ointment were almost certainly submitted with the intention of mocking medical practices of the past. Such an aim is evident in the way the recipe differs from its source, in that Doctor Rare advises throwing the cooked goose away, "least any body eat thereof," while Fries insists that it "must all be eaten" once the ointment is gleaned from the drippings.[103] Fries's recipe falls in line with other sixteenth-century and seventeenth-century gout remedies derived from animal fat. Nicholas Culpeper's popular 1659 medical guide, *School of Physick*, for instance, includes among several recommended gout treatments a "special remedy" made from frogs and a puppy: "Take a young Whelp in *March*," he instructs, "kill him, and flea him, and pull out his guts, and fill up his belly with Water-frogs, sow up his belly close again, then roast him, and save the dripping."[104] In the eighteenth century, however, the drippings of geese, kittens, puppies, and frogs had become increasingly displaced by fat from farm animals such as sheep, hens, ducks, and hogs. By the time Doctor Rare submitted his remedy to "Mr. Printer," recipes for ointments no longer used flayed kittens and puppies. The recipe thus seems suspiciously out of time, and the method of preparing the kitten may also give reason for pause. To skin and "cast away the head and entrails" of a "young cat" would be a straightforward procedure for those familiar with cleaning dead animals, but "to contund" with a mortar – a tool most often used for grinding herbs and making pastes – may not have been.

It was typical also for eighteenth-century satirists to use inflated terms to describe what they thought abhorrent or laughable, including the gout that was sometimes called "The Disease of Kings." The first clue that the recipe was not submitted in earnest lies in its claim to be "exactly transcribed" even though the source, which was likely known to the writer, is presented as the temporally vague and unnamed "very antient Dutch author" of a presumably distant past. The second is the description of gout as an "honourable Malady." Though gout had become a fashionable disease by the time the treatment appeared in *The Nova Scotia Gazette*, such a perverse popularity does not also mean that its sufferers were unequivocally or universally admired. As Hogarth's illustrations remind us, the prestige attached to debilitating afflictions of excess was often held up to ridicule, and not everyone thought honourable the over-indulgence that was both the perceived and actual cause of gout and other disorders of excess.

The elevated status implied by the name "Doctor Rare" further signals the recipe's parodic intent. Long the target of ridicule and satire, physicians were often regarded as no more honourable or "rare" than the many maladies they professed to treat, and they had long been ridiculed in print as much for their inefficacious and sometimes harmful practices as their reputed avarice. A 1700 collection mocking unscrupulous healers, published under the telling title *The Harangues or Speeches of Several Famous Mountebanks in Town and Country*, features a chapter titled "The Infallible Mountabank, or, Quack Doctor."[105] In it, the speaker also refers to himself as "A Doctor rare, / Who Travels much at Home!" Urging his audience to "SEE! Sirs, see here!" and to "take my Bills" (or advertisements), the mountebank claims to "cure all Ills" that include

The Cramp, the Stich,
The Squirt, the Itch,
The Gout, the Stone, the Pox;
The Mulligrubs,
The Bonny Scrubs,
And all Pandora's Box.[106]

The poem also appears in a nearly identical 1750 work under the slightly altered title *The Harangues, or Speeches, of Several Celebrated Quack-Doctors, in Town and Country*, which was republished in 1762.[107] Like the earlier version, the mid-century edition of *Harangues* presents numerous speaking characters that include one "Dr. Rock," "The horse-doctor," and a "Doctor rare." As the later book's subtitle indicates, both books conclude with "The Character of a Quack," several recipes, and "Three Mountebank Songs." The recipes specify mock ingredients that include the "sovereign tree of Tyburnia" and "a hen, trodden by one cock" and claim, satirically, to treat disorders ranging from scurvy to barrenness.[108] As much as the self-promoting doctors who made them, remedies from strange ingredients and bearing inflated claims were often the subject of ridicule, and the "For the Gout" remedy of this "Doctor RARE" brings this tradition to Nova Scotia.

Herbal Remedy for Gout

The following herbal remedy for gout comes from the diary of Henry Nase (1753–1836), where it appears along with a treatment for "Rheumatism" between entries dated 19 December 1785 and 22 March 1786.[109] A Loyalist from New York, Nase began his diary with his 1776 enlistment in the King's American Regiment and kept it for over two decades. Nase eventually settled in New Brunswick, where he contracted to build a house for Major John Coffin under whom he had served, and in 1786 established Mount Hope Farm on the banks of the Nerepis River. A justice of the peace and lieutenant colonel in the local militia, Henry Nase may now be best known for the Grand Bay–Westfield ferry that carries his name.

Gout

Four ounces leaves of speedwell[110] Two ounces alder Bark – 3do wintris bark[111] ½ pd angelica root 4 ounces Fennel Bark boil these together in 2 gal[ons] of soft water, strain the decoction in a earthen Pan, let it stand all night to settle. Pour it off in the morning and disolve 3.^{tb} treble refined sugar; Two p.^{d} virgin honey – gently simmered into a thin syrup – a larger teacup full, night & morning – to each dose or time of taking, a teaspoonful of D^{r}. Huxham's essense of antimony.

Nase's internal remedy for gout differs dramatically from the topical ointment rendered from a kitten-stuffed goose submitted by "Doctor RARE" to *The Nova Scotia Gazette and the Weekly Chronicle*. Herb-based concoctions like this one abound in eighteenth-century English medicine, however, and they were used to treat a multitude of ailments. The 1716 pharmacopeia of the Royal College of Physicians of London, *Pharmacopoia* [sic] *Londinensis: Or, the New London Dispensatory*, recommends black alder as a purge and claims it to be profitable for gout and other diseases as a dose mixed with cinnamon, ginger, and fennel – a concoction that shares some similarities with Nase's medicine.[112] *Collectanea Medica, the Country Physician* by William Salmon (1644–1713) includes "A Drink of Black Alder, by Matthiolus" that includes, like Nase's remedy, speedwell, black alder bark, "winter's cinnamon," fennel root and seed, leaving out only angelica.[113] All of Nase's herbal ingredients were commonly used in the eighteenth century to treat gout – although not everyone agreed on their usefulness.

Speedwell (also known as veronica) is recommended by, for instance, physician John Armstrong (1709–1779), who wrote in 1737 that it might be used in cases where "the Blood must be diluted" and specifies its use in a tea concocted from the "milder vulnerary [or healing] Herbs."[114] Fellow physician Richard Brookes (1721–1763) in 1754 also included veronica in a tea aiming "To promote Perspiration."[115] *A New and Complete Dictionary of Arts and Sciences* (1755) professes that speedwell is a good antiscorbutic and notes that "it has lately been celebrated in the gout and rheumatism."[116] Speedwell is also described in the widely read work of Dutch physician Herman Boerhaave (1668–1738) as "A little Plant common in our Pastures" that is "celebrated against Obstructions of the *Viscera*," or bowels; Boerhaave, however, disputes the herb's efficacy in treating gout, noting that "There was an Opinion some few Years ago set on Foot, that it would cure the Gout, and many drank it constantly as Tea, but it did not produce the Effect, and fell again into Disuse."[117] A study from McGill University in 1998 suggests, however, that speedwell is one of the northeastern North American plants that contains the XO (the enzyme xanthine oxidase) inhibitor that actually is effective in treating gout. The article's inclusion of speedwell in its list of plants traditionally used by Indigenous peoples to treat gout, however, is rather suspect in that it offers no direct evidence that it was employed by a particular First Nation.[118] Perhaps speedwell came to be used by Indigenous peoples, but it's important to note that the plant was first introduced to North America by Europeans and is not included in Virgil Vogel's *American Indian Medicine.*

Other ingredients in this recipe were also sometimes used in treating gout in European medicine (alder was commonly used in Indigenous medicine, although not to treat gout, and angelica was used by the Cherokee to treat "asthma symptoms, hay fever, and headaches" and also "combined with dogwood in traditional sweats and ceremonies" – but again, not to treat gout).[119] In European medicine, black alder was valued topically for its diuretic and astringent properties. The tree was described by physician and chemist William Lewis (1708–1781) as "common in moist woods in divers parts of England"; Lewis also notes that the tree's inner bark "purges violently," and thus recommends the use of other "safer and less precarious purgatives" that are also available in "plenty."[120] "An Electary against the Rheumatism," a recipe recommended by the Royal College of Physicians of London and Edinburgh, uses "Winter's Bark in Powder" in treating disorders of the joints, which could include gout in a time when the term *gout* was used to describe "a range of arthritic conditions."[121] Winter's bark is also specified along with fennel and angelica seed in "A Potion against the Gout," a concoction proclaimed effective also against jaundice, scurvy, and the "French Pox" by the anonymous author of *A Collection of Receipts in Physic* (1752).[122] Sugar and honey, the final ingredients of Nase's "thin syrup," would have served not only to sweeten the concoction. Honey has also long been valued for its antibacterial and antiseptic properties and was used by the ancients in topical treatments for wounds or, from Aristotle, to treat sore eyes.[123] The indicated honey, especially in the large quantity of two pounds, was likely included for its perceived medicinal value. According to Charles Butler (1560–1647), "the Father of English Beekeeping" who published *The Feminine Monarchie* (1623), honey can also be used "as a laxative and diuretic, as a cough medicine, an eye balm, a highly nourishing restorative, an aphrodisiac, a preservative, a mouthwash for ulcers, a gargle for quinsy and sore throats, a treatment for snakebites, a sobering agent for those that have partaken of mild narcotics, and a calming agent after stomach upsets."[124]

Nase's recipe concludes by noting that the "teacup full" of syrup is to be taken along with "a teaspoonful of Dr. Huxham's essense of antimony." John Huxham (1692–1768) was a member of the Royal College of Physicians of Edinburgh and the author of several eighteenth-century printed medical treatises. His *Of the Constitution of Air and Epidemic Diseases* describes essence of antimony as a simple made of antimony and dry wine, very efficacious for obstructions, sweats, and chronic disorders, like rheumatism.[125] A chemical element used even by the Assyrians in medicinal concoctions intending to promote "sweating, vomiting, and purging" with the aim of expelling "undesirable humours from the body," the medical use of antimony "declined during the eighteenth and nineteenth centuries" as it became increasingly recognized as poisonous.[126] Though it is unclear whether Nase's recipe specifies purchasing "Dr. Huxham's essense of antimony" or whether one was expected to concoct it, the "List of Quack Medicines" recorded by fellow Loyalist Dr William James Almon suggests that a number of pre-made medicinal concoctions may have been available for purchase in the colonial Maritimes.[127]

Advice to the Gouty

This advice to the gout sufferer was published in the 16 February 1790 issue of *The Royal Gazette and the Nova Scotia Advertiser* and signed only by "M."[128] Though treatises on the disease abound in the eighteenth century, what appears in *The Royal Gazette* may be a somewhat paraphrased and truncated version of a letter to the editor that was included in the 1789 edition of London's *Universal Magazine*. Signed there by one "Benevolus," the letter is printed in that magazine as "A Hint to Persons Afflicted with the Gout,"[129] and it is likely also derived from another unnamed source. Both letters urge moderation to counter the effects of luxury and excess, but *The Royal Gazette* version differs in speaking out against bleeding patients to achieve humoral balance, the practice of phlebotomy long thought key to health. The recipes appended to the end of each letter differ somewhat as well. The "M" who claims authorship of *The Royal Gazette* letter seems not to endorse purging of any kind as a remedy for gout and omits the "half an ounce of hiera picra," a purgative derived from aloes and canella bark that is specified in the *Universal Magazine*.

ADVICE to the GOUTY:

THE gout acknowledges for its predisposing use, either hereditary taint, luxury, or irregularity. Of the first of those, I shall say nothing, as every one knows palliation[130] to be the only relief hereditary diseases can admit of: But the two last are objects worthy the regard of invalids affected in this way.

Luxury, more immediately and more severely, irregularity (which always included intemperance, and is in fact, occasional luxury, as luxury is habitual intemperance; and repeated irregularity) more gradually, and though less severely, yet not less certainly, produces gout; and all, in a modus operandi, not much differing from each other. This, sufferers from podagrical[131] paroxysms know too well, either to doubt or deny, however averse they may be from acknowledging it.

From this conviction, when severity of pain urges to a remedy affecting the general conduct, one is at hand, founded on very illogical data; namely a meagre diet, grounded on the principles of this very fallacious syllogism.

If intemperance, luxury, or irregularity, be the cause of gout, their reverse must be the cure.

Irregularity, &c. is the cause – therefore, low living must be the cure.

But this is as wise reasoning as to say, that "I am full

of blood – bleeding is my remedy – therefore I must ruin my constitution by an excess of phlebotomy!" But the sober truth is this – Intemperence, luxury and irregularity, induce, what physicians call, indirect ability, or, in plainer words, produce general weakness, by means of overloading nature, as in the case of luxury and intemperance: or over-stretching her, by violent and ill timed exertions, as in the case of irregularity. Now, in this case, what does a regular course of low living do for the patient? Why, over and above the force put on the constitution by the sudden transition, it adds direct to indirect debility; disables the body from throwing off its load, by depriving it of the strength sufficient to effect a salutary and critical paroxysm; and so only disposes, by an inadequate effort, to cast it upon the vital parts; and so destroy the patient!

But the medium lies here; it consists in destroying the cause indirect debility; without inducing a worse, that which is direct.

I. Let luxury, intemperance, and irregularity, be cut off - by a regular, moderate, nutritious, easily digested diet; with proper portions of exercise and rest; equally avoiding fatigue and indolence: and by regulating the passions.

II. Let acquired constitutional injury, be repaired by the warm, bracing, stomachic medicines; among which nothing exceeds the following: Steep two ounces of dried Seville orange-peel, and one ounce of best rhubarb, in a quart of brandy for four days, shaking the bottle every day. Let a large spoonful of the tincture be taken with three of pepper-mint water, two hours before and after dinner. M.

The recipe that appears at the end of "Advice to the Gouty" is in two parts. The first takes a holistic approach, advising a regimen that has the patient avoid "luxury, intemperance, and irregularity" by regulating the "passions" and finding a more healthful balance through rest, exercise, and "a regular, moderate, nutritious, easily digested diet." The second recommendation offers a medicinal remedy, advising that the patient repair "constitutional injury" with the ingestion of "warm, bracing, stomachic medicines." The best of these, the writer claims, is a concoction made from "Seville orange-peel" and the "best rhubarb" steeped in brandy. Along with "three of pepper-mint water," the writer advises that the tincture be taken in one large spoonful before and after dinner.

Orange peel contains a number of medicinally useful chemicals that include anti-inflammatories, and it appears as an ingredient in numerous eighteenth-century medical remedies. It is frequently specified in gout remedies, including several by physician George Cheyne (1672–1743) that were published in his 1722 *An Essay of the True Nature and Due Method of Treating the Gout.* Cheyne played a major role in disseminating medical information, and it was from him that "Many 18th-century doctors took their cues on gout," though he drew heavily from his predecessor Thomas Sydenham (1624–1689), who in 1683 published his renowned *Treatise on the Gout.* Like the author of "Advice to the Gouty," Sydenham saw bleeding and purging as unhelpful and even harmful to gout patients. Because Sydenham believed that bleeding and purging drove "'peccant humours' further into the extremities," he concluded that they could only harm the body parts most afflicted by gout.[132] But the *Gazette* letter writer also implicitly disagrees with Cheyne, who "commended a largely dietary regime" and a "lowering diet" to treat gout.[133] Contrary to Cheyne, "Advice to the Gouty" does not endorse a "meagre diet" and "low living," recommendations the writer argues are predicated on a "fallacious syllogism" that denies a potential for harm akin to that of bleeding and purging.

Medicinal rhubarb (*Rheum palmatum*), the remedy's second ingredient, was valued for its roots that were ground into a medicinal powder; it differs from the familiar garden variety (*Rheum rhaponticum*) grown for its stems.[134] Known in the Middle Ages as "Turkish rhubarb,"[135] Chinese medicinal rhubarb was first imported to Russia and its seeds later smuggled to Scotland by James Mounsey (1710–1773), erstwhile physician to the Tsar. As a milder alternative to other purgatives, medicinal rhubarb was initially "so difficult to obtain that it generated an economic frenzy" that subsided only when British growers began to produce quantities sufficient to meet demand.[136] Rhubarb soon became widely used in eighteenth-century British medicine, and Mounsey was in 1770 "awarded the gold medal of the Royal Society of Arts" for his efforts.[137]

Given that excessive alcohol consumption was recognized as a cause of gout, brandy seems an odd medium in which to steep the medicinal orange peel and rhubarb, especially since rhubarb-infused brandy was also used as a purgative.[138]

Brandy is also distilled from wine, which was thought to generate "a 'tartarous' matter within the body" that contributed to the gout.[139] As physician Timothy Bennet (1703–?) asserts in *An Essay on the Gout*, "all Salts, and tartarous Salts among the rest, are some of the Materials that furnish out the Gout," and the afflicted should therefore seek out only "an inflammable Spirit" of the kind that "abound not with such kind of Salts."[140] Brandy was also "in some cases distilled using lead-containing equipment" that is now understood to cause or exacerbate the disease.[141] Yet, because spirits were thought by distillers as akin to those "coursing through the human body" and could "thus prolong life," alcoholic beverages were "an important element in the medical pharmacopeia"[142] and appear as the main ingredient in countless receipts for "spiritous tinctures."

The "pepper-mint water" to be taken along with the brandy-based tincture appears regularly in eighteenth-century remedies, both as a simple tincture and in combination with other ingredients that sometimes include spirits. In his *Domestic Medicine*, physician William Buchan (1729–1805) notes that in treating colic, "A glass of good pepper-mint water will have nearly the same effect as a glass of brandy, and in some cases, is rather to be preferred."[143] In his *Advice to Gouty Persons*, physician Richard Kentish (1730–1792) agrees that purgatives "are now very properly decried in all gouty cases." Instead, Kentish advises that "[a]rthritics should keep the body open by the use of some warm cathartic," recommending a "tincture of senna, or spirituous tincture of rhubarb" taken as a tablespoon stirred into "a glass of water, or pepper-mint water"[144] and "[a] large spoonful of Huxham's tincture of bark in a glass of pepper-mint water" as "a very good stomachic medicine."[145] Native to Europe, peppermint "has long been the most popular 'medicinal mint'" and appears in many herbals; both peppermint and spearmint were brought to North America by colonists and were likely readily available in the colonial Maritimes.[146]

SCURVY

Scurvy was another of the eighteenth century's most common diagnoses, suffered especially by soldiers and sailors forced to remain on ships for long sea voyages. Scurvy was thus often defined as a disease of the sea or of land and, for much of the eighteenth century, was thought to be a "putrid disease" caused by the putrefaction or decay of the humours. This putrefaction could have a variety of causes, such as perspiration, poor diet (a lack of vegetables, too much salt meat and fish, rotten food), moist air, stagnant water, damp housing, and lack of exercise. Cures for scurvy would thus seek to counteract the putrefaction and improve the humoral "viscosity." In the 1780s, some also theorized that scurvy was a nervous disease caused by a disordered nervous system rather than an imbalance in one of the humours, even though the nervous system disorder was thought to result from the same factors believed to putrefy the humours. According to this newer theory, treatments would stimulate the nervous system through the consumption of brandy, opium, or water infused with carbon dioxide. The late eighteenth century thus marked a period of reform in scurvy treatments, with naval physician Sir Gilbert Blane (1749–1834) arguing that the dryness, cleanliness, and ventilation of accommodations would help to prevent scurvy when accompanied by a diet that included citrus juices, which became standard issue in the navy in 1795; diet was, however, just one perceived cause of the malady, and the relationship to the ascorbic acid we now know as vitamin C – the lack of which is now known to be scurvy's root cause – was not yet fully understood.[147]

A Certain Radical Cure for the Scurvy

This recipe was published in *The Royal Gazette and Miscellany of the Island of Saint John* on 30 January 1793.[148] The island's second newspaper, *The Royal Gazette* was printed in Charlottetown between 1791 and 1794 by William A. Rind (1763–1842), a printer who learned his trade in Virginia before moving to St John's Island in 1788, where he worked as a journeyman printer for James Robertson (1747–1816).[149] *The Royal Gazette* regularly published the lieutenant governor's proclamations and often reprinted items from Halifax and London newspapers.[150] When Robertson left the island in 1789, Rind became the king's printer. He married Elizabeth Bagnall, the daughter of a Loyalist, in 1790 before returning to the United States in 1798, where he continued to work in the printing business.[151]

Scurvy cures are often found in pre-1800 recipe collections, but this particular remedy was not a common one. It did, however, appear in *The Weekly Entertainer*, a magazine printed in Sherborne (in Dorset, England) on 31 March 1783.[152] This English version did not have the note to the printer from A.R., who may have been located on St John's Island, but it did claim in its title to "not cost more than three-pence per Week," a promise this version leaves out.

AN EXTRACT.

A certain radical Cure for the SCURVY.

It has proved most effectual in this tor-
menting disorder, attended with irritation,
continual blotches in the face, &c. after
every other application has failed, and par-
ticularly those famous expensive drops,
ad other nostrums, whose reputation the
writer hereof has found to be much superior
to their merit, he therefore desires, from the
sole principle of humanity, that what he
has experienced to be so great a benefit,
may be universally known, for it came to
his knowledge by mere accident.
"Take two ounces of cream of tartar
one ounce of Sulphur, one ounce of
AEthiops mineral;[153] pound them fine,
and mix them in half a pound of
treacle,[154] taking half a spoonful an
hour after breakfast, and the same
quantity going to rest; if this should
purge too much, take it only once in
24 hours, every evening. Continue
the practice, and the effect will soon
demonstrate its utility."
Mr. Printer, This I was desired to copy,
and tend to you, that you might insert the
same in your paper, for the benefit of the
afflicted, by a subscriber. Your's, A.R.

This recipe seems to work as a purge, a treatment predicated on the understanding of scurvy as a disease caused by putrefaction. Gilbert Blane writes in 1789 that while there is no "article of *Materia Medica*" that will cure scurvy in the absence of proper diet, medicines do help to "increase the fluid secretions" and thereby cause the body to purge itself (through diarrhea, urination, sweat) or help to encourage circulation.[155] Like the recipe published in the Charlottetown newspaper, a collection of remedies published in Boston as well as England, titled *The Medical*

Pocket-Book (1791) and credited to the British physician John Elliot, recommends cream of tartar and sulphur for treating scurvy (land scurvy in particular); it also recommends a liquor made of molasses as an antiseptic, a substance meant to prevent putrefaction, to treat sea scurvy.[156]

CONSUMPTION

Though afflicting humans for at least six millennia, consumption is perhaps most familiar to us in the languishing sufferer of the nineteenth century, when the notoriously poor living and working conditions of the Industrial Revolution accelerated the spread of the disease then renamed tuberculosis.[157] The disease that would become "the leading killer of the nineteenth century"[158] was prevalent also in the eighteenth, described by Edinburgh physician William Buchan as "a wasting or decay of the whole body from an ulcer, tubercles, or concretion of the lungs, an empyema, a nervous atrophy, &c."[159] Previously known in Greek as *phthisis* and believed to be caused by a lifestyle-weakened constitution or inherited disposition, its cause was sometimes posited as environmental. In his 1729 *The Family Companion for Health*, Edward Strother (1675–1737) admits a cause "either hereditary or accidental," drawing also on humoral theory in observing the "Moisture and Warmth" of Bath, London, "and all its adjacent towns," from which he concludes, "The most common Consequence of this Weather, is a Consumption."[160] The disease's infectious origins were, however, first hypothesized in the 1720 treatise *A New Theory of Consumptions*, where English physician Benjamin Marten (fl. 1722) begins the first chapter of his groundbreaking work by noting that "There is no Country in the World more Productive of Consumptions than this our Island."[161] Thought to have been imported to North America by European settlers, tuberculosis spread to Indigenous populations across the continent as settlers moved into their territories, with those in the east being exposed in the seventeenth and eighteenth centuries.[162]

To Make Milk-Water

The following remedy appeared in the 1791 issue of *The Nova Scotia Calender, or an Almanack*.[163] Given the disease's prevalence, remedies for treating consumption appeared regularly in English publications. The same recipe is found in at least two other eighteenth-century recipe collections: *Dr. Lower's, and Several Other Eminent*

Physicians Receipts (first printed in 1700 and then several more times in the early eighteenth century) and *The Family Pocket-Book* (1762), which claims on its title page "the ingenious Dr. Lower's Works" as one of its sources.[164] A similar concoction for treating ailments that include "Spitting of Blood" specifies the use of very similar herbs – "*Carduus benedictus*," "Goat's-Rue," mint, wormwood, rue, and angelica – mixed with "new Milk" also appears in the 1707 herbal of London physician John Pechey (1655–1716).[165]

To make Milk-water, very useful in all sorts of Fevers and consumptions.

Take of cardus, two handfuls;
of rue, goat's rue, angelica, wormwood, mint, and balm, of each
one handful; put them all, being
well bruised, into a cold still, with
a gallon of milk, and draw off with
a very gentle fire, lest it should run
thick; you may draw off almost
three quarts, drink a glass of it at
any time, sweetened with sugar.

Cures for consumption sometimes recommended removal to the country, "where the air is pure, dry and free,"[166] as well as a diet heavy in milk and milk products. Looking to the past rather than proposing an innovative new technique, this remedy focuses on milk, adding to it herbs that were readily available for inclusion in homemade remedies. The first mentioned is cardus, the *Carduus benedictus* also known as holy or blessed thistle originating in the Mediterranean region and introduced to North America as well as other parts of Europe. Famously mentioned in *Much Ado About Nothing* (3.4.71–74) by William Shakespeare (1564–1616), the plant had been grown in England and used to treat a variety of ailments since at least the Middle Ages. In use today as an expectorant and as a treatment for digestive ailments, the plant was familiar enough in early modern England that renowned herbalist Nicholas Culpeper advised that he would "spare a labour in writing a description of this, as almost every one that can but write at all, may describe them from his own knowledge" – a perspective that persisted into the eighteenth century with the continued publication of his work.[167] Goat's rue, as

Joseph Miller (1668/9–1748) explains in his *Botanicum Officinale; or a Compendious Herbal*, "is accounted Cordial, Surdorific [sudorific, causing perspiration], and Alexipharmic [expelling a toxic substance from the body], and good against pestilential Distempers" as well as "all kind of Fevers, the Small Pox and Measles,"[168] while angelica – for Miller, "Stomachick, Cordial, *Alexipharmick*" – was available also in North America (and specified also in Henry Nase's remedy for gout).[169] Wormwood, or *Artemisia absinthium*, a herb also familiar from the Shakespeare plays *Hamlet* and *Romeo and Juliet*, may be native to North Africa and southern Europe but has been naturalized in North America as well as Europe, and "descriptions are found in almost all medicinal books of the Western World";[170] as its name suggests, wormwood has been used primarily to treat worm infestations and other digestive ailments.[171] The recipe also includes mint and balm, both of which would have been readily available in the colonial Maritimes.

An Admirable Receipt for a Consumption

This recipe was published in *The Nova Scotia Gazette and the Weekly Chronicle* on 3 May 1774.[172] It had previously appeared in *The Pennsylvania Chronicle and Universal Advertiser* on 27 April 1767 with a preface from Philanthropus that cited *The London Chronicle* as its source.[173] We have not been able to find a reference to this recipe in that London periodical, but it was printed, without the title, in *The Universal Museum* in London in February 1767 in a letter to the printer from Benevolus.[174] Nearer the date of its appearance in *The Nova Scotia Gazette*, the version of the recipe found in *The Universal Museum* also appeared in *The Royal American Magazine*, printed in Boston, for May 1774.[175]

An Admirable RECEIPT for a Consumption.

TAKE of Madeira (or good generous Mountain[176]) wine, two quarts; balsams of Gilead[177] and Tolu,[178] each two ounces; gum olibanum[179] in tears, (groisly[180] powdered) two ounces; flowers of Benjamin, half an ounce. Let the mixture stand near the fire for three or four days, frequently shaking the vessel; then add thereto, of Narbonne honey,[181] four ounces; extract of Canadian maiden hair, eight ounces. Shake the bottle well, and strain off the liquor. The dose, two tea spoonfuls to be taken once in four hours, in coltsfoot-tea, or water, sweetened with capillaire.

Unlike "Milk-water," this remedy eschews dairy.[182] But as with a plant mixture for treating consumption that "may be infused in water or wine" in William Buchan's remedies, this recipe specifies mixing the concoction with madeira or "Mountain wine."[183] With the "balsams of Gilead and Tolu," from Asia and South America, and Narbonne honey from France, it is likely that the recipe originated in Europe. Narbonne honey was a valuable commodity; an eighteenth-century advertisement identifies it as a "fragrant honey" from France and recommends it "for preventing Coughs, Colds, Fevers, Consumptions, &c." – its high value cemented by the claim it is frequently adulterated.[184]

Despite its European origins, however, the recipe specifically calls for Canadian maidenhair, or *capillaire du Canada*, the North American variety of maidenhair fern. Christopher Parsons suggests that French colonists had highly valued the plant they called *capillaire du Canada,* and in the eighteenth century it became "the principal pharmaceutical remedy transported from New France to the old."[185] As a commodity "prized for the slight hint of the exotic," Canadian maidenhair was exported in large quantities to France, which "ensured that the capillaire du Canada became a principal vehicle through which French consumers experienced the French colony" – before they gave it up in peace negotiations with Britain.[186] The 1767 version of the recipe that appeared in *The Universal Museum* in London includes a further note on the fern: "The Canadian maiden-hair, which we now import from thence in great plenty, is infinitely superior to that which grows in England. A strong infusion made of this herb, sweetened with honey, or sugarcandy, is the best ptisan which can possibly be drank by consumptive people, and will of itself cure any recent cough."[187]

European knowledge of medical uses of maidenhair fern may have come from Indigenous peoples of North America, although – as is typical of European recipe culture – the recipe does not mention this history. However, Pehr Kalm, a Finnish-Swedish botanist who wrote an account of his travels in North America recounts one incident of settler acquisition of knowledge of Canadian maidenhair: "Several people in Albany and Canada, assured me that its leaves were very much used instead of tea, in consumptions, coughs, and all kinds of pectoral diseases. This they have learnt from the Indians, who have made use of this plant for these purposes since times immemorial."[188] His work was published in English in 1770, although it had appeared earlier in Sweden. In this recipe, the relatively newer knowledge – for European physicians – of the maidenhair fern is combined with the addition of ingredients from around the world, as well as drawing on long-standing medicinal practices such as using honey and wine.

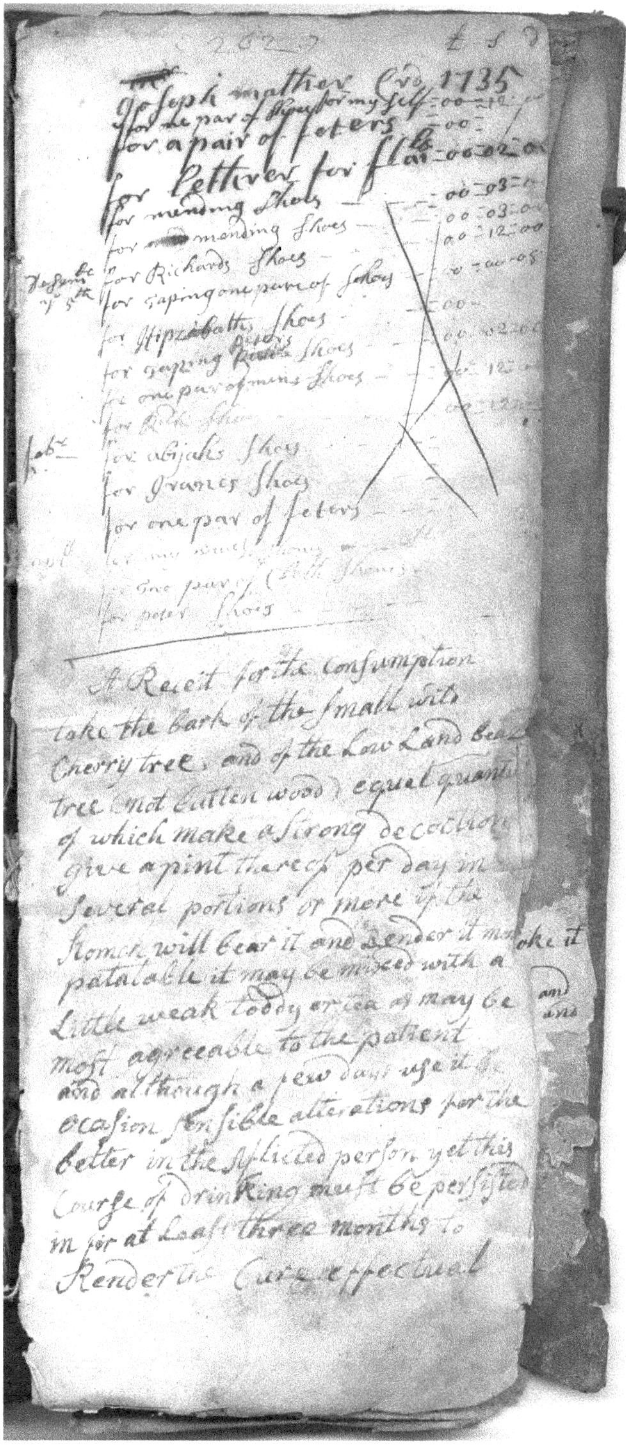

Figure 3.2
Cornwallis Account Book.

A Receit for the Consumption

This recipe is one of three included in a 1790 account book by an unknown creator that records the purchase and sale of dry goods, agricultural products, and services in Cornwallis Township in King's County, Nova Scotia.[189] We have not found another source for this "Receit," but it is one of several medicinal remedies held in Maritime archives that include tree bark, and one of many others aiming to treat consumption; as the English translation of *Dictionnaire Oeconomique* by Noël Chomel (1633–1712) put it in 1758, "Multiudes [*sic*] of Receipts there are for the Cure of this Distemper."[190]

A Receit for the consumption

take the Bark of the small wild Cherry tree, and of the Low Land bea[ch]tree (not butter wood) equal quantities of which make a strong decoction give a pint thereof per day in several portions or more if the stomach will bear it and Render it most palatable it may be mixed with a Little weak toddy or tea as may be most agreeable to the patient and although a few days use it be ocasion sensible alterations for the better in the Afflicted person yet this course of drinking must be persisted in for at least three months to Render the Cure effectual.

"The small wild Cherry tree" whose bark is specified in this remedy may be the *Prunus avium* native to Asia Minor that was imported to Europe and used medicinally since the Greeks and Romans as a cough suppressant, diuretic, and astringent.[191] It is also possible that the recipe had been imported to Nova Scotia by the New England Planters who founded a number of Nova Scotia townships between 1759 and 1764[192] and might therefore also refer to black cherry native to North America. As the botanical name *Prunus serotina* suggests, the bark of the black cherry tree had long been used by Indigenous peoples as a sedative useful also in suppressing coughs, its astringent properties helpful in treating respiratory ailments and colds,[193] and the North American black cherry is yet widely used in many familiar over-the-counter cough treatments.

The addition of bark from the "Low Land bea[ch] tree" may also suggest that the remedy was imported from England, where forests of lowland beech cover much of the southern part of the country. The European beech was, however, also imported to North America and can be found throughout the northeast, as well as in Ontario. That the recipe may also refer to the native American beech is also implied in that it is likewise used for medicinal purposes: the confusion over which species the recipe's author indicates is further complicated by *The History of the County of Worcester* by Peter Whitney (1744–1816), who notes that in this region of Massachusetts "low lands are stored with ash, beech, birch, maple, and hemlock."[194]

As with many recipes, this one does not include specific instructions for making the "strong decoction" to be consumed regularly to a pint per day and mixed with "a Little weak toddy or tea" to render the medicine more palatable to taste and more agreeable to the stomach. Though the patient might see some benefit within "a few days use," the recipe insists that the regimen be maintained for "at least three months to Render the Cure effectual."

THE STONE

The stone is the early modern term used to describe kidney and bladder stones. In the medieval and early modern periods, the stone was believed to be caused by corrupted humours that obstructed the body's healthful state of openness. Treatments typically involved addressing the blockage, which could include bloodletting, purges, inducing vomiting, steam baths, and other treatments that could draw the stone to the surface of the body where it could be removed.[195]

Effectual Cure for the Stone

This recipe was printed in *The Royal Gazette and the Nova Scotia Advertiser* in Halifax on 15 April 1794, having travelled some distance in print before its appearance.[196] The Halifax paper, another of Anthony Henry's publications, notes that the recipe had previously been printed on 22 February 1794 in the *Columbian Centinel*, a Boston newspaper printed between 1790 and 1799.[197] The version in the *Columbian Centinel*, like the one in *The Royal Gazette*, identifies its source as an Alexandria newspaper – likely *The Columbian Mirror and Alexandria Gazette*, a newspaper active in Alexandria, Virginia, from 1792 to 1800. Before being printed in Halifax, the recipe had already appeared in newspapers in Baltimore, Norfolk (VA), Elizabethtown (NJ), New York, Hartford (CT), Worcester (MA), and Providence (RI).[198] The recipe continued to be published in American newspapers until at least 1811 and is one of the more popular recipes discussed in this book.[199]

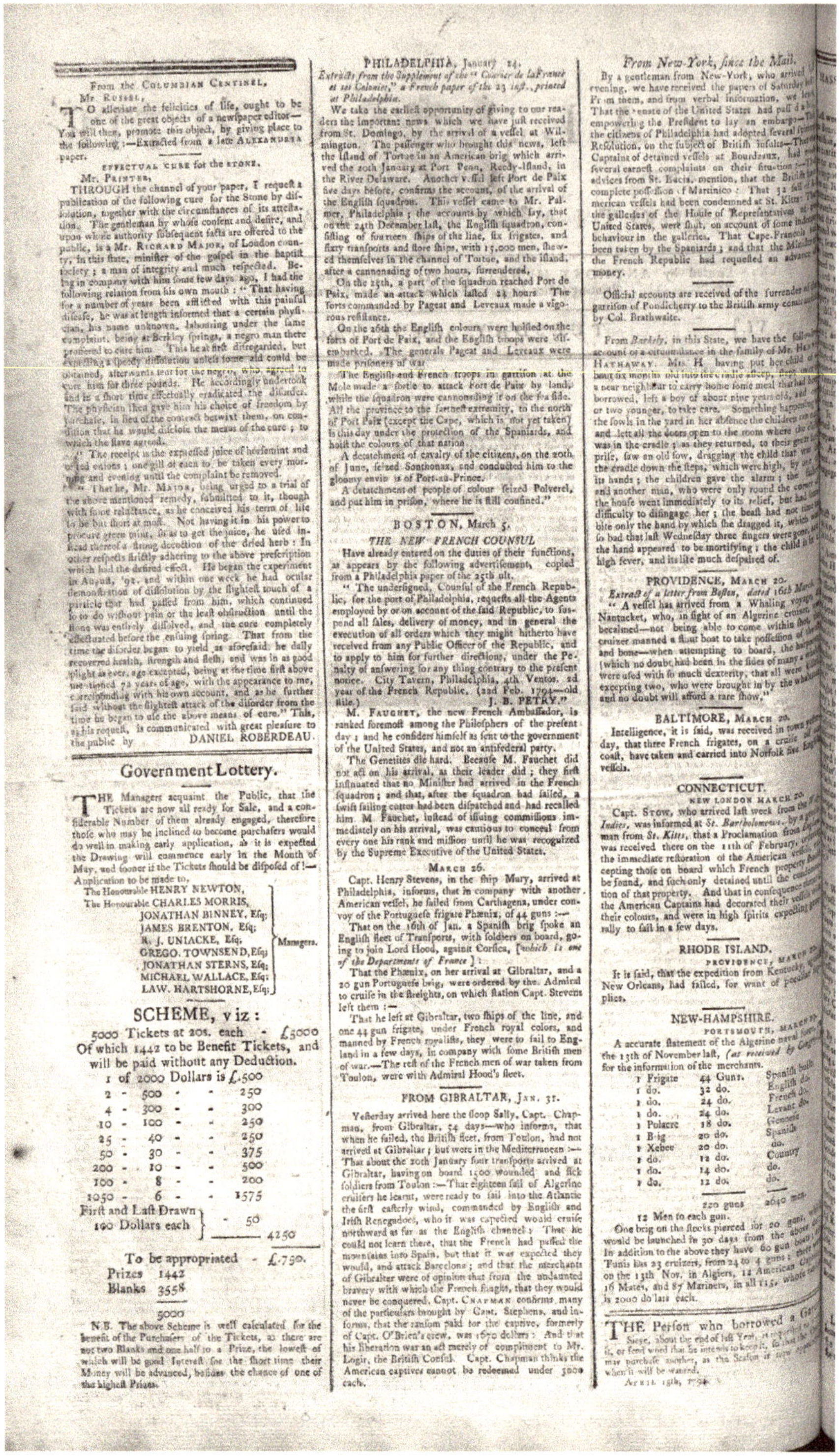

From the COLUMBIAN CENTINEL,

Mr. RUSSEL,

TO alleviate the felicities of life, ought to be one of the great objects of a newspaper editor— You will then, promote this object, by giving place to the following :—Extracted from a late ALEXANDRIA paper.

EFFECTUAL CURE for the STONE.

Mr. PRINTER,

THROUGH the channel of your paper, I request a publication of the following cure for the Stone by dissolution, together with the circumstances of its attestation. The gentleman by whose consent and desire, and upon whose authority subsequent facts are offered to the public, is a Mr. RICHARD MAJOR, of Loudon county, in this state, minister of the gospel in the baptist society ; a man of integrity and much respected. Being in company with him some few days ago, I had the following relation from his own mouth : "That having for a number of years been afflicted with this painful disease, he was at length informed that a certain physician, his name unknown, labouring under the same complaint, being at Berkley springs, a negro man there proffered to cure him. This he at first disregarded, but expecting a speedy dissolution unless some aid could be obtained, afterwards sent for the negro, who agreed to cure him for three pounds. He accordingly undertook and in a short time effectually eradicated the disorder. The physician then gave him his choice of freedom by purchase, in lieu of the contract betwixt them, on condition that he would disclose the means of the cure ; to which the slave agreed.

"The receipt is the expressed juice of horsemint and [illegible] onions ; one gill of each to be taken every morning and evening until the complaint be removed.

"That he, Mr. MAJOR, being urged to a trial of the above mentioned remedy, submitted to it, though with some reluctance, as he conceived his term of life to be but short at most. Not having it in his power to procure green mint, so as to get the juice, he used instead thereof a strong decoction of the dried herb : In other respects strictly adhering to the above prescription which had the desired effect. He began the experiment in August, '92, and within one week he had ocular demonstration of dissolution by the slightest touch of a particle that had passed from him, which continued so to do without pain or the least obstruction until the stone was entirely dissolved, and the cure completely effectuated before the ensuing spring. That from the time the disorder began to yield as aforesaid he daily recovered health, strength and flesh, and was in as good plight as ever, age excepted, being at the time first above mentioned 72 years of age, with the appearance to me, corresponding with his own account, and as he further said without the slightest attack of the disorder from the time he began to use the above means of cure." This, at his request, is communicated with great pleasure to the public by DANIEL ROBERDEAU.

Government Lottery.

THE Managers acquaint the Public, that the Tickets are now all ready for Sale, and a considerable Number of them already engaged, therefore those who may be inclined to become purchasers would do well in making early application, as it is expected the Drawing will commence early in the Month of May, and sooner if the Tickets should be disposed of !— Application to be made to,

The Honourable HENRY NEWTON,
The Honourable CHARLES MORRIS,
JONATHAN BINNEY, Esq;
JAMES BRENTON, Esq;
R. J. UNIACKE, Esq;
GREGO. TOWNSEND, Esq;
JONATHAN STERNS, Esq;
MICHAEL WALLACE, Esq;
LAW. HARTSHORNE, Esq; } Managers.

SCHEME, viz :

5000 Tickets at 20s. each - £5000
Of which 1442 to be Benefit Tickets, and will be paid without any Deduction.

1	of 2000 Dollars is	£.500	
2	500	250	
4	300	300	
10	100	250	
25	40	250	
50	30	375	
200	10	500	
100	8	200	
1050	6	1575	
First and Last Drawn 100 Dollars each		50	
			4250

To be appropriated - £.750.
Prizes 1442
Blanks 3558

5000

N.B. The above Scheme is well calculated for the benefit of the Purchasers of the Tickets, as there are not two Blanks and one half to a Prize, the lowest of which will be good Interest for the short time their Money will be advanced, besides the chance of one of the highest Prizes.

PHILADELPHIA, January 24.

Extracts from the Supplement of the "Courier de la France et ses Colonies," a French paper of the 23 inst., printed at Philadelphia.

We take the earliest opportunity of giving to our readers the important news which we have just received from St. Domingo, by the arrival of a vessel at Wilmington. The passenger who brought this news, left the Island of Tortue in an American brig which arrived the 20th January at Port Penn, Reedy-Island, in the River Delaware. Another vessel left Port de Paix five days before, confirms the account, of the arrival of the English squadron. This vessel came to Mr. Palmer, Philadelphia ; the accounts by which say, that on the 24th December last, the English squadron, consisting of fourteen ships of the line, six frigates, and sixty transports and store ships, with 15,000 men, shewed themselves in the channel of Tortue, and the island, after a cannonading of two hours, surrendered.

On the 25th, a part of the squadron reached Port de Paix, made an attack which lasted 24 hours. The forts commanded by Pageat and Leveaux made a vigorous resistance.

On the 26th the English colours were hoisted on the forts of Port de Paix, and the English troops were disembarked. The generals Pageat and Leveaux were made prisoners of war.

The English and French troops in garrison at the Mole made a sortie to attack Port de Paix by land, while the squadron were cannonading it on the sea side. All the province to the farthest extremity, to the north of Port Paix (except the Cape, which is not yet taken) is this day under the protection of the Spaniards, and hoist the colours of that nation.

A detatchment of cavalry of the citizens, on the 20th of June, seized Sonthonax, and conducted him to the gloomy envir[illegible] of Port-au-Prince.

A detatchment of people of colour seized Polverel, and put him in prison, where he is still confined."

BOSTON, March 5.

THE NEW FRENCH COUNSUL

Have already entered on the duties of their functions, as appears by the following advertisement, copied from a Philadelphia paper of the 25th ult.

"The undersigned, Counsul of the French Republic, for the port of Philadelphia, requests all the Agents employed by or on account of the said Republic, to suspend all sales, delivery of money, and in general the execution of all orders which they might hitherto have received from any Public Officer of the Republic, and to apply to him for further directions, under the Penalty of answering for any thing contrary to the present notice. City Tavern, Philadelphia, 4th Ventos. 2d year of the French Republic. (22d Feb. 1794—old stile.) J. B. PETRY."

M. FAUCHET, the new French Ambassador, is ranked foremost among the Philosphers of the present day ; and he considers himself as sent to the government of the United States, and not an antifederal party.

The Genetites die hard. Because M. Fauchet did not act on his arrival, as their leader did ; they first insinuated that no Minister had arrived in the French squadron ; and that, after the squadron had failed, a swift sailing cutter had been dispatched and had recalled him. M. Fauchet, instead of issuing commissions immediately on his arrival, was cautious to conceal from every one his rank and mission until he was recognized by the Supreme Executive of the United States.

MARCH 26.

Capt. Henry Stevens, in the ship Mary, arrived at Philadelphia, informs, that in company with another American vessel, he sailed from Carthagena, under convoy of the Portuguese frigate Phœnix, of 44 guns :—

That on the 16th of Jan. a Spanish brig spoke an English fleet of Transports, with soldiers on board, going to join Lord Hood, against Corsica, [*which is one of the Departments of France*] :

That the Phœnix, on her arrival at Gibraltar, and a 20 gun Portuguese brig, were ordered by the Admiral to cruise in the streights, on which station Capt. Stevens left them :—

That he left at Gibraltar, two ships of the line, and one 44 gun frigate, under French royal colors, and manned by French royalists, they were to sail to England in a few days, in company with some British men of war.—The rest of the French men of war taken from Toulon, were with Admiral Hood's fleet.

FROM GIBRALTAR, JAN. 31.

Yesterday arrived here the sloop Sally, Capt. Chapman, from Gibraltar, 54 days—who informs, that when he sailed, the British fleet, from Toulon, had not arrived at Gibraltar ; but were in the Mediterranean :— That about the 20th January four transports arrived at Gibraltar, having on board 1500 wounded and sick soldiers from Toulon :—That eighteen sail of Algerine cruisers he learnt, were ready to sail into the Atlantic the first easterly wind, commanded by English and Irish Renegadoes, who it was expected would cruise northward as far as the English channel : That he could not learn there, that the French had passed the mountains into Spain, but that it was expected they would, and attack Barcelona ; and that the merchants of Gibralter were of opinion that from the undaunted bravery with which the French fought, that they would never be conquered. Capt. CHAPMAN confirms many of the particulars brought by Capt. Stephens, and informs, that the ransom paid for the captive, formerly of Capt. O'Brien's crew, was 1670 dollars : And that his liberation was an act merely of compliment to Mr. Logir, the British Consul. Capt. Chapman thinks the American captives cannot be redeemed under 3000 each.

From New-York, since the Mail.

By a gentleman from New-York, who arrived [illegible] evening, we have received the papers of Saturday [illegible] From them, and from verbal information, we lea[rn] That the Senate of the United States had pass'd a [bill] empowering the President to lay an embargo—Th[at] the citizens of Philadelphia had adopted several [illegible] Resolution, on the subject of British insults—Th[at] Captains of detained vessels at Bourdeaux, had [illegible] several earnest complaints on their situation [illegible] advices from St. Eustatia mention, that the Britis[h] complete possession of Martinico : That 32 sail of [Ame-]rican vessels had been condemned at St. Kitts : Th[at] the galleries of the House of Representatives of [the] United States, were shut, on account of some inde[cent] behaviour in the galleries. That Cape-Francois [had] been taken by the Spaniards ; and that the Minist[er of] the French Republic had requested an advance [of] money.

Official accounts are received of the surrender of [the] garrison of Pondicherry to the British army comma[nded] by Col. Brathwaite.

From *Barkely*, in this State, we have the foll[owing] account of a circumstance in the family of Mr. H[illegible] HATHAWAY. Mrs. H. having put her child of [illegible] bout six months old into the cradle asleep, [illegible] a near neighbour to carry home some meal that had [been] borrowed, left a boy of about nine years old, and [one] or two younger, to take care. Something happen[ing to] the fowls in the yard in her absence the children [went out] and left all the doors open to the room where the c[hild] was in the cradle ; as they returned, to their great [sur]prise, saw an old sow, dragging the child that wa[s in] the cradle down the steps, which were high, by on[e of] its hands ; the children gave the alarm ; the [illegible] and another man, who were only round the corne[r of] the house went immediately to its relief, but had no[t time] difficulty to disingage her ; the beast had not tim[e to] bite only the hand by which she dragged it, whic[h was] so bad that last Wednesday three fingers were gone, [and] the hand appeared to be mortifying ; the child is [in a] high fever, and its life much despaired of.

PROVIDENCE, MARCH 20.

Extract of a letter from Boston, dated 16th March.

"A vessel has arrived from a Whaling voyage [at] Nantucket, who, in sight of an Algerine cruiser, [was] becalmed—not being able to come within [illegible] cruiser manned a flunt boat to take possession of [her] and bone—when attempting to board, the har[poons] (which no doubt had been in the sides of many a [whale]) were used with so much dexterity, that all were [killed] excepting two, who were brought in by the wha[lers] and no doubt will afford a rare show."

BALTIMORE, MARCH 20.

Intelligence, it is said, was received in town yes[ter]day, that three French frigates, on a cruise o[ff our] coast, have taken and carried into Norfolk five Eng[lish] vessels.

CONNECTICUT.

NEW LONDON MARCH 20.

Capt. STOW, who arrived last week from the W[est] *Indies*, was informed at *St. Bartholomews*, by a g[entle]man from *St. Kitts*, that a Proclamation from [illegible] was received there on the 11th of February, [for] the immediate restoration of the American vessels, [ex]cepting those on board which French property [should] be found, and such only detained until the con[demna]tion of that property. And that in consequence [of this] the American Captains had decorated their vessels [with] their colours, and were in high spirits expecting [to be] ready to sail in a few days.

RHODE ISLAND.

PROVIDENCE, MARCH 20.

It is said, that the expedition from Kentucky, [against] New Orleans, had failed, for want of pecun[iary sup]plies.

NEW-HAMPSHIRE.

PORTSMOUTH, MARCH [illegible]

A accurate statement of the Algerine naval force [on] the 13th of November last, (*as received by Cap[tain]* [illegible]) for the information of the merchants.

1	Frigate	44 Guns.	Spanish built
1	do.	32 do.	English do.
1	do.	24 do.	French do.
1	do.	24 do.	Levant do.
1	Polacre	18 do.	Genoese
1	Brig	20 do.	Spanish
1	Xebec	20 do.	do.
1	do.	12 do.	Country
1	do.	14 do.	do.
1	do.	12 do.	do.
		220 guns	2640 men

12 Men to each gun.

One brig on the stocks pierced for 20 guns, [which] would be launched in 30 days from the above [date]. In addition to the above they have 60 gun boats [illegible] Tunis has 23 cruizers, from 24 to 4 guns ; The [illegible] on the 13th Nov. in Algiers, 12 American Cap[tains] 16 Mates, and 87 Mariners, in all 115, whole [illegible] is 2000 dollars each.

THE Person who borrowed a G[illegible] Siege, about the end of last Year, is requested to [illegible] it, or send word that he intends to keep it, so that the [owner] may purchase another, as the Season is now [approaching] when it will be wanted.

APRIL 15th, 1794.

Figure 3.3
Effectual Cure for the Stone, *The Royal Gazette and the Nova Scotia Advertiser*, 15 April 1794.

From the Columbian Centinel

Mr. Russel,[200]

To alleviate the felicities of life, ought to be one of the great objects of a newspaper editor. You will then, promote this object, by giving place to the following, extracted from a late Alexandria paper.[201]

EFFECTUAL CURE for the STONE

Mr. Printer,

Through the channel of your paper, I request a publication of the following cure for the stone by dissolution, together with the circumstances of its attestation. The gentleman by whose consent and desire, and upon whose authority subsequent facts are offered to the public, is a Mr. Richard Major, of Loudon County,[202] in this state, minister of the gospel in the Baptist Society, a man of integrity and much respected. Being in company with him some few days ago, I had the following relation from his own mouth: "That having for a number of years been afflicted with this painful disease, he was at length informed that a certain physician, his name unknown, labouring under the same complaint, being at Berkley Springs,[203] a negro man there proffered to cure him. This he at first disregarded, but expecting a speedy dissolution unless some aid could be obtained, afterwards sent for the negro, who agreed to cure him for three pounds. He accordingly undertook and in a short time effectually eradicated the disorder. The physician then gave him his choice of freedom by purchase, in lieu of the contract betwixt them, on condition that he would disclose the means of the cure; to which the slave agreed.

"The receipt is the expressed juice of horsemint and of red onions; one gill[204] of each to be taken every morning and evening until the complaint be removed.

"That he, Mr. Major, being urged to a trial of the above mentioned remedy, submitted to it, though with some reluctance, as he conceived his term of life to be but short at most. Not having it in his power to procure green mint, so as to get the juice, he used instead thereof a strong decoction of the dried herb. In other respects strictly adhering to the above prescription which had the desired effect. He began the experiment in August, '92, and within one week he had ocular demonstration of dissolution by the slightest touch of a particle that had passed from him, which continued, so to do without pain or the least obstruction until the stone was entirely dissolved, and the cure completely effectuated before the ensuing spring. That from the time the disorder began to yield as aforesaid, he daily recovered health, strength and flesh, and was in as good plight as ever, age excepted, being at the time first above mentioned 72 years of age, with the appearance to me,

> corresponding with his own account, and as he further said without the slightest attack of the disorder from the time he began to use the above means of cure."
> This, at his request, is communicated with great pleasure to the public by
> Daniel Roberdeau[205]

Importantly, this recipe draws attention to how the knowledge of an enslaved man became part of the dominant white scientific culture. The cure's ingredients, horsemint and red onions, are readily available in what is now the eastern United States, though horsemint does not appear to be native to Nova Scotia. Tellingly, the recipe does not name the enslaved man – as it does Daniel Roberdeau (1727–1795) and Richard Major (1722–1796) – so he does not receive credit for his cure in the way that the white men do. In early modern recipes, sources of recipes were often named, working to construct authority for the cure; submitted to the newspaper by Roberdeau – politician, military leader, and member of the Continental Congress before his death in Winchester, Virginia, in 1795 – the recipe uses Roberdeau's status to enhance the recipe's authority. Recounting how the remedy was proved, the recipe further emphasizes the white patients helped by the remedy – the white physician and the minister respectively – but fails to mention any enslaved people the recipe's inventor may have also successfully treated. The social status of the doctor and minister matter, too, in securing the recipe as one worthy to be shared in print.

Nonetheless, the recipe does record that the unnamed enslaved man was able to use the gratitude of his white patients advantageously. When given the choice between earning three pounds for simply curing the physician or earning his freedom in exchange for the recipe itself, the enslaved man was presumably able to use his knowledge to change his legal status – if the promise of freedom was indeed kept. The exchange of a man's life for a recipe offers an extreme illustration of the value of recipe knowledge in the early modern world.

CANCER

In the eighteenth century, *cancer* (or canker) did not necessarily refer to the "malignant neoplastic disease" we think of today, but was more usually used to describe "any of various types of non-healing sore or ulcer" collectively known as ulcerating cancers.[206] In *Domestic Medicine*, Scottish physician William Buchan explains in "Of a Scirrhus and Cancer" that a cancer can be distinguished from the scirrhus, which is a "hard indolent tumour" of the glands, when an "ichorous matter of an abominably foetid smell is discharged from the sore"; the latter, Buchan explains, "is called an open or ulcerated cancer," and he goes on to note that those over "the age of 45, particularly women, and those who lead an indolent sedentary life, are most subject to this disease."[207] In his long entry "On the Cure of Ulcerated Legs," Halifax physician William James Almon includes "the cancerous ulcer" among the eight kinds of ulcers afflicting the lower limbs. As well as identifying some leg ulcers as cancerous, Almon recorded two plant-based recipes for treating ulcerating cancers, one based on dock root and the other on red oak, a tree indigenous to North America that was used for a variety of medicinal purposes.[208] Fellow Loyalist physician William Paine also recorded a plant-based cancer treatment, made in this case from a decoction of *Phytolacca americana*, the native plant commonly known as poke or pokeweed. In contrast, the ulcerating cancer treatment published in *The Nova Scotia Calender* relies on mercury chloride, a chemical compound. Taken together, the herbal and chemical cancer remedies can thus be seen to replicate some of the tensions and contradictions of the eighteenth-century medical milieu, where chemical and Galenic physicians both competed and corroborated.

Cure for Cancer

One of Dr William James Almon's cancer treatments is credited to the August 1793 edition of the *Boston Magazine*.[209] The recipe had also been published in Connecticut's *Windham Herald* on 6 July 1793, where it appeared verbatim, save an additional attribution to the "Nat. Gaz.,"[210] presumably the semi-weekly *National Gazette* published in Philadelphia from October 1791 to October 1793.[211] The remedy also appears with no references to other magazines in *The Columbian Almanac*, also published in Philadelphia in 1793.[212] The circulation of this recipe in 1793 appears to have been rooted in a very similar one that had appeared a few years earlier in a number of Philadelphia papers, including *The Independent Gazetteer* on 18 August 1787 and the *Pennsylvania Packet* on 21 August 1787 as the recipe of one William Leigh; this recipe was also published in *The Boston Gazette* on 3 September 1787. All of these examples cite *The Maryland Gazette* of August 1787 as their source.[213]

Cancer cure of from the Boston Magazine for August 1793.

> Take a bushel of red oak bark and burn it to ashes: take the ashes and boil them in three Gallons of water, until the water is reduced to a gallon: then strain it and boil it again until it is reduced to a thick substance similar to butter milk or cream: then spread plaister of it on [silk or lint], and renew the plaister once in two hours, until the roots of the cancer are well cured. It will sometimes take four and sometimes six plaisters, but do not be discouraged if it should take twelve.

A topical remedy for ulcerous cancers, this heavily reduced decoction of red oak bark ashes is to be boiled down to the thickness of "butter milk or cream" and applied to plasters between four and twelve times until "the roots of the cancer are well cured." Given that red oak is native to eastern North America, this is one of the few early modern recipes from what is now the Maritimes that appear to be of exclusively colonial origin. Named the provincial tree of Prince Edward Island in 1905, the red oak ranges from Nova Scotia to Ontario and grows in the eastern seaboard states as far south as Georgia. "Some Account of the Present State of Nova Scotia," published in England in *The Weekly Entertainer* in 1786, describes the area around Shelburne, Nova Scotia, as "clothed with fine woods, consisting of birch, maple, spruce, pine, and red oak" – woods the Loyalists cut down to make timber.[214] Though Almon copied a popular and frequently reprinted recipe, red oak was not a frequent ingredient in English medicines. Physician James Stuart (1746–1813), "a native of Virginia," specifies red oak bark in combination with rose leaves, alum, and honey to make a gargle for treating swollen salivary glands.[215] Earlier in the seventeenth century, one of the few references to red oak in English recipes appears in a collection created by Salvator Winter, whose book describes him as originating from Naples and his recipes the product of his travels through Europe, Asia, and Africa; one recipe in Winter's collection uses red oak in a cure for sore throat.[216] It is possible that Europeans learned about medicinal uses of the red oak tree from Indigenous peoples, but we have not found a clear reference to such a knowledge exchange relating to red oak and cancer. An anthropologist writing at the beginning of the twentieth century reports that the Wolastoqiyik and Mi'kmaq at that time used red oak bark steeped with "the buds or young cones of a fir tree" as a treatment for diarrhea, similar to the Rappanhannocks, a tribe in Virginia, and the Houmas, from what is now Louisiana, who used it in the treatment of dysentery.[217] The Cherokee used red oak "with other tree barks as a wash for sores and itching skin."[218]

Rob Phytolae

Like the remedy above, this recipe from the 1769 notebook of New Brunswick physician William Paine uses a native North American plant, in this case, pokeweed or poke.[219] The date of the entry suggests that it was recorded during Paine's time studying medicine with Dr Edward Augustus Holyoke of Salem, Massachusetts.[220] We have not found a printed source for this recipe.

Rob[221] Phytolae,[222]
Take y^e Leaves, tender Branches
and the Berries ripe and unripe
bruise them in a Marble Mortar
to a Magma, strain and press
out very strongly all Juices
thro, a course Cloath, pour the
expressd Juice into a broad shal-
=low broad Dish, to the Depth
of half an Inch, let it stand
in the Sun, till the Moisture
is evaporated, and the Mass
reduced to a Rob or Extract.
This Rob has been credibly
reported, to have cured Cancers
by applying it to the Part
It gives great Pain upon y^e
Application

The technique, which calls on the user to create juice and then allow it to evaporate, was recorded in an 1800 diary entry by Hester Lynch Thrale (1741–1821), where she explains that "The Juice squeez'd & set in a Pewter dish in ye Sun till thick, cures Cancers." Thrale notes, too, that "Phytolacca or Pokeweed is a domestic Plant in Virginia and New York," and it "grows in all their Plantations."[223] Though her father, John Salusbury (1707–1762), had in 1749 "set out to repair the family fortunes as part of Lord Halifax's expedition to Nova Scotia,"[224] her comment suggests that knowledge of the plant's medicinal benefits migrated to but did not originate in England (and the plant itself migrated to Africa and Europe in the seventeenth century).[225] Though the remedy's origins go unmentioned here, it seems almost certain that colonial settlers learned how to use the plant from Indigenous peoples, including its recommended use in treating the skin disorders known as cancer.[226]

At the University of Pennsylvania between 1790 and 1810, several settler physicians wrote dissertations on Indigenous medicines, including one Benjamin Shultz, of Pennsylvania, who studied poke.[227] Shultz's thesis plainly exposes the racist, colonial power dynamics of the knowledge exchange around the plant. He explains the need for his work through the argument that America has many native plants that might "be brought to a state of culture and perfection," a framing that takes plants from the realm of nature to culture through his study of them (as if the Indigenous people he goes on to reference did not themselves have culture and study); even more explicitly, he explains that his goal is to "bring to public view an important object, hitherto unexamined except by savages."[228] Yet even as he discounts Indigenous knowledge with racist epithets, when he goes on to do experiments with poke, he uses that knowledge, but without citing where he gleaned it, for the most part. He does, however, take the opportunity to cite English and American physicians by name at every turn while highlighting only the supposed inferiority and otherness of Indigenous peoples.[229] When he records that the Cherokee use poke to treat "venereal chancres [ulcers]," he claims the plant is not effective because many of them suffer from the disease – an act of othering that pretends Europeans did not also suffer the same, allows successful use only by the settlers, and discounts the full range of uses by the Cherokee and others.[230] Similarly, Shultz recounts the use of poke leaf in curing a cancerous sore by an unnamed Black man, but names only the settler observer and reporter, Dr Wistar.[231] One of the primary conclusions of his work is that poke is very successful in treating cancer, although he does not point to Paine's particular technique.[232] It's not clear who Paine's credible reporters are, but his use of the Latin name for the plant appropriates it and its purported benefits into European systems of knowledge.

Method of Curing Cancers

Another cancer remedy, this recipe was published in *The Nova Scotia Calender, or an Almanack* of 1789.[233] The recipe was in 1788 quoted in the English publication *The Monthly Review*, where it is attributed to Dr [Benjamin] Moseley (1742–1819)'s *Treatise on Tropical Diseases*, published in London the previous year.[234] Untitled in *The Nova Scotia Calender*, the item would later appear in *The Edinburgh Practice of Physic, Surgery, and Midwifery* in a section titled "Cancer of the Breast."[235] In North America, the remedy earned further mention in an 1828 guide to veterinary and domestic medicine, *The New England Farrier, and Family Physician*, where it appears in a condensed version that does not include full instructions but does acknowledge that "Dr. Mosely [*sic*] says, the above method is infallible."[236] The version of Moseley's remedy published in *The Nova Scotia Calender* differs from that found in the first edition of Moseley's book, which specifies that "no other preparation is necessary, in habits otherwise healthy."[237] Moseley later amended the third edition to what was published in *The Nova Scotia Calender* to read instead that "[n]o other preparation is necessary, unless the patient is gross, and requires a cooling regimen."[238]

> The following method of curing cancers, is said to be infalliable,
> "Spread a plaister of diachylon[239] with gum, upon thin leather, the size of the cancer: suppose the plaister to be as large as a crown piece, or a Spanish dollar, sprinkle on it a scruple of corrosive sublimate of mercury, finely powdered; and so in proportion to a larger or smaller plaister. This plaister must be applied to the cancer, and remain on it forty-eight hours; but if there is any apprehension that it has not done its office in that time, it must remain longer. Then, take it off and apply a poultice of bread and milk with a little olive oil, which must be renewed frequently, until the cancer comes entirely out, by the roots as it were. The part is then to be dressed, digested, and cured as a common ulcer. A purge or two with calomel[240] must precede the application. No other preparation is necessary, unless the patient is gross, and requires a cooling regimen. Bark is sometimes necessary to forward the digestion and cure."

Unlike those recorded by fellow physicians Almon and Paine, Moseley's treatment is not entirely plant based; rather, his treatment calls for the use of a diachylon plaster, an adhesive bandage made from oil and a variety of plants, to be sprinkled with "a scruple of corrosive sublimate of mercury" and applied to the ulcerating cancer. Also known as calomel and mercury chloride, the mercury compound was used relatively sparingly throughout the eighteenth century, when it was applied topically to treat skin disorders and taken internally for syphilis. Now recognized "to be highly toxic and invariably fatal in sufficient doses," especially when it is the specified "corrosive" kind, mercury sublimate would later be used in treatments for ailments ranging from constipation to teething pain.[241] The harshness of the treatment is evident in the need to follow it with a soothing poultice made from the ordinary kitchen ingredients of bread, milk, and olive oil.

Though the instructions end by noting that "[b]ark is sometimes necessary to forward the digestion and cure," the author does not specify what kind of bark in a comment that seems more of an afterthought than integral to the remedy.

MISCELLANEOUS

Method of Treatment for Death by Drowning

The following method to recover a drowned person was printed in *The Nova Scotia Gazette and the Weekly Chronicle* on 7 March 1786.[242] This paper was printed in Halifax by Anthony Henry between 1770 and 1789 and was Henry's third Halifax newspaper.[243] The text that appears in the Nova Scotia newspaper is excerpted from publications by the Royal Humane Society, specifically *Plans and Reports of the Society Instituted at London in the Year MDCCLXXIV for the Recovery of Persons Apparently Drowned* (1775) and *Reports of the Humane Society Instituted for the Year 1774* (1777).[244] The entries are not identical, however: the accounts published in England include a fourth method – giving the drowned person a spoonful of water or warm wine or brandy when signs of life return – that is not reprinted in the Nova Scotia newspaper.

First called the Society for the Recovery of Persons Apparently Drowned, the Royal Humane Society was organized in 1774 and active until 1808 in London. It received royal patronage in 1787. Its aim was to promote the study of techniques to aid people in recovering from accidents, with a particular interest in whether people who looked dead could be restored to life.[245] Named in the recipe, William Hawes (1736–1808) was one of the group's founders, and he served after 1777 as its secretary.[246] James Horsfield [Horsfall], the other contact named in the text, was a fellow of the Royal Society and the Humane Society's treasurer.[247] The Massachusetts Humane Society, founded in 1786, also focused on the recovery of drowned persons and published its recommendations for treatments in American newspapers.[248]

Methods of Treatment to be used for the Recovery of Persons apparently dead by drowning.

I. IN removing the body to a convenient place, great
care should be taken that it be not bruised, nor shaken
violently, nor roughly handled, nor carried over any

one's shoulders with the head hanging downwards, nor rolled upon the ground, or over a barrel, nor lifted up by the heels; for experience proves that all these methods are injurious, and often destroys the remains of life. The unfortunate object should be cautiously conveyed in the arms of two or more persons, or in a carriage upon straw, laying as on a bed, with the head a little raised, and kept in as natural and easy a position as possible.

II. The body being well dried with a cloth, should be placed in a bed, or blanket, properly warmed, but not too near a large fire; bottles of hot water should be laid to the bottoms of the feet, in the joints of the knees, and under the arm pits, and a warming pan moderately heated, or hot bricks wrapped in cloths, should be rubbed over the body, and particularly along the back. The natural and kindly warmth of a healthy person laying by the side of the body, particularly by that of a child, has been found in many cases very efficacious. The windows or doors of a room should be left open, and no more people admitted into it than is absolutely necessary, as the life of the person greatly depends upon his having the benefit of a pure air. The shirt or cloaths of an attendant, or the skin of a sheep fresh killed, may also be used with advantage. Should these accidents happen in the neighbourhood of a warm bath, brew-house, bake-house, glass-house, soap manufactory, or any fabrick were warm lees ashes, embers, grains, sand, water, &c. can be easily procured, it would be very proper to place the body in any of these, moderated to a degree of heat, but very little exceeding that of a healthy person.

III. The body being placed in one or other of these advantageous circumstances as speedily as possible, various stimulating means should next be employed; the most edficacious one, blowing with force into the lungs, by applying the mouth to that of the patient, closing at the same time his nostrils with one hand, and gentle the air again, by pressing the chest with the other, imitating the strong breathing of a healthy person; the medium of a handkerchief or cloth may be used to render the operation less indelicate; – throwing the smoke of tobacco up the fundament[249] into the bowels, by means of a pipe or fumigator, such as are used in administering clysters;[250] a pair of bellows may be employed while the other can be procured; – rubbing the belly, chest, back and arms, with a coarse cloth, or dry salt, so as not to rub off the skin, or with a flannel dipt in brandy, rum, or gin; – applying spirits of harthorne,[251] volatile salts, or any other stimulating substance, to the nostrils, and rubbing them upon the temples very frequently; – tickling the throat with a feather, so as to excite a propensity to vomit, and the nostrils also with a feather snuff, or any other stimulant so as to provoke sneezing: the body should at intervals be shaken also, and varied in its position.

One or other of these methods should be preserved in until the patient be restored.
We have been as circumstantial as possible in the aforesaid directions, that if one conveniency should be wanting, the attendants may not be at a loss for others.
Where the patient has lain but a short time senseless, blowing into the lungs and bowels has been in some cases found sufficient: yet a speedy recovery is not to be expected in general. The above methods are therefore to be continued with spirit for two hours or upwards, although there be not the least symptoms of returning life: the vulgar notion that people will recover in a few minutes or not at all, and the ignorant foolish rediculing of those who are willing to preservere, as if they were attempting impossibilities, have most certainly caused the deaths of many, who might otherwise have been saved.
Most of the above means are happily of such a nature, that they may be begun immediately, and that by persons who are not acquainted with the medical art; yet it is

> always adviseable to seek the assistance of some regular practitioners as soon as possible, as it is presumed that such a one will be more skillful and expert, and better able to vary the methods of procedure, as circumstances may require.
>
> The Society[252] think it proper to observe, that most of the above means of restoration are applicable to various other cases of apparent deaths, whether from hanging, apoplectic[253] and convulsive fits, cold suffocation by damps or noxious vapour proceeding from coal mines, the confined air of wells, cisterns, caves or the must of summoning liquors.
>
> Whenever any good has been produced by the means recommended, the person who has superintended the cure, is desired to write a circumstantial account of it to *James Horsefield*, Esquire, Treasurer, Middle Temple, or *Mr. Wm. Haws*, Secretary to the Society, Pelsgrave Place, Strand.
>
> The Society pay the rewards within the limits of their institution, in the following manner;
>
> Four guineas whenever life has been restored.
>
> Two guineas in every unsuccessful attempt, provided the mode of treatment prescribed by the Society has been used two hours.
>
> One guinea to publicans, &c. who receive the bodies readily into their house.

The Royal Humane Society arose in part because drowning was the most prevalent form of sudden violent death in London that, according to one study, accounted for over 42 per cent of such deaths.[254] Though early modern people depended on fire and water for life and commerce, those elements could also be dangerously life-threatening, and being able to recover those who had drowned was a socially important form of medical knowledge. In Nova Scotia, Handley Chipman's notes include the story "Of restoring a drowned person" that recounts how in 1765 a three-year-old child fell into the water and was found without breath or heartbeat but was restored by being laid on a bed of ashes and rubbed with hot cloths.[255] In his *Enquiry into the Causes of Suspended Animation from Drowning, with the Means of Restoring Life* (1792), David Hosack (1769–1835) points to "the late improvements for the recovery of the drowned" as evidence of the "happy" progress that has been made in recent medical research, an approach that positions recipes like this one as a mark of modernity.[256]

While some of these methods, such as warming the body and blowing air into the lungs, seem familiar to today's readers, that is likely not the case with the remedy's recommendation to "throw [...] the smoke of tobacco up the fundament into the bowels." The application of medicines through the anus was a familiar enough practice within early modern medicine. Clysters – or medicines injected into the rectum – had been used for a long time, and from the seventeenth century onward the treatment could include the insertion of tobacco smoke. For example, one seventeenth-century medical treatise on the virtues of tobacco and coffee indicates that "to let in the smoke of Tobacco at the fundament ... hath done much good."[257] Similarly, William Salmon's popular family medicine dictionary recounts among tobacco's many medical virtues how "A Pipe lighted, and the Smoak forced up the Fundament, eases the Colick, or Pains of the Belly; it also cures the Fits of the Mother, and Faintings."[258] The earliest reference to using this technique to revive a drowned person that we have found in print is seen in a 1745 edition of an essay by Richard Mead (1673–1754) that prescribes drowning as a cure for the biting of a mad dog, and then subsequently cures the drowning by blowing the "smoak of Tobacco into the intestins" before the body is warmed by rubbing with warm cloths.[259] However, an 1805 study of the effects of tobacco smoke on the drowned notes that the method was used by the Humane Society of Amsterdam in 1667.[260] According to a reporter detailing the technique in 1766, the method works by "irritating" the intestines and "exciting the muscles subservient to respiration to renew their action."[261]

Tobacco, of course, entered European culture through contact with Indigenous peoples in the Americas, and it is possible that the idea to use tobacco to cure drowning also came from this contact. The French surgeon Sieur de Dièreville's *Relation of the Voyage to Port Royal in Acadia or New France* (1708) includes among its medical observations the Mi'kmaw use of balsam fir turpentine, moss, and birch bark to set broken bones effectively within a longer narrative describing how they "cure themselves of death itself." Insultingly, de Dièreville goes on to describe the Mi'kmaq as "wretched People [...] very liable to be drowned" because of their reliance on canoes for transportation – as if Europeans were not themselves also frequent victims of drowning, and as if the Mi'kmaq were not skilled in navigating the waters that comprised their extensive transportation and exchange networks.[262] Moreover, even as he denigrates their paddling abilities, de Dièreville goes on to report on how the Mi'kmaq were able to help a drowned person, providing a level of detail that seems aimed at allowing the practice to be replicated in Europe:

> They then fill with Tobacco smoke the bladder of some animal, or a long section of large bowel, commonly used as receptacles for the preservation of their Fish & Seal oil, & having tied one end securely, they fasten a piece of Pipe or Calumet into the other, to serve as an injection Tube; this is introduced into the backside of the Men who have been drowned, &, by compressing it with their hands, they force into them the smoke contained in the bowel; they are afterwards tied by the feet to the nearest tree which can be found, & kept under observation; almost always follows the satisfaction of seeing that the smoke Douche forces them to disgorge all the water they had swallowed. Life is restored to their bodies, and before long this astonishing & beneficent result is made manifest by the twitching movements of the suspended Men. Don't forget this blessed restorative, attested by a thousand experiences; its virtue, in time of need, would be no less effective among your friends, than among the Indians.[263]

Here de Dièreville appropriates Indigenous knowledge he deems valuable and disseminates it with the expectation that Europeans will find it useful; he thus positions Mi'kmaw and Wolastoqey medical knowledge as collected to serve his own interests. Describing a remedy he was not given the opportunity to learn about, he laments that "I should have brought back from Acadia a remedy, which in France would have been profitable to me, as it would have been advantageous to the Public."[264] *History of New France* (published in French in 1744) by the Jesuit priest Pierre-François-Xavier de Charlevoix (1692–1761) also reports on what he calls a curious way (or *assez singular*) of restoring the drowned among the Mi'kmaq, describing filling a bladder with tobacco smoke, attaching a reed to one end, inserting the reed into the anus, and forcing the smoke into the body by pressing the bladder. The Mi'kmaq, he says, then hang the drowning victim by the feet, upon which the smoke in his belly forces the patient to discharge all the water he had swallowed from his mouth.[265] Although this method was taken up by leading scientists on both sides of the Atlantic, and even used as an example of medical progress, the instructions never credit any Indigenous people for the technique when it is shared across Europe as a cure for drowning. The method still had traction in 1805 amongst settlers when medical student Daniel Legare at the University of Pennsylvania performed his experiments, starting first by injecting smoke "per anum" into himself to observe the effects and then by cutting up and drowning many dogs, trying to revive them with smoke, and observing the effects. Although he could never revive a dog he had drowned, he concludes that this is so not because the smoke is a sedative, as others had claimed, but because it is too stimulating.[266]

A Receipt for Deafness

Appearing in a transcript made of the Gagetown, New Brunswick, church records for the years 1786–1841, this recipe was recorded just above a baptismal record for "St. John," that is, St John's Anglican Church, for 5 March 1788, of "Bettee Negro Wench. / Sarah ye Dar. of – Mary Feney / Charles – ye son of Bettee."[267] These details do not appear to have any particular relationship to the described treatment, but this record illustrates the wide range of places in which people recorded recipes. Including a recipe alongside baptismal records signifies its importance, suggesting that it may need to be recorded and remembered as crucially as baptism. Because deafness was often given religious connotations by Protestants, it may be less surprising that a recipe for treating the ailment was copied into church records. It was thought that it was through hearing the word of God that one came to faith, and the early modern Anglican church thus emphasized the importance of hearing as a means of understanding God; hence deafness often served as a metaphor for faithlessness that needed to be cured.[268] Despite its religious context, however, this recipe takes a medical approach and, unlike many of the recipes included here, we have not discovered any other sources for this remedy.

A Receipt for deafness

Slice black Radishes on a puter[269] Plate
sprinkle fine salt on them from the
liquid it affords wet a wadd of cotten
wool & put it in ye Ear.

The eighteenth century marked a period of change in the history of deafness. Before the eighteenth century, deafness was not a "social category of disability," and there were no schools for the deaf and little discourse about deafness (exceptionally, John Bulwer [1606–1656], a member of the Royal Society in London, wrote about sign language in 1644 and Daniel Defoe [1660?–1731] devised the novel *Duncan Campbell* [1720] featuring a deaf character as its hero). By the end of the eighteenth century, however, schools for the deaf had been established across Europe, thereby instituting the beginning of what we now call "special education."[270]

This recipe does not address the cause or kind of deafness – whether the impaired hearing came from tinnitus or age-related degeneration, as a side effect of measles, mumps, smallpox, or a cold, or from working in a noisy environment – and it does not define whether the deafness was partial, profound, congenital, or late in onset.[271] All forms of deafness are imagined to be treated in one way, and the remedy's methodology – if not the ingredients – is not unlike those found in early modern recipe books. *A Thousand Notable Things* by Thomas Lupton (fl. 1572–1594) – a recipe book published first in 1579 but reprinted into the nineteenth century – includes one recipe that recommends putting the warmed juice of the buds, leaves, bark, or branches of an elder tree into the ear, while another recommends red onion juice "put into the deaf Ear cold, three or four nights when the Party goes to bed."[272]

Other ingredients could also be used with the same method of application. A popular eighteenth-century family recipe book recommends for deafness, dipping "fine clean black Wool in Civet, put into the Ear," keeping it moist in the ear for three weeks to a month.[273] Alongside the red onion and civet remedies, another collection includes "An approved Remedy for present Deafness" that entails applying the breast milk of a woman who has recently had her first male child directly from the nipple into the ear,[274] while instructions for ear care in *Dictionnaire Oeconomique*, a dictionary that offers many medical recipes published in France in 1725 and in England in 1758, also specifies the use of radishes. For "the Noise and Tingling of the Ears," the dictionary instructs the user to "take as many Radishes as you please, the Oil of sweet or bitter Almonds, Coloquintida, and White-wine," indicating that the radishes should be pounded and the resulting liquid mixed with the other ingredients and put into the ears with cotton.[275] All of this suggests that this Gagetown recipe may be an individual adaptation of common methodologies and approved ingredients.

Turlington's Balsam

The following recipe was recorded in Latin, using medical abbreviations, in a notebook belonging to Jonathan Odell (1737–1818).[276] Born in New Jersey, Odell graduated in 1757 with a master's degree from the College of New Jersey, which later became Princeton University. He was a member of the American Philosophical Society, founded in 1743 by Benjamin Franklin, and after 1774, of the newly formed New Jersey Medical Society. He served as a surgeon in the British Army before becoming ordained in the Church of England; he was also a poet, and this is one of several recipes transcribed into the notebook with a recipe for ink, poetry, and other literary notes. From the 1760s onward, Odell was writing and publishing poetry, work that would establish him as an antagonist to the American Revolution. He moved to New Brunswick in 1784, where he would become provincial secretary, a major landowner in Fredericton, and an original member of the board of trustees of the College of New Brunswick that is now the University of New Brunswick. Odell died in Fredericton in 1818.[277]

Turlington's Balsam was a proprietary medicine sold by Robert Turlington, who began marketing his Balsam of Life after declaring bankruptcy in his trade as a weaver in east London. He secured a patent for the medicine, made of twenty-seven ingredients, in 1744 and extended the patent to North America in 1748.[278] As a patent medicine, the medicine's recipe was Turlington's secret, but once the patent expired in 1758, the medicine continued to be marketed, albeit in a variety of formulations, and copycat recipes emerged. An apothecary in Massachusetts, for example, recorded in his daybook three different recipes for Turlington's Balsam between 1796 and 1812.[279] Different recipes for Turlington's Balsam appeared also in print. Later editions, published after 1776 and including editions published in America, of George Buchan's popular *Domestic Medicine* include a recipe for a "Vulnerary Balsam" that, it says, also goes by the name "Turlington's drops"; this remedy specifies three ounces of benzoin, two ounces of balsam of Peru, half an ounce of hepatic aloes, and two pints of rectified spirit of wine.[280] In 1834, the Philadelphia College of Pharmacy published a streamlined list of ingredients for Turlington's Balsam in an apparent attempt to encourage consistency in formulation and an authoritative standard; this shortened list – benzoini, styracis liquid, aloes socatrinae, balsam peruviani, myrrhae, radicis angelicae, balsam tolutani, extract glycyrrhizae, and alcoholis – is similar but not identical to Odell's.[281] A specific source for Odell's recipe has not been found, although his is not unlike other recipes, and its ingredients represent a selection of those included in the balsam patented by Turlington.[282]

Turlington's Balsam

Rx Bals: Tolu:[283] [ounce] iii

Styracis[284] [ounce] ii

Benzoini[285] [ounce] iii

Aloes socotrina,[286]

Myrrhae[287]

Olibani[288]

Rad: Angelica[289] sicc:

Croci Angelic : ^~aa[290] [ounce] fs

Contusa singula infudentur
quinque semanas in [pound] iiii Sp:
Vini imptimi rectificati,[291] & prius
liduum floribus Hypenici imbuti:
Tinctura demum pura decoletur.

Although he did not publish the recipe, Turlington had presented the evidence for the many good effects of "Turlington's Balsam of Life" in a pamphlet published in London in 1744. The pamphlet's title page indicates the medicine was available for sale on Lombard Street for three shillings and six pence per bottle, and the proclaimed benefits, conveyed through a series of testimonies from patients, often with the names of witnesses, include relief from pain, rheumatic disorders, stone, bruises, gout, cuts, cholic, cough, and sinking spirits, among other things.[292] Not sold only in London, Turlington's Balsam continued to be available in North America, including what is now known as the Maritime provinces, until at least the middle of the nineteenth century. *The Port-Roseway Gazetteer and the Shelburne Advertiser*, for example, published an ad in its 27 January 1785 edition that includes Turlington's Balsam among the drugs and medicines available at John Boyd's "medicinal store" located on Water Street in Shelburne.[293] William Smith, proprietor of a store in Market Square in Saint John, advertised Turlington's Balsam in the *New Brunswick Courier* in 1832 as one of the medicines he had received on a ship from London; he did so again in 1834.[294] Turlington developed distinctive bottles for the medicine to prevent counterfeits.[295] Odell's recipe represents one of many attempts to create such a counterfeit of the proprietary remedy.

A Lip Salve

This recipe comes from the notebook of Sarah Creighton Wilkins.[296] Though Wilkins's recipe collection is not confined to those associated with the conventionally feminine – she does reference techniques and recipes used by professional physicians, for instance – she did choose to include a recipe that draws attention to the relationship between health and beauty in the early modern period and beyond. We were not able to find another printed source for this recipe, which might suggest that it is one of Wilkins's own devising or the work of someone in her social network that was copied into her collection. It does, however, use ingredients and methods commonly used in making lip salve recipes. Sarah Harrison's *The House-Keeper's Pocket-Book* (1751) offers a similar recipe "To make Lip

Salve" that calls for half a pound of butter, half an ounce each of virgin's wax, benjamin, "Ackarony-root" (alkanet root), fine sugar and a bunch of white grapes – all melted over a fire, strained, and made into cakes.[297]

A Lip Salve everyone approves

4 oz[s] fresh Beef Marrow
2 [ounces] Virgins wax[298]
½ Alcany Root[299]
½ Storax[300]
½ Gum Benzoin[301]
1 Slic'd Apple
½ once loaf Sugar
6 spoonfuls of Port
4 of any good White wine
Boil until it is a good Coloar
Strain it into small pots
To cool when you take it out dry
the bottoms. Wipe y[r] cups before you put
the salve in.

While published instructions for making such lip salves aim to grant them a medical purpose in treating dry and sore lips, they also have an aesthetic function in making the lips soft and supple and therefore more beautiful. Even more important to women, beauty was often constituted as a sign of good health. *Beeton's Domestic Recipe Book* from 1870 outlines such a connection in the preface to its lip salve recipes, noting that "Good lips are indispensable in the general estimate of female loveliness. The lips should be fine, smooth, soft, and of a ruby tint. Good health alone can impart to the lips their peculiar beauty; and the appearance of the lips, especially of the under lip, is generally considered as a strong index of the state of the health"; when the lips have been chapped by cold, lip salves like the one produced by the recipe provided, can be helpful.[302] That the red dye of alkanet root is very commonly used in recipes for lip salve in eighteenth- and nineteenth-century recipe books suggests just how closely health and beauty are linked (as it does nothing to help chapping but does change the lips' colour).[303] Like the recipe in *Beeton's Domestic Recipe Book*, which measures the end of the boiling stage by the concoction's "good red or pink colour," Mary Kettilby's "good Salve for Sore Lips or Nipples" also highlights the aesthetic in stipulating that the wax and salad oil used in this recipe should be "colour[ed] with Alcany-roots" and boiled until it is "of a fine Red."[304]

Remêdes Contre les Engelures

This recipe (and the next) comes from a small twelve-page book of recipes recorded in French.[305] There is no name attached to the recipes, but the date, 5 July 1755, appears above "Remede contre la difficulte d'uriner," a series of different remedies for difficulties with urination. Consisting of approximately sixteen recipes, this book constitutes the only written French-language recipes we found in our archival research in the Maritime region.[306] There are recipes for toothache, the stone and other urinary tract problems (pissing blood, as well as difficulties urinating), rheumatism and gout, and a cure for the stomach. The booklet also includes "Autre Ptisarme Merveilleuse Contre toutes sortes de maux veneriens" [another marvelous cure against all sorts of venereal diseases], a remedy for syphilis that may suggest the recipe collection belonged to someone with a surgical practice, given that the disease was more often the purview of surgeons than domestic practitioners. The only other recipe in the *Early Modern Maritime Recipes* database of this kind is one for "venereal warts and other Excrescences" in Dr William Paine's recipes.[307] Part of the Miller Family Fonds at the Nova Scotia Archives, the French recipe compilation is part of a collection of documents that start with Jacob Miller (1742–1825), a German Loyalist from New York who moved to Halifax in the 1780s with his wife Elizabeth and six children.[308] This is, however, the only document in the fonds that appears in French. We have not found another source for this remedy for frostbite.

Remêdes Contre les Engelures des doigts, des pieds etc: non entamées.

Prenés de l'huile d'olive et un peu de sel ammoniac, é chaffés les - ensemble et oignés en Chaudent la partie affligée autant qu'il est possible de la tenir devant le feu, reïterés une fois ou deux si la premiere ne suffit pas.

Translation

Remedies Against Chilblains/Frostbite of the fingers, the feet etc: not burst.

Take some olive oil and a bit
of sal ammoniac, and heat them
together and anoint while heating
the afflicted part as much as
possible in front of the fire,
repeat one time or two if the
first does not suffice.

Today understood as frostbite, *engelures* was often translated in eighteenth-century English as chilblains. *Encyclopedie Françoise, Latine et Angloise, ou dictionnaire universel des arts et des sciences* (1761) defines *engelure* by linking it to "Pernio" in Latin and "Chilblain" in English; *engelure* is "Enflare aux pieds ou aux mains, accompagnée d'inflammation, de douleur, &c." (a swelling of the feet or hands, accompanied by inflammation, pain, etc.).[309]

Recognition of the ill effects of excess cold has a long history, one in which the effects of cold and heat were related. The influential Greek physician Hippocrates, writing in the fourth century BCE, argued that cold and heat had a healthy, moderate effect on the body when they were mixed together but, when taken to their extremes, heat and cold cause pain, with, for instance, cold causing pain that becomes hot in response. He wrote that

> all those who after walking through snow or other cold are exceedingly chilled in their feet or hands or head – how they suffer in the night from burning and itching when they return to a warm place and wrap themselves up! And on some people blisters appear just as they do on those who have been burned by fire; and they do not suffer this until they have warmed up.[310]

The English surgeon John Aitken thus follows Hippocrates in linking cold and heat, explaining of chilblain that "Cold, like heat […] is capable of altering and destroying the animal as well as vegetable organization. It excites or extinguishes the vital qualities of the whole system, or a portion of it, according to the degree of its action, which is regulated by its quantity, duration, and the circumstances of the body on which it operates."[311] English surgeon and physician Daniel Turner, whose treatise on diseases of the skin was also translated into French, gives a more extended analysis of the malady. He says that the symptoms of chilblain (translated as *engelure*) are "Great Redness sometimes with unequal bunching out in the Skin, burning Heat, Smart, Tingling and Itching affecting chiefly the Skin of the Hands and Fingers, also of the Feet and Toes in the Winter-Season." The cause, he adds, "is said to arise from Blood diffused by the capillary Vessels of the *Cutis,* and not return'd by the Circulation, nor able to breath out by the Pores, on Account of the Constipation of them in the Cuticle, by the Cold still more contracted at this Time, there stagnate vitiate the Glandules and breaking the Unity of the Fibres ulcerate and raise Blisters on the Parts."[312] For both Aitken and Turner, chilblains are the result of a lack of movement or kind of stagnation or constipation in the blood. The more severe form of ulceration is caused by this lack of circulation, the pressure of which causes the skin to burst. This recipe for *engelures* "non entamées," likely means not ulcerated, burst, or cut. The Miller manuscript also offers a recipe "Si le Engelures sont entâmées," which directs the user to apply a hot ointment of virgin wax, olive oil, and eau de vie.[313]

The ingredients employed by the recipe in the Miller manuscript seem to work within an eighteenth-century approach to curing cold with heat. If the problem is for Turner a lack of circulation, the cure in his view is to enable movement by adding warm plants and hot flannels or, as cook maids do, using a bath of brine or salt water. Turner also reports that people in cold regions use a bath of cold water and rub the afflicted parts with snow, which Turner explains with reference to the German surgeon Guilelmus Fabricius Hildanus (1560–1634), who had said that "the Heat suddenly concentr'd, riseth up with a redoubled force to expel the Adversary."[314] Turner's text also provides cures of white wine and alum and of turnip, sourced in the seventeenth-century works of Daniel Sennert (1572–1637) and Theodore Mayerne (1573–1655).[315] Turner also offers the common plaster "Diap. Bol. Ol. Ros. & Acet., which both strengthened the Part, and kept off the Fluxion," for which the French translation provides more information, expanding the abbreviations as "un emplâtre faite de diapalme, de bol, d'huile-rosat & de vinaigre, qui fortisioit & garantissoit en même tems la partie de la congestion des humeurs" (a plaster made of diapalma, bol, oil of roses, and vinegar, which fortified and guaranteed at the same time the part of the congestion of the humours).[316]

Remedies "*contre les engelures*" are not hard to find in print in French, although we have not found a version with instructions exactly like this one. The use of olive oil seems to align with Galen's description of olive oil as a useful substance in health and sickness because it was wet and potentially hot, easily turning to flame and thus having a heating effect on bodies.[317] Turner's recipe may use oil of roses and diapalma (of palm oil) for the same reason. *Pharmacopée Royale, Galenique et Chymique* recommends butter or "l'Huile figée de Cire" (hard wax oil) as remedies "contre les engelures," among other things.[318] And also using oil, "Onguent de Raves contre les Engelures" (Turnip ointment for chilblains) calls for making an ointment with four ounces of oil of turnips and one ounce each of "réfine de pin," yellow wax, turpentine, and ram fat, although a note at the end says that "L'huile de semence de jusquiame est meilleure pour les engelures, que celle de raves" (the oil of henbane seed is better for chilblains than that of turnip).[319]

Sal/sel ammoniac, or salt of Ammon in Egypt (ammonium chloride), commonly used in medieval and early modern medicine, does not seem to be a common ingredient in recipes for chilblains/*engelures*.[320] However, a recipe for "Lotion contre de engelures" does call for making a lotion of "eau-de-vie" (brandy), sal ammoniac, and camphor.[321] The logic for using sal ammoniac in a remedy for chilblains/*engelure* may reflect eighteenth-century chemistry more than Galenic medicine. *Philosophical Transactions Giving Some Account of the Present Undertakings, Studies, and Labours, of the Ingenious, in Many Considerable Parts of the World*, for the years 1737 and 1738, reports that "Salt mix'd with Water, increases its Cold" and that "Of all Salts, Sal Ammoniac gives the greatest Degree of Cold."[322] In a remedy for chilblains, the use of sal ammoniac would seem to follow the logic of those that use snow as a remedy: that applying cold causes heat within the body to rise up and expel the cold. This may be the rationale behind several similar recipes that use salt. A "Remede efficace contre les Engelures" in *Journal Oeconomique* (1758) has a recipe practised in Sweden from the botanist Carl Linnaeus (1707–1778) that calls for the afflicted to "imbiber à plusieurs reprises avec de l'Esprit de Sel les parties affectées de ce mal" (soak repeatedly with the Spirit of Salt the parts affected by the pain).[323] Linnaeus's recipe (his putative work was reprinted in a different form in *Affiches d'Austrasie* in 1766) is not unlike, then, that of the cookmaids Turner observed soaking the frozen body part in brine, a more homely salted water than Linnaeus's distillation.[324]

The use of the term *frostbite* to describe the damaging effect of cold on the body emerged only in the late eighteenth century. The OED gives the date of its first use as 1798, where it appears in a list of maladies that could be remedied by Blackhead's Essence of Pitchfork, a patent medicine.[325] However, the *American Museum*, a magazine printed in Philadelphia, published a "Cure for frost bites" on 1 December 1788, which recommends rubbing the affected area "three or four times before the fire with the fat of dunghill fowls" (a breed of chicken) then wrapping it in flannel.[326]

A cure for frostbite is obviously useful for settlers in the eighteenth-century Maritimes. This French recipe, like many of the English ones, is engaged with the ideas, practices, and ingredients of learned European medicine but is not entirely separate from domestic household medicine.

Autre ptisarme merveilleuse contre toutes sortes de maux veneriens

Another recipe in French from the Miller manuscript;[327] this remedy for syphilis appears to be from *Dictionnaire oeconomique* (1709) by Noël Chomel (1633–1712), where it is included under "Tisane" with other medicinal decoctions in a narrative form as "Tisanne merveilleuse pour toute sorte de Maux Veneriens." This work was printed several times in eighteenth-century Paris. The copyist has introduced changes, noting the ingredients at the beginning of the recipe as well as in the instructions, while using the words *preparation* and *usage* as section titles rather than as part of the narrative (for example, the original instead incorporates "Pour la preparation" and "l'usage suivant" at the beginning and end of the second paragraph). Further, while Chomel's version has "Faites infuser dans le vin blanc pendant une nuit le bois de Gayac & la Salsepareille," the version in the Miller manuscript specifies the amount of white wine as "5. quartes Mesure d'angleterre."[328] Three other recipes in the manuscript also refer to English measurements. "Remêde pour l'estomac" calls for "½ pinte d'angleterre, de laict," "Contre la Gravelle" for the same measure of a nettle juice remedy, and "Remêde Contre la Goute et le Rumathisme, bien éprouvé" for "une pinte mesure d'angleterre, de laict."[329] These references to English measures may suggest the copyist acquired the recipes more directly from an English source or that the recipe is being used in a context where English measures are commonly used or readily available. Chomel's *Dictionnaire oeconomique* was translated into English and published several times in England, but this recipe is not included in the English translation, which differs significantly from Chomel's original.[330]

Autre Ptisarme Merveilleuse
Contre toutes sortes de maux
veneriens.

Bois de Gayac[331] rappé de chacune
Ecorce de Gayac concassée 4 once
Salsapareille[332] Coupé [...] ^en^ bien petis morceaux
4 once.

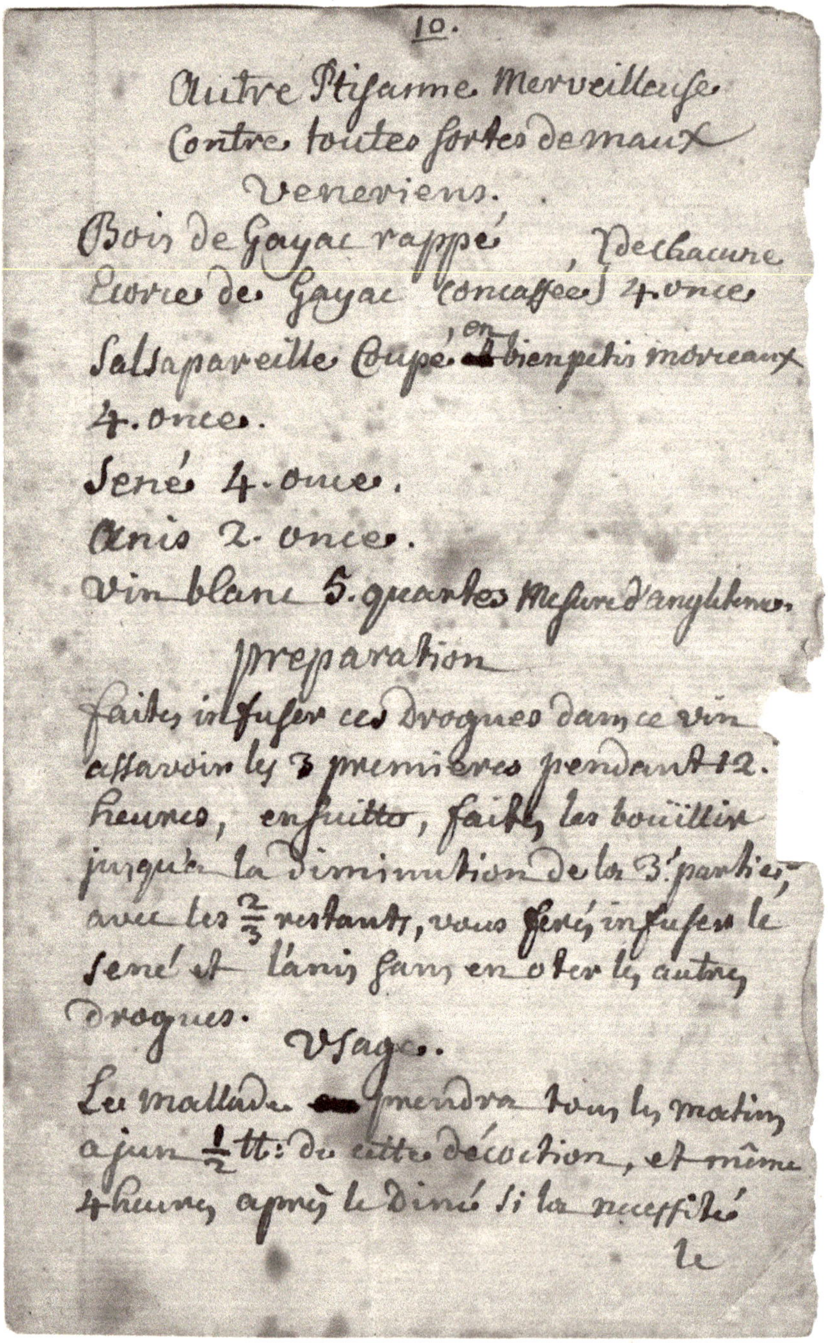
10.

Autre Ptisarme Merveilleuse
Contre toutes sortes de maux
veneriens.

Bois de Gayac rappé } de chacune
Ecorce de Gayac (concassée) } 4. once
Salsapareille Coupé en bien petits morceaux
4. once.
Sené 4. once.
Anis 2. once.
Vin blanc 5. quartes Mesure d'angleterre

Preparation

faites infuser ces drogues dans ce vin
assavoir les 3 premieres pendant 12.
heures, ensuitte, faites les bouillir
jusqu'a la diminution de la 3.e partie,
avec les 2/3 restants, vous ferés infuser le
sené et l'anis sans en oter les autres
drogues.

Usage.

Le mallade prendra tous les matins
a jeun 1/2 tt: de cette décoction, et même
4 heures apres le diné si la necessité
le

Figure 3.4
Autre Ptisarme Merveilleuse, Booklet of Remedies in French.

Sené[333] 4. once.
Anis 2. once.
Vin blanc 5. quartes Mesure d'angleterre

Preparation
faites infuser ces Drogues dans ce vin
assavoir les 3 premieres pendant 12
heures, ensuitte, faites les bouïllir
jusqu'a la diminution de la 3.ᵉ partie,
Avec les 2/3 restants, vous ferés infuser le
Sené et l'anis sans en oter les autres
drogues.

Usage.
Le mallade en prendra tous les matins
ajun ½ tt: de cette décoction, et même
4 heures après le Diné si la necessité
le demande, il continuera d'en prendre
ainsi 10 ou 12 jours sans être obligé
de garder aucun Regime et pourra
librement vaquer a les occupations
sans souffrir la froidure.

Translation
Another Marvelous Medical Drink
Against all sorts of
venereal diseases
grated Guaiac Wood of each
crushed Guaiac Bark 4 ounces
Sarsaparilla Cut [...] ^in^ very small pieces
4 ounces.
Senna 4. ounces.
Anise 2. ounces.
white Wine 5. quarts English measurement

Preparation
infuse these Drugs in the wine

Combine the first 3 for 12
hours, then, bring them to a boil
until reduced by a 3rd part,
With the remaining 2/3, you will infuse the
Senna and the anise without removing the other
drugs.

Usage.
The ill person will take every morning
without eating ½ tt[lb?]: of this decoction, and again
4 hours after dinner if necessary.
The ill person will continue to take this for
10 or 12 days without being obligated
to keep any regimen/diet and can
freely attend to duties
without suffering from cold.

The recipe aims to treat what we now know as *syphilis*, a term adopted for the disease in the nineteenth century. The malady had from the fifteenth century instead been known in Latin as *morbus gallicus*, in English as *French pox*, or in French, as here, as *maladie vénérienne*; later, the name *lues venerea* was adopted all over Europe.[334] This recipe uses two of the ingredients most widely associated with the treatment of syphilis in early modern Europe: guaiacum and sarsaparilla. European knowledge of these trees, both of which are native to the Americas, was the result of Spanish colonialism. The most influential early purveyor of information of plant knowledge from Spanish colonies was physician Nicolas Monardes (1493–1588), who never visited the Americas but from the port of Seville collected information for his 1569 herbal that would be translated into multiple European languages, including French and English, and was published in England as *Joyfull Newes Out of the Newe Found Worlde* (1577 and after).[335] Guaiac, also called *Lignum vitae* or *Lignum sanctum*, began to be used in Europe in the early sixteenth century as a treatment for syphilis, inspired by a belief that this disease had originated in the Americas and therefore the most effective cures also originated there. Guaiacum was meant to act as a purge, purifying the corrupted blood that fed the pox. Although guaiacum had lost its reputation as a miracle cure by the end of the sixteenth century, it continued to be prescribed for centuries.[336] Monardes was not far off when he wrote that knowledge of guaiacum's healing powers spread from the man who was cured, to other

Spaniards also cured, to Seville, to all of Spain and "from thence through all the world."[337] Sarsaparilla was also used widely in pox medicines in sixteenth-century Europe and continued to be used into the nineteenth century for its ability to provoke sweat.[338] Sarsaparilla, Monardes indicates, comes from "new Spaine, and the Indians did use it for a great medicine, with the which they did heale many divers diseases."[339] By the eighteenth century, Europeans valued sarsaparilla to the degree that they produced it for export through the exploitation of enslaved labourers on plantations in Jamaica.[340] As well as the tree, sarsaparilla is also the name of a plant that grows in more northern regions and was used in eastern North America by Innu, Penobscot, Houma, Catawba, Creek, Meskwaki, Ojibwe, and Potawatomi peoples for the treatment of other disorders.[341]

The method of boiling the wood of the trees to make a medicinal drink was learned from Indigenous peoples in the Americas. Repeating an account also conveyed by Gonzalo Fernandez de Oviedo and Ulrich von Hutton, Monardes describes how a Spaniard in Santo Domingo learned about guaiacum by receiving a cure for the disease:[342]

> There was an Indian that gave knowledge thereof to his Maister, in this maner. A Spanyarde that did suffer great paines of the Pox, which he had by the companie of an Indian woman, but his servaunte being one of the Phisitions of that countrie, gave unto hym the water of Guaiacan, wherewith not onely his greevous paynes were taken awaie that he did suffer but healed verie well of the evill.[343]

Refusing to acknowledge the given knowledge as a gift, the account describes not a grateful recipient but a Spaniard who assumes the role of "Maister" despite the Taino person's status as physician, asserting in doing so the imperialist entitlement that brought not healing but death and destruction to the Taino people. Monardes then goes on to describe the method of making a decoction, steeping the wood and bark, broken in pieces, in water over a soft fire until two-thirds of it has evaporated, describing a method similar to that found in "Autre Ptisarme Merveilleuse Contre toutes sortes de maux veneriens," albeit the French decoction is instead reduced only by one-third.[344] Monardes also explains how the Spanish learned about sarsaparilla from Indigenous peoples in "New Spain," a moniker that reinforces Spanish ambitions while subsuming the land's diverse inhabitants into a single, undifferentiated other. The described method of preparing sarsaparilla is similar to that of guaiacum. According to Monardes, they boil broken pieces of sarsaparilla to create a thick drink by pounding the wood as it cooks, which the patient took without eating anything else – a method Europeans also used but had more recently moved away from, replacing it with the steeping create another cure for the pox; this method is likewise informed by Indigenous methods, for Monardes reports that another people in the region of the Guaiaquil River (Rio Guyas, in Ecuador) – probably the Manteño-Huancavilca – also used this steeping technique to create a decoction by boiling the wood in water.[345] Although Europeans had long made medicines by steeping, that guaiacum and sarsaparilla were even regarded as medicines is the direct result of colonial contact, and Europeans persisted in using Indigenous methods as they were incorporated into European medicine.

Unlike many other treatments that recommended a special diet and confinement, this remedy recommends no such restrictions, noting instead that the patient can carry on with life while taking it. Monardes, on the other hand, reports of the guaiacum treatment that it should be taken in a warm room, that the patient be "kept from the colde and from ayre," and that he should eat only raisins, almonds, and biscuit. As for sarsaparilla, one treatment requires that it be taken for two or three days without eating anything else, while another requires that it be taken in a warm chamber in the morning and in the evening, and again with no other food but raisins, almonds, and biscuit.[346] The remedy in the Miller manuscript does not, however, require this kind of attention to regimen.

In this recipe, guaiacum and sarsaparilla are mixed with smaller amounts of senna and anise, which have a longer tradition in European medicine. Chomel says that senna (*senné*) comes from Tuscany and Egypt, which produces the best; like guaiacum and sarsaparilla, it was used as a purgative as well as in other applications.[347] Several of the virtues of anise, which was widely cultivated in early modern Europe (Chomel identifies good anise from Spain), relate to comforting the digestive system; it may be included in this remedy for that reason or to make the remedy more palatable.[348] This remedy has long roots, stretching back to two hundred years of European syphilis treatments, but was not yet out of fashion in 1755; the first *Pharmacopoeia of the United States of America* (1820) recommends a "Compound decoction of Sarsaparilla" of sarsaparilla, guaiacum, sassafras, licorice, mezereon (a kind of English shrub), and water, as well as a syrup of sarsaparilla and guaiacum made with the further addition of roses, acacia gum, senna, ginger, and water.[349]

CHAPTER FOUR

Agriculture

In what is now known as Canada's Maritime provinces, the history of humans interacting with the land to feed themselves begins with Indigenous peoples. Native people were involved, as Jason Hall argues, "in a centuries-long process of adapting plants and cultivation and harvesting practices to the diverse soils and climate of the region."[1] For the Wolastoqiyik, these adaptations included growing maize, beans, kidney beans, and pumpkins. They altered the landscape of the Wolastoq River's banks to make it "a food-yielding and medicinal landscape."[2] Living along the Wolastoq, they had established long-distance links with Indigenous peoples throughout northeastern North America. Through these networks, the Indigenous peoples of the region gained knowledge of cultivating the corn that had been domesticated in Mexico.[3] Though the Mi'kmaq also grew corn, they mostly lived in nomadic communities that relied primarily on fishing and hunting to obtain food. Fishing and hunting, however, came with responsibilities and obligations to the land. On the lands on which Mi'kmaw family groups had long hunted and fished, the community aimed "to maintain a material and spiritual balance between its own needs and those of the animal population."[4] The Mi'kmaq also engaged in fish farming, using man-made ponds to keep fish and weirs to catch them.[5] Europeans, however, mostly failed to understand the Indigenous peoples' approach to the land. So while the Mi'kmaq and Wolastoqiyik introduced and tended to crops of sunchokes and groundnuts, for instance, settlers defined as agricultural land only that with the deforested, single-cropped fields familiar to them.[6]

In keeping with European standards and expectations about agriculture, the colonial government of Nova Scotia argued as early as 1783 that the Mi'kmaq needed to become farmers in the European mode and to abandon what they saw as their "wandering" ways. These governmental expectations were associated with European ideas of "civilization." Seeing land mostly as private property, the British valued only those improvements they identified with fences and ploughed land, both of which served as signs that it was being efficiently used – and a standard they applied to deem Indigenous peoples undeserving inhabitants who should be replaced.[7] Intensive European-style agriculture, as Daniel Paul observes, thus served as an instrument of colonization. Not only did settlers deem Indigenous peoples uncivilized and unworthy of land because of their approach to its management, settler governments persisted throughout the nineteenth century and into the twentieth century in encouraging European agricultural practices among Indigenous communities, despite the unsuitability of the land on which the communities were forced to survive.[8] At the same time, nineteenth-century settlers cleared land, built fences, and allowed grazing animals on reserve lands, commandeering still more arable land from the Mi'kmaq.[9] John Reid writes about how settler agriculture served the colonial enterprise:

> Agriculture, with its land clearances and its demands for the pasturing of livestock, was a potentially lethal threat to aboriginal hunting-gathering economies. Although eighteenth-century Europeans would have seen agricultural development at one level as a natural and beneficial use of the soil, imperial strategists were aware that it also represented an efficient means of undermining aboriginal societies where they had become obstacles to strategic or economic ambitions.[10]

Moreover, even as settlers criticized Indigenous peoples for their less intrusive approach to land management, some of the practices of Mi'kmaw and Wolastoqey food production became foundational to settler agriculture. As Jason Hall argues, "the Maliseet and Mi'kmaq helped create some of the first fields credited to pioneering colonists on both the Annapolis River and the Wəlastəqw"; what settlers chose and upheld as their own farmland had often been already cultivated by Indigenous peoples, and "Native plant sites may have provided a foundation for settler agriculture throughout Acadia."[11]

The British, of course, were not the first Europeans to take up farming in the region, even though the agricultural recipes and instructions published in Maritime newspapers and magazines were in English. Settling first around Port Royal, Acadian farmers diked the marshlands in the area and at the head of the Bay of Fundy, using the land to grow wheat, legumes, and grains, such as oats, rye, flax, and barley.[12] The practice of diking among the Acadians began in the seventeenth century and drew on European reclamation practices.[13] At Louisbourg, the French also built gardens that grew cereals, vegetables, and fruit trees from imported plants and seeds and built pens for sheep, cattle, pigs, and poultry that were initially stocked with imported animals; like the later work of the English, French colonial agriculture was informed by European scientific experiments, as well as garden engineering that sought to control space along geometric lines and proportions.[14] After the Acadian deportations that began in 1755, English settlers, including the Yorkshire settlers who arrived in 1774–75, took over the marshlands that the Acadians had transformed into viable farmland; those Acadians who were able to return beginning in the 1780s were thus compelled to settle in other, less agriculturally fertile areas, given that ruling authorities had also passed their land along to the New England Planters as well as other English speakers, such as Scots and their Gaelic-speaking countrymen.[15]

These newcomers were not always immediately successful farmers. Though Horton Township (around Grand Pré and Wolfville) was one of the region's best agricultural areas, fewer than one-third of the English-speaking settlers, who by the 1760s had inhabited the formerly Acadian farms, produced enough food to feed themselves.[16] Yorkshire settlers did, however, extend marshland reclamation, applying knowledge gleaned from farming Yorkshire's waterlogged fields to the land of Nova Scotia.[17] Land use data available from censuses taken between 1767 and 1771 in Annapolis suggest that by that time English-speaking settlers used land for hay and to grow grain (wheat, oats, rye, and barley) and produce small amounts of peas and beans as well as cabbages, pumpkins, turnips, and potatoes.[18] In the 1760s and 1770s, before the Loyalist influx that dramatically increased the number of settlers in Nova Scotia, the relationship of English settlers to the imperial state's ambitions was less compelling, however, than the relationship between the colonists and their Indigenous neighbours and how the treaties of the 1760s, which did not cede land to the British, worked in practice. Unlike the Loyalists who came later, the English settlers in this period made more limited incursions into Indigenous territories and mostly practised agriculture in ways that had many affinities with Acadian cultivation.[19] The treaties restricted new British settlements and incursions into new territories that impeded on Mi'kmaw rights to hunt and fish.[20]

Many of the Loyalists who began arriving in the 1780s saw land as "important as a source of future wealth and as a visible mark of status," and prominent Loyalists received large land grants from the colonial government. Some of the major grant holders imagined themselves as estate holders on the English model, wherein tenant farmers and labourers would do the actual work of farming,[21] but this model was not especially successful in the region because of a lack of willing labourers. Small farms thus came to dominate Loyalists agriculture in Nova Scotia and New Brunswick, although for many successful farming continued to be a struggle.[22] Land grants to Loyalists also caused conflict with Yorkshire settlers who thought themselves equally deserving.[23] Yet the most productive settler farms in the Maritimes before 1800 continued to be found in the diked Fundy marshlands, as well as in the Saint John River Valley and in the Lunenburg area.[24] The Kennebecasis and Annapolis Valleys were also important agricultural areas.[25]

Black Loyalists were also involved in agriculture, although on structurally different terms than white Loyalists. Some Black Loyalists remained enslaved during the eighteenth century and worked on white-owned farms. While free Black Loyalists were promised land and provisions, when they did get land, it was of poor quality and segregated from white settlements as they were "settled in separate areas, on smaller plots of remote, often uncultivable land," and inequitable distribution meant that "[t]heir share of provisions and tools was substantially less – sometimes only a third as much as the Whites received – although their hunger and their need were surely as great."[26] This dire situation contributed to the departure in 1791 of over one thousand Black Loyalists to Sierra Leone, in search of a more favourable political and social climate.

Despite the diversity of people who occupied the land, the instructions included in this chapter speak mostly to how white English-speaking settlers engaged with and represented agricultural practices (though agriculture could, of course, proceed without interventions from Halifax newspapers). What the texts that follow make clear are the ways in which European agriculture was a component of natural philosophy and how, as with scientific knowledge more generally, European thinkers sought to make advancements for reasons of public good and commercial profit. In England, the sites and forms for agricultural knowledge-making included artefacts of print culture such as books and periodicals, the private communications of letters and conversations, the public communications of speeches, the commercial efforts of seed shops and farms, equipment and material objects designed to facilitate agricultural production, and agricultural animals bred according to innovative principles.[27] Reflecting the influence of these and other sources, agricultural instructions printed in Maritime newspapers document the transfer of knowledge across the Atlantic as well as the circulation of knowledge within what had become the United States and in Britain's northern colonies.

These instructions do not necessarily represent established practices, however. There was some suspicion among European and settler farmers of what would at the end of the eighteenth century be described as "book farming": agricultural knowledge gained from books rather than practical experience. Some of the criticisms levelled against book learning arose from a sense that books encouraged an approach to farming that was too theoretical, complicated, speculative, or expensive. Through the sixteenth and seventeenth centuries in England, agricultural knowledge of raising crops and livestock had been formed primarily through practice, by doing the work and learning through conversation and demonstration. Publications about agriculture nevertheless increased in volume through the seventeenth and into the eighteenth century, bearing witness to a growing emphasis in the value of experimentation. Importantly, however, English agricultural publications were often aimed not at farmers but at gentlemen and landowners who could direct the labour of others, and they came with the attendant sense that such printed knowledge could alleviate the gentleman's need to rely on the experiential knowledge of servants and tenants.[28] This conflict between theoretical and practical knowledge, book learning and experience, is discernible also in Maritime history. Major Benjamin Griffiths, who owned land near Woodstock, was criticized by American surveyor Charles Turner for preferring English books about agriculture to "that good old pedagogue: Experience." Turner felt that Griffiths was too little concerned with differences of climate and soil between England and New Brunswick. George Leonard, who had a large property and grand house in the Kennebecasis Valley, was also interested in English agricultural methods, but when he had a threshing machine built on the basis of an English description, its "flails stuck in all directions" according to one unimpressed observer.[29] Yet the instructions reproduced here from Maritime print and manuscript sources do display an enthusiasm for innovation and experiment characteristic of the period.

Maple Sugar

These instructions were printed in *The Nova Scotia Magazine* on 3 October 1790.[30] The "late Philadelphia Publication" identified in the title is likely *Remarks on the Manufacturing of Maple Sugar; with Directions for Its Further Improvement*, a pamphlet printed in Philadelphia in 1790, as "Collected by a Society of Gentleman"; the

"Remarks" were also printed in two parts in a Philadelphia magazine, *Universal Asylum, & Columbian Magazine*, in August and September 1790.[31] These instructions were frequently reprinted and were included in some 1790 and 1791 periodicals published along the eastern seaboard of America and in London, where it appeared as both a pamphlet and in the periodical press.

Despite the length of this text – originally over four thousand words in its entirety before being abbreviated here – it maintains most of a recipe's standard features in providing an explanation of the ingredients and tools required for making maple sugar, explaining a process, and pointing to an expected result. Its stated goal is to spread the method widely.

REMARKS on the MANUFACTURING of MAPLE SUGAR; with Directions for its future Improvement.

[From a late Philadelphia Publication.]

HE who enables another to obtain any necessary of life, either cheaper or more independently than heretofore, adds a new source of happiness to man; and becomes more or less useful, in proportion to the number of those who participate in the benefits of his discovery. The transitions, however made from one stage of improvement to another, are not sudden, but gradual; which probably arises from that strong and almost universal disinclination, in the mind, at departing from the beaten path, or from long established customs. Hence men, frequently, at first, treat with neglect or contempt, that, which afterwards, on better information, and a thorough knowledge of facts, they believe, and without reserve, adopt in their subsequent practice. Were we to introduce, and embrace as a maxim – "That every new proposition, merely on account of its novelty, must be rejected" – our knowledge would no longer be progressive, and every kind of improvement must cease. That the juice of the Sugar Maple would produce a saccharine substance, answering the purposes of sugar has been known many years, and particularly by the inhabitants of the Eastern States; – but that there was a sufficient number of this kind of tree, in the States of New-York and Pennsylvania, only, to supply the whole of the United States with this article, is a fact which was not so well ascertained, or so satisfactorily authenticated, until within a year or two past; – and that the sugar of this tree was capable of being grained, and produced, in quality, equal to the best imported – was in some measure problematical until within even two or three months past, when the arrival of several chests in the city of Philadelphia, made last spring on the Delaware; removed every doubt in the minds of those who have seen it, as to the truth of this last fact.

The object which this publication has particularly in view, is, "A communication of such observations and directions on manufacturing the Maple Sugar, as will be most useful to those, who, from situation, interest or patriotism, may be induced to engage in and carry on this business." – A person who had, many years, been acquainted with the usual way of making this article being desirous of improving the method – obtained the instructions of a refiner of sugar in this city, and, with these before him, began his experiments, in February last, at Stock-port, about three miles below the junction of the Mohock and Popatchtunck branches of the Delaware. He soon discovered that the business was yet in its infancy, that great and even essential improvements might be made therein, which would require a departure from the methods heretofore in general use, in boiling down the green sap, graining the syrup, &c. and which if attended to and adopted, would enable him to produce sugar, in colour, grain and taste, equal, if not superior in reputation, to any imported. His sentiments and hopes, on this head, have been fully confirmed, by the result of his experiments; for the sugar he has made, and sent down to this city, is equal to the best sugars imported from the West-India islands.

The person above mentioned, whose judgment on this subject is much to be relied on, as well from his experience in the business, as his established character for candour and integrity – is clearly of opinion – that four, active, industrious men, well provided with materials, and conveniencies proper for carrying on the business, may turn out, in a common season, which lasts from four to six weeks, forty hundred weight of good sugar, that is, ten hundred to each man. If four men can effect this, how great must be the product of the separate or associated labours of the many thousands of people who now inhabit, or may inhabit the immense tracts of lands, which abound with the Sugar Maple tree! What a new and extensive field opens from these considerations! What an interesting and important object to the cause of humanity, presents itself to our View! An object that deserves the countenance of every good citizen, and that highly merits even national encouragement.

[...]

Detail and description of the necessary Utensils and Materials.

KETTLES; Sixteen, of about fifteen gallons each.

IRON LADLES; Two, the bowls to contain three or four quarts, each, for shifting the syrup: [...]

TRAMMELS or POT-RACKS; Sixteen, one for each kettle [...]

SCREW AUGERS; Four, of an half, three quarters, and one inch, for boring the trees. [...]

BUCKETS; Eight or ten, of three gallons each, at least, for collecting the sap.

BOARDS; Eight or ten round pieces, to lay on the surface of the sap, at the top of the Buckets, to prevent its splashing over.

COOLERS; Three or four tubs, of about fifteen gallons each (kettles will answer the purpose) to receive the syrup from the boilers [...]

YOKES; Four, to go across the shoulders of the persons employed in collecting the sap, having a bucket suspended at each end.

TROUGHS; Eight hundred should be made of white pine, white ash, water ash, aspen, linden or bass wood, poplar, common-maple, or Sugar Maple: [...] STORE TROUGHS: Where large cisterns, fit for the purpose, cannot be had, which will generally be the case in a new country, troughs may be had of the white-pine, by falling a large tree of that kind, and fixing it in a level position; the upper side to be dug out in the shape of a manger for feeding cattle: [...] SHEDS, WALLS, &c. The exposed manner in which sugar has been usually made, in the back country, is attended with many inconveniences, especially in windy weather, when the ashes, leaves, &c. may be blown into the boilers, and thereby discolour the syrup, or injure its flavour: neither can the keeping up a proper degree of heat be always effected in an exposed situation. To remedy these inconveniences it is recommended that a back wall, for the fire-place, be erected eighteen or twenty inches high, and to extend a sufficient length for all the boilers employed. [...] For graining the syrup, after it is brought to a proper state in the boilers, it will be right to have a separate shed or building in which two of the sixteen kittles should be fixed; for this service, charcoal is much better than wood, as the heat or flame should be confined to the bottoms of the kettles, and be uniform and regular, to guard against burning or scorching. A wall, as above described, should be made at the fire-place, as well as at each end; and the hearth or bottom laid with flat stones, on which charcoal is to be placed.

AND IRONS: Pieces of cast-iron, something like and irons, and to serve the same purpose, will be very useful: They should, in the long part, be two feet and an half, and two inches square; the turn at the inner end, four inches downwards, and a small turn upwards, at the outer end of about two inches, to prevent the wood from rolling. Of these, there should be a number to suit the extent of the fire-place, to be placed at the distance of five or six feet from each other.

SUGAR MOULDS: These should be made of seasoned boards, or of such wood as will not impart a taste to the sugar. To answer the end of earthen moulds, used in the West-Indies, and in our refining houses, the use of sugar moulds has been, in the present year, well supplied, by making then of wood, somewhat resembling a millhopper, about twenty seven inches long, and ten or twelve inches wide, at the top, and tapered to the width of one inch, at the lower end.

FRAMES, to place the moulds in, above described, should be formed so as to admit the moulds to rest in them, about half their depth.

GUTTERS, spouts, or narrow troughs, – should be fixed within the frames, under the moulds, in a descending position; the lower ends to enter covered casks or vessels, so that when the plugs or stoppers are drawn from the bottom of the moulds, which may be done in about twenty-four hours after they are set, the molasses that will run therefrom, may fall into these gutters and pass readily into the covered vessels, which, if open, would be exposed to dust and dirt.

PRICKERS: [...]

A few hours after the moulds are unstopped, the prickers should be run up the bottom of them, three or four inches, to make way for the whole quantity of molasses to pass off.

SEASON for TAPPING: – By trials, made in the month of February, it will readily be discovered, when this valuable tree ought to be bored, for the purpose of extracting the sap, as in that month, either earlier or later, according to the season, it generally begins to yield a sufficient, quantity for commencing the business.

TAPPING or BORING: – Four hundred trees, each tree bored with two holes, as nearly as may be on the south side; and also with two holes on the north side of the tree, in the early part of the season, with screw augers from two to four quarters of an inch, according to the size of the tree; and towards the middle of the season, a like number of trees to be bored in the same manner, is recommended, as a better mode for the management of four hands, than if the whole number of eight hundred trees were tapped at the first running of the sap. [...]

PRESERVING the SAP: – It is observed, that in the early part of the season,

the sap will keep two or three days without injury; but as the spring advances, and the frost becomes less intense, it will be necessary to boil the sap the day after It is collected, or it may ferment and sour.
LIME: – To every half barrel, or fifteen gallon kettle, a table spoonful of slack'd lime, should be put in, while the sap is warming, and before it boils; this promotes the rising of the scum and forming of the grain.
BOILING: – A smart fire should be kept up, while the sap is boiling, and the watery part evaporating. – As the scum rises to the top, be careful to skim it off. When the liquor is reduced one half in quantity, lade the second kettle from the end, into the end one; and when the contents of three or four kettles can be contained in one, then let the whole be laded into that, at the end; filling up the empty kettles, without delay, with fresh sap. As the liquor in the end kettles, removed from those which have been mentioned, becomes a syrup, it should be strained through a good blanket, or woollen cloth; and care must be taken, not to suffer it to boil too long, so to be too thick to be strained in this manner. It should, when thus cleansed from its impurities, stand in buckets or other suitable vessels, twelve hours or more, that the particles of lime, and other remaining sediment, may settle to the bottom; after which, it should be so gently poured off into a kettle or boiler, as not to carry with it any of these settlings. However, they need not

be wholly lost; they will mostly contain a considerable quantity of sugar or syrup; by pouring fresh sap on them, stirring them well together, and suffering them to stand a while to settle, a great part of the valuable sweets contained in such sediment may be saved. [...]

GRAINING. – The syrup, having stood twelve hours, or upwards – is then to be gently poured into a kettle or boiler as above-mentioned; which would be best placed over a fire made of charcoal, as before hinted; unless the kettle is so fixed in a furnace, or in such a situation, that the flame can be confined to the bottom; for if it be suffered to pass on the sides, it endangers the syrup's being burned. – This operation should also be performed with a smart fire, to be uniformly and equally kept up – in which, as well as in boiling the green sap, the use of butter, hog's lard, or other fat, it not only very useful and advantageous, but absolutely necessary. – When, in the course of boiling, the fat rises towards the top, a piece of fat equal in size to a nutmeg, thrown in, will keep it down. Particular care should be taken to prevent, by these means, the the rising of the syrup when graining, which may require a larger proportion of butter, &c. It is found that the evaporation is much more expeditious, and is believed the quantity of sugar made, is larger, when careful guard is kept to prevent the sap, and particularly the syrup, when graining, from rising, by the timely introduction of a piece of fat, as above described. - […] The managing a sugar-works in the West-Indies, and in the refining houses in North America, has been found to require much judgment and experience, to conduct the business to the best advantage; indeed, it seems hardly possible, to communicate to persons who have little knowledge of the matter, and in terms clearly to be understood, full information, as to the different appearances of the syrup, in the time of boiling, and to point out the moment when some material movements or changes ought to be made; nevertheless, from the foregoing hints and directions, which are grounded on observation and experience, it is hoped, much use may be derived, and that from year to year, greater advances and Improvements may be made in this valuable business.

CLAYING or WHITENING the SUGAR: - To promote the molasses passing more freely from the sugar, when draining in the moulds, and to improve its colour, in two or three days after the moulds are unstopped at the lower end, mix white clay with water, so as to reduce it to a thin mortar; with this cover the top of the moulds one inch and a half thick, when this covering appears dry, remove it, and supply the place with a fresh covering of about two inches thick.

[…]

MOLASSES and VINEGAR. – When the trees of the second tapping become poor, in quantity and quality, which may be about the tenth of April, or perhaps sooner, then a number of fresh tapped trees will yield a sap, of which may be made good molasses, and also excellent vinegar. In all sugar plantations, it will be advantageous to cut out the different sorts of timber, which grow intermixed with the sugar Maple, and even those of that species which are not thriving, promising trees. The timber so cut out will serve for fuel for the boilers, and leave greater openings for the rays of the sun to enter, which will have a tendency to improve and enrich the remaining trees. The ground so cleared of all except the maple tree, it has been observed, is particularly favourable for pasture and the growth of grass. [...] How far a careful cultivation of them, the stirring and manuring the soil in which they stand, may improve their value, remains to be ascertained in future, though it may be expected that this, like almost all over trees and plants, may from a natural state be greatly and essentially improved by the hand of art. Experiments, therefore, will not be unworthy the attention of those citizens, situated in the more interior parts of the States, if it shall, thereby, be found that these trees can be readily propagated, either from the seed or young plants, and be brought to thrive, so as to be equal in their product, if not superior, to those who have been strewed over the country, without the aid of man. To what an extent of cultivation may not this lead! There will be no risk or disadvantage attending the experiment; and it certainly deserves encouragement.

These instructions aim at transforming the long-standing Indigenous practice in the northeast of making a sweetener from maple sap. The goal was to establish a large-scale maple sugar industry to rival that of cane sugar in the Caribbean. The scale of production is evident in the size and number of tools, the recommendation of a fire that fits sixteen kettles, and the placement of the fire in a purpose-built building rather than a home or outdoor space. The instructions also reveal a vested interest in efficiency, in producing the greatest amount of sugar with a few – in this case, merely four – labourers. Developed in Stockport, Pennsylvania, with the help of "a refiner of sugar," the method explicitly draws on practices used in the manufacturing of cane sugar in the Caribbean, including moulds "used in the West-Indies" and the addition of lime and fat – adulterations that are not typically used in manufacturing maple sugar but were in the making of cane sugar. The fat, the recipe indicates, works toward ensuring that "evaporation is much more expeditious." Also with an eye to efficiency, the instructions imagine creating "sugar plantations" of maple trees by "cut[ting] out the different sorts of timber, which grow intermixed with the sugar Maple," thus replicating the monoculture of Caribbean sugar plantations. Where eighteenth-century sugar cane plantations relied on large numbers of enslaved labourers, however, this maple sugar project represents the work of a group of abolitionist Quakers in Pennsylvania, including Henry Drinker (1734–1809), who led the project, and his agent at Stockport, Samuel Preston (1756–1834).[32] Though the instructions do not specifically say whether the four men should be paid for their work, they do explicitly argue for settler expansion, envisioning that "many thousands of people who now inhabit, or may inhabit the immense tracts of lands, which abound with the Sugar Maple tree!" With its enthusiasm about moving into new land to create plantations of maple trees to produce sugar, the instructions link maple sugar making to nation building.

Like other agricultural recipes considered here, this one is deeply informed by ideologies of settler colonialism. It does not acknowledge maple sugar's Indigenous origins but gestures only to "long established customs" that will be superseded by "better information," with which the recipe makers position themselves as the voice of improvement and progress even though Europeans had observed and admired this Indigenous practice for over a century and a half.[33] When the recipe was printed in Nova Scotia, it appeared in a place with a history of Mi'kmaw maple sugar making that preceded European contact and from where there is strong evidence of European learning about maple sugar making. For instance, Chrestien LeClercq recorded in the 1690s that in Mi'kmaki the people reduce maple sap through boiling to a syrup, "which hardens to something like sugar, and takes on a reddish color. It is formed into little loaves which are sent into France."[34] The value that the recipe places in efficiency, economy, and profit persists in settler thought, as Nishnaabeg writer Leanne Betasamosake Simpson explains in her critique of settler approaches to maple syrup: "they completely miss the wisdom that underlies the entire process because they deterritorialize the mechanics of maple syrup production from Nishnaabeg intelligence, and from Aki (land). They appropriated and recast the process within a hyperindividualism that negates relationality."[35] The instructions for making maple sugar in the "Remarks" explicitly reject relationships with Indigenous peoples, who are mentioned neither as inhabiting the land where the maple trees grow nor as the source of the original method. Publication of the instructions in print plays a role in disavowing relationships; when the instructions acknowledge the difficulty of learning to make maple sugar with the assertion that "indeed, it seems hardly possible, to communicate to persons who have little knowledge of the matter," it imagines that these remarkably extensive and detailed instructions will successfully convey the method even in the absence of human interaction and in-person knowledge exchange. The instructions also reject a sustainable relationship with the land and its natural diversity, which must not support an interconnected and interdependent ecology but, to maximize profits and efficiency, grow only maple trees. Importantly, however much the instructions present themselves as rational, optimistic, and progressive, the proffered method was not successful or widely adopted, and Henry Drinker died in debt in 1809.[36] Regardless, Maritime settlers did make maple sugar, as suggested by the probate records of one Yorkshire settler who operated two big pots in the sugar woods in 1797.[37]

Seedling Potatoes

These instructions were printed on 28 March 1795 in William Minns's *The Weekly Chronicle*.[38] The paper tended to focus on local and international news but also included agricultural instructions like these.[39] Before appearing in *The Weekly Chronicle*, the instructions had been printed in England in the 1773 fourth volume of *Georgical Essays* by Alexander Hunter (1729?–1809), a founding member of the York Agricultural Society, as "Experiment XI. On the Method of Raising Seedling Potatoes."[40] Also in 1773, *The Pennsylvania Packet*, a Philadelphia newspaper, published a slightly abbreviated version of Hunter's instructions, identifying him as a doctor from York.[41]

On the method of raising SEEDLING POTATOES.

TAKE of the apples[42] of any sort of potatoes, hang them up in a warm room, during the winter, and in the spring separate the seeds from the pulp, by washing the apples in water, and pressing them with the fingers. Then dry the seeds upon paper – otherwise when the apples are thoroughly ripe press out the seeds and dry them on paper.

In the month of April sow these seeds in drills, in a bed of earth well dug and manured with rotten dung. When the plants are about an inch high, draw a little earth up to them with a hoe, in order to lengthen their main roots. When they are about three inches high, dig them up with a spade, and separate them carefully from each other, in order for planting out in the following manner.

Prepare a piece of fresh ground by trenching it well. Dig up the seedling plants as before directed, and plant them out in the ground thus prepared, in such a manner that there shall be sixteen inches between every plant. As they advance in growth, let them receive one or two earthings up, in order to lengthen the main root, and to encourage the shoots under ground.

By this management they will in the course of one season, arrive at the size of hen's eggs, and the haulm or stalks will be as vigorous as if sets or cuttings had been planted, and although this may seem impossible, at least, very improbable to the unexperienced readers, yet one experiment properly conducted, will convince them otherwise, as I have experienced upon the peninsula of Halifax.

By the method commonly used by unexperienced Farmers in general of raising potatoes from seed, they are always two and probably three years in bringing them to their full size. By the above method of transplanting with wide distances, many of the potatoes nearly attain their full size in one season.

It is observable that these seedlings produce potatoes of all the different kinds; and sometimes new sorts are procured.

Potatoes when propagated from sets or cuttings, after a number of years, are found to decrease in bearing; for which reason they should be brought back every 10, 12, or 14 years to their original.

For want of attention to this circumstance, I have known potatoes to run out, that they hardly return treble seed. The farmer complains his land is tired of them, but the true cause is the age of the sets.

The encrease of potatoes raised from seed is truly astonishing. They continue in vigour from about ten to fourteen years, according to the soil, after which the produce gradually declines.

When Minns printed these instructions in the Halifax newspaper some twenty-two years after their initial publication, he introduced several changes to Hunter's original essay, seemingly to make the instructions more relevant to Nova Scotia conditions. He does not name his source. The time recommended for separating the seeds from the pulp has changed from "February" to "spring," likely reflecting Nova Scotia's longer winter. Minns has added a second method for drying the seeds to the end of the first paragraph, and where Hunter refers to Lancashire farmers, this recipe describes "unexperienced farmers."[43] The reference to experience on the peninsula of Halifax also does not appear in the original. The changes that include the text's use of "I" to describe an experimenter and the trial conducted in Halifax render the city a site of scientific experiment with potatoes – an agricultural crop that is now very much associated with the Maritimes (if not with Halifax).

European interest in potato growing was burgeoning in this period, and the crop would eventually replace the sunchoke as the dominant starchy tuber in English and settler diets. It is well-known that potatoes were first cultivated by the Indigenous peoples of the Andes, and from there, the cultivation of varieties of potatoes spread throughout the region we now call South America. When the Spanish colonized the region, they brought knowledge of the potato to Europe, where it was grown on a small scale starting in the sixteenth century. In England, it was in the eighteenth century that potatoes moved from being a garden crop to a field crop that resulted in a marketable product. Famously, the potato also became an especially important crop in Ireland.[44]

Potatoes were not unknown to Minns's audience of English-speaking settlers in Nova Scotia. The tuber became a regular crop throughout New England and other eastern states by the middle of the eighteenth century; by the 1760s, potatoes were being both exported and imported from Europe by New Englanders.[45] In Nova Scotia, the British had harvested potatoes in Halifax in 1750, and the French imported seed potatoes from France for planting in 1757 on Île Royale, while Acadians grew potatoes throughout the region in the 1750s.[46] Potato growing was sufficiently established by 1792 that 1200 bushels of potatoes were listed on the Bill of Fare that outlined the food supplies provisioned for the thousand free Black men, women, and children departing Nova Scotia for Sierra Leone; saltfish and potatoes with butter were expected to provide dinner four days a week during the voyage.[47] Further documenting the growing importance of the potato (while also lamenting the declining fortunes of the elite whom he thought should govern the colony), New Brunswick Loyalist Edward Winslow (1746/7–1815) complained that "Our gentlemen have all become potato-planters, and our shoemakers are preparing to legislate."[48] Minns's recipe thus seems aimed at promoting an improved method rather than an entirely new practice.

To Multiply the Increase of Corn

The following instructions for increasing corn production appeared in the 23 September 1791 edition of *The Royal Gazette and Miscellany of the Island of Saint John.*[49] The article had been previously printed in American newspapers that include *The Christian's, Scholar's, and Farmer's Magazine* (June and July 1790), *American Museum* (September 1790), *The New York Daily Gazette* (27 October 1790), and *Pennsylvania Packet* (29 October 1790), later reappearing in *The Halifax Gazette* on 1 April 1793 as well as in other American newspapers.[50] The "small French work" to which the beginning of the instructions refers is *Agronome: Dictionnaire portatif du cultivateur,* a two-volume dictionary of agricultural terms and ideas by Pons-Augustin Alletz (1703–1785) printed in 1760 and 1764 in Paris.[51] The entire volume does not appear to have been translated and published in the Americas, but extracts did appear in newspapers and in almanacs that include *The Pennsylvania, Delaware, Maryland and Virginia Almanack* for 1791.[52]

> Extract from a small French Work, now circulating in America, under the Title of *Agronome; or, The Farmer's Pocket Dictionary.*
>
> **To multiply the increase of Corn of any kind.**
>
> TAKE of the dung of the cow, goat, sheep, and pigeon, and of salt-petre,[53] each one pound; put them all into two or three gallons of water, and let them stand covered several days; strain the liquid thro' a sieve or coarse cloth, and let your seed corn moisten therein for eight hours; take it out, and put it into a convenient corner of your granary; stir it well and often during several hours after. This recipe is adapted to 160 pounds weight of corn.
>
> ANOTHER.
>
> Put 20 pounds of lime into a barrel, and pour on it ten gallons of rain or river water; then put 120 pounds of corn into a basket, and let it remain eight hours; take it out, and plunge it into another vessel, in which there is a quantity of water, and wherein you have previously dissolved three pounds of common salt or salt-petre.

In 1791, corn was not a new plant for Nova Scotia.[54] At the time of contact with Europeans, Indigenous peoples had cultivated corn from what is now Montreal to what is now Santiago.[55] Before 1492, the many peoples who grew maize used it for food and drinks and conferred the crop with spiritual and social meanings.[56] After colonial contact, Europeans took the plant to Europe, to Asia, and to Africa (along with beans), where it became part of local cultures before the end of the sixteenth century. In New England, English settlers learned about growing maize from the Powhatan and Wampanoag, exchanges that were sometimes coercive, as in the two Powhatan men, Kemps and Tassore, who were held captive by the colonists in Virginia and forced to reveal how to sow corn.[57] In what is now called the Maritimes, the Mi'kmaq may have started growing maize between 1350 and 1550.[58] The Wolastoqiyik had developed knowledge of maize through their extensive trade contacts, and its cultivation in the Wolastoq watershed, as Jason Hall argues, "began as part of a broad pattern of Native horticultural innovation and adaptation before Europeans visited the region."[59] Their methods drew on extensive knowledge of the river, soils, irrigation, and weather and the selection of short-season strains of maize, as well as growing corn alongside squash and beans.[60] The Acadians were growing corn in Port Royal by 1700.[61] This recipe shows English-speaking settlers looking to Europe for agricultural recommendations despite the food's origins on this side of the Atlantic.

The method described here treats seeds with the aim of increasing yield. The materials used – dung, saltpetre, and lime – were employed as fertilizers in the seventeenth and eighteenth centuries in England. While fertilizers were usually applied directly to the soil, here they are mixed with water and applied to the seeds. This method of fortifying, or "fructifying," seeds dates back to at least the seventeenth century in England, when farmers and experimenters attempted to steep seeds in ingredients such as alum, quicklime, salts, urine, manure, and other organic matter in attempts to improve germination and ultimately the yield and quality of the crop. The use of salts emerged through the influence of Paracelsus, a chemical physician who believed salt to be one of the principal elements of life, in opposition to Galenic medicine that upheld earth, air, fire, and water as the primary elements. Salt was thought to prevent disease and rot, while saltpetre could serve this role while also increasing a seed's fertility. Some thought that the active ingredient in manures (a catch-all term for fertilizers) was salt; for Paracelsus, as well as for Van Helmont and the other like-minded thinkers collectively known as vitalists, all matter had seeds that were animated by nature, and fructifying waters like those advocated in this recipe were believed to improve germination by activating and encouraging the animating force.[62] In the seventeenth century, this technique was a new one, and it was associated with innovation and scientific experiment: "For the agricultural reformer, it was the manipulable nature of seeds, plants, manures, salts, and the steeping liquids that could be made from them which suggested that scientific control of the processes of germination and plant growth was possible for agricultural improvement."[63] Recipes for seed steeps were commonly published, and the practice was actually adopted by farmers (which is not the case with all of the recipes included here).[64] That the instructions printed in Charlottetown and Halifax in the eighteenth century aiming "to multiply the increase of Corn of any kind" are relatively brief may suggest that it was the ingredients of the steep that provided the key information rather than the technique itself, which evidently needed no explanation.

Fertilizer

This recipe is found in a 1791 letter from Benjamin Marston (1730–1792) to his cousin, Edward Winslow, in Saint John, New Brunswick.[65] Marston was a Loyalist from Massachusetts who, with other refugees loyal to the British crown, fled to Nova Scotia in 1776. Providing an account of his activities between 1776 and 1787, Marston's journal is a notable historical source. In 1791, Marston was in London, where he had gone in 1787 in an attempt to regain property in Marblehead, Massachusetts, that had been taken from him during the American Revolution. In the remainder of this letter, Marston refers to his "Robinson Crusoe adventures," describes his continued financial challenges, and sends greetings to his relatives in Saint John, including a challenge for a Captain Agnew to a game of chess that notes his improved abilities in the game. Marston was never able to return to New Brunswick, however. He died in August 1792 in western Africa, where he had gone with other British settlers attempting to establish a colony. He was there as a paid surveyor.[66]

London April 3. 1791
My dear Ned
The following information I think may be of
some worth to you in NB - A farmer from
somewhere about Bristol[67] sometime last year gave
notice to all the farmers in G Brittain & Ireland that

> he had discovered a Ferment (as he called it) a few bush
> els of wch would most effectually manure an acre of
> Land & would produce a most exuberant Crop – I was
> told by a Gentleman who saw them of some Oats the
> produce of this new manure of a most extraordina
> -ry size – What this ferment was he did not explain
> to the public at that time – But I have since been
> informed It is nothing more than the Lime of the
> Plaister of Paris reduced in it's unslaked State to a
> perfect powder by either Grinding or pounding & y^{n}
> strewed over the Land in the Broad Cast way about
> 6 bushells to ye Acre – & I suppose must be then plough
> -ed in – Whether it would be best to mix this powder
> with some fine mould before strewing it on the land
> I don't know – Experiment will readily decide that
> I had seen before I had this information an aw^{o}
> from America of the beneficial effects of manuring
> wth plaister of Paris pulverized as experienced in some
> parts of Pensylvania – It would produce 2 tons good
> English hay paire from the most miserable Land
> I think twill be worth making the experiment &
> I heartily wish it success – For it would afford me a very
> great satisfaction to be in any way instrumental to the im
> provement of NB – altho I am not so fortunate as to be able
> to come among you –

Like the printed recipes, this letter shows how knowledge circulated between Europe and America and confirms Marston's engagement in the quest for what eighteenth-century educated Europeans saw as a more scientific approach to agriculture. Marston here recommends spreading plaster of Paris (a kind of gypsum mined in Paris) as a fertilizer to "manure" the fields, a practice that became popular in Germany during this period. In 1768, John Friederich Mayer's *Die Lehr vom Gips* (*The Doctrine of Plaster*) urged the use of plaster of Paris as a fertilizer, and the practice was taken up by German-American farmers in Pennsylvania, where plaster was used to replace non-animal fertilizers such as lime, marl, and ashes.[68] Marston's letter suggests that he had learned about the use of gypsum as fertilizer from two sources: a farmer in Bristol who had tried the technique and from Pennsylvania.

In a series of contradictory letters, *On the Effects of Gypsum, or Plaster of Paris, as a Manure* (1791), a publication of the Agricultural Society of Canada, evaluates Nova Scotia's gypsum for use as a fertilizer. One letter claims gypsum imported from the Bay of Fundy had been ineffectual as fertilizer, while another argues that gypsum from Nova Scotia "is of great repute"; still another reports that experiments reveal it to be as effective as the gypsum from France. One account attributes the purported deficiencies of Nova Scotia gypsum to where it was mined, arguing that gypsum mined from the surface is less effective than that from deeper in the ground.[69] Expressing his belief that "I think twill be worth making the experiment," Marston encourages the continuation of agricultural experiments with gypsum in New Brunswick. Nova Scotia remained until relatively recently a major site for quarrying gypsum, which continues to be used in fertilizer as well as in manufacturing drywall and cement.[70]

Method of Making Potash

These instructions were printed in Halifax in *The Royal Gazette and the Nova Scotia Advertiser* on 17 January 1792.[71] We have not found the exact method in American or British newspapers or books that "Philanthropy" puts forward to Anthony Henry and his Nova Scotia readers, which may suggest a method devised locally. However, the proffered method is clearly in dialogue with other common methods for making *pot-ash*, a term that would later become more closely associated with mined fertilizers. Describing how to render fertilizer from wood ashes, William Lewis's (1708–1781) *Experiments and Observations on American Potashes* (1767) reports that, in America, hardwoods burned in household fireplaces were collected for potash making, the ashes made into lye by soaking them in water for a week or more, and the liquid then boiled down in pots, leaving an evaporated salt behind.[72] Hinting that the addition of plant material such as ferns, marsh plants, and seaweed is intended to increase the salt content, Lewis suggests that seawater can also be added to speed the process; Thomas Stephens (?–1780) in *The Method and Plain Process for Making Pot-Ash* (1755), suggests that ferns and other annuals produce a large proportion of salt but "require too much Labour in collecting."[73] The instructions in *The Royal Gazette and the Nova Scotia Advertiser* appear to be experimenting in making potash with ingredients found in Nova Scotia.[74]

Mr. Henry,
Please do insert in your respectable Paper, the following
method of making Pot Ash[75] – it may be very profitable

to the industrious farmers of *Nova-Scotia*, as this method of making Pot-Ash differs materially from that process generally known and practiced, by its yielding more salts from the same quantity of Ashes - and by a strict attention to the rules here laid down, they may be able in a short time to make the sharpest and most refined Pot-Ash, such as will sell at the London market for the highest price – and by application in the business among the farmers, it may produce a great quantity of that article, which will make a large exportation, that may be very condusive to our Wheel, &c. in the first place it will be necessary to mention the various sorts of materials, which may be collected in most places, from which the sharpest salts may be extracted from their Ashes – and then to shew the process to make Pot-Ash.

The first article to begin with is sea-weed, sea-thong or sea-lace, and all herb or plants which abound with a good Quantity of alkatious[76] salts will serve for this purpose, rushes, reads and sedge, which growes in mashes, poole and ditches of water; all sorts of bitter herbs, as cardus, beans, century, hops, southern-wood, worm-wood, as also Tobacco, the body of the plant and its stalk, with all sorts of milky plants, as dandelyons, celandine, sow-thistles, and leguminous plants abound with abundance of this salt, as bean-stalks and pods, peas-straw, &c. very sharpe[77] salt is extracted from fern, it grows in great abundance all over the Country, all these materials must be cut down when in their full prime, – because then they yield more, better and whiter salt, and dried by the heat of the sun, then gather them on heaps and burn them on iron grates; the Ashes falling through into a pit made underneath with a stone hearth to receive them, these Ashes when cold, must be carried into a dry place, and may be mixed with the Ashes of hard wood, all hard wood trees, if cut down in their prime when most fullest of sap, they contain a larger quantity of alkatious salt, then those that are cut in the fall of the year, because then the sap leaves the tree and of course the less salts from their Ashes – great care should be taken in the burning of hardwood for the sake of their Ashes – that way of burning them in piles on the ground is a great loss of their salt, they ought to be burnt on iron barrs or grates as mentioned above, and their Ashes carried to a dry place. In order to undergo the process, now to be mentioned – [t]wo iron kettles well be necessary, one of them to be cast with a spout about three feet long to be fourteen inches in the side above the bottom, this kettle when set, is to make the lye in; the spout is for the convenience of drawing off the lye in wooding fats or tubs, the other kettle is to boil the pure clear lye in, to evaporate the water and produce the salts. – All our Ashes being well made fill up your long spout iron kettle with fair water, and make a fire with dried wood, when the water begins to boil, put in ten-pounds of Tarter[78] calcined to a whiteness to every hundred pounds of Ashes, stirring it with a long wooding ladle in the kettle till all the Ashes is incorporated with the water and the salts extracted, the water being one third part boiled away, fill the kettle again with fresh water, and continue the boiling till half be consumed – when the lye is thus made, slack your fire and empty your lye into wooden fatts or tubs prepared for this use, let it stand so six days that the Ashes may settle to the bottom and the lye become clear, pour that lye into other tubs leaving the Ashes behind, and let it stand two days longer the lye will become very limped and clear, all the earthly faces precipitating and settling at the bottom, continue thus three times, and you will have a clear and limpid lye which will yield a very fine and perfect salt – this being done fill the other kettle with this refined and clarified lye in your tubs, gently boiling it to evaporate the water till it begins to thicken and shoot its salt which it commonly does in about twenty four hours time, so that the salt begins to appear on the surface of the kettle; let the fire be gentle and easy as soon as the salts begins to shoot, for fear the salt should stick to the kettle, which

> a great fire will cause it to do and so burn it, which often happens to those that do not take such precaution, take a scimmer full of holes and take out the salts, letting the lye drop from it, and put this salt in a dry wooding tub, the better to dry out all the moisture, and then put it into well glazed earthen pans and moderately heat in an oven or furnace till it is perfectly dried, take it out and keep it in a covered vessel from the dust and air; and the matter is compleat.
>
> N. B. In mixing such a proportion of the Calx of Tarter with the Ashes, is to make the greater quantity of salt, because it makes a stronger attraction of the salt out of the Ashes, and also makes the salt whiter, and by this means may be got seven or eight pound weight of salts out of fifty weight of good Ashes, without which, such a quantity could not be extracted, and to notice that the Tarter ought to have five or six hours calcination, for so it becomes whiter and more easily dissolveable in water.
>
> PHILANTHROPY.
>
> *Halifax*, Jan. 17, 1792.

Potash was used in making soap, glass, drugs, bleaches, and dyes, as well as the fertilizer that is the focus of these instructions. England imported potash and saw its colonies in the Americas as likely sources of the product, although manufacturers in other European countries, such as Sweden and Germany, were more practiced in its production. Manufacturing of potash was happening in the New England colonies by the 1750s, and Governor Hopson in Nova Scotia (from 1752 to 1755) commissioned Thomas Stephens, who was building a potash furnace in Massachusetts, to build one also in Nova Scotia. The letter writer urges that the potash produced in Nova Scotia be exported.[79] In 1789–90, the United States exported about 7,050 tons of potash, valued at $661,634, which made it the most valuable exported chemical, and potash exports came to be valued at over a million dollars in the early nineteenth century.[80] The name "Philanthropy" – which denotes love of humankind – as well as the suggestion that this industry will be "very condusive to our Wheel [commonwealth], &c." links the industry to social benefits.

Advocating a method designed to maximize profits in making a potash "such as will sell at the London market for the highest price," these instructions take little account of the ecological damage wrought by burning old growth forest to obtain ashes. These dangers are evident in Stephens's *Method and Plain Process for Making Pot-Ash*, which imagines along the eastern coasts of North America "some hundred Leagues of Woods to cut" and even more to the west. For him, this use of native forests gives potash two advantages over lumber as an export: while it is difficult to carry lumber across the ocean, potash is a portable commodity, and for those clearing land, "the Occupier" can quickly convert his wood into a commodity simply by burning it.[81] Stephens also links potash production to British cultural dominance: "But if we view it in a national Light, the Advantage is more striking, as by clearing the Lands backwards, it will be a means for ever to prevent the Encroachments of the French, who will not be able to annoy our Settlements, if we dislodge their skulking Friends the Indians; who can do little, but under Covert, or from behind a Tree."[82]

Not only does settler potash production offer a way to imagine all land as available to the English for economic exploitation, the process of making it was also seen to support British military strength, as clearing land was imagined as helping both to prevent attacks from the French and undermine Indigenous resistance to English settlement, here imagined as "skulking," a word connoting native presence on the land as illegitimate, yet persistent.

A Certain Cure for the Measles in Swine

This recipe for treating an infestation of tapeworm larvae in the flesh of pigs was published in the March 1791 edition of *The Nova Scotia Magazine*.[83] Defined as "a Distemper in Swine" in the 1704 *Dictionarium Rusticum & Urbanicum: Or, a Dictionary of All Sorts of Country Affairs*,[84] the symptoms of measles in swine were articulated in more detail in *The Complete Grazier* (1776), which explains that swine suffering from the disorder "will have a much hoarser voice than usual; their tongues will be pale, and their skin thick set with little blisters, about the bigness of peas."[85] Credited here to the *Dublin Universal Magazine*, the instructions for "A Certain Cure" were earlier published without the title in the agricultural reference, *A New and Compendious System of Husbandry* (1787), published by George Winter (fl. 1787–1801) of the Bath Agricultural Society.[86] It had also appeared in Philadelphia in *The American Magazine, or Universal Magazine* in 1788.[87] The recipe, still attributed to the *Dublin Universal Magazine*, would also be reprinted later in *The Royal Gazette and Miscellany of the Island of Saint John* in Charlottetown on 25 March 1794 (see figure 4.1).

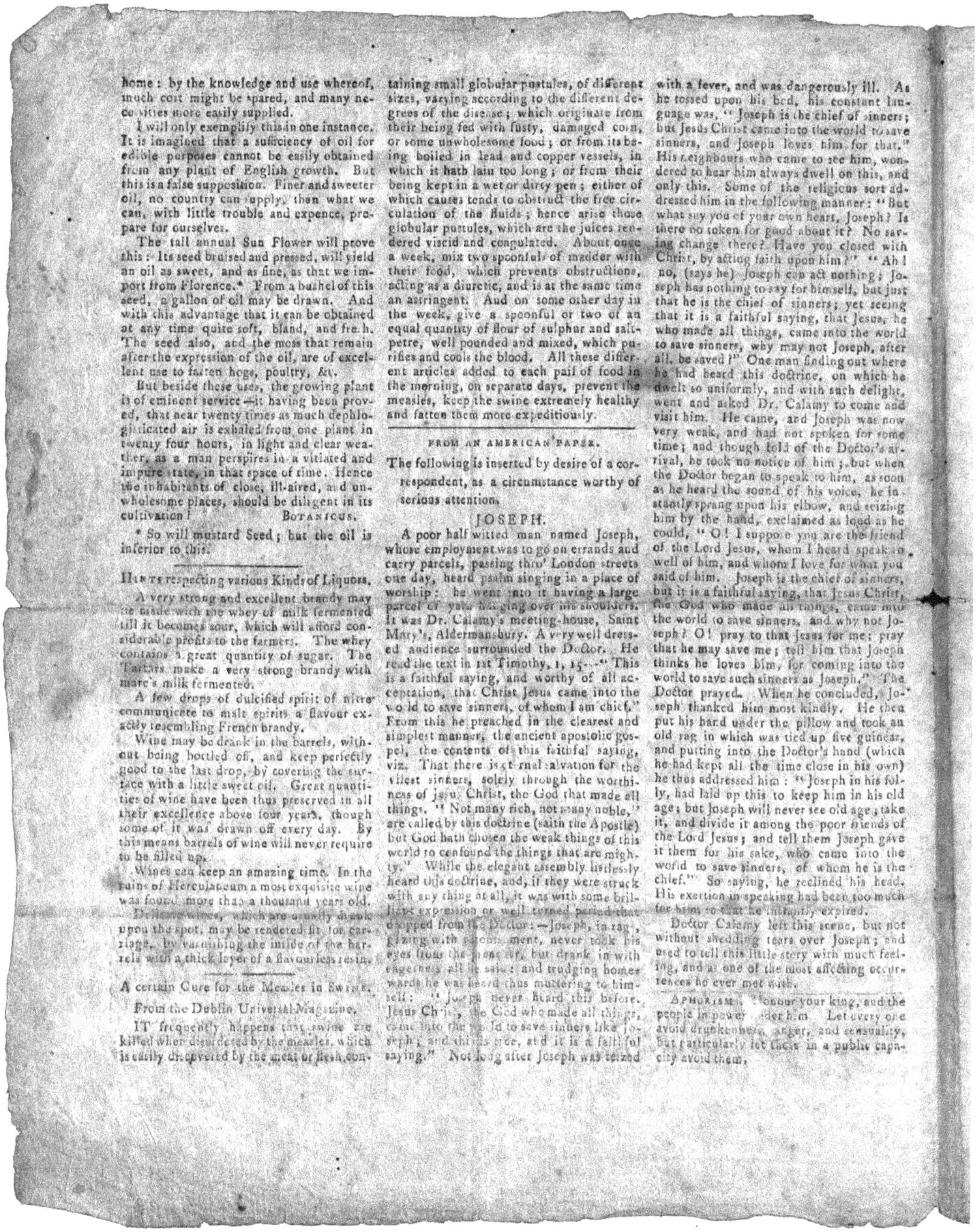

home: by the knowledge and use whereof, much cost might be spared, and many necessities more easily supplied.

I will only exemplify this in one instance. It is imagined that a sufficiency of oil for edible purposes cannot be easily obtained from any plant of English growth. But this is a false supposition. Finer and sweeter oil, no country can supply, than what we can, with little trouble and expence, prepare for ourselves.

The tall annual Sun Flower will prove this: Its seed bruised and pressed, will yield an oil as sweet, and as fine, as that we import from Florence.* From a bushel of this seed, a gallon of oil may be drawn. And with this advantage that it can be obtained at any time quite soft, bland, and fresh. The seed also, and the moss that remain after the expression of the oil, are of excellent use to fatten hogs, poultry, &c.

But beside these uses, the growing plant is of eminent service—it having been proved, that near twenty times as much dephlogisticated air is exhaled from one plant in twenty four hours, in light and clear weather, as a man perspires in a vitiated and impure state, in that space of time. Hence the inhabitants of close, ill-aired, and unwholesome places, should be diligent in its cultivation!

BOTANICUS.

* So will mustard Seed; but the oil is inferior to this.

HINTS respecting various Kinds of Liquors.

A very strong and excellent brandy may be made with the whey of milk fermented till it becomes sour, which will afford considerable profits to the farmers. The whey contains a great quantity of sugar. The Tartars make a very strong brandy with mare's milk fermented.

A few drops of dulcified spirit of nitre communicate to malt spirits a flavour exactly resembling French brandy.

Wine may be drank in the barrels, without being bottled off, and keep perfectly good to the last drop, by covering the surface with a little sweet oil. Great quantities of wine have been thus preserved in all their excellence above four years, though some of it was drawn off every day. By this means barrels of wine will never require to be filled up.

Wines can keep an amazing time. In the ruins of Herculaneum a most exquisite wine was found more than a thousand years old.

Delicate wines, which are usually drank upon the spot, may be rendered fit for carriage, by varnishing the inside of the barrels with a thick layer of a flavourless resin.

A certain Cure for the Measles in Swine.

From the Dublin Universal Magazine.

IT frequently happens that swine are killed when disordered by the measles, which is easily discovered by the meat or flesh containing small globular pustules, of different sizes, varying according to the different degrees of the disease; which originate from their being fed with fusty, damaged corn, or some unwholesome food; or from its being boiled in lead and copper vessels, in which it hath lain too long; or from their being kept in a wet or dirty pen; either of which causes tends to obstruct the free circulation of the fluids; hence arise those globular pustules, which are the juices rendered viscid and coagulated. About once a week, mix two spoonfuls of madder with their food, which prevents obstructions, acting as a diuretic, and is at the same time an astringent. And on some other day in the week, give a spoonful or two of an equal quantity of flour of sulphur and saltpetre, well pounded and mixed, which purifies and cools the blood. All these different articles added to each pail of food in the morning, on separate days, prevent the measles, keep the swine extremely healthy and fatten them more expeditiously.

FROM AN AMERICAN PAPER.

The following is inserted by desire of a correspondent, as a circumstance worthy of serious attention.

JOSEPH.

A poor half witted man named Joseph, whose employment was to go on errands and carry parcels, passing thro' London streets one day, heard psalm singing in a place of worship: he went into it having a large parcel of yarn hanging over his shoulders. It was Dr. Calamy's meeting-house, Saint Mary's, Aldermansbury. A very well dressed audience surrounded the Doctor. He read the text in 1st Timothy, 1, 15--"This is a faithful saying, and worthy of all acceptation, that Christ Jesus came into the world to save sinners, of whom I am chief." From this he preached in the clearest and simplest manner, the ancient apostolic gospel, the contents of this faithful saying, viz. That there is eternal salvation for the vilest sinners, solely through the worthiness of Jesus Christ, the God that made all things. "Not many rich, not many noble," are called by this doctrine (saith the Apostle) but God hath chosen the weak things of this world to confound the things that are mighty." While the elegant assembly listlessly heard this doctrine, and, if they were struck with any thing at all, it was with some brilliant expression or well turned period that dropped from the Doctor:—Joseph, in rags, gazing with astonishment, never took his eyes from the preacher, but drank in with eagerness all he said; and trudging homewards he was heard thus muttering to himself: "Joseph never heard this before. Jesus Christ, the God who made all things, came into the world to save sinners like Joseph; and this is true, and it is a faithful saying." Not long after Joseph was seized with a fever, and was dangerously ill. As he tossed upon his bed, his constant language was, "Joseph is the chief of sinners; but Jesus Christ came into the world to save sinners, and Joseph loves him for that." His neighbours who came to see him, wondered to hear him always dwell on this, and only this. Some of the religious sort addressed him in the following manner: "But what say you of your own heart, Joseph? Is there no token for good about it? No saving change there? Have you closed with Christ, by acting faith upon him?" "Ah! no, (says he) Joseph can act nothing; Joseph has nothing to say for himself, but just that he is the chief of sinners; yet seeing that it is a faithful saying, that Jesus, he who made all things, came into the world to save sinners, why may not Joseph, after all, be saved?" One man finding out where he had heard this doctrine, on which he dwelt so uniformly, and with such delight, went and asked Dr. Calamy to come and visit him. He came, and Joseph was now very weak, and had not spoken for some time; and though told of the Doctor's arrival, he took no notice of him; but when the Doctor began to speak to him, as soon as he heard the sound of his voice, he instantly sprang upon his elbow, and seizing him by the hand, exclaimed as loud as he could, "O! I suppose you are the friend of the Lord Jesus, whom I heard speak so well of him, and whom I love for what you said of him. Joseph is the chief of sinners, but it is a faithful saying, that Jesus Christ, the God who made all things, came into the world to save sinners, and why not Joseph? O! pray to that Jesus for me; pray that he may save me; tell him that Joseph thinks he loves him, for coming into the world to save such sinners as Joseph." The Doctor prayed. When he concluded, Joseph thanked him most kindly. He then put his hand under the pillow and took an old rag in which was tied up five guineas, and putting into the Doctor's hand (which he had kept all the time close in his own) he thus addressed him: "Joseph in his folly, had laid up this to keep him in his old age; but Joseph will never see old age; take it, and divide it among the poor friends of the Lord Jesus; and tell them Joseph gave it them for his sake, who came into the world to save sinners, of whom he is the chief." So saying, he reclined his head. His exertion in speaking had been too much for him, so that he instantly expired.

Doctor Calamy left this scene, but not without shedding tears over Joseph; and used to tell this little story with much feeling, and as one of the most affecting occurrences he ever met with.

APHORISMS. Honour your king, and the people in power under him. Let every one avoid drunkenness, anger, and sensuality, but particularly let those in a public capacity avoid them.

Figure 4.1
A certain Cure for the Measles in Swine, *The Royal Gazette and Miscellany of the Island of Saint John*, 25 March 1794.

A CERTAIN CURE FOR THE MEASLES IN SWINE.

[*From the Dublin Universal Magazine*.]

IT frequently happens that swine are killed when disordered by the measles, which is easily discovered by the meat or flesh containing small globular red or white pustules, of different sizes, varying according to the different degrees of the disease; which originate from their being fed with fusty, damaged corn, or some unwholesome food; or from its being boiled in lead and copper vessels, in which it hath lain too long; or from their being kept in a wet or dirty pen; either of which causes tends to obstruct the free circulation of the fluids; hence arise those globular pustules, which are the juices rendered viscid and coagulated. – About once a week, mix two spoonfuls of madder in their food, which prevents obstructions, acting as a diuretic, and is at the same time an astringent. And on some other day in the week, give a spoonful or two of an equal quantity of flour of sulphur and saltpetre, well pounded and mixed, which purifies and cools the blood. All these different articles added to each pail of food in the morning, on separate days, prevent the measles, keep the swine extremely healthy, and fatten them more expeditiously.

Specifying ingredients that include madder, sulphur, and saltpetre, "A Certain Cure for the Measles in Swine" differs from other remedies for the disease. The *Dictionarium Rusticum*, for instance, describes a treatment of wine and whey mixed with the iron oxide commonly known as red ochre, while *The Complete Grazier* does specify sulphur in its "most sure" treatment for the disease, but instead mixes the element with alum and bayberry.[88] What is most distinct about the remedy published in *The Nova Scotia Magazine*, however, is that it draws on humoral theory to substantiate the treatment's efficacy. Particularly influential in the early modern period, the belief that the bodily humours were the primary determinants of health and disease is most famously associated with the Roman physician Galen but had shaped the course of human medicine from the time of the Greek Hippocrates. Predicated on the supposition that achieving equilibrium among the bodily humours of blood, phlegm, black bile, and yellow bile would prevent and cure disease, humoral medicine focused on regulating the bodily qualities of hot, cold, moist, and dry with the aim of achieving the optimal balance thought necessary to good health.

The "Certain Cure" thus aims to encourage in swine "the free circulation of the fluids" impeded by the consumption of "fusty corn" or other "unwholesome food," the use of "lead and copper vessels" in preparing the feed, and too much time spent by the animals in "a wet and dirty pen." The recommended treatment is twofold. First, the farmer is to weekly add to the pig's feed "two spoonfuls of madder," a plant of Mediterranean origin best known as a pigment but also used to treat blood disorders in humans. Lauded as "diuretic" and "astringent," madder ostensibly "prevents obstruction" by counterbalancing the moist humour and presumably facilitating the dry. Second, the instructions specify that the swine be fed a mixture of sulphur and saltpetre that purportedly "purifies and cools the blood." In cooling the blood, the mixture would act as a corrective to redress an overabundance of heat that might compromise the health of a bodily fluid whose efficacy was thought to depend on the proper balance of hot and moist. Correcting the blood first with madder and then with sulphur and saltpetre will ostensibly "prevent the measles." Though the remedy proper does not offer "A Cure for the Measles in Swine" as the title claims, it does promise to "keep the swine extremely healthy, and fatten them more expeditiously."

Receipt for Curing the Wood Evil, Frog Ill, Rickets, Goggles, or Shaking in Sheep

The following discussion of various disorders that may also have afflicted Nova Scotian sheep appeared in the 13 January 1795 edition of *The Royal Gazette and the Nova Scotia Advertiser*.[89] The article had been earlier published by Robert Fraser (n.d.), without the introductory paragraph (which seems to come from Nova Scotia), in his *General View of the County of Devon*, where it is credited to an "A.B."

who goes unmentioned in the Nova Scotia newspaper.[90] *The Royal Gazette and the Nova Scotia Advertiser* does, however, acknowledge both Mr Fraser and the earlier publication date of 31 May 1794. Raised in Nova Scotia since the seventeenth century, sheep were first imported to Port Mouton in 1604,[91] with the Acadian population counting 407 animals by 1671.[92]

London.

Mr. FRASER'S REPORT OF DEVON DISEASE OF SHEEP.

The following extract from this valuable report, cannot fail to be very acceptable to our numerous readers in the country. It may perhaps induce people to attend more than hitherto to the diseases of this most useful animal

The stocks in the western part of England being very subject to the disease called the Goggles, &c. the following remedy for it, which comes from a respectable quarter, is recommended to the readers attention.

Receipt for curing the Wood Evil, Frog Ill, Rickets Goggles, or shaking in sheep

The disorders in sheep have been so little attended to, that it is difficult to le[a]rn the names of them; and when the names are obtained they are, in different counties applied to diseases accompanied with such very different, symptoms, that unless the nature of the disease be previously described, any receipt may be as useless or injurious in one country as it is beneficial in another.

The disorder for which the following receipt is recommended, is a weakness and perfect debility in the loins; which in different counties, is called by the names above mentioned. But shaking does not seem to be at all applicable to it, because the sheep is affected with no sympton of that kind. The goggles is a disease which affects the head, and is occasioned sometimes by a worm and sometimes by water. In time it makes the sheep turn always on one side and give the appearance of the whole side and loins being affected; but the seat of that disease is in the head. The frog, or hoof of the sheep is not at all hurt, and there[f]ore I would wholly reject the name of the frog ill, for the present. The rickets, a descriptive of the disease known under that name among children, is accompanied with a weakness in the loins, and therefore may be applied to the present complaint; but as that name denotes other ailments also, I would affix the name of wood-evil only to the following disorder:

In the winter 1792, I had a sheep which apparently had lost the use of his hinder legs: if raised from the ground he could not stand: and my shepherd baliff, and workmen agreed that he was past all recovery, and must die very soon. Under these circumstances it was impossible to do any harm, and, recollecting, that for some time past, the nights had been very cold and wet, I concluded that the sheep was chilled and benumbed; therefore I blooded him, and prepared the following medicine:

Take penny royal, wild scabeous, and shepherds purse. of each half a handful; bruise them well, and boil them in three pints of a[l]e; then strain off the liquid part, by hard squeezing and pressing the herbs; add cumrain seeds, fenugreek seeds, and caraway seeds, of each one ounce, and of London treacle two ounces: put these in a bottle and stop it close.

I gave the sheep nearly half a pint in the afternoon; the same quantity in the morning and evening of the next day, and the remainder of the bottle on the day after, when the sheep got up, walked away has ailed nothing since, and has been fatted.

The medicine is not the worse for keeping, and will be found useful in many sudden complaints: but if given for a fever, omit the carminative seeds.

May 13, 1794.

After establishing that the "remedy comes from a respectable quarter," the article narrows the catch-all "shaking" to the various afflictions of wood evil, frog ill, rickets, and goggles. Beginning with goggles, the author describes the disorder as caused "sometimes by a worm and sometimes by water" that gives "the appearance of the whole side and loins being affected." Though goggles may present physically, he argues, it actually "affects the head" and is therefore not an accurate term for the physical disorder the proffered remedy aims to treat. Because "The frog, or hoof of the sheep is not at all hurt" by the targeted affliction, the author will also "wholly reject the name of frog ill" as inaccurate to the disorder his remedy promises to correct and as therefore misleading. Similarly "accompanied with a weakness in the loins," rickets may be more apt a term, but is still too broad to convey the specifics of the intended disease. Thus working to remedy the confusion caused by "different counties" using similar terms to describe "diseases accompanied with such very different symptoms," Fraser rejects goggles, frog ill, rickets, and shaking to finally settle on "wood-evil," thus offering a remedy not intended to treat all the disorders claimed in the rather misleading title. Given that "wood-evil" is yet defined as a "Local name for dysentery or a similar disease in sheep and cattle,"[93] however, it seems unlikely that Fraser succeeded in correcting the ambiguities he meant to redress.

Following a rather convoluted attempt to distinguish wood-evil from the article's several listed diseases, the author explains bleeding as the first step in treating the affliction. As with the Galenic practices of human medicine, bleeding would have been administered with the aim of balancing the humours of an animal who seemed "chilled and benumbed." The sheep was then given five doses of a remedy Fraser claims to have cured a sheep who "has ailed nothing since." The article ends by asserting that the resulting medicine keeps well and "will be found useful in many sudden complaints," a broad and unspecific claim given the amount of ink already shed in narrowing the recipe's usefulness specifically to wood-evil.

Instructions for making the medicine first specify bruising a handful each of pennyroyal, wild scabious, and shepherd's purse, all of which were commonly used in herbal remedies and would have been readily available in England. Of the mint family and grown throughout Europe, pennyroyal is found also in an American variety whose range includes Nova Scotia. The herb has recently been shown to have antibacterial properties[94] and had long been used in Britain to treat a variety of human disorders such as colds and stomach complaints; pennyroyal also appears regularly in remedies for women, and it was sometimes used as an abortifacient. Wild or field scabious, a member of the honeysuckle family indigenous to Europe and naturalized in North America that has both antibacterial and antifungal properties, was traditionally used to treat coughs and sore throats as well as skin disorders that included scabies.[95] Shepherd's purse, a common weed of European origin that grows throughout North America, has likewise "been proved with multiple healthy benefits,"[96] and was in the eighteenth century valued for drying and astringent properties thought to treat blood and menstrual disorders. After instructions that include boiling the bruised herbs in "three pints of ale," straining off the liquid, and "hard squeezing and pressing" what remains, the recipe calls for the addition of one ounce each of cumin and fenugreek seeds, likely imported from India, and one ounce of native caraway seeds. Except in the case of fevers, where the "carminative seeds" are to be omitted, the recipe is finished with two ounces of "London treacle" that, like the cumin and fenugreek, would also have been imported.

Ringbone or Spavin and a Charge

These two recipes are found in the pocket and account book of William Chapman (c.1730–1813?) on display at Fort Beauséjour National Historic Park.[97] The notebook contains mostly accounts covering the years between 1764 and 1776. The volume appears to have been begun in England and carried to Fort Cumberland by William Chapman and then used by a later generation of the family; a Thomas Chapman, likely William's second son who was aged seventeen when he arrived with his family in 1774, signed the book as his in 1778.

William Chapman with his wife Mary and their nine children emigrated from England to the Chignecto Peninsula in the area near Fort Cumberland, or Fort Beauséjour, which had been built by the French in 1751, but was taken and renamed by the English after 1755. The Chapman family and many of those who arrived with them from Great Britain were Methodist, and in 1788 Chapman deeded the land for a church to John Wesley, the denomination's leader in England, for five shillings.[98] Chapman was a farmer who, according to the ship's log, left England because of rent increases "by his landlord Lord Cavendish and all necessaries of life being so dear."[99] In the colony, he was able to build a fashionable brick house, now called Chapman House, in Fort Lawrence (now in Nova Scotia).

The Chapman family was part of a group of English settlers, many from Yorkshire (hence they are dubbed the "Yorkshire Settlers"), who were encouraged to migrate by the lieutenant governor of Nova Scotia; only Protestant farmers and artisans who had at least fifty pounds were allowed to apply, and they were given ten acres of cleared land. The area where the Chapman family moved had been an Acadian

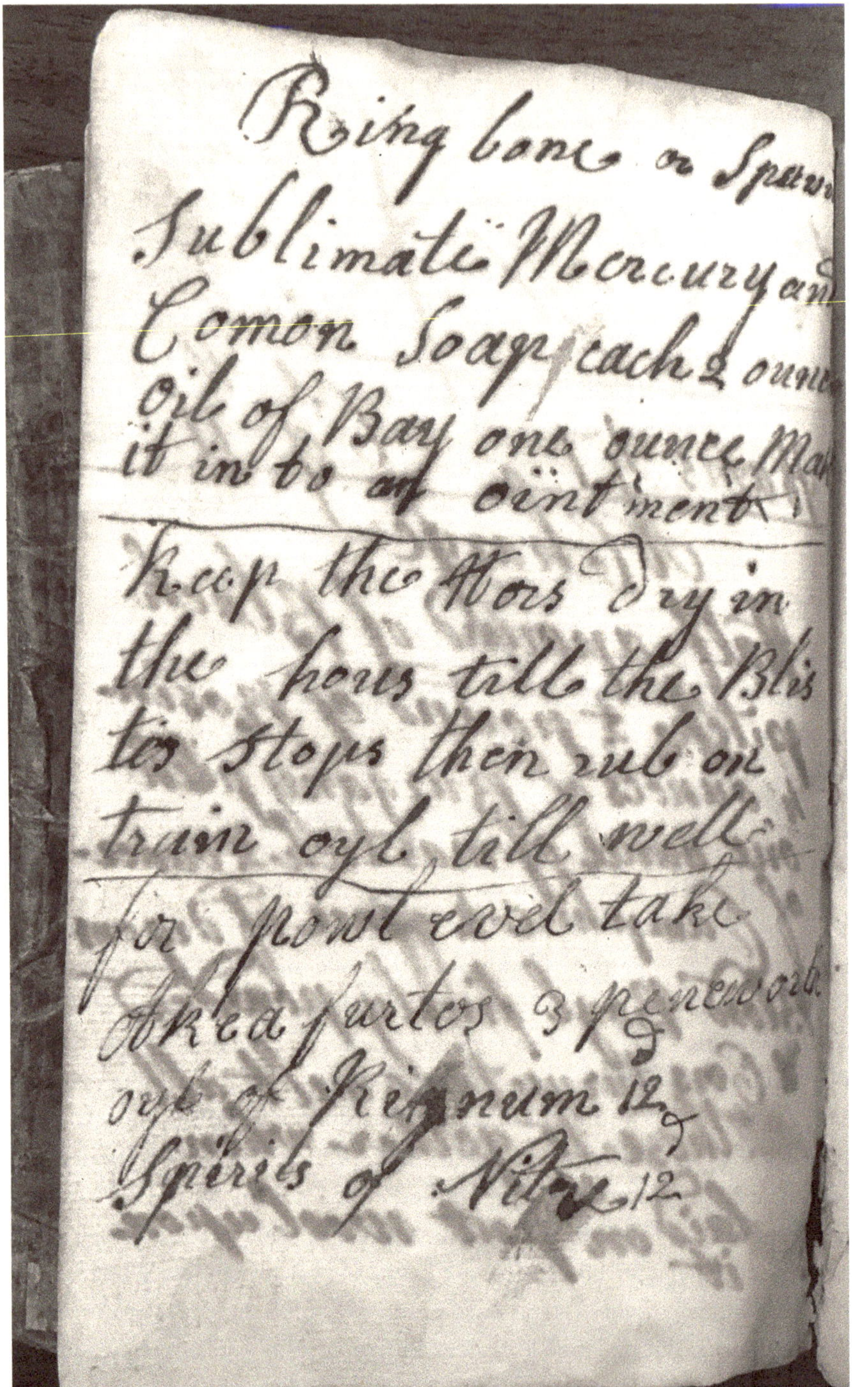
Ring bone or Spavi
Sublimate Mercury and
Comon Soap each 2 ounce
Oil of Bay one ounce Mak
it in to an ointment

Keep the Hors dry in
the hous till the Blis
ter stops then rub on
train oyl till well

for fowl evel take
Akea furtes 3 penewort
oyl of Rignum 12 d
Spirits of Niter 12

Figure 4.2
Ring bone or Spavin.

stronghold and the site of Beaubassin, an Acadian village before the deportations of 1755 and 1758.[100] Chapman claims ownership of the book with an inscription dated 25 November 1764: "Steal not this Book for fear of Shaim for hear you see the owners name Willm Chapman of Hawnby Hall." Another similar message gives voice to the book itself:

> Who so ever do on me
> look I am William Chap
> man Pockit Book and
> what so ever you on me
> say I pray you Carre me
> not a way for here the
> owner did me ly and he
> will fetch me by and by.

The use of the volume over the course of a century, along with comments of like kind that frequently appear in similar early modern collections, suggest something of the value of recipes and accounts in family histories. The two recipes appear between accounts dated 1765 and 1771; though we have not been able to find other sources, they are not unlike other eighteenth-century veterinary recipes.

A Charge[101]

Half a pound of Black
pitch ½ pound of Rosin[102]
4 ounces of Burgany pitch[103]
one ounce of mastich.[104] ½ ounce
of Camphire[105] ½ ounce of drgons
Blood[106] Boyl finely powderd
& Cors turpetine melt all
these to gether when
laid on put wool upon
it

Ring bone[107] **or Spavin**[108]

Sublimate Mercury and
Comon Soap each 2 ounce
Oil of Bay one ounce Make
it in to an ointment:

keep the Hors dry in
the hous till the Blis
ter stops then rub on
train oyl[109] till well:

In Europe, veterinary medicine was not institutionalized and professionalized until the founding of veterinary schools in Lyon in 1761 and in London in 1791. The first formal veterinary education in what is now Canada started in 1862 in Toronto.[110] Before the emergence of veterinarians, farriers (the craftsmen responsible for shoeing horses) often played a role in horse health care, while "leeches" (an archaic name for those who provided healthcare to animals) and cattle doctors, who likely learned their trade through informal apprenticeship, provided some of the care for larger domesticated animals; farmers themselves and others who worked closely with animals (such as shepherds) provided most of the health care offered to animals living with humans, with men taking care of the larger animals, such as cows, and women the smaller ones, such as chickens. In print, texts on husbandry and agriculture, human medicine, and almanacs all provided information on domestic animal health care for readers.[111] That Chapman and other farmers like him were responsible for the health of their own animals is not unusual.

Galenic theory underpinned early modern veterinary medicine. In Galen's theory of human physiology, health was the consequence of balance among four humours and the positive influence of non-naturals (air, food and drink, sleeping and waking, moving and rest, emptiness and repletion, and the mind) on that balance. Illnesses were caused by imbalance, although the theory also held that individuals could have different dominant humours. In animal medicine, as in human medicine, a regimen that attended to the non-naturals could promote health, while animal species could be defined by different dominant humours. Horses, for instance, could be generally choleric, while still differing in their individual temperaments.[112] Paracelsian medicine, which saw salt, sulphur, and mercury as key elements, played a role in animal medicine as it did in human medicine – often making itself known in the use of a chemical cure. Medicines for animals often sought to remedy the malady by redressing a humoral deficiency (with cold food for a disease caused by heat, for instance) or by addressing an excessive humour (through purging or bleeding, for example).[113]

The recipes in the Chapman notebook both aim to treat horse ailments of a type found also in eighteenth-century farriery texts. The charge – a plaster topically applied – includes a number of ingredients that were commonly used in eighteenth-century pharmaceuticals. Dragon's blood is, according to one contemporary pharmacopeia that lists it under gums, "the Weepings of a Tree which bears a Fruit not unlike a Cherry; the Skin of which pulled off, they say resembles a Dragon."[114] William Merrick's *The Classical Farrier* (1789), which explains the specific relevance of medicinal ingredients for horses, says much the same, and adds that "this drug is experienced to be of an agglutinating quality. It is a powerful drier, an astringent, and has a sharp diuretic virtue."[115] Camphor, it says, "is a pellucid gum [...] brought into Europe from China, or the island of Borneo [...] of a singular efficacy in removing external inflammations, whether of the eyes or otherwise."[116] And Burgundy pitch is "a very drawing and sticking medicine; it is therefore to be used with other ingredients, for a hot charge, or strengthening plaister."[117]

Although there were different types of charges, the ingredients in this Maritime recipe for a charge are well-known in recipes of this kind in British medicine. A recipe in one farrier collection for "A blistering charge" differs, however, in using not just black pitch, "rosin," turpentine, mastic, and dragon's blood – all ingredients used in the Chapman family recipe – but also euphorbium (a gum used as a purgative), cantharides (a kind of beetle used to irritate the skin), and aqua fortis (a kind of corrosive acid) to create what is meant to be a healing blister.[118] The effect of the Chapman recipe may be more like that imagined by another charge that appears in a variety of books among recipes to cure a joint strain. This one is made with black pitch, Burgundy pitch, and turpentine, laid with a spatula on the joint, "as hot as the Horse can well bear it." The charge should then be peeled off and another put on.[119] The effect here seems more restorative and strengthening than blistering.

The recipe to treat the spavin is a corrosive concoction that aims at removing a "hard swelling on the inside of the Hock"; spavin were thought to be caused by working a horse too hard before it was grown, by hereditary weakness, from other illnesses, from violent treatment, or from diet.[120] Mercury sublimate, its principal ingredient, was a common if somewhat controversial mainstay in early modern medicine. Surgeons used it to treat the pox (what we know as syphilis), skin diseases, and cancers in humans; exposure to mercury used to burn off pox lesions or otherwise consume unwanted flesh would cause negative effects including sweating (which was part of the cure for pox), as well as sores in the mouth and loose teeth. Because of the compound's powerful, even dangerous effects, surgeons often claimed its use as their exclusive domain while criticizing those they deemed unlearned – such as women and horse-leeches – for using it in their own medical practices.[121]

Mercury sublimate was nevertheless used in veterinary medicine by healers who were not learned physicians. With a note of caution that it must be "judiciously administered," William Merrick's *The Classical Farrier* suggests that the compound is a "most excellent medicine" in treating horses, for "it opens the pores, small vessels, and ducts of the glands; resolves obstructed humours in the remotest parts of the body, and performs wonders in cutaneous pustules, scabs, and other eruptions of the skin."[122] He recommends the application of fire or a caustic ointment to remove a bone spavin; the recipe for the caustic ointment that follows mixes mercury sublimate with other ingredients.[123] A similar recipe for spavin conveys the expectation that the cure will cause the horse substantial pain; in this recipe, where mercury sublimate is put under the skin, the horse's head should be tied to a rack so that he will not be able to bite "the sore place" and, after three hours, "the Anguish will be over, and so let him fall to his Meat." The spavin will then rot "and go away" and the sore that remains can be treated.[124] The train oil specified in the Chapman notebook may also be meant for post-treatment healing. Although the cure seems harsh, eighteenth-century people did care about their animals. One farrier's recipe book posits curing a horse's ailments as an act of love: "There is no Man who is a Lover of Horses, but would be glad to be acquainted with such Methods to preserve them sound when they are so, as well as to recover them from any Indisposition or Disaster that may at any time befall them."[125]

CHAPTER FIVE

Household

The recipes in this chapter approach the household both as a site of construction and a space for everyday life. Centred on family, sociability, and reproduction, houses were built not only to provide shelter but also to create a space in which complex human relations were enacted. As dwellings that require resources to make, houses signal their owners' economic and political status and convey social, personal, and emotional values expressed through architecture, design, and decoration. Houses are rarely the same across time and culture, however. In *Homeplace: The Making of the Canadian Dwelling over Three Centuries* (1998), Peter Ennals and Deryck W. Holdsworth divide early settler houses into three categories, whose styles reflected the comparative wealth of their respective owners. For the wealthiest, houses in the high style or polite homes were the work of particular architects in established but evolving styles; the vernacular houses that were sometimes linked to high style tended to be more amateurish and predictable, guided less by innovation and more by established conventions and structural systems; and the folk houses that came to be associated with distinct regional identities, their styles necessitated in part by the availability of materials and the demands of place.[1] In Nova Scotia, New Brunswick, and Prince Edward Island before 1850, few houses fell under the high or polite category, but vernacular homes, which included Cape Cod, salt box, and colonial Georgian styles, were constructed throughout the region from 1770 to the 1830s.[2]

Folk styles were also evident. Some eighteenth-century builders drew on Irish and Scottish traditions, while Acadians had built houses in French styles since the seventeenth century, drawing on folk traditions while developing construction techniques and using materials particular to the region.[3] For instance, Louis de Gannes de Falaise, a French military captain who arrived in Port Royal in 1696, built a wood-framed, post-and-beam, one-and-a-half-storey house in Annapolis Royal in 1708 (after his death, the house was owned by member of Nova Scotia's governing council, Alexander Cosby, and his son, Phillips Cosby, who became an admiral in the British Navy).[4] Seventeenth- and eighteenth-century Acadians often built frame houses that used wattle and daub with clay and straw in the walls; John Adams, a Boston merchant who came to Annapolis Royal in 1710 when the British seized the fort, also built a one-storey frame house with the assistance of Acadian workers and the wattle and daub technique.[5] Unfortunately, Acadian houses largely did not survive the 1755 *Grand dérangement*. Although different European ethnic groups drew on different folk building traditions, they often shared a "hall-and-parlour form" of one and a half storeys with two large rooms on the main floor, and a fireplace.[6]

Constructing houses in the eighteenth-century Maritimes was a complex activity, marked by layers of political and social significance. First, building is a way of claiming land. Situating the history of housing within a European drive to "harness a varying set of natural resources needed for European sustenance and manufacture, and by a wish to colonize territory and settle population," Ennals and Holdsworth see Canadian "shelter as one element of a complex mix that includes access to land, resources, markets, and wages by a variety of migrant streams."[7] Settlers also incorporated European social values into their construction practices. As Peter Ward writes in *A History of Domestic Space: Privacy and the Canadian Home*, "early European settlers established an inequality of domestic space in their communities during the first years of settlement. Colonial elites built houses reflecting their claims to status, wealth, and dignity while the less privileged built with an eye to utility, cost, and imitation. The social hierarchy was endlessly reproduced in a hierarchy of spaciousness. The homes of the wealthy defined norms of comfort and roominess that other families strove to emulate as best they could."[8] This "hierarchy of spaciousness" made itself known also in the Maritimes. Ronald Rees suggests that upon first arrival to what they called Nova Scotia (but then included New Brunswick), wealthier Loyalists imagined creating "a ruling class of landowners" who would receive from the crown substantial grants for land, which would then be worked by tenant farmers and labourers.[9] Building large houses helped both to represent and reinforce an imagined class structure. For instance, John Saunders, a Loyalist from Virginia who became one of the largest landholders in New Brunswick, was granted almost six thousand acres of land above Fredericton. There he built "The Barony" to replicate his Virginia house, now fashioned from wood rather than brick. Other large homes were constructed by those with means in the Saint John River Valley, the Kennebecasis Valley, Saint John, and the Annapolis Valley.[10] With wealthy landowners not actually labouring as farmers, this approach ultimately failed due to an absence of workers, and many houses had to be sold and "estates" broken up. Prince Edward Island's history was slightly different, with absentee English and Scottish landlords renting land to island tenants but not building large country houses.[11]

Only a few of the thousands of Loyalists received such large land grants. Most Loyalists were not from privileged backgrounds but were primarily non-commissioned soldiers, farmers, merchants, tradesmen, artisans, and skilled labourers that included shoemakers, bricklayers, bakers, blacksmiths, bookbinders, tailors, cabinet makers, and the like.[12] A more established Loyalist farmhouse was often characterized by a symmetrical plan that featured a central door and staircase, two windows on each side of the doorway, and five windows on the second storey.[13] Town dwellers would have been more likely to build a single-storey gable-roofed house in the salt box style or a Cape Cod cottage of a storey and a half, while those with greater means tended to build two-storey Georgian townhouses.[14] These house styles were not unique to the late eighteenth-century Loyalists who came to New Brunswick and Nova Scotia. Earlier, the diarist, merchant, and New England Planter Simeon Perkins, who was born in Connecticut and moved to Liverpool, Nova Scotia, in 1762, had built a Cape Cod cottage that he expanded in 1781 to create a new kitchen and additional bedroom.[15]

Utilitarian and necessary, houses are also decorative spaces that further reflect social consciousness and aspirations as well as consumption practices, at least to the extent that houses themselves might be rented or owned and hold a variety of goods acquired to render them functional and comfortable.[16] Money and status determined the number and quality of a home's furnishings and housewares as well as its size, level of comfort, degree of protection against heat and cold, and the extent of privacy it afforded. Among Maritime settlers of European origin, the French-speaking inhabitants of Louisbourg lived in close quarters, with extended families sharing households. Because rooms were regularly altered by the construction of partition walls when more people came to live in a house, furniture needed to have multiple uses. Even when eighteenth-century settlers were able to build more spacious accommodation, extant household items, such as furnishings, continued to have long-term value. Because consumer goods had to be imported from France and New England, Louisbourg inventories may have described furniture and household goods as utilitarian "hors de service," but those items were recorded as an important and valuable part of a household's possessions. Archaeologists have, for example, found many broken but repaired pieces of pottery, such as a French bowl reconstituted with wire, a broken platter stapled together with lead, and a broken English bottle that had been ground down to be repurposed as a container; pieces of broken dishes could also be repurposed as game pieces.[17]

The attention to goods was not unique to Louisbourg. Successful Lunenburg merchant Casper Wollenhaupt, whose foreign Protestant parents had moved to Nova Scotia from Germany in 1751, left many possessions on his death. The probate record for his estate lists items room by room in the family's two-and-a-half storey house. His possessions encompassed a clock, four looking glasses (two of which were very expensive and appraised at ten pounds), candlesticks, three Windsor chairs, ten mahogany chairs, three mahogany tables (among several other tables), more chairs, at least two desks, several beds (including two servants' beds in the kitchen), a wide variety of kitchen utensils, and silver dining accessories that even included a silver mustard pot. Much of this furniture likely came from American and British sources, but it is possible that the Windsor chairs were made in Halifax.[18] William Trueman, the collector of the leather tanning recipe that follows in this chapter, was one of several Yorkshire settlers able to build a brick or stone home in the eighteenth century near what is now Sackville, New Brunswick; the family enjoyed sufficient wealth to build a stately brick house on Beauséjour Ridge, with a "magnificent view," a wide hall, central staircase, and four rooms on each floor with a kitchen at the back. They also owned an American tall case clock and an armchair in the English Chippendale style in local wood, possibly made by William Trueman, a qualified joiner whose varnish recipe is also included in this chapter.[19] The recipes for cement and cleaning products in this chapter reflect the concern for the long-term care of things.

The recipes also engage with clothing. Like other household goods, settler clothing was acquired from abroad and manufactured locally, drawing heavily on foreign styles. While both French and British soldiers wore uniforms provided by their military, much civilian clothing was also imported from Europe, with French settlers importing French clothing and British colonists obtaining theirs (or the cloth to make it) from Britain. French law prohibited cloth weaving in the colonies, but British settlers were not so constrained and manufactured "homespun" at home (it wasn't until the nineteenth century that clothing production was industrialized and ready-made at a large scale, as in Halifax and Saint John).[20] The clothing worn by French settlers at Louisbourg was fashioned in contemporary French styles that worked also to preserve class distinctions: clothing for those of lower status tended to be more suitable for work. Hence upper-class people sported leather shoes, while those of the lower classes who worked outdoors wore wooden shoes or clogs. For lower- and middle-class women, respectability could also mean wearing a white bonnet and neckerchief.[21] Drawing on long-standing techniques, rural diaries of nineteenth-century New Brunswick women continued to document the work of shearing sheep, washing the wool, spinning, knitting, and weaving, as well as weaving the homespun cloth that was produced both for the family's use and to be traded or sold.[22] In eighteenth-century society, consumer goods held value much longer than they do today, with clothing lasting years instead of months and furniture passed down for generations. The recipe to remove ink from linen is intended to ensure this is possible.

Maintaining stylish household goods in the eighteenth-century may extend beyond practical need and also evoke culture. Loyalist Jonathan Odell, whose ink recipe is also included here, had household furniture that included New York styles and British imports as well as New Brunswick-built furniture made in English fashion; reflecting his identity, his property was, as Jane Cook puts it, "forged from both American experience and British longings."[23] As they had in Nova Scotia, eighteenth-century furniture makers had begun to manufacture their products in New Brunswick, where Odell lived, but used local woods rather than species common in New England and the middle American states.[24] Bonnie Huskins's study of the goods and habits of Shelburne Loyalists argues that ideas about manners and polite behaviour that informed European society from the Renaissance into the eighteenth century also influenced the behaviour of Nova Scotia Loyalists.[25] Although the majority of Shelburne Loyalists were artisans, mechanics, and farmers, rather than elite, they nevertheless valued genteel manners, conversation, and culture (reading and writing, entertainment), and they acquired clothing and household furnishings, such as a mahogany furniture, a Hepplewhite sideboard in the neoclassical style, and the china and silver required to engage in polite entertaining.[26] Some of their contemporaries were critical of such middling consumption of "fashionable clothing, elegant furniture, fine wine, and other embodiments of polite society," however, regarding it as inappropriate to their class origins. Huskins sees this critique as "part of a larger trans-Atlantic debate about the dilution and democratization of gentility."[27] While Shelburne's critics held to the more narrow traditional perspective that defined gentility through rank and, to some degree, through Britishness, Shelburne Loyalists wanted to fashion "new genteel identities" in Nova Scotia.[28]

The recipes and instructions included in this section thus speak to the construction of houses, to the furnishings and objects that support their utility and the comfort of the inhabitants, and to the home's decoration. Although the various instructions that follow do not pertain to substances now thought to be the subjects of recipes (we largely buy cleaning products rather than make them, for instance), they present the same features of recipes for making food and other consumables – a description of ingredients and their amounts, an outline of the process for incorporating them, an anticipated result, a consideration of advantages presented or technique used, and the authority or source for the knowledge. Given their value in a culture where goods were less disposable than in our own, many of the recipes in this chapter point to the importance of good construction and preserving and cleaning household goods and clothing. The ink and paint recipes also document how people sought to manufacture items essential to learning and the arts, which were key to fashioning and maintaining the gentility Huskins describes. Though not the only people to make homes in what would become Canada's Maritime provinces, only English-speaking settlers seem to have had their recipes for domestic practices archivally preserved.

A Fire Proof and Water Proof Cement

Pasted into Anthony Allaire's diary and order book, this recipe for making a cement to repair broken china and crockery appears in the middle of the notebook on an added page that includes four recipes for desserts as well as instructions for making a "Thorough Servant."[29] Recipes for making cement to glue broken ceramics appeared in numerous print publications. Though the exact source of Allaire's clipping is unknown, the same recipe for fireproof and waterproof cement was published in newspapers that include *The Ladies' Literary Cabinet* (New York, 25 May 1822) and *Minerva* (New York, 14 February 1824), as well as in numerous print recipe collections such as *The Housekeeper's Book*, *The New York Cook Book*, and *Mrs. Gillette's Cook Book*, where it appears under the title "Cement for China and Glass."[30] The dates of these recipes may suggest that Allaire's order book was repurposed for domestic uses, with recipes added years after the order book's compilation.

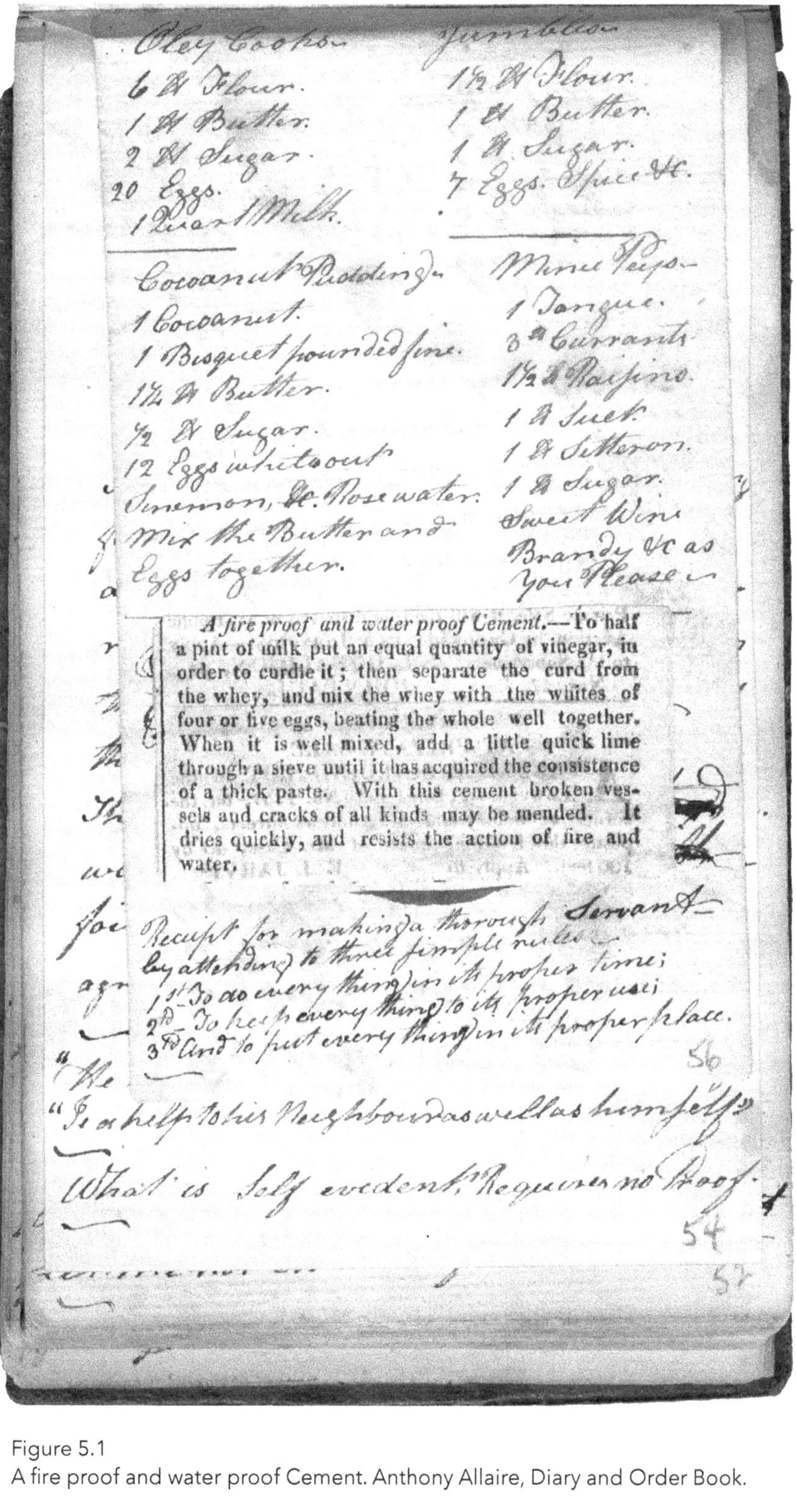

Oley Cooks—
6 lb Flour.
1 lb Butter.
2 lb Sugar.
20 Eggs.
1 Quart Milk.

Jumbles—
1½ lb Flour.
1 lb Butter.
1 lb Sugar.
7 Eggs. Spice &c.

Cocoanut Pudding—
1 Cocoanut.
1 Bisquet pounded fine.
1½ lb Butter.
½ lb Sugar.
12 Eggs whites out
Sinemon, &c. Rosewater.
Mix the Butter and
Eggs together.

Mince Pies—
1 Tongue.
3 lb Currants
1½ lb Raisins.
1 lb Suet.
1 lb Citteron.
1 lb Sugar.
Sweet Wine
Brandy &c as
you Please—

A fire proof and water proof Cement.—To half a pint of milk put an equal quantity of vinegar, in order to curdle it; then separate the curd from the whey, and mix the whey with the whites of four or five eggs, beating the whole well together. When it is well mixed, add a little quick lime through a sieve until it has acquired the consistence of a thick paste. With this cement broken vessels and cracks of all kinds may be mended. It dries quickly, and resists the action of fire and water.

Recept for making a thorough Servant—
by attending to three simple rules—
1st To do every thing in its proper time;
2d To keep every thing to its proper use;
3d And to put every thing in its proper place.

56

"He
"Is a help to his Neighbour as well as himself"

What is Self evident, Requires no Proof.

54

Figure 5.1
A fire proof and water proof Cement. Anthony Allaire, Diary and Order Book.

> ***A fire proof and water proof Cement.*** – To half a pint of milk put an equal quantity of vinegar, in order to curdle it; then separate the curd from the whey, and mix the whey with the whites of four or five eggs, beating the whole well together. When it is well mixed, add a little quick lime through a sieve until it has acquired the consistence of a thick paste. With this cement broken vessels and cracks of all kinds may be mended. It dries quickly, and resists the action of fire and water.

China tableware had initially been imported to England before the efforts of Josiah Wedgwood made English porcelain widely available in the last half of the eighteenth century, and china had "changed from being unknown in 1675 to being a normal part of household equipment by 1715."[31] A kind of "china fever" took hold in eighteenth-century Anglo consumer culture and endured well into the nineteenth and beyond.[32] Though lesser-quality china was affordable even to the lower classes, the quality of one's household dishes and decorative objects was an important marker of status for the upper classes. Retaining some value as cultural capital, broken dishes were often repaired and displayed if no longer usable. Common techniques included piecing together by drilling holes and lacing or riveting the broken pieces, as well as rejoining the pieces using adhesives that, like those also found in seventeenth-century Chinese manuscripts, often included egg whites combined with lime and an acidic substance (this recipe calls for vinegar, while some Chinese recipes specified mulberry juice).[33]

To Put into Beds, to Prevent Visitors

The following instructions for making an insect repellent are found in Sarah Creighton Wilkins's manuscript notebook, which includes entries dated 1779 through 1833.[34] Though we have not found a specific source for this recipe, it does appear toward the end of the volume and is probably from the nineteenth century. The specified visitors are likely bedbugs.

To put into Beds, to prevent visitors

2d. Red Precipitate

2d. green ointment

Mix up in Oil-

Pesticides and insect repellents were a common component of eighteenth- and nineteenth-century domestic recipe collections. Similar recipes that appeared under less evocative and metaphorical titles than Wilkins's usually described the recipe as being one to kill or destroy insects. For example, in her popular eighteenth-century recipe collection, *The Compleat Housewife*, Eliza Smith offers "An infallible Receipt to destroy Bugs," which recommends rubbing quicksilver (as mercury was sometimes called) and egg whites on the bedstead.[35] Wilkins's recipe also specifies mercury in the compound known as red precipitate, which was used from the middle of the seventeenth century to treat the skin.[36] The mercury compound used in these recipes draws attention to the convergence of pesticides with the history of European chemical medicine, with the mercury long used in early modern medicine deployed also as an insecticide toward the end of the seventeenth century.[37] The green ointment Wilkins's recipe uses likely also derives from chemical medicine. Between 1650 and the end of the eighteenth century, the ointment appeared in a number of different medical concoctions, including herbal mixtures, though one of its forms leaned toward the chemical in a concoction as corrosive as red precipitate. In his 1705 *The Family Dictionary*, for instance, medical practitioner William Salmon describes a green ointment made of butter, burgundy pitch, resin, beeswax, and powdered verdigris (copper acetate) that is claimed to be a "wonderful Cleanser and Healer of all sorts of Wounds and Ulcers."[38] While some pesticides relied on less harmful herbal ingredients, the use of mercury in pesticides, as well as in medicine, highlights how caring for the home could require knowledge of chemistry.

Bedbugs were regarded with some horror. A nineteenth-century English manual for maids articulates some of the feelings about this pest: "It would be difficult to point out a more loathsome insect than the bug, for its appearance is objectionable and its smell when touched or crushed is most sickening and disgusting. Everything has its use throughout the whole range of creation, but it is not an easy matter to determine the precise utility of this filthy insect."[39] Bedbugs had first been reported in England in 1583 and had arrived in the Americas with settlers, first infesting port towns and then moving inland.[40] Bedbugs, says one historian, offer a "forgotten private history of bodily discomfort, stress, painstaking labor, and excruciating shame."[41] Bedbug bites were not just painful but also shameful. Having bedbugs in the home was stigmatized and getting rid of them helped to ensure a family's respectability. Racialized and immigrant populations were often unjustly blamed for living in the kind of unsanitary conditions associated with bedbugs. Thus preventing and ridding of bedbugs and other pests was thought key to keeping a healthy home, a perspective that – much as today – positions the home and its homemaker as central to public health.[42] The importance of pesticides in the history of cleaning is further evident in the inclusion of pesticides in the very first collection of recipes published in Nova Scotia. Comprising an eight-page section of the 1820 *The Nova Scotia Almanac* titled "Collection of Highly Approved and Valuable Receipts, for Domestic Economy," recipes to keep off flies and to destroy rats and mice appear alongside instructions for making food, drinks, and medicines.[43]

For Cleaning Tables

This recipe is also from Sarah Creighton Wilkins's notebook.[44] We have not identified a particular source for this recipe, though furniture polishes are frequently found in recipe collections published in the eighteenth and nineteenth centuries. A similar recipe that includes the same ingredients appeared in an 1800 manual, *Domestic Management: or The Art of Conducting a Family; with Instructions to Servants in General*, as a polish for mahogany; however, Wilkins's recipe calls for a pint of linseed oil rather than the quart specified in the *Domestic Management* version.[45]

For Cleaning Tables

4 Pennyworth of Alkanet root[46]
2 Pennyworth of Rose Pink[47]
A pint of cold drawn linseed oil[48]
Mix this in a Earthend Pan let
it remain all Night, then rub some of it over your Tables with a linnen Rag &
when it has has lain some time rub it up with a rag if the Tables are Dirty wash
them Clean with Vinegar before you use it

Like the recipe for shoe polish later in this section, this recipe for furniture polish shows how practical household knowledge could draw on a wide variety of areas of expertise. *Domestic Management* commends the combination of linseed oil, alkanet root, and rose pink (specifying that it costs eighteen pence) because the furniture will need to be oiled only once a week and because its ingredients can be bought "at any colour-shop" – that is, a shop that prepares and sells pigments, dyes, paints, and the like.[49] That book's imagined audience is the mistress of the house, but its furniture polish recipe appears in the section directed particularly to the housemaid whose duty it was to polish the furniture on a daily basis; the polish thus promises economy in labour. That this printed version indicates ingredients available at a "colour shop" also points to their use in painting and other applications.[50] Although the art of painting has historically been accorded more cultural esteem than table polishing, Wilkins's recipe suggests that the two activities require some of the same practical knowledge concerning how to mix and use colours. That the polish is elsewhere used specifically for mahogany may also imply that Wilkins, like other of her Loyalist contemporaries, owned a valuable mahogany (or at least a dark or reddish coloured) table.

How to Take Ink Spots out of Linen

The following offers more instructions for cleaning that appear in Sarah Creighton Wilkins's notebook.[51] This is the only laundry-related recipe included in Wilkins's collection, however, and we have not found another specific source.

> **How to take Ink Spots out of Linnen**
>
> Dip the Ink d places in the Melting of a mould Candle[52] then wash it The spots will disappear

Wilkins's instructions offer some insight into the history of laundry, where stain removal entails a process separate from washing. As John Townshend in *The Universal Cook; or, Lady's Complete Assistant* (1773) explains, immediately upon receiving the laundry, the laundry-maid should go through the clothes and identify any pieces with stains, and "if there happens to be any stains of ink, red-wine, or any sort of fruit, you must be sure to get them clean before you begin to wash."[53] Several guides for servants include recipes like Wilkins's but do not recommend this particular technique for an ink stain. Both *The Universal Cook* and the household manual of Eliza Fowler Haywood (1693?–1756), *A Present for a Servant-Maid* (1744), recommend leaving the ink-stained linen in vinegar and salt for two nights, putting fresh vinegar and salt on the second day, and then rubbing the spot.[54] *The Complete Man and Maid Servant* (1764) recommends removing spots of ink or wine from cloth or linen by rubbing the spot with lemon juice, or in the case of linen specifically, rubbing the spot with lemon juice while stretching the cloth over a pot of boiling water.[55]

Until the 1860s, a time when doing laundry became increasingly mechanized, and the emergence of steam laundries in the 1890s, laundry was done by hand, most often by non-elite women. Before machines took over, the preferred methods were trampling the clothes with the feet or using a wooden bat known as a beetle to pound the clothes against rocks, and neither method relied on soap. If a cleansing agent were used, it was frequently lye made by running water through a box of ashes with holes in the bottom. In Victorian England, being a laundress was one of the main occupations of working-class married women.[56] In nineteenth-century Halifax, laundry was important work for African–Nova Scotian women, who had few legal wage-earning opportunities outside of domestic service, laundry, and sewing. In an 1871 census of Halifax and Dartmouth (which significantly under-represented African Nova Scotians), 31 of the 120 women counted with professions worked in laundry, second only to those working as servants, but these numbers declined with the rise of commercial laundries in the subsequent decade.[57] We do not know who did the Wilkins family's household laundry, but it is unlikely that Sarah Creighton Wilkins did the laundry herself.

Wearing clean and pressed linen was a long-standing signifier of cleanliness and gentility in Europe, and these values were imported to Anglo-America. Worn next to the skin, and often under other articles of clothing, linen shirts and shifts were widely available, and eighteenth-century men and women often owned more linen shirts than any other article of clothing. Their cleanliness, as well as the quality of the fabric, could function as markers of distinction among social classes, with those at the top of the social order expecting their linen to be very white and washed and changed often. The cleanliness of linen was also thought to have an effect on health, with dirty linen trapping the body's humidity and encouraging diseases.[58] Kathleen M. Brown argues that, for Europeans in North America and the Caribbean, white linen was also associated with racialized whiteness: "the freshly laundered white shirt helped a European gentleman to identify his peers by revealing the wearer's good taste, refinement, and membership in a global community defined by civility."[59] That instructions for cleaning linen were common in eighteenth- and nineteenth-century domestic recipe books suggests something of the persistent importance of the removal of spots. Being able to remove spots might also suggest frugality, in helping to ensure that linen had a longer life.

Shoe Blacking

Although its indicated ingredients are commonly found in instructions for making shoe polish, we have not been able to locate a particular source for the following recipe from Sarah Creighton Wilkins's notebook.[60] Maria Rundell's *A New System of Domestic Cookery* [...] *Adapted for the Use of Private Families Throughout the United States* (1814) does include a similar recipe for "Fine Blacking for Shoes" that calls for four ounces of ivory black, three ounces of sugar, a tablespoon of oil, and a pint of beer as well as the same amount of ivory black as Wilkins's recipe; it differs, however, in using oil rather than the egg whites called for in Wilkins's recipe as well as less beer and slightly less sugar.[61] It may be that Wilkins devised her own concoctions based on experiential knowledge of some common practices.

Shoe Blacking

¼ of a pound Ivory Black
The White of 4 Eggs well beat
2 Ozs of Coarse Sugar
Mix well in a quart of Beer

Most often called *blacking*, the first commercial shoe polishes were produced in Europe, North America, and Australia beginning in the nineteenth century. Ready-made shoe polish did not become widely available until the twentieth century, however, when soldiers returning from the First World War increased demand for products that would produce highly polished footwear.[62] Before the commercialization of manufacturing, shoe polish was made at home, and Wilkins's recipe appears to be aimed at making shoes shiny as well as black. The entry for "Blacking" in *Pantologia: A New Cabinet Cyclopaedia* (1819) says that ivory black mixed with linseed oil is a common shoe black; it adds that using beer and sugar will make the shoes even more shiny. Adding egg white will also contribute to the shine, although egg white is "supposed to hurt the leather, and make it apt to crack."[63] Interestingly, in using ivory black, Wilkins's recipe, as in her instructions for making furniture polish, deploys materials used in painting. *A Treatise on the Art of Painting* (1797) defines the ivory black made by burning as one of the materials most generally used in oil painting, but advises that it is "to be used with precaution, not only on account of its bearing a high price, but, without instruction, being difficult to use."[64] That Wilkins's household recipes do not appear to have direct sources may suggest that she too is experimenting, engaging with contemporary knowledge of various kinds, while developing her own preferred method. The art treatise's comment on the difficulty of using ivory black may suggest the level of skill required by household makers.

Chymical Liquid for Cleaning BootTops

The following instructions appear in the preserved papers of Loyalist physician William Paine.[65] Paine's notebook credits the recipe to the "Universal RBook," a reference to the *Universal Receipt Book* first published in 1814 that includes sections on "Cookery, Preserving, Pickling, Distilling, and All the Branches of Domestic Economy," as well as "Some Advice to Farmers." Paine's transcription from this source does, however, omit its conclusion that the recipe will "not only restore the colour to leather, but all spots caused by ink, grease, fruit stains, &c. will be completely removed by it."[66] Paine copied this shoe polish recipe into a collection that is otherwise largely medical.

Chymical Liquid for cleaning BootTops[67]

Mix in a Phial one drachm of Oxymuriate of Potash
with two Ounces of distilled Water, when the Salt is dissolved
add two Ounces of Muriatic Acid. Then shaking Well
Together in another Phial, three Ounces of rectified Wine
with half an Ounce of the essential Oil of Lemon, unite
the Contents of the two Phials, and keep the liquid thus
prepared closely corked for use.
Apply with a clean Sponge, and dry in a gentle
heat, afterwards pollish with a proper Brush.
Universal RBook.
Kutchimmoke.[68] Be of good cheer.

This recipe differs significantly from the instructions for making shoe polish found in Sarah Creighton Wilkins's notebook. Although both use ingredients that could also be used as food, Paine's recipe relies on chemicals while Wilkins's turns to paint ingredients. The oxymuriate of potash, or potassium chlorate, in Paine's recipe is a chemical compound used for a variety of purposes that include manufacturing matches and explosives as well as disinfecting.[69] The potassium chlorate is to be dissolved in distilled water before adding muriatic acid, a solution of hydrogen

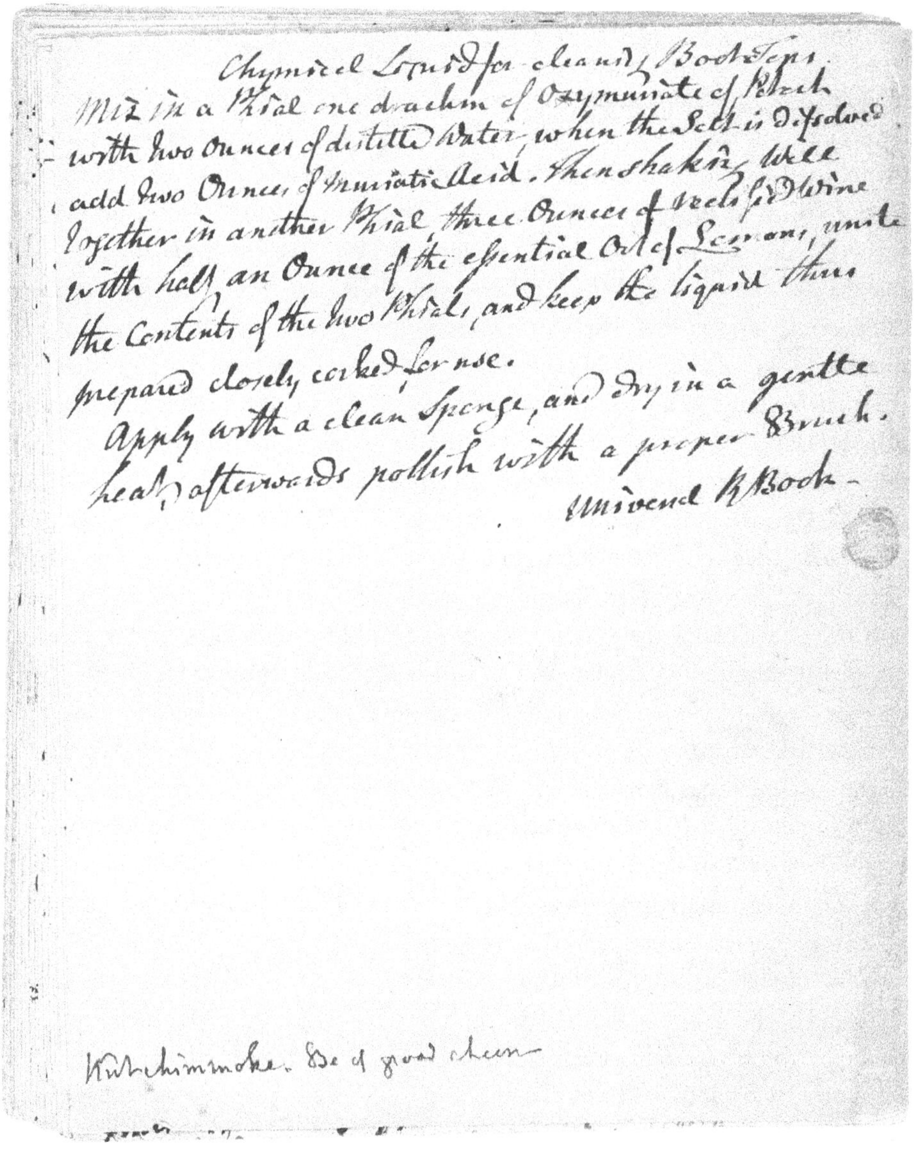

Chymical Liquid for cleaning BootTops.
Mix in a Phial one drachm of Oxymuriate of Potash
with two Ounces of distilled Water, when the Salt is dissolved
add two Ounces of Muriatic Acid. Then shaking well
together in another Phial, three Ounces of rectified Wine
with half an Ounce of the essential Oil of Lemons, unite
the Contents of the two Phials, and keep the liquid thus
prepared closely corked for use.
Apply with a clean Sponge, and dry in a gentle
heat, afterwards pollish with a proper Brush.
Universal R Book -

Figure 5.2
Chymical Liquid for cleaning BootTops. Paine Family Papers.

chloride also known as hydrochloric acid used in leather tanning as well as for cleaning concrete and other masonry.[70] The mixture is completed with the addition of rectified wine, a highly concentrated form of alcohol, and essential oil of lemon, ingredients that would facilitate shine.

A curious thing about this recipe is that it signs off with the exhortation *Kutchimmoke*, translated as "be of good cheer." This note does not appear in other printed versions of this recipe. The word *kutchimmoke* is, however, recorded in Roger Williams's "Key into the Language of the Indians of New England," which was printed in 1794 and 1810 in *Collections of the Massachusetts Historical Society* and then in *Collections of the Rhode Island Historical Society*, as "A Key into the Language of America" in 1827.[71] Roger Williams (1606–1683) was a non-conformist English minister who had arrived in New England in 1631 and gained a parliamentary patent for establishing the colony of Providence Plantations, which became Rhode Island.[72] His experience with the Wampanoag and Narragansett peoples included that of "language learner, interpreter, trader, scribe, colony official, would-be missionary, captor, and slave trader."[73] His *A Key into the Language of America* had been printed in London in 1643.[74] It was reprinted in the nineteenth century because, as an introduction in the Rhode Island reprint explains, it "presents the character of the Natives in a new and favourable light, and appears to have been admirably calculated to facilitate that intercourse with them."[75] Although the word *kutchimmoke* does not appear in a contemporary Algonquin dictionary, Williams was recording not one but many related eastern Algonquin languages, including Narragansett, Mohegan-Pequot, and Wôpanâak, spoken by the Wampanoag.[76] It seems very likely that Paine encountered the word as "be of good cheer" through one of these iterations of Williams's work. It is not clear why Paine has situated the word, which Williams links to funereal practices, beneath a recipe for a boot cleaner.

Williams elaborated that kutchimmoke is expressed while "stroking the cheek and head of the father or mother, husband or wife of the dead," but he links it also to dress: "the men also, as the English wear black mourning clothes, wear black faces, and lay on soot very thick, which I have often seen clotted with their tears. This blacking and lamenting they observe in a most doleful manner, divers weeks and months, yea a year, if the person be great and public."[77] What does seem clear is that Paine's engagement with an Indigenous language occurs through settler perspectives. His gesture thus exists within a broader context where colonists were adopting into their food and medicines some aspects of Wampanoag ecological understanding, but in doing so "vastly altered the interdependent, reciprocal relationships [with the land] that Wampanoags had learned through painstaking trial and error, and labored for generations to balance."[78] The Wampanoag, for their part, also engaged with English culture, in the aftermath of King Philip's War, seeking ways to return to their homelands by "selectively borrow[ing] European cultural practices by carefully weighing outside demands against their own needs and priorities";[79] English literacy, law, agriculture, especially animal husbandry, and Christianity all became "strategies for countering the new phases of colonial hegemonic assertions over place."[80] It is in such a complex context of unequal cultural exchange that Paine concluded a shoe polish recipe with what he encountered as an Indigenous expression of solace used at funerals to comfort the grieving. It seems to illustrate the broader settler colonial practice of detaching Indigenous practices from their broader relational contexts when they draw them into settler culture – and also perhaps how the adopted knowledge is misunderstood.

The Process of Leather Tanning

This recipe is found in the John and William Trueman notebook, copied upside down to others and recorded by an unknown hand.[81] We have not been able to locate a print source for this recipe.

The Proses of ^Leather^ Tanning

If the Hide is dry sok
them till quite soft &

---

then put them in Lime
fatt and let the lime be quick
taking them out 2 times a day
to air till you find the hair
com of, then scrape the flesh
of and put them in ^soft^ watter,
scraping them every day
till the watter com clear from
them; then lay them in your
fatt with Bark and stirr
your fatt well & let them
be coverd with ouse[82] Air
them at first puting in
as conveinent if the ous
is weak add more Bark
it will require fresh bark
about once a month _____

when you lay them away
mind to have Bark between
till ready to take out --
NB black birch bark and
Hemlock Equall Quantity

Tanning preserves leather from rotting and helps to make it waterproof. The process that had been used for centuries saw little technological change until around 1850.[83] The recipe represents an abbreviated version of the tanning process, suggesting that it would be used by someone who was already somewhat familiar with the work. The instructions in this recipe exclude the first step, which is to clean the hide thoroughly to ensure that all dirt and residual flesh have been removed. Soaking the hide in lime, the first step detailed here, then removes hair. This step of the process can take a month or more of soaking. The hides would then normally be subject to further scraping and to an alkali bath, usually made of ingredients such as salt, water, dung, or potash, to stop the working of the lime. This recipe gives the most details on the tanning stage, where hides are covered in tannin-producing bark, and it also recommends hemlock, one of the commonly used barks, and black birch, which was less common.[84] Tanners could prepare the bark by drying it and grinding it to a coarse powder and by mixing the bark with water. The Trueman instructions do not mention preparing the bark this way or adding water, but water is essential to create the ooze that treated the hides in a process that could take from twelve to eighteen months to complete.[85]

In eighteenth-century England, New England, and the mid-Atlantic states, leather tanning would usually be done at a commercial tannery rather than at home. Instructions for tanning leather are not commonly found in print and, unlike shoe polish, are not usually found in recipe collections for domestic use. That this recipe was written down at all may suggest that the work was being undertaken outside of a tannery. The use of hemlock and black birch further suggests that the recipe may have originated on the North American side of the Atlantic, given that black birch is native to eastern North America and not Great Britain and, like hemlock, is native to what is now New Brunswick.[86] The spelling and language, together with the absence of a published source, may also indicate that the method was conveyed orally and recorded after the Truemans had settled in North America.

A Cheap Method of Making a Watch-Coat for Soldiers

These instructions for transforming a shirt into a waterproof coat appeared in *The Nova Scotia Gazette* on 20 August 1767.[87] The periodical was printed weekly in Halifax from 1766 to 1770 by Robert Fletcher, who arrived in Halifax from England to become government printer. Though the newspaper normally published proclamations, laws, and public notices, it also frequently included material on other topics that were reprinted from English sources.[88] These instructions for making the watch-coat appear to have been copied nearly verbatim from William Smith's *An Historical Account of Bouquet's Expedition Against the Ohio Indians in 1764* (1766).[89]

***A cheap Method of making a Watch-Coat for Soldiers, chiefly those* in America.**

TAKE a large check shirt of about half a crown a yard, for it should be pretty fine: cut off the wristbands, and continue the opening of the breast down to the bottom; sew up the sides from the gussets downwards; rip out the gathers in the fore parts of the collar as far as the shoulder straps, and resew it plain to the collar. The shirt will then become a sort of Watch-coat, like a bed-gown with wide sleeves.

Take a quantity of linseed oil, and boil it gently till one half is diminished, to which put a small quantity of litharge of gold, and when it is well incorporated with the oil, lay it on with a brush upon the Watch-coat, so that it shall be every where equally wet.

Let the Watch-coat be hung in a garret, or other covered place, and so suspended that one part shall not touch another. When it is dry a a second mixture of the same kind should be laid on with a brush as before. When the second coat of painting is dry, the paint will not come off, and the garment is an effectual preservative from the rain; it is very light to carry, and being pretty full on the back, will not only keep the

> man dry, but also his pack and ammunition. This Watch-coat will be equally serviceable to sailors at sea, in rainy weather, and if generally used, would save many lives.

The instructions for making this watch-coat require altering a checked shirt to produce a cape-like garment that is then waterproofed with an application of linseed oil mixed with "a small quantity of litharge of gold." Linseed oil has long been used to waterproof wood and fabric, but it will not dry properly without an additive. The litharge of gold specified in this recipe is a combination of lead oxide and red lead that was often used in making paint (providing more evidence of the way that ingredients and knowledge were frequently deployed in a variety of applications used in different contexts). Similar to this recipe, another recipe from the Trueman notebook, "How to Make Fat Drying Oyl," calls for "litharge of lead" added to linseed oil and other ingredients to facilitate "Drying paint."[90] The linseed and litharge mixture is to be applied to the shirt with a brush in two coats, between and after which it is to be hung in an attic "or other covered place" with presumably good air circulation to facilitate drying. The result is a garment loose enough to cover and protect not only the wearer, but also the user's "pack and ammunition."

This recipe emerges from a military context where British soldiers were fighting Indigenous peoples. In Smith's text, the instructions appear as a footnote in "Reflections on the War with the Savages of North-America," with an observation connecting the coat to the war: "As the Indian war will require frequent incursions into a wild country, where a man sick or wounded, is in several respects more detrimental to the service than a man killed, every thing that may contribute to the health of the men is of moment."[91] Also highlighting the method's military origins, the footnote explains that it was "contrived by an officer, whose name I do not remember" and that "The sleeves are left long and wide, to receive the butt end of a firelock." It points out the coat's usefulness to the soldier who, by "drawing the watch coat close to his body," will be kept comfortable so that "leaning against the trunk of a tree, he may pass a tolerable night, both warm and dry." The coat may also act as camouflage, in that "it might be useful to mix some dark or greenish colour with the oil of the second coating, to make the watch-coat less remarkable in the woods."[92] These instructions appear in a chapter that represents Indigenous peoples both as "savages" and as without the vulnerabilities of those of "civilized nations." So on the one hand, Indigenous people are compared to "beasts of prey [...] almost insensible to the common feelings of humanity," while on the other, they have many advantages, "both natural and acquired," including good health and physical prowess (strength, endurance, good sight and hearing); from childhood, "they have been inured to bear the extremes of heat and cold," even as they go almost naked, exposed to the scorching sun or nipping frosts." In this formulation, the watch-coat seems to be fashioned contradictorily both as a means to address the weakness of Europeans in a North American context and as a confirmation of their superior humanity and civility.[93]

Method of Taking Spots of Grease from Paper

This recipe appears in the collection of Dr William James Almon.[94] There are multiple printed options for the immediate source of Almon's handwritten recipe. The instructions appeared in English, with a preface, under the title "Process for Removing Spots of Grease from Books and Prints. By M. Deschamps, Jun. Member of the Philosophical Society at Lyons. From *Bibliotheque Economique*, Vol. 1" in the *Philosophical Magazine*, published in London in October 1798.[95] Almon's version also has not copied the prefatory material. The French text referenced is a periodical printed in Paris, *Bibliothèque Physico-Économique, Instructive et Amusante*, for the year 1791. It provides the same preface and set of instructions, with the further detail that M. Deschamps is a young master of pharmacy.[96] The instructions appeared again under a slightly different title, yet still gesturing to the French source, in the *Monthly Magazine, & American Review* that was printed in New York, on 1 June 1799.[97] The text without the preface found in the original was also printed in *The New Family Receipt Book*, a recipe collection first published in London in 1810 but printed many times afterwards in Britain and the United States.[98] Here the recipe appears between instructions for storing milk and butter and for sowing wheat in ridges and among hundreds of recipes pertaining not only to closely related practices, such as cleaning books and making ink, but also practices in agriculture, fishing, brewing, distilling, construction, animal care, laundry and cleaning, dyeing, gardening, paints, perfumes, cosmetics, pesticides, cookery, and medicine – among other things.

Method of taking spots of grease from paper

After having gently warmed the paper stained with grease, wax, oil. or any fat body whatever, take out as much as possible of it by means of blotting paper. Then dip a small brush in the essential oil of well rectified spirit of turpentine, heated almost to ebullition (for when

> cold it acts only very weakly) and draw it gently over both sides of the paper which must be carefully kept warm. This operation must be repeated as many times as the quantity of the fat body imbib'd by the paper or the thickness of the paper may render necessary When the greasy substance is entirely removed, recourse may be had to the following method to restore the paper to its former whiteness, which is not completely restored by the first process dip another brush in highly rectified spirit of Wine, and draw it in like manner over the place which was stained, and particular--ly round the Edges, to remove the border that would still present a stain, by employing these means with proper caution, the spot will totally disappear; the paper will resume its orriginal whiteness; and if the process has been employed on apart written on with common ink, or printed with printers ink, it will experience no alteration.

The English preface to the recipe translated in the *Philosophical Magazine* and the *Monthly Magazine* suggests why it was important to remove grease spots from paper: the cleanliness of the book. Contending that a book's sense passes more readily "through the organs of sight" when the book is "well printed, carefully preserved, and neat," the preface argues that "a bad, confused edition, or a dirty stained and disgusting copy" obscures the author's thoughts, and "the dirtiness of the paper, which offends the eye, makes the subject lose much of its charms and attraction." The method, it says, was created by "M. Deschamps, at the request of a man of letters" whose books had been damaged by candles and lamps.[99]

Frequently reprinted, some appearances of this recipe suggest that it was not only learned men who might need to repair their books. The instructions were also printed in the *Lady's Monthly Museum* (1 October 1802) and in an abbreviated form in *Juvenile Miscellany* (1 January 1833), a magazine for children printed in Boston. The latter version instructs children how to repair their books but advises them to practise beforehand by attempting "the experiment first on a useless piece of paper."[100] Given that Almon himself owned a large library,[101] this recipe seems likely to have been meant to help to sustain his books in good condition.

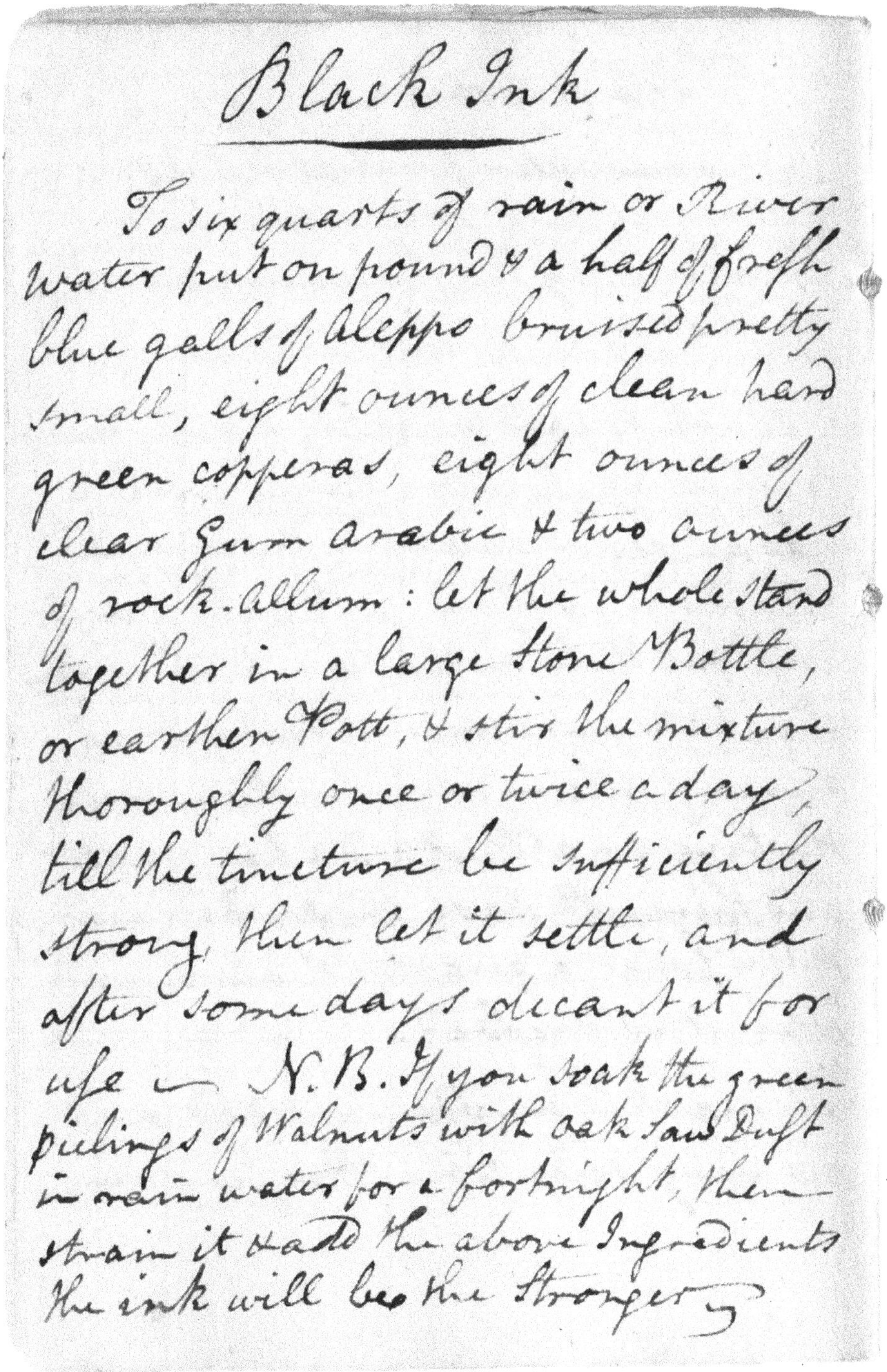
Black Ink

To six quarts of rain or River water put on pound & a half of fresh blue galls of Aleppo bruised pretty small, eight ounces of clean hard green copperas, eight ounces of clear Gum arabic & two ounces of rock-Allum: let the whole stand together in a large Stone Bottle, or earthen Pott, & stir the mixture thoroughly once or twice a day, till the tincture be sufficiently strong, then let it settle, and after some days decant it for use — N.B. If you soak the green peelings of Walnuts with Oak Saw Dust in rain water for a fortnight, then strain it & add the above Ingredients the ink will bee the stronger —

Figure 5.3
Black Ink. Jonathan Odell, Notebook.

Black Ink

This recipe is one of several copied into the middle of a commonplace book kept by Jonathan Odell.[102] It is a slightly abridged version of a recipe that appears in George Fisher's *The Instructor: or, Young Man's Best Companion: Containing, Spelling, Reading, Writing, and Arithmetick in an Easier Way Than Any Yet Published; and How to Qualify Any Person for Business, Without the Help of a Master* that was printed in London in 1735 and reprinted multiple times throughout the eighteenth century.

Black Ink

To six quarts of rain or river water, put one pound and a half of fresh blue galls of Aleppo[103] bruised pretty small, eight ounces of clean hard green copperas,[104] eight ounces of clear gum arabic[105] and two ounces of rock alum.[106] Let the whole stand together in a large stone bottle, or earthen pot, and stir the mixture thoroughly once or twice a day, till the tincture be sufficiently strong, then let it settle, and after some days decant it for use. N.B. If you soak the green peelings of walnuts with oak saw-dust in rain water for a fortnight, then strain it and add the above ingredients, the ink will be the stronger.

Gall was used in making ink from the ninth century onwards, and oak galls have been used in making ink, dyeing, and medicine around the world. The Aleppo gall, found in Hungary, Turkey, Greece, and western Asia, has been valued in Europe since Hippocrates, and Pliny recorded medicinal uses while also noting its use in tanning and dyeing, with Aleppo gall considered the best.[107] As a politician, minister, and scholar, Odell was deeply invested in writing. Given the date of the source, this recipe for ink may have been recorded during Odell's years as a student in New Jersey and came with him to New Brunswick. Many of his papers, which were written in ink he may have made himself, survive in the New Brunswick Museum archives.

Paint

This recipe is part of a longer passage on painting preserved in the *Diary of Thomas Wright* held in the Prince Edward Island Public Archives.[108] The notebook also includes surveying notes, measurements, observations on the weather, accounts, poetry, songs, and two medical recipes. Thomas Wright (c. 1740–1812) was an English surveyor who came to what is now the Maritime provinces in 1764 as a deputy to Samuel Holland, the surveyor general of the northern district of eastern North America. Wright assisted with surveying St John's Island, Cape Breton, Anticosti Island, the coast of the Bay of Fundy, and parts of New England. In 1773, he was named surveyor general of St John's Island, a position he held until his death in 1812. In 1775, he was kidnapped along with the acting governor of the island and taken to Massachusetts, until George Washington arranged his release and he could return home, where he married Susanna Turner and had eleven children, one of whom succeeded him as surveyor general. The Wright family lived first in Charlottetown before moving to Morell and then to nearby Cherry Valley, where Wright acquired land.[109] With Samuel Holland, Wright also submitted a report to the Royal Society on the transit of Venus (3 June 1769), which he had observed from the Saint Lawrence River.[110]

The source for the recipes for flesh colour and "pure lake" (a red pigment) is John Barrow's *Dictionarium Polygraphicum* (London, 1735).[111] The source for the instructions for painting the sky and for carnation is Godfrey Smith's *The Laboratory, or School of Arts* (London, 1738).[112]

Of mixt and compound Colours

[...]

To make a flesh colour, Mix a little lake[113] and red lead with white, a very small quantity of each, you may make it as light or as red as you please, by putting more or less white in it. If you would have a swarthy complexion to distinguish a mans flesh from a woman's, put a little yellow oker[114] among your flesh colour; and for your shadow, put a little more lake, and a small quantity of burnt umber.

[...]

To make a pure lake. Take urine ten pounds, boil it in a kettle, and
skim it with an iron skimmer, till it comes to eight pounds; to which add gum
lake half a pound, allum[115] two ounces and a half; boil all till it is well colourd,
which you may try by dipping a piece of linen cloth in it; then add sweet allum
in powder a sufficient quantity; strain it and let it stand; strain it again thorough
a dry cloth, till the liquor be clear; that which remains in the cloth or bag is
the pure lake. –

[...]

To paint or colour a clear sky

Take clear blue verditer,[116] mixed with a little white; with this begin at the top of your

landskip or picture, and having laid on the blue for some space, break it with a little lake or purple, working it with a clear pencil, one colour imperceptibly into another, apply more white and masticote[117] in order to make it – fainter & fainter towards the horizon working all the white the colours imperceptible one into another from the horizon on to the blue sky; after which, you may lay some stronger strokes of purple over the light, in as to make the appear like clouds at a distance – For a firey red sky use red lead and a little white instead of the purple streaks or clouds, working them according to art, imperceptibly one with another. –
Clouds you are to lay ^with^ white & black, sometime mix a little purple therewith: but the less & surest direction you can have is from nature herself

[...]
Of carnation or flesh colour. –

In carnation or flesh colour, use for young women & children flake white burnt oaker and a little vermillion; some add a little lake, but that must be but sparingly; having laid in the colour for the carnation you shade the lips, cheeks, chin, knees, and toes, with fine lake & vermillion, and the naked parts, with sea coal and a little lake, or brown red, or with brown oaker and lake, or else with indian ink[118] or lake; for a brownish complexion, mix a little brown oaker among the carnation colour - Some artists lay the dead colouring[119] of the carnation for young women on with white; they shade it with paper black and bring in the carnation colour where it is required. –

These instructions entail Wright's bringing European painting traditions to the Maritimes. The ingredients and colour names used by Wright are common also to eighteenth-century painting treatises, some of which have a long European history. Wright's notebook includes a fuller set of instructions that incorporate a list of the "seven painting Colours" that distinguishes between changeable and permanent colours; it also distinguishes simple colours made from plants and mineral colours derived from metals, and offers instructions for preparing and grinding colours. The recipes for flesh colour and pure lake appear in a section entitled "Of mixt and compound Colours," as they do also in the *Dictionarium Polygraphicum*. Interestingly perhaps, Barrow recommends using urine in making colours throughout his work, while another part of the instructions from *The Laboratory, or School of Arts* (not included here but copied by Wright into his notebook) calls for mixing in a little earwax if the colours fail to stick to the paper.

It is possible that Wright used paint in his surveying work. He was skilled at rendering landscape scenes, as well as delineating coasts used to make maps, and his landscape drawing of the town and harbour of Louisbourg in 1766 survives.[120] As part of Holland's survey team, Wright was involved in producing some of the most intricate and detailed maps of the time. Although the geographic knowledge they conveyed did not help prevent the British from losing control of large chunks of the territory in the American Revolutionary War, Stephen Hornsby argues that the surveys helped to facilitate the growth of the British empire over the longer term. The surveys of the 1760s illustrate Britain's exertion of greater control over its North American colonies – a control abetted by the military – and Britain's martial as well as "scientific mastery"; they also "fixed and arranged the geographic space of northeastern North America in preparation for colonial settlement," an arrangement that included demarcating not just boundaries of land and sea but also imperial names and meridian lines deriving from Greenwich that arranged the world around Britain.[121]

The record of paint colours for skin suggest that Wright may have been a surveyor and scientist, but he was also interested in eighteenth-century art. Although the recipe for painting the sky suggests that "the less & surest direction you can have is from nature herself," the recipe for carnation suggests that when looking at skin, the artist turns less to nature than convention; the paint colours for skin tones are set, thus conveying the artifice of painting and of early modern European ideals of female beauty. Painters were rendering not exactly what they saw but producing desirable types from their subjects. "To make a flesh colour" suggests that men are more "swarthy" than women; indeed, representing the skin tone of men requires the addition of yellow ochre to red and white, the two colours most often praised as beautiful in early modern verse. "Of carnation or flesh colour" similarly presents the idea that the skin tone of young women and children should be similar to each other and pinker than that of other portrait sitters. The colour carnation is also specified in early modern cosmetics, such as "A Water to give the Cheeks a Carnation Colour" published in *The New London Toilet*, a 1778 book on beautifying.[122] In a period when women were often called "the fair sex," these recipes for paints were part of a discourse concerning European female bodies, one in which skin colour was painted less according to how it actually looked than by the expectation that skin could distinguish people by class, gender, age, and race.[123] That flesh is equated with carnation, or pink, also conveys the extent to which it is implicitly presumed that people with other skin tones will not be the subjects of portraits.

Mortar

This recipe was printed in the November 1791 issue of *The Nova Scotia Magazine.*[124] Other recipes that appear in the issue include directions for making parmesan cheese and for growing potatoes. Except for the letter to the editor from one "E.F.," the instructions for making mortar published in *The Nova Scotia Magazine* had appeared earlier in London in *The Annual Register* [...] *for the year 1771* in the section headed "Useful Projects" under the title "Method of making Mortar which will be impenetrable to moisture, from *Mr Dossie's* second volume of Memoirs of Agriculture, just published."[125] The original source, where the instructions appear in an extended form, is found in *Memoirs of Agriculture* (1768) by Robert Dossie (1717–1777), also printed in London.[126] There are no clues given as to the identity of E.F.

TO THE EDITOR OF THE NOVA SCOTIA MAGAZINE. SIR,

if you will insert the enclosed Method of making Mortar, which will be impenetra-ble to Moisture, in your useful Magazine, you will oblige a Subscriber, and, very pro-bably, thereby confer an Obligation on the Public.

I am, Sir, your most obedient and humble Servant, E. F.

METHOD of making MORTAR, which will be impenetrable to MOISTURE.

TAKE of unslacked[127] lime and fine sand in the proportion of one part lime to three parts sand, as much as a labourer can well manage at once; and then, adding water gradually, mix the whole well together, till it be reduced to the consistence of mortar. Apply it immediately, while it is yet hot, to the purpose either of mortar, as cement to brick or stone, or of plaister, for the furnace of any building. It will then ferment for some days in drier places, and afterward gradually concrete, or set and become hard. But in a moist place, it will continue soft for three weeks or more; though it will at length attain a firm consistence, even if water have such access to it, as to keep the surface wet the whole time. After this it will acquire a stone like Hardness, and resist all moisture. The perfection of this mortar depends on the ingredients being thoroughly blended together, and the mixture's being applied immediately after to the place where it is wanted. In order to this, about five labourers should be employed for mixing the mortar, to attend one person who applies it. This method of making mortar, Mr. Dossie says, was discovered by a gentleman of Neuschattel, the back part of whose house being cut out of a rocky hill, the spring from the rock greatly annoyed it, and produced a continual damp, which nothing could cure till he tried the mortar above described, which effectually answered his purpose, and which by time grows so tenacious and firm, that he was induced to believe the method of composition was the same with that pursued by the antients.

We are told that chalk lime, which is the kind most commonly used in London, is unfit for the purpose, on account of the stints it contains, which render it necessary to be skreened before it can be temper-
[page break]
ed with water and sand. Previous to skreening, however, the lime must be slacked: and the slacking it before it be mixed with sand, prevents its acting on that ingredient, so as to produce their incorporation; which power it loses in a great degree after its combination with the quantity of water that saturates it.

The lime for this purpose, therefore, must

> be that made of lime-stone, shells, or marble; and the stronger it is, the mortar will be proportionably better.
> Besides an attention should be paid to the kind of lime to be used in making this mortar; what is intended for it, should be carefully kept from the access of air, as it will readily attract moisture, and lose proportionably that power of acting on the sand to produce an incorporation. It is also advised to exclude the sun and wind from the mortar for some days after it is applied, that its drying too quickly may not prevent the due continuance of the fermentation, which is necessary to favour the action of the lime on the sand.
> This mortar is attended with very particular advantages; for it may be used, and will even attain a perfect induration, though moisture have access to it when it is applied; and while it is fermenting and setting, it is extremely beneficial for preventing the oozing of water through the floors of walls of houses, where the common method used would have no effect. When a very great hardness and firmness are required in this mortar, the using of skimmed milk, instead of water, either wholly or in part, will produce the desired effect; and in this circumstance, likewise, the preparation is imagined to resemble that of the antients.

The use of burnt lime in mortars dates back thousands of years to Mesopotamia; the Roman architect Vitruvius (fl. 70–15 BCE) recommended in his work on architecture that white limestone be burned and mixed with three parts sand and water.[128] In the eighteenth century, lime would still be made by burning limestone to remove carbon dioxide, leaving calcium oxide (or quicklime) that would then be soaked in water to make a lime putty, to which sand was added to make mortar. We now know that different types of limestone grant different properties to the mortar, with dolomitic limestone's high levels of magnesium producing the strongest.[129] The instructions' rejection of London's chalk lime fits with this principle. The use of shells as a source of lime was also common practice in the northeast. In seventeenth-century New England, for instance, settlers first obtained lime from mollusk shells and natural deposits of limestone; they calcified the rocks and shells by burning, which were then slaked with the addition of water. The shells were often found in "kitchen middens," buried heaps of domestic waste left by the Indigenous inhabitants of the region. The calcification of lime required a kiln, which pushed air through an inverted cone layered with limestone and fuel. Because limestone quarries had been constructed in that region as early as the 1660s, natural limestone was a less expensive source of lime than shells, and the discovery of limestone deposits allowed masonry construction to spread throughout New England.[130]

In the Maritimes, evidence suggests that the French used limestone quarried in what is now Saint John as early as the 1630s; records show that at the beginning of the eighteenth century, it was used in construction at Annapolis Royal. Limestone was also shipped from Saint John to New England, Newfoundland, and Nova Scotia during the late eighteenth century, with kilns being available to burn the rock before shipping; in this period, there were at least four quarries in the Saint John area. By 1838, there were at least sixteen kilns operating in a four-mile stretch of the Saint John River. Saint John lime developed a good reputation, and in the nineteenth century, the British government called for its use in Halifax because of its durability.[131] The extraction of limestone is one of the earliest industries in what is now Canada. A 2001 Government of Canada publication titled "A Chronology of Minerals Development in Canada" reports that in 1736, "First Nations people oppose[d] the landing of ships near [what is now] Saint John, New Brunswick, for the purpose of transporting quarried limestone to Port Royal," which "was possibly the first reported dispute concerning title to minerals."[132]

As well as illustrating how European knowledge was applied to the manufacture and use of local building materials, the recipe captures the gestures to social authority commonly seen in early modern recipe culture. This recipe, for example, starts with the experiment: the Neuchâtel man who tried multiple methods to create dry rooms and finally succeeded with this process. To enhance the authority of the method, the instructions document the experimenter's status as a "gentleman." In

Dossie's extended version, the experiment is further witnessed by a "Lord M –" who is claimed to have observed the dry rooms the gentleman had created with the use of this particular mortar.[133] The recipe also invokes a Roman past, when the preparation is "imagined to resemble that of the antients"; Dossie had explained that the method was confirmed by Pliny and Vitruvius to have been used in Rome, and, what is more, the survival of Rome's ancient buildings "are proofs of the excellence of this method" and a model that London should follow because her own buildings were too quickly decaying.[134] Providing this recipe some twenty years later to Nova Scotia readers, "E.F." may be seeking not only to make houses drier, but also to secure for the region's buildings the "perpetual durability" Dossie ascribes to those of Rome.[135]

There were innovations in mortar technology in the eighteenth century, but the proposals made in these instructions were not the significant ones. The innovation in these instructions seems to be that the initial lime is unslaked before water is added to the lime and sand. The possibility of using skimmed milk instead of water to mix the sand and lime is also not standard procedure. The real innovation in the quest for a water-resistant mortar was the observation by English engineer John Smeaton (1724–1792) that calcined limestone with a greater percentage of clay produced the best mortar, rather than the whitest limestone as others had thought; in 1796, a James Parker was granted a patent in England for a cement made from burning stones of clay (first called Parker Cement, and then Roman Cement).[136]

To Make a Fine Varnish

The recipe can be found in Handley Chipman's notebook, where it appears alongside a number of medical recipes.[137] In addition to serving as justice of peace and then judge of probate of King's County, he was also a farmer, distiller, and cabinet maker (hence explaining the need for varnish). Chipman's recipe appears to be copied exactly from "A Method of Making a very good Lacque [*sic*], or Varnish, in a Letter from Paris," which appeared in the 1 December 1763 edition of London's *Universal Magazine.*[138]

To make a fine Varnish

Take clear lye of potash, or tartar,[139] add to it a very small quantity of a Solution of Alum,[140] put the Lye into a very fine, glass Vessel, take Some Powdered Cochineal[141] carefully sewed up in a bag of Linen, which st[ir] about in the Lye, till no colour

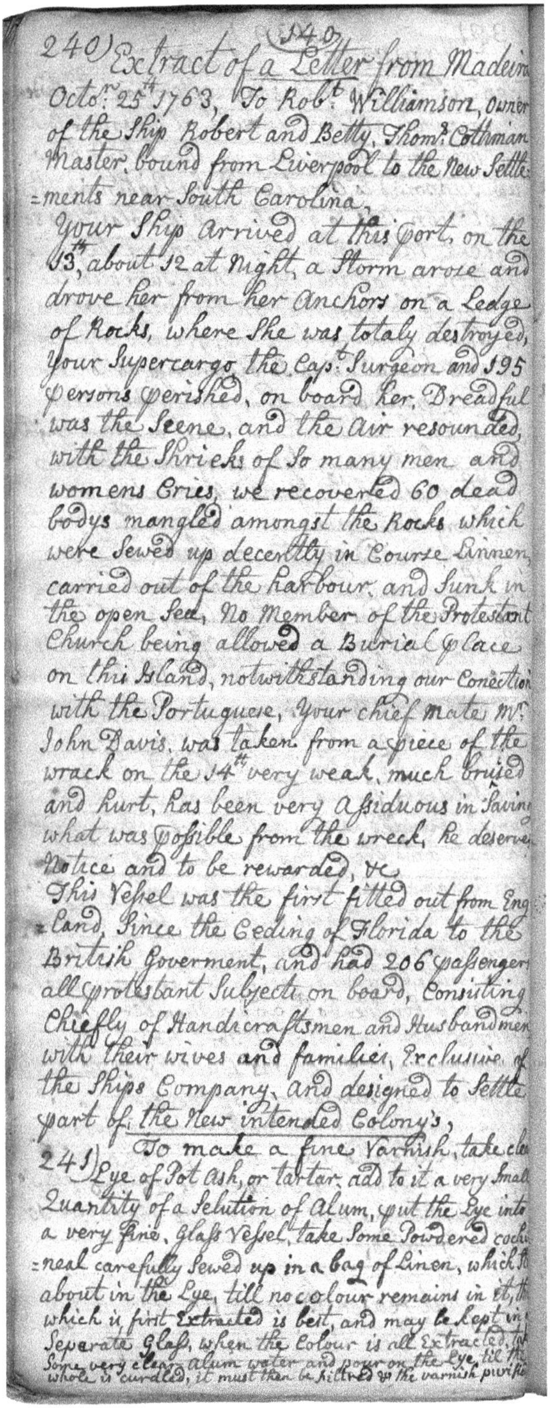
240) Extract of a Letter from Madeira Octo.r 25th 1763, To Robt. Williamson, owner of the Ship Robert and Betty, Thoms. Cothman Master, bound from Liverpool to the New Settle=ments near South Carolina.

Your Ship arrived at this Port, on the 13th, about 12 at Night, a Storm arose and drove her from her Anchors on a Ledge of Rocks, where She was totaly destroyed, Your Supercargo the Capt. Surgeon and 195 Persons Perished, on board her. Dreadful was the Scene, and the Air resounded, with the Shrieks of So many men and womens Cries, we recoverted 60 dead bodys mangled amongst the Rocks which were Sewed up decentlty in Course Linnen, carried out of the harbour, and Sunk in the open Sea, No Member of the Protestant Church being allowed a Burial Place on this Island, notwithstanding our Conection with the Portuguese, Your chief mate Mr. John Davis, was taken from a piece of the wrack on the 14th very weak, much bruised and hurt, has been very assiduous in Saving what was Possible from the wreck, he deserves Notice and to be rewarded, &c

This Vessel was the first fitted out from Eng=land, Since the Ceding of Florida to the British Goverment, and had 206 passengers all Protestant Subjects on board, Consisting Chiefly of Handicraftsmen and Husbandmen with their wives and families, Exclusive of the Ships Company, and designed to Settle part of the New intended Colony's,

241) To make a fine Varnish, take clear Lye of Pot Ash, or tartar; add to it a very Small Quantity of a Selution of Alum, put the Lye into a very fine, Glass Vessel, take Some Powdered cochi=neal carefully Sewed up in a bag of Linen, which St[ir] about in the Lye, till no colour remains in it, th[at] which is first Extracted is best, and may be kept in [a] Separate Glass, when the Colour is all Extracted, tak[e] Some very clear alum water and pour on the Lye, til the whole is curdled, it must then be filtred & the varnish purifie[d]

Figure 5.4
To make a fine Varnish, Handley Chipman's Notes.

remains in it, that which is first Extracted is best, and may be kept in a Seperate Glass, when the Colour is all Extracted, take Some very clear Alum water and pour on the Lye, til the whole is Curdled, it must then be filtred & the varnish purified.

The recipe in *Universal Magazine* explains that there are three types of varnish (or lacque) –Venice lacque, columbine lacque, and liquid lacque – and that the Venice varnish is, despite its name, made in Paris. Claiming the standard methods of making it are "all troublesome, and very expensive," this method is recommended as a cheaper and easier way "to make a very fine varnish."[142] The cochineal in this mixture would dye it red.

For Varnish

Another, perhaps more standard, recipe for varnish appears in the notebook attributed to John and William Trueman.[143] The recipe for varnish does not appear to be in William Trueman's handwriting. Although the name Amelia Trueman is written in pencil at the bottom of the recipe, the recipe is in black ink and in a different handwriting than her name.[144] Whoever wrote down this recipe, it is clear that the notebook was used and valued across generations.

No original or exact source for the recipe has been found. The Trueman recipe does, however, share some ingredients, including "spirit of wine," with a recipe published in *England's Happiness Improved: or, An Infallible Way to Get Riches, Encrease Plenty, and Promote Pleasure* (London, 1699), a title that puts varnish in the interesting cultural position of promoting English happiness, wealth, and pleasure, probably because of its perceived aesthetic value. The recipe in this volume calls for eight ounces of seed lac, four ounces of gum sandarac, four pounds of spirit of wine, an ounce of guttagamba (another name for gamboge, a gum), and half an ounce of "sanguis draconis" (dragon's blood) – all ingredients that appear also in the Trueman recipe.[145] Dragon's blood, as it was known, is a resin collected from the fruits of palm trees, such as *Calamus draco*, the so-called dragon palm that grows in Asia and South America.[146]

For Varnish

1 Quart of duble Rettifid

spirts of wine

4 ounce of salack[147]

1 ounce of seed Lack

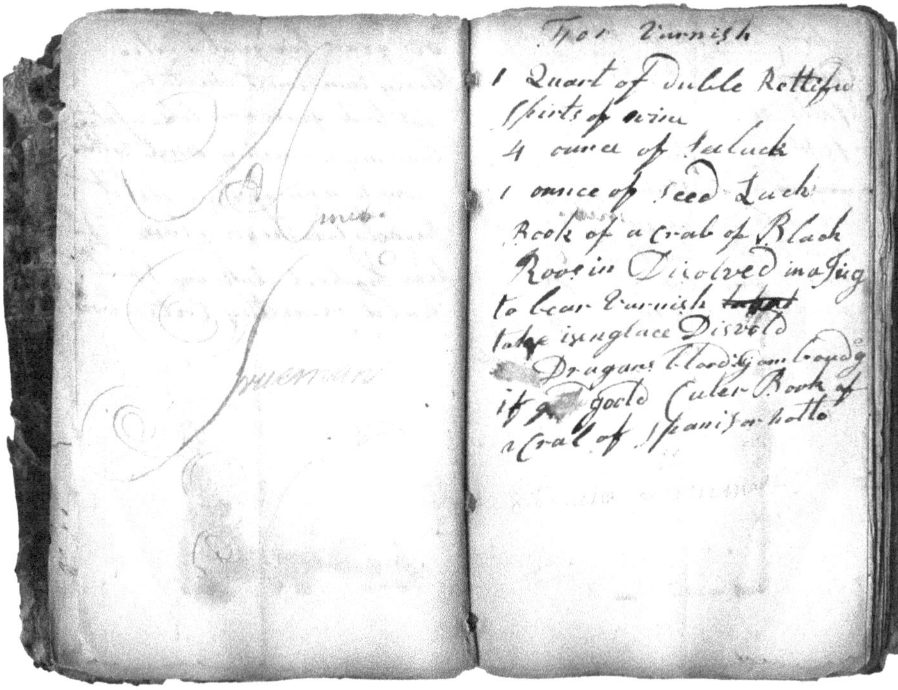

Figure 5.5
For Varnish. Trueman Family Fonds.

Book of a crab of Black
Roosin Disolved in a Jug
to bear varnish ~~tabat~~
tako isonglaco Disvold
Dragans blood: Gambloudge
if get goold Culer Book of
a Crab of Spanis or notto[148]
Amelia Trueman

For Varnish[149]

1 quart of double rectified
spirits of wine[150]
4 ounces of [sandarac][151]
1 ounce of seedlac[152]
[Book of a crab] black

resin dissolved in a jug to bear varnish. Take isinglass dissolved, dragon's blood, gamboge. If get gold color, book of a crab of Spanish or annotto.
Amelia Trueman

This recipe is unclear at some points, which highlights the way in which recipes could be used as reminders by those who were already familiar with the method of making the product. Such truncated recipes may, however, be less useful to subsequent users; in this case, what "R / Book of crab" means remains unknown. However, the recipe does fall within the norms of eighteenth-century varnish recipes in the way that the recipe in the Chipman manuscript using potash and alum does not. In the eighteenth century, three types of varnish were typically used, each identified with the key solvent employed to dissolve a resin: spirit varnishes, which had been used from the seventeenth century; essential oil varnishes, often relying on turpentine, which came into use before 1750; and fixed oil varnishes, which mixed the resin with a drying oil (most commonly linseed oil), which had been in use since the medieval period. With its inclusion of spirit of wine, this recipe is of the first type, a spirit varnish. In England, varnishes were not made in factories until the 1790s, and in America not until the 1820s, so craftsmen developed, fabricated, and employed their own recipes. Making varnish generally required grinding a resin into a coarse powder, putting the particles and solvent into a vessel to heat it, and then filtering it through cotton.[153]

Glue

Captain John MacDonald (1742–1810) sent these instructions to his sister Nelly (Helen) MacDonald in a booklet.[154] Originally from Glenaladale, Scotland, and the eighth laird of Glenaladale, MacDonald organized an emigration scheme to St John's Island for himself and other Catholics with the help of the Roman Catholic Church. They arrived in 1772, with MacDonald himself acquiring land in lots 35 and 36 (near Tracadie Bay in what is now Prince Edward Island). Between 1775 and 1792, however, MacDonald was often away from the island. First, he served as a captain and company commander in a regiment of Highlanders who were fighting for the British in the American colonies. Between 1782 and 1792, he was often in London, engaged in legal conflicts around his property on St John's Island. During his time away, Nelly MacDonald took care of his property in Tracadie, to which he returned in 1792.[155]

These instructions are part of a much longer discourse on how to build a house that John MacDonald wrote to his sister. He described this text in a letter of 29 April 1784 as "a little stitched book with a white paper cover" entitled "Private Instructions & Hints regarding the building of the House, & procuring Material, which are not to be shewn to anyone." The booklet contains, he says, "all the advice & hints I can give you at this distance to assist you in the Method of carrying on the work & procuring the Materials." He asks his sister to "read the same over attentively," although he allows "perhaps you will find it of some use along with the Resources of your own mind & Ingenuity – You'll better not let anyone see it." The booklet in effect advises Nelly on how to become his general contractor by directing her in how to acquire timber and arrange for the cutting of boards, hire a good carpenter, oversee the digging of the cellar, supervise the mason's building of the foundation and fireplace, and direct the plastering of walls, among other things. As for the glue necessary to construction, MacDonald writes that

> Some glue may be wanted:
> I forgot to order some in proper time, but
> you know glue May be made by boiling
> calf or sheep skins, as I have often seen
> in the highlands – I believe glue may also
> be made of fish & probably the french
> may teach you the secret –

Here, MacDonald positions glue-making as an activity that Nelly will herself undertake, alongside her management of the building project and its financial negotiations. She is asked to rely on her own tacit knowledge of the process of boiling skins ("you know glue May be made") and also to turn to the French for their knowledge of a different process, making glue from fish. Interestingly, he expects that the French will tell Nelly their secrets, while also expecting her to keep his secrets from everyone else.[156] "The French" to whom MacDonald refers are likely Acadian. The French had from 1726 established settlements, including at Tracadie, on the island they called Île Saint Jean and the Mi'kmaq called Abegweit. In 1758, the British deported around three thousand Acadians from Île Saint Jean (the population included some four thousand Acadian refugees expelled from Nova Scotia in 1755). By 1784, the Acadian population included those who had been able to stay, as well as those who had returned after being shipped to France.

Other Acadians had perished from shipwreck or from illness, some stayed in France, and others went to the Caribbean and to Louisiana.[157] The recipe suggests both the transfer of building techniques across cultures and the involvement of women in construction.

These two methods of glue-making mentioned – using animal skin or fish – are not unique to St John's Island. Animal and fish glues had been used by the Romans: Pliny's *Natural History*, for instance, mentions that boiling ox hide produces glue, with the bull's hide making the best glue.[158] Recipes for glue are not common in published recipe books before 1800. Instead, recipes tend to call for the use of specific types of glue and seem to assume that the user already knows how to make the specified adhesive. The first European commercial glue factory, which manufactured glue from hides, was located in Holland, and the first British patent for glue, made from fish, was issued in 1750. Both protein-based adhesives, fish and animal glues were commonly used in woodworking, which seems to be the intended purpose here.[159]

Afterword

The story Maritime recipes tell shouldn't end with this book. There may be other ways of reading the recipes discussed here, more connections to be made, more details to be investigated, and more contexts brought to bear. Other researchers could develop their own methodologies and analyses of these and of the dozens of other fascinating recipes we did not have the space to discuss here. Researchers working on historical recipes in other parts of the English-speaking world may find links between their archival materials and those discussed in this book, creating a still more expansive picture of recipe circulation and culture in the early modern Atlantic world. The archive of recipes we have so far gathered probably remains incomplete; it seems likely that there will be hitherto unknown recipes from the region preserved in attics and personal collections, as well as in archives outside the region. If you happen to have any pre-1800 Maritime recipes you'd like to share, please let us know. It could be especially important to have more recipes that document marginalized knowledges, such as those belonging to Indigenous, Black, and Acadian people. Future research projects focused on physically making the food and drink recipes would also enrich our understanding of eighteenth-century experiential knowledge. The same may be said of other kinds of recipes – but with an important caveat: medicinal, household, and agriculture recipes must be prepared only with a thorough understanding of the dangers inherent in using or ingesting some of the ingredients, which can be poisonous, flammable, or otherwise dangerous.

For interested readers more familiar with the work of more recent recipe writers – luminaries like Irma S. Rombauer, Julia Child, Jean Paré, and Martha Stewart – we hope this book provides an unexpected history, one that shows not only how what is now a fixed and familiar genre has a long and varied history not defined exclusively by the space of the kitchen. For recipe scholars, we hope to have shown that recipes were collected not only in Britain and the United States, but also in this northern corner of the British Atlantic world. Future studies might look further at connections and distinctions between the Maritime recipes studied here and the pre-revolutionary American medical recipe collections that Hillary M. Nunn has recently examined. As Nunn explains, "To examine recipes is to examine movement."[1] We hope that our work has also highlighted some of the many ways that what we now call the Maritimes was not isolated but participated in and contributed to larger movements of people, things, and knowledge around the Atlantic world. Despite their often simple and frequently truncated form, eighteenth-century recipes are not uncomplicated texts – and that is as true in the Maritimes as it is elsewhere. When used in culinary spaces, recipes helped to assuage hunger, articulate taste, and create communal experiences. Outside the domestic, culinary instructions were useful also in commercial contexts, used in manufacturing food at a large scale and in preserving it for transport across long distances, either for sale or to feed a military or seafaring force. Beyond the culinary, settler recipes in the eighteenth-century Maritimes were part of a genre that has long been crucial to the histories of medicine, both human and animal; of agriculture, in offering fertilizing and planting techniques; of construction, as in instructions for making mortar or paint; and of the day-to-day running of a household, where recipes were used to make products that helped to clean homes and clothing and, in some instances, to make houses and garments impermeable to water.

As they do today, historical recipes allowed knowledge to move across time and across physical and social spaces. Some recipes preserved old ways and family members' techniques, thus becoming a record of proven, tried-and-true approaches. Recipes sometimes also point to the future, arguing for innovation and new ways of doing things in proposing techniques that may or may not have been adopted or successful. The recipes in this book also demonstrate some of the ways that knowledge moved geographically, from Europe to North America and back again, from Indigenous peoples to settlers and colonial powers, from settlers in one part of the Americas to those in another and, further afield, from Asia and Africa to Europe and its colonies. Though sometimes offering or encouraging the adoption of local knowledge, the eighteenth-century settler recipe culture of what is now

Nova Scotia, New Brunswick, and Prince Edward Island seems most interested in practical knowledge gleaned from elsewhere, the region thus serving as a hub from which essential knowledge both departed and arrived. The knowledge that recipes recorded and disseminated also moved across social spaces, in many ways permeating eighteenth-century hierarchies of knowledge. In a world that (in print if not in daily life) seemed most to value the knowledge of elite, university-educated men, recipes both borrowed and provided the knowledge claimed by professional physicians and learned societies, while also demonstrating how knowledge rooted in the experiences of the less privileged – women, non-elite white men, the enslaved, and the colonized – also moved into dominant discourses, where it might be validated and thus gain legitimacy from institutions of knowledge or by appearing in print. Knowledge also moved across disciplines, with the understanding of an ingredient's usefulness in one field, such as medicine or agriculture, informing its use in another, like cookery or domestic cleaning.

As well as recording techniques, enabling knowledge circulation, and inspiring innovation, the recipes in this book demonstrate the social importance of knowledge and knowledge-making. Recipes matter, in other words, because accurate, useful, and effective knowledge matters. Creativity and innovation in ways of living are key not just to personal survival but also to culture. Recipes offer knowledge that allowed eighteenth-century makers to utilize commodities as readily available as garden herbs and as exotic as South American woods, as rare as Balsam of Gilead and as powerful as hydrochloric acid, and to make that knowledge a part of the style and taste of everyday life as well as to meet the basic needs of food, clothing, and shelter. Tied further to culture by conveying knowledge aimed at addressing social needs, recipes address the need to preserve food, nourish the poor, or feed a crowd on festive occasions. Recipes address the universal and particular in showing, for instance, how communities might survive epidemics while focusing also on applications meant to reduce pain or cure diseases in distinct and separate bodies; likewise, recipes may record an individual's approach to a particular problem, but they also track a broader response in a seeking and sharing of knowledge that encompassed the local community and beyond.

Recipes are documents that explain the "how" of knowledge creation. They record who counts as a knowledge maker in the eighteenth century, both those deemed experts by virtue of education or class privilege and those whose authority rests more heavily on experience, in having tested and tried a process and proved its merits. Recipes can document the importance of precision in measurement and technique, particularly in new processes, but they can also more casually leave the recipe's success to the maker's tacit knowledge and experience. With their many notations of sources, recipes also convey how important it was for knowledge to have a genealogy. Recipes' construction of that history can also take the form of disavowal, however, as they elide or occlude sources – an approach that especially defined the approach in settler recipes to Indigenous knowledges in a colonial context. The recipe archive affords only traces of peoples and cultures whose ideas and practices were not written in European languages nor deemed worthy for preservation by colonial powers. But if the Maritime recipe archive privileges the politics, culture, and society of the settlers who recorded them, recipes nevertheless exist as a palimpsest of gestures and subtexts that also record the oral and traditional cultures of knowledge that helped to shape them. As they tell the story of an appropriative, selective, and wide-ranging knowledge culture, eighteenth-century Maritime recipes by and large record the tastes, preferences, and wants of those who enjoyed literacy, access to pen and paper, and the privilege that allowed their recipes to survive both in manuscript and print. Valuable practical knowledge, as we all know, does not always need to be written down to be useful.

Eighteenth-century recipes show that the "how" of knowledge creation is embedded in history, in the political history that forced the movements of peoples around the Atlantic world, in the imperialist history that justified the extraction of knowledge and materials, and in the colonial history that expected settler expansion and made goods available to colonial powers. Recipes are intricately engaged with and shaped by social values concerning gender, sexuality, education and literacy, religion, and domestic and family life, and they are core to the history of science and technology. Recipes reflect history, and they can tell history, but they also help to make it.

APPENDIX

List of Recipes

FOOD

Meat and Fish

Soup and Stew

Bread

Condiments

Sweets

Food for Health

Miscellaneous

DRINK

Beer

Wine

MEDICINE

Rabies

Ringworm

Smallpox

Gout

Scurvy

Consumption

The Stone

Cancer

Miscellaneous

AGRICULTURE

HOUSEHOLD

Notes

INTRODUCTION

1 Lorenzo Veracini, "Introducing Settler Colonial Studies," *Settler Colonial Studies* 1, no. 1 (2013): 3.

2 Alfred W. Crosby, *The Columbian Exchange: Biological and Cultural Consequences of 1492*, 30th anniversary ed. (Westport, CN: Praeger, 2003).

3 Examples of this research include Robert Appelbaum, *Aguecheek's Beef, Belch's Hiccup, and Other Gastronomic Interjections: Literature, Culture, and Food Among the Early Moderns* (Chicago: University of Chicago Press, 2006); Michelle DiMeo and Sara Pennell, eds., *Reading and Writing Recipe Books, 1550–1800* (Manchester: Manchester University Press, 2013); Laura Lunger Knoppers, "Opening the Queen's Closet: Henrietta Maria, Elizabeth Cromwell, and the Politics of Cookery," *Renaissance Quarterly* 60, no. 2 (2007): 464–99; Kristine Kowalchuk, *Preserving on Paper: Seventeenth-Century Englishwomen's Receipt Books* (Toronto: University of Toronto Press, 2017); Rebecca Laroche, "Becoming Visible: Recipes in the Making," *Early Modern Women: An Interdisciplinary Journal* 13, no. 1 (2018): 133–43; Seth Stein LeJacq, "The Bounds of Domestic Healing: Medical Recipes, Storytelling and Surgery in Early Modern England," *Social History of Medicine* 26, no. 3 (2013): 451–68; Elaine Leong, "Collecting Knowledge for the Family: Recipes, Gender and Practical Knowledge in the Early Modern English Household," *Centaurus* 55, no. 2 (2013): 81–103; Elaine Leong, *Recipes and Everyday Knowledge: Medicine, Science, and the Household in Early Modern England* (Chicago: University of Chicago Press,

2018); Elaine Leong and Alisha Michelle Rankin, eds., *Secrets and Knowledge in Medicine and Science, 1500–1800* (Farnham, UK: Ashgate, 2011); Hillary Nunn, *Recipes on the Move in Early Modern England and British North America: Domestic Medicine, Mobility, and Manuscript Culture* (Amsterdam: Amsterdam University Press, 2025); Sandra Sherman, *Fresh from the Past: Recipes and Revelations from Moll Flanders' Kitchen* (New York: Taylor Trade Publishing, 2004); Pamela H. Smith, Amy R.W. Meyers, and Harold John Cook, eds., *Ways of Making and Knowing: The Material Culture of Empirical Knowledge* (Ann Arbor: University of Michigan Press, 2014); Wendy Wall, *Recipes for Thought: Knowledge and Taste in the Early Modern English Kitchen* (Philadelphia: University of Pennsylvania Press, 2016).

4 Pamela H. Smith, "Making as Knowing: Craft as Natural Philosophy," in *Ways of Making*, 17–47, esp. 40.

5 Leong, *Recipes and Everyday Knowledge*, 7.

6 Hosted by the University of New Brunswick, the EMMR database is open access and available at https://emmr.lib.unb.ca/.

7 See Metonicus, "To Preserve the Face from Being Deformed by the Small-Pox," *Nova Scotia Calender, or an Almanack* (1791), https://emmr.lib.unb.ca/recipes/preserve-face-being-deformed-small-pox.

8 Manuscript Notebook of Dr William James Almon, Almon Family Fonds, MG 1 vol. 10, microfilm reel 10045, Nova Scotia Archives. Recipes from Almon's *Notebook* are also available on the EMMR database at https://emmr.lib.unb.ca/recipes-for/430; William Paine Papers, University of New Brunswick Loyalist Collection, MIC–Loyalist FC LFR.P3W5P3. Recipes from the Paine Papers are also available on the EMMR database at https://emmr.lib.unb.ca/sources/william-paine-papers.

9 *What's Cooking: Food, Drink and Eating in Old-Time Nova Scotia*, Nova Scotia Archives, Halifax, NS, https://archives.novascotia.ca/cooking/.

10 Elizabeth Driver, *Culinary Landmarks: A Bibliography of Canadian Cookbooks, 1825–1949* (Toronto: University of Toronto Press, 2008), xxi. EBSCOhost.

11 Driver, *Culinary Landmarks*, xxi.

12 Driver, *Culinary Landmarks*, 41–2.

13 Driver, *Culinary Landmarks*, 41–2.

14 Driver, *Culinary Landmarks*, 13, 10, 67.

15 Marie Tremaine. *A Bibliography of Canadian Imprints, 1751–1800* (Toronto: University of Toronto Press, 1999), 597, 599–600, 646–7.

16 Looking at the English-language context, Sara Pennell and Michelle DiMeo, "Introduction," in *Reading and Writing Recipe Books*, ed. DiMeo and Pennell, 9, count

several hundred domestic manuscript recipe collection surviving in archives in Britain and the US for the period 1550–1800.

17 *Oxford English Dictionary*, s.v. "recipe (n.)."

18 Francisco Alonso-Almeida, "Genre Conventions in English Recipes, 1600–1800," in *Reading and Writing Recipe Books*, ed. DiMeo and Pennell, 68–90.

19 Leong, *Recipes and Everyday Knowledge*, 4.

20 Girolamo Ruscelli, *The Secretes of the Reverende Maister Alexis of Piemount*, trans. William Warde (London: John Kingston, 1558), Early English Books Online (EEBO).

21 Hugh Plat, *The Jewell House of Art and Nature Conteining Divers Rare and Profitable Inventions* (London: Peter Short, 1594), EEBO.

22 Alisha Rankin, "Recipes in Early Modern Europe," in *Encyclopedia of the History of Science*, ed. Christopher J. Phillips (Carnegie Melon University, March 2023), https://doi.org/10.34758/fvw2-w336.

23 Mary E. Fissell, "The Marketplace of Print," in *Medicine and the Market in England and Its Colonies, c.1450–1850*, ed. Mark S.R. Jenner and Patrick Wallis (Houndmills, UK: Palgrave Macmillan, 2007), 108–32; Leong, *Recipes and Everyday Knowledge*, 13.

24 Holly Dickinson, *Women of the Healing Arts: Domestic Medicine in Nova Scotia, 1750–1850* (MA thesis, Dalhousie University, 2021), 47–76.

25 John Partridge, *The Treasurie of Commodious Conceits, & Hidden Secrets and May be Called, the Huswives Closet, of Healthfull Provision* (London: Richard Jones, 1573), EEBO.

26 Mary F. Williamson, "Recipes and Household Literature," in *History of the Book in Canada*, vol. 1, *Beginnings to 1840*, ed. Patricia Lockhart Fleming, Gilles Gallichan, and Yvan Lamonde (Toronto: University of Toronto Press, 2004), 275.

27 Driver, *Culinary Landmarks*, xxi. Throughout "fl." is used as an abbreviation for "flourished." For those writers whose dates of birth and death are unknown, flourished marks the dates in which they were known to be active.

28 Driver, *Culinary Landmarks*, 163; Anne Marie Lane Jonah and Chantal Véchambre, *Le gout francais au Canada atlantique, 1604–1758: Une histoire gastronomique/French Taste in Atlantic Canada, 1604–1758: A Gastronomic History* (Sydney, NS: Cape Breton University Press, 2012), 68–70.

29 Lane Jonah and Véchambre, *Le gout francais*, 68–70; Harvey Amani Whitfield, *Biographical Dictionary of Enslaved Black People in the Maritimes*, ed. Donald Wright (Toronto: University of Toronto Press, 2022), 163, https://doi.org/10.3138/9781487543846-024.

30 Williamson, "Recipes and Household Literature," 276.

31 For more on this, see Henry Notaker, *A History of Cookbooks: From Kitchen to Page over Seven Centuries* (Oakland: University of California Press, 2017), 28–46.

32 Michelle DiMeo, "Authorship and Medical Networks: Reading Attributions in Early Modern Manuscript Recipe Books," in *Reading and Writing Recipe Books 1550–1800*, 41–2.

33 Steven Shapin, "The House of Experiment in Seventeenth-Century England," *Isis* 79, no. 3 (1988): 375–8.

34 Elaine Leong and Sara Pennell, "Recipe Collections and the Currency of Medical Knowledge in the Early Modern 'Medical Marketplace,'" in *Medicine and the Market in England and Its Colonies, c. 1450–1850*, 134.

35 Notaker, *A History of Cookbooks*, 30.

36 Leong and Pennell, "Recipe Collections," 141–3.

37 Notaker, *A History of Cookbooks*, 30.

38 Michelle DiMeo, "Communicating Medical Recipes: Robert Boyle's Genre and Rhetorical Strategies for Print," in *The Palgrave Handbook of Early Modern Literature and Science*, ed. Howard Marchitello and Eveyln Tribble (London: Palgrave Macmillan UK, 2017), 213, ProQuest Ebook Central.

39 On fashion and recipes, see Margaret J.M. Ezell, "Cooking the Books, or, the Three Faces of Hannah Woolley," in *Reading and Writing Recipe Books*, 166.

40 Notaker, *A History of Cookbooks*, 145–7; DiMeo, "Communicating," 213.

41 DiMeo and Pennell, "Introduction," 7.

42 John J. McCusker, "Weights and Measures in the Colonial Sugar Trade: The Gallon and the Pound and Their International Equivalents," *The William and Mary Quarterly* 30, no. 4 (1973): 602, 612.

43 McCusker, "Weights and Measures," 610.

44 Julian Hoppit, "Reforming Britain's Weights and Measures, 1660–1824," *English Historical Review* 108, no. 426 (1993): 86–94.

45 Ronald Edward Zupko, *A Dictionary of English Weights and Measures: From Anglo-Saxon Times to the Nineteenth Century* (Madison: University of Wisconsin Press, 1968), 69–72.

46 Zupko, *A Dictionary*, 15–17, 72, 78–9, 80–1, 128; H. Arthur Klein, *The World of Measurements: Masterpieces, Mysteries, and Muddles of Metrology* (New York: Simon and Schuster, 1974), 28–39.

47 Zupko, *A Dictionary*, 7–9.

48 Zupko, *A Dictionary*, 50, 111–12, 153.

49 McCusker, "Weights and Measures," 600, 610.

50 Bruce Curtis, "From the Moral Thermometer to Money: Metrological Reform in Pre-Confederation Canada," *Social Studies of Science* 28, no. 4 (1998): 559–65.

51 "Mi'kma'ki," Mi'kmawey Debert Cultural Centre, 12–13, https://www.mikmaweydebert.ca/home/wp-content/uploads/2022/01/Mikmaki.pdf.

52 "Wolastokuk (Ancestral Territory)," Wolastoqiyik First Nation, https://malecites.ca/en/territory.

53 David Bell, *Loyalist Rebellion in New Brunswick: A Defining Conflict for Canada's Political Culture* (Halifax: Formac, 2013); Margaret R. Conrad and James K. Hiller, *Atlantic Canada: A History*, 2nd ed. (Oxford: Oxford University Press, 2010); Margaret Conrad, *At the Ocean's Edge: A History of Nova Scotia to Confederation* (Toronto: University of Toronto Press, 2020); N.E.S. Griffiths, *The Acadians: Creation of a People* (Toronto: McGraw-Hill Ryerson, 1973); Elizabeth Mancke and Carole Shammas, eds., *The Creation of the British Atlantic World* (Baltimore: Johns Hopkins University Press, 2005); Daniel Paul, *We Were Not the Savages: A Mi'kmaq Perspective on the Collision Between European and Native American Civilizations* (Halifax: Fernwood, 2000); John Reid, *Nova Scotia: A Pocket History* (Blackpoint, NS: Fernwood, 2009); Harvey Amani Whitfield, *North to Bondage: Loyalist Slavery in the Maritimes* (Vancouver: UBC Press, 2016).

54 Elizabeth Mancke, "Spaces of Power in the Early Modern Northeast," in *New England and the Maritime Provinces: Connections and Comparisons*, ed. Stephen J. Hornsby and John G. Reid (Montreal: McGill-Queen's University Press, 2005), 32–49.

55 Mancke, "Spaces of Power," 33.

56 Paul, *We Were Not the Savages*, 12.

57 Conrad and Hiller, *Atlantic*, 48–50; Reid, *Nova Scotia*, 17–18.

58 N.E.S. Griffiths, "1600–1650: Fish, Fur, and Folk," in *The Atlantic Region to Confederation: A History*, ed. Phillip Buckner and John G. Reid (Toronto: University of Toronto Press, 2017), 52–64, eBook Academic Collection (EBSCOhost); Conrad and Hiller, *Atlantic*, 39–51; Reid, *Nova Scotia*, 19, 68–70.

59 John G. Reid, "1686–1720: Imperial Intrusions," in *The Atlantic Region*, 83–4.

60 Conrad and Hiller, *Atlantic*, 64–5.

61 "The Treaties of 1725–6," qtd. in Conrad and Hiller, *Atlantic*, 75.

62 Reid, "1686–1720," 85.

63 George Rawlyck, "1720–1744: Cod, Louisbourg, and the Acadians," in *The Atlantic Region*, 89–90. Rawlyck sets the population of Louisbourg in 1737 at 1963, while Conrad and Hiller, *Atlantic*, 71, say it was "approaching 3000" by 1744.

64 Conrad and Hiller, *Atlantic*, 71–2.

65 Stephen E. Patterson, "1744–1763: Colonial Wars and Aboriginal Peoples," in *The Atlantic Region*, 99–115; Reid, *Nova Scotia*, 56–60.
66 Conrad and Hiller, *Atlantic*, 79; Reid, *Nova Scotia*, 57–60.
67 Reid, *Nova Scotia*, 21.
68 Conrad and Hiller, *Atlantic*, 77; Patterson, "1744–1763," 106.
69 Conrad and Hiller, *Atlantic*, 84; Paul, *We Were Not the Savages*, 157.
70 Conrad and Hiller, *Atlantic*, 82–5.
71 Paul, *We Were Not the Savages*, 161.
72 Tremaine, *A Bibliography*, 646–7
73 Patterson, "1744–1763," 113; Conrad and Hiller, *Atlantic*, 87–90.
74 Conrad and Hiller, *Atlantic*, 90–1; Reid, *Nova Scotia*, 77.
75 Reid, *Nova Scotia*, 80–2; M. Bumsted, "1763–1783: Resettlement and Rebellion," in *The Atlantic Region*, 116–31.
76 Paul, *We Were Not the Savages*, 170.
77 Bumsted, "1763–1783," 129–31; Ann Gorman Condon, "1783–1800: Loyalist Arrival, Acadian Return, Imperial Reform," in *The Atlantic Region*, 132–46; Conrad and Hiller, *Atlantic*, 97–8.
78 Reid, *Nova Scotia*, 83.
79 Reid, *Nova Scotia*, 84.
80 Reid, *Nova Scotia*, 84; Conrad and Hiller, *Atlantic*, 98.
81 Gorman Condon, "1783–1800," 132–47.
82 Conrad and Hiller, *Atlantic*, 100; Paul, *We Were Not the Savages*, 173.
83 Reid, *Nova Scotia*, 24.
84 Reid, *Nova Scotia*, 25.
85 Graeme Wynn, "1800–1810: Turning the Century," in *The Atlantic Region*, 148–50.
86 Conrad and Hiller, *Atlantic*, 90. Reid, *Nova Scotia*, 27, says that the Mi'kmaq in Nova Scotia by 1800 were not interested in being counted and for this and other reasons were moving away from colonial sites, the proximity to which informed British population counts.
87 Reid, *Nova Scotia*, 84.
88 Qtd. in Reid, *Nova Scotia*, 24.
89 Crystal Fraser and Zoe Todd, "Decolonial Sensibilities: Indigenous Research and Engaging with Archives in Contemporary Colonial Canada," in *Decolonising Archives* (n.p.: L'Internationale Books, 2016), 33, 35, 39, https://e-artexte.ca/id/eprint/30628/1/03-decolonisingarchives_pdf-final.pdf.
90 Harvey Amani Whitfield, "White Archives, Black Fragments: Problems and Possibilities in Telling the Lives of Enslaved Black People in the Maritimes," *Canadian Historical Review* 101, no. 3 (2020): 326–7.

91 Whitfield, "White Archives, Black Fragments," 328.

92 Ian McKay, "Race, White Settler Liberalism, and the Nova Scotia Archives, 1931–1976," *Acadiensis* 49, no. 2 (2020): 7.

93 Lane Jonah and Véchambre, *Le gout francais*, 194–5.

94 Booklet of Remedies in French, 1755, Miller Family Fonds, MG1 vol. 693, Nova Scotia Archives. The booklet is also available on the *EMMR* database at https://emmr.lib.unb.ca/recipes-for/541. The booklet is dated by the NSA to around 1755 and is therefore assumed to have predated the deportation of the Acadians. Yet, as recipe transcriber and translator Danielle Arseneau notes in her essay "Growing Acadian Medicine: From the Acadian Homeland to Nova Scotia Gardens," *Early Modern Maritime Recipes: Essays*, 2017, 1–8, https://emmr.lib.unb.ca/essays, the booklet "is a mysterious inclusion in the Miller Family Fonds" (3). It is possible that the remedy collection originated with the Pernette family of Petite Rivière, to whom the Miller family was related. Regardless of the booklet's provenance, however, it seems likely that the recipes it records – as recipes most often were – had been shared by others and may have circulated among the region's French-speaking population, including the Acadians.

95 Pernette Papers, Miller Family Fonds, MG 1 vol. 585, no. 1, microfilm reel 23505, Nova Scotia Archives. The collection is also available on the *EMMR* database at https://emmr.lib.unb.ca/recipes-for/589.

96 Rawlyk, "1720–1744," 95.

97 Marielle Boudreau and Melvin Gallant. *A Taste of Acadie*, trans. Ernest Bauer (Fredericton: Goose Lane, 1991), Canada Commons.

98 Laurie Lacey, *Micmac Medicines: Remedies and Recollections* (Halifax: Nimbus Publishing, 1993), Canada Commons.

99 Greg Bak, "Counterweight: Helen Samuels, Archival Decolonization, and Social License," *The American Archivist* 84, no. 1 (2021): 427.

100 Rose Knockwood-Morris, foreword to *Micmac Medicines: Remedies and Recollections*, by Laurie Lacey (Halifax: Nimbus Publishing, 1993), vi–vii.

101 Whitfield, "1388. Unnamed Woman (c. 1752, age 35)," in *Biographical Dictionary*, 224.

102 Whitfield, "1397. Unnamed Woman (c. 1779, age 21)," in *Biographical Dictionary*, 225; Whitfield, "1408. Unnamed Woman (c. 1787, age 23)," in *Biographical Dictionary*, 227.

103 Whitfield, "1154. Unnamed Boy (c. 1786, age 14)," in *Biographical Dictionary*, 191; Whitfield, "1213. Unnamed Man (c. 1799, age 20)," in *Biographical Dictionary*, 200.

104 Londa Schiebinger, *Secret Cures of Slaves: People, Plants, and Medicine in the Eighteenth-Century Atlantic World* (Stanford, CA: Stanford University Press, 2017), 3.

105 The Manuscript Notebook of Sarah Creighton Wilkins, 1779–1833, MacDonald

Family Fonds, MG 1 no. 1, microfilm reel 10618, Nova Scotia Archives. Recipes from the *Notebook* are also available on the *EMMR* database at https://emmr.lib.unb.ca/recipes-for/273.

106 Joel Perlmann and Dennis Shirley, "When Did New England Women Acquire Literacy?," *The William and Mary Quarterly* 48, no. 1 (1991): 64, estimate that New England settler women (their study does not mention Black or Indigenous women) born after 1765 had an illiteracy rate of about 19 per cent; see also E. Jennifer Monaghan, "Literacy Instruction and Gender in Colonial New England," *American Quarterly* 40, no. 1 (1988): 34–5.

107 Judith Fingard, "Attitudes Towards the Education of the Poor in Colonial Halifax," *Acadiensis* 2, no. 2 (1973): 15–42. The Black population of the Maritimes, most of whom came to Nova Scotia after the American Revolution as freed or enslaved people, came from a context of enslavement in the American colonies where reading and writing was often prohibited by law, although there were individuals and organizations in the northern states who sponsored schools for enslaved people, with a particular eye to teaching Bible reading. See E. Jennifer Monaghan, "Reading for the Enslaved, Writing for the Free: Reflections on Liberty and Literacy," *The American Antiquarian Society* 108, no. 2 (1998): 309–24. Indigenous peoples in New England had a different relationship to English-language literacy. Mohegan, Niantic, Narragansett, and Pequot people were often the focus of missionary endeavours by settler New Englanders who sought to teach them reading and writing in English; Hilary E. Wyss, "Mary Occom and Sarah Simon: Gender and Native Literacy in Colonial New England," *The New England Quarterly* 79, no. 3 (2006): 410, argues that "Native women adapted some Euroamerican practices to sustain their traditional roles in Native societies" and used reading and writing letters to maintain family connections.

108 Julian Gwyn, "Female Litigants Before the Civil Courts of Nova Scotia, 1749–1801," *Histoire Sociale/Social History* 36, no. 72 (2003): 318–19.

109 Gwendolyn Davies, "Private Education for Women in Early Nova Scotia: 1784–1894," *Atlantis* 20, no. 1 (1995): 10–11.

110 Shapin, "The House of Experiment," 378.

111 Lynette Hunter, "Sisters of the Royal Society: The Circle of Lady Ranelagh," in *Women, Science and Medicine: 1500–1700*, ed. Lynette Hunter and Sarah Hutton (Thrupp, UK: Sutton, 1997), 182–8.

112 Leong, *Recipes*, 7.

113 Alix Cooper, "Homes and Households," in *The Cambridge History of Science*, vol. 3, *Early Modern Science*, ed. Katharine Park and Lorraine Daston (Cambridge: Cambridge University Press, 2006), 224–5.

114 Cooper, "Homes and Households," 226–9.

115 Susan Scott Parrish, *American Curiosity: Cultures of Natural History in the Colonial British Atlantic World* (Chapel Hill: UNC Press, 2006), 7, EBSCOhost.

116 Anya Zilberstein, "Making and Unmaking Local Knowledge in Greater New England," *Journal for Eighteenth-Century Studies* 36, no. 4 (2013): 567, https://doi.org/10.1111/1754-0208.12083.

117 Peter Ward, *A History of Domestic Space: Privacy and the Canadian Home* (Vancouver: UBC Press, 2007), 15, ProQuest Ebook Central.

118 Ronald Rees, *Land of the Loyalists: Their Struggle to Shape the Maritimes* (Halifax: Nimbus, 2000), 42–5; Peter Ennals and Deryck Holdsworth, *Homeplace: The Making of the Canadian Dwelling over Three Centuries* (Toronto: University of Toronto Press, 1998), 71–5.

119 Ward, *A History*, 71–2.

120 Fiona Lucas, *Hearth and Home: Women and the Art of Open-Hearth Cooking* (Toronto: James Lorimer, 2006), 7–10.

121 Sara Pennell, *The Birth of the English Kitchen, 1600–1850* (New York: Bloomsbury Academic, 2016), 8–11, 15, EBSCOhost.

122 Ennals and Holdsworth, *Homeplace*, 3.

123 Rachel Bryant, *The Homing Place: Indigenous and Settler Literary Legacies of the Atlantic* (Waterloo, ON: Wilfrid Laurier University Press, 2017), 4.

124 Kathryn Kish Sklar, "Reconsidering Domesticity Through the Lens of Empire and Settler Society in North America," *American Historical Review* 124, no. 4 (2019): 1250.

125 Hilary Eklund, Jennifer Park, Debapriya Sarkar, and Ayanna Thompson, "Becoming Undisciplined: On Pathways to Environmental and Racial Justice in Early Modern Studies," *PMLA/Publications of the Modern Language Association of America* 139, no. 5 (2024): 801, https://doi.org/10.1632/S0030812924000683.

126 Kish Sklar, "Reconsidering Domesticity," 1265.

CHAPTER ONE

1 Dorothy Duncan, *Canadians at Table: Food, Fellowship, and Folklore: A Culinary History of Canada* (Toronto: Dundurn Press, 2011), 60, says of this period that "Bread was the foundation of every meal."

2 Duncan, *Canadians at Table*, 1–82, considers the pre-Victorian period.

3 Anne Marie Lane Jonah and Chantal Véchambre, *Le gout francais au Canada atlantique, 1604–1758: Une histoire gastronomique / French Taste in Atlantic Canada, 1604–1758: A Gastronomic History* (Sydney, NS: Cape Breton University Press, 2012).

4 Lane Jonah and Véchambre, *Le gout francais*, 194–5. The document survives in the Archives Nationales d'Outre Mer, Paris.

5 Eric D. Tourigny, "Maintaining Traditions: Food and Identity Among Early Immigrants to Upper Canada," *Historical Archaeology* 54, no. 2 (2020): 355, https://doi.org/10.1007/s41636-020-00237-5.

6 Tourigny, "Maintaining Traditions," 357.

7 Victoria Dickenson, "Cartier, Champlain, and the Fruits of the New World Botanical Exchange in the 16th and 17th Centuries," *Scientia Canadensis: Canadian Journal of the History of Science, Technology and Medicine / Revue canadienne d'histoire des sciences, des techniques et de la médecine* 31, no. 1–2 (2008): 30–1.

8 Dickenson, "Cartier, Champlain," 32.

9 Dickenson, "Cartier, Champlain," 38–9, 43–4.

10 N.E.S. Griffiths, *From Migrant to Acadian: A North American Border People 1604–1755* (Montreal and Kingston: McGill-Queen's University Press, 2005), 174–5.

11 Griffiths, *From Migrant to Acadian*, 176.

12 Marielle Cormier-Boudreau and Melvin Gallant, *A Taste of Acadie*, trans. Ernest Bauer, (Fredericton: Goose Lane, 1991), xiii–xiv, Canada Commons.

13 W. Jeffrey Bolster, *The Mortal Sea: Fishing the Atlantic in the Age of Sail* (Cambridge, MA: Harvard University Press, 2012), 12–13.

14 Griffiths, *Migrant to Acadian*, 28–9.

15 R.W. Dunfield, *The Atlantic Salmon in the History of North America* (Ottawa: Department of Fisheries and Oceans, 1985), 10.

16 Marc Lescarbot, *Nova Francia: A Description of Acadia, 1606*, trans. P. Erondelle, ed. E. Denison Ross and Eileen Power (New York: Harper, 1928), 283, Internet Archive.

17 A.J.B. Johnston, "The Early Days of the Lobster Fishery in Atlantic Canada," *Material History Review* 33 (1991): 56–60.

18 Dunfield, *Atlantic Salmon*, 15–16.

19 Lescarbot, *Nova Francia*, 283.

20 Dunfield, *Atlantic Salmon*, 52–3, 65.

21 Dunfield, *Atlantic Salmon*, 58, 80.

22 Bolster, *Mortal Sea*, 49; Daniel Paul, *We Were Not the Savages: A Mi'kmaq Perspective on the Collision Between European and Native American Civilizations* (Winnipeg: Fernwood Publishing, 2000), 23, 182, Canadian Electronic Library / DesLibris; Kerry Prosper and Mary Jane Paulette, "The Mi'kmaq Relationship with Kat (American Eel)," *Social Research for Sustainable Fisheries* 8 (March 2002): 1–8, https://people.stfx.ca/rsg/srsf/researchreports1/FactSheets/Factsheet7.pdf.

23 Russel Lawrence Barsh, "Netukulimk Past and Present: Míkmaw Ethics and the Atlantic Fishery," *Journal of Canadian Studies* 37, no. 1 (2002): 16–17.

24 Barsh, "Netukulimk Past," 25–7, 17, 23.

25 Barsh, "Netukulimk Past," 27; Paul, *We Were Not the Savages*, 182.

26 Nathalie Cooke, *What's to Eat? Entrées in Canadian Food History* (Montreal and Kingston: McGill-Queen's University Press, 2009), 3.

27 Ann Gorman Condon, "1783–1800: Loyalist Arrival, Acadian Return, Imperial Reform," in *The Atlantic Region to Confederation: A History*, ed. Phillip A. Buckner and John G. Reid (Toronto: University of Toronto Press, 2017), 132–47, eBook Academic Collection (EBSCOhost).

28 Lescarbot, *Nova Francia*, 117.

29 Lescarbot, *Nova Francia*, 118.

30 Lane Jonah and Véchambre, *Le gout francais*, 119–20.

31 Bonnie Huskins, "From Haute Cuisine to Ox Roasts: Public Feasting and the Negotiation of Class in Mid-19th-Century Saint John and Halifax," *Labour / Le Travail* 37 (Spring 1996): 37, https://doi.org/10.2307/25144034.

32 Huskins, "From Haute Cuisine," 15–18.

33 Huskins, "From Haute Cuisine," 19–20.

34 Robert P. Harvey, "Black Beans, Banners and Banquets: The Charitable Irish Society of Halifax at Two Hundred," *Nova Scotia Historical Review* 6, no. 1 (1986): 16–35. Harvey doesn't make clear whether women were included in the group.

35 Harvey, "Black Beans," 19.

36 Sarah F. McMahon, "Laying Foods By: Gender, Dietary Decisions, and the Technology of Food Preservation in New England Households, 1750–1850," in *Early American Technology: Making and Doing Things from the Colonial Era to 1850*, ed. Judith A. McGaw (Chapel Hill: University of North Carolina Press, 1994), 179–80.

37 T. Sarah Peterson, *Acquired Taste: The French Origins of Modern Cooking* (Ithaca: Cornell University Press, 1994), 133–47.

38 Jennifer Stead, "Navy Blues: The Sailor's Diet, 1530–1830," in *Food for the Community: Special Diets for Special Groups*, ed. C. Anne Wilson (Edinburgh: Edinburgh University Press, 1991), 75–6, 81.

39 Cooke, *What's to Eat?*, 4.

40 Alison Norman, "'Fit for the Table of the Most Fastidious Epicure': Culinary Colonialism in the Upper Canadian Contact Zone," in *Edible Histories, Cultural Politics: Towards a Canadian Food History*, ed. Franca Iacovetta, Marlene Epp, and Valerie J. Korinek (Toronto: University of Toronto Press, 2012), 45.

41 Katharina Vester, *A Taste of Power: Food and American Identities* (Oakland: University of California Press, 2015), 17, EBSCOhost.

42 Vester, *A Taste of Power*, 20.

43 Garrett Clopper, "Planting Journal, Accounts and Recipes," 1790–1899, Beverly Robinson Papers, S37A–2, F46, New Brunswick Museum Archives and Research Library. See also Anthony Allaire, Diary and Order Book, 1780–1794, Beverly Robinson Papers, S37A, F19, New Brunswick Museum Archives and Research Library.

44 Jonas Howe, "The King's New Brunswick Regiment," *New Brunswick Historical Society* 1 (1894): 51, Google Books.

45 Howe, "The King's New Brunswick Regiment," 13, 50.

46 Howe, "The King's New Brunswick Regiment," 42; Joseph Wilson Lawrence, *The Judges of New Brunswick and Their Times* (Saint John: n.p., 1907), 127, Archive.org.

47 Anthony Allaire, *Diary of Lieut. Anthony Allaire* (New York: New York Times and Arno Press, 1968).

48 Sal-prunella is "fused nitre cast into cakes or balls" according to OED *Online*, "sal-prunella, n." One eighteenth-century dictionary defines *sal prunella* as "purified salt petre" and a substance used in medicines to cool the body and to provoke urine. See John Harris, *Lexicon Technicum: Or, An Universal English Dictionary of Arts and Sciences*, vol. 1, 2nd ed. (London: Dan. Brown, et al., 1708), sig. 6E3*v*, Eighteenth Century Collections Online (ECCO).

49 Megan E. Edwards, "Virginia Ham: The Local and Global of Colonial Foodways," *Food and Foodways* 19, no. 1–2 (2011): 66, https://doi.org/10.1080/07409710.2011.544175; Jennifer Stead, "Necessities and Luxuries: Food Preservation from the Elizabethan to the Georgian Era," in *Waste Not, Want Not: Food Preservation from Early Times to the Present Day*, ed. C. Anne Wilson (Edinburgh: Edinburgh University Press, 1991), 68.

50 Stead, "Necessities and Luxuries," 68.

51 "Admiral Pocock's Receipt," in *The Burlington Almanack for the Year of Our Lord 1774*, ed. Timothy Trueman (Burlington, NJ: Isaac Collins, 1773), sig. E*v*, ECCO. The recipe also appeared in *American Museum, or, Repository of Ancient & Modern Fugitive Pieces, &c. Prose & Poetical* 2, no. 6 (1 December 1787), 591, American Antiquarian Society (AAS) Historical Periodicals Collection, Series 1, EBSCOhost; William Augustus Osbaldiston, *The Universal Sportsman: or, Nobleman, Gentleman, and Farmer's Dictionary of Recreation and Amusement* (Dublin: n.p., [1795?]), 630, ECCO; *New Jamaica Magazine* 3 (February 1799), 132, Google Books. This last periodical was printed in Jamaica in 1798 and 1799.

52 Tom Pocock, "Pocock, Sir George (1706–1792), naval officer," in *Oxford Dictionary of National Biography* (Oxford: Oxford University Press, 2004), online.

53 "Admiral Pocock's Receipt," in *The Burlington Almanack*, sig. E*v*.

54 Townsend, qtd. in George Yagi, Jr, "Surviving the Wilderness: The Diet of the British Army and the Struggle for Canada, 1754–1760," *Journal for the Society for Army Historical Research* 89, no. 357 (2011): 66–8.

55 Lane Jonah and Véchambre, *Le gout francais*, 73.

56 Scrapbook containing Trueman Family Papers, 1755–1851, Trueman Family Fonds, Accession 0102, Mount Allison University Archives.

57 "Raw or unrefined sugar obtained from the juice of the sugar cane by evaporating it and draining off the molasses." See OED *Online*, s.v. "muscovado, n."

58 Saltpetre, or potassium nitrate, is a component of gunpowder. It was used in early modern medicines as well as in culinary recipes like this one. See OED *Online*, s.v. "saltpetre, n."

59 "Admiral Pocock's Receipt," in *The Burlington Almanack*, sig. E*v*.

60 H.C., "Salt or Corned Beef," *New England Farmer, and Gardener's Journal* 15, no. 45 (17 May 1837), 355, AAS Historical Periodicals Collection, Series 1, EBSCOhost.

61 McMahon, "Laying Foods," 195.

62 McMahon, "Laying Foods," 195–6.

63 Letter from Jonathan Bliss to Mary Bliss, 5 June 1798, Bliss Family Fonds, vol. 1604, no. 50, microfilm reel 22,713, Nova Scotia Archives.

64 Phillip Buckner, "Bliss, Jonathan," in *Dictionary of Canadian Biography*, vol. 6 (Toronto: University of Toronto Press; Quebec: Presses de l'Université Laval, 2003–), http://www.biographi.ca/en/bio/bliss_jonathan_6E.html.

65 J.A. Houlding, "Dundas, Thomas (1750–1794), Army Officer and Politician," in *Oxford Dictionary of National Biography* (Oxford: Oxford University Press, 2004), online.

66 Lady Eleanora Dundas, Collection of Medical and Cookery Receipts, ca. 1785, Accession Number 41932, MS 2242, Wellcome Library, https://wellcomelibrary.org/item/b1903149x#?c=0&m=0&s=0&cv=4&z=-0.4868%2C-0.1322%2C2.1548%2C1.3536.

67 Mrs Dundas, *Dundas of Finask: Some Memorials of the Family* (Edinburgh: David Douglas, 1891), 74–91, https://electricscotland.com/webclans/dtog/dundasoffingasks00dunduoft.pdf.

68 Garrett Clopper, "Planting Journal, Accounts and Recipes," 1790–1899, Beverly Robinson Papers, S37A-2, F46, New Brunswick Museum Archives and Research Library.

69 Stead, "Necessities and Luxuries," 74–7.

70 Sue Shephard, *Pickled, Potted, and Canned* (New York: Simon and Schuster, 2000), 62–78.

71 S. Taylor, *The Complete Family Cook*, 4th ed. (London: J. Annereau, 1796), 98, ECCO.

72 "To Pickle Berwick Salmon," *The Nova Scotia Gazette*, 13 August 1791, Nova Scotia Newspapers on Microfilm, vol. 2. no. 51, microfilm reel 9466, Nova Scotia Archives.

73 Marie Tremaine, *A Bibliography of Canadian Imprints, 1751–1800* (Toronto: University of Toronto Press, 1999), 601–2, EBSCOhost.

74 "The Following Receipts," *The Virginia Gazette* no. 841, 2 July 1767, 1, https://research.colonialwilliamsburg.org/DigitalLibrary/va–gazettes/VGSinglePage.cfm?issueIDNo=67.PD.30&page=1&res=LO.

75 A kitt (or kit) was a barrel that held twenty-five pounds and was a standardized unit of measurement used in the fish trade. See Dunfield, *Atlantic Salmon*, 159.

76 "The History of the Salmon and Sea-Trout Net Fisheries of the Tweed and the Eye," *The Tweed Foundation* (2014): 1–6, https://www.tweedfoundation.org.uk/S4.1_The_Salmon_–_Sea–trout_Net_Fisheries_of_the_Tweed_–_Eye.pdf.

77 Dunfield, *Atlantic Salmon*, 159.

78 Dunfield, *Atlantic Salmon*, 160.

79 Dunfield, *Atlantic Salmon*, 160.

80 Anonymous, *The Gentleman Angler* (London: A. Bettesworth, 1726), 168–9, ECCO. The recipe was reprinted several times. It appeared in *The Complete Family-Piece: and, Country Gentleman, and Farmer's, Best Guide*, 2nd ed. (London: A. Bettesworth et al., 1737), 215–16, ECCO, as well as George Smith, *The Angler's Magazine; or, Complete Fisherman* (Dublin: James Hoey, Jr, 1760), 74, ECCO.

81 Eliza Smith, *The Compleat Housewife: Or, Accomplish'd Gentlewoman's Companion*, 5th ed. (London: J. Pemberton, 1732), 77–8, ECCO.

82 On vinegar and salt as preservatives, see Francis McFadden and Corinne Trang, "Deconstructing Haute Cuisine: Food Preservation as a Factor in the Culinary Arts," *Journal of Historical Sociology* 15, no. 4 (2002): 515–19.

83 "To Carry Fish Alive to a Great Distance," *Weekly Chronicle*, 26 March 1791, Nova Scotia Newspapers on Microfilm, vol. 5, no. 2, microfilm reel 8165, Nova Scotia Archives.

84 Tremaine, *Bibliography*, 617–18.

85 George L. Parker, "Minns, William," in *Dictionary of Canadian Biography*, vol. 6 (Toronto: University of Toronto Press; Quebec: Presses de l'Université Laval, 2003–), http://www.biographi.ca/en/bio/minns_william_6E.html.

86 Sylvanus Urban, "To Carry Fish Alive, to a Great Distance," *The Gentleman's Magazine* 22 (London, July 1752), 308, Google Books; "To Carry Fish Alive, to a Great Distance," *The London Magazine* 22 (Dublin, July 1752), 363, HathiTrust.

87 "To Carry Fish Alive to a Great Distance," *Shamrock* 2, no. 46 (24 October 1812), [4], Readex: America's Historical Newspapers.

88 A kind of crystalized sugar made by boiling the sugar. OED *Online*, s.v. "sugar candy, n. and adj."

89 Izaak Walton and Charles Cotton, *The Complete Angler, or Contemplative Man's Recreation*, 5th ed. (London: J.F. and C. Rivington, 1791), 5, 19, ECCO.

90 Walton and Cotton, *The Complete Angler*, 160–1, 221, 246.

91 Amelia Chambers, *The Ladies Best Companion; Or, A Golden Treasure for the Fair Sex* (London: J. Cooke, [1775?]), 122, ECCO.

92 Dunfield, *Atlantic Salmon*, 112.

93 Paul, *We Were Not the Savages*, 51–2.

94 "To the Printer," *Nova Scotia Gazette* 2, no. 78, 4 February 1768, Nova Scotia Newspapers on Microfilm, vol. 2, no. 78, microfilm reel 9466, Nova Scotia Archives.

95 Lynn Murphy and Brenda Hicks, *Nova Scotia Newspapers: A Directory and Union List 1752–1988* (Halifax: Dalhousie University School of Information Sciences, 1990), 1: 205.

96 "Extract of a letter from Nayland, Suffolk, Jan. 5," *Pennsylvania Packet* (Philadelphia), no. 3189 (21 April 1789), Readex: America's Historical Newspapers.

97 From the central German state of Hesse.

98 Maria Rundell, *A New System of Domestic Cookery; Formed upon Principles of Economy: and Adapted to the Use of Private Families* (London: John Murray, 1810), 104, Google Books.

99 Rundell, *A New System*, 104.

100 Esther Copley, *The Cook's Complete Guide on the Principles of Frugality, Comfort, and Elegance: Including the Art of Carving, and the Most Approved Method of Setting-Out a Table* (London: George Virtue, 1810), 323, Google Books.

101 "Advertisement," in *Cottage Comforts with Hints for Promoting Them*, 12th ed. (London: Simpkin and Marshall, 1834), n.p., Nineteenth Century Collections Online.

102 "Preface," *Cottage Comforts*, III.

103 Christof Mauch, "Images of America – Political Myths – Historiography: 'Hessians' in the War of Independence," *Amerikastudien / American Studies* 48, no. 3 (2003): 411–23, JSTOR.

104 "Extract of a letter sent to the Bath Society by the Rev. H.J. Close," *Nova Scotia*

Packet and General Advertiser, Nova Scotia Newspapers on Microfilm, no. 65, microfilm reel 4823, Nova Scotia Archives.

105 Tremaine, *Bibliography*, 612–14; Gertrude Tratt, "Humphreys, James," in *Dictionary of Canadian Biography*, vol. 5 (Toronto: University of Toronto Press; Quebec: Presses de l'Université Laval, 2003–), http://www.biographi.ca/en/bio/humphreys_james_5E.html.

106 H.J. Close, "Article XVI. On the Culture of Potatoes," *Letters and Papers on Agriculture, Planting, &c.* 3 (1786), 111–17, ECCO.

107 Close, "On the Culture of Potatoes," 111–17.

108 Close, "On the Culture of Potatoes," 116.

109 "Agriculture," in *Encyclopaedia Britannica; or, a Dictionary of Arts, Sciences, and Miscellaneous Literature on a Plan Entirely New* (Dublin: James Moore, 1790), 1: 298–9, ECCO; "Agriculture," in *Encyclopaedia; or, A Dictionary of Arts, Sciences, and Miscellaneous Literature* (Philadelphia: Thomas Dobson, 1798), 1: 298–9, ECCO.

110 Close, "On the Culture of Potatoes," 115.

111 Close, "On the Culture of Potatoes," 115.

112 John Reader, *Potato* (New Haven: Yale University Press, 2009), 111, 115, 118, EBSCOhost.

113 "Harrico of Mutton," *Almon Scrapbook*, 1700–1954, Almon Family Fonds, MG 1 vol. 14, microfilm reel 14894, Nova Scotia Archives.

114 According to the Nova Scotia Archives, the *Almon Scrapbook* "was compiled by Senator William Johnstone Almon, M.D., (1816–1901) and later continued by his granddaughter Susanna Almon." See "What's Cooking? Food, Drink and the Pleasures of Eating in Old-Time Nova Scotia," Nova Scotia Archives, https://archives.novascotia.ca/Cooking/archives/?ID=1118.

115 "Receipt of Our Dear Mary Byles of Granada," *Almon Scrapbook*, 1700–1954, Almon Family Fonds, MG 1 vol. 14, microfilm reel 14,894, Nova Scotia Archives.

116 Though Mather Byles III had an aunt by the same name, she was the Mary Byles who "lived unmarried with her father in Boston and continued to live at their Boston house after his death" in 1788. See "Guide to the Collection: Byles Family Papers, 1757–1915," Massachusetts Historical Society, https://www.masshist.org/collection–guides/view/fa0314.

117 *OED Online*, s.v. "haricot, n."

118 Elizabeth Raffald, *The Experienced English House–keeper, for the Use and Ease of Ladies, House-keepers, Cooks, &c.* (Manchester: J. Harrop, 1769), 89–90, ECCO.

119 François Massialot, *The Court and Country Cook: Giving New and Plain Directions*

How to Order All Manner of Entertainments, trans. J.K. (London: W. Onley, for A. and J. Churchill, 1702), 105, ECCO. For an earlier edition, see also François Massialot, *Le Cuisinier royal et bourgeois, qui apprend à ordonner toute sorte de repas, & la meilleure maniere des ragoûts les plus à la mode & les plus exquis*, 2nd ed. (Paris: de Laurent Rondet, 1693), BnF Gallica.

120 [Joseph Marie] Brossais du Perray, *Historical Remarks and Anecdotes on the Castle of the Bastille*, trans. from the French, 1774 (London: T. Cadell and N. Conant, 1780), 9, ECCO.

121 du Perray, *Historical Remarks*, 8.

122 Mrs Frazer, *The Practice of Cookery, Pastry, Pickling, Preserving, &c.* (Edinburgh: Peter Hill, 1791), 56–7, ECCO.

123 Susanna MacIver, *Cookery and Pastry, as Taught and Practised by Mrs Maciver, Teacher of Those Arts in Edinburgh* (Edinburgh: the author, 1782), 55, ECCO.

124 George Dalrymple, *The Practice of Modern Cookery; Adapted to Families of Distinction, As Well As to Those of the Middling Ranks of Life* (Edinburgh: the author, 1781), 243–4, ECCO.

125 Elizabeth Cleland, *A New and Easy Method of Cookery* (Edinburgh: C. Wright and Company, 1759), 45, 91, ECCO.

126 Frazer, *The Practice*, 56; MacIver, *Cookery*, 55; Cleland, *New and Easy Method*, 45.

127 Dalrymple, *The Practice*, 244.

128 John Farley, *The London Art of Cookery, and Housekeeper's Complete Assistant* (London: J. Fielding, 1783), 71–2, ECCO.

129 "American Chestnut in Nova Scotia," Canadian Chestnut Council, https://www.canadianchestnutcouncil.ca/index.cfm?page=NovaScotia.

130 M. Parmentier, "A Method to Make Potatoe-Bread [*sic*] Without the Admixture of Flour," *Nova Scotia Magazine*, 4 April 1791, Nova Scotia Newspapers on Microfilm, nn. 207, microfilm reel 8063, Nova Scotia Archives.

131 Tremaine, *Bibliography*, 653–6.

132 Phyllis R. Blakeley and John Grant, eds., *Eleven Exiles: Accounts of Loyalists of the American Revolution* (Toronto: Dundurn, 1982), 28–58.

133 *The Annual Register, or a View of the History, Politics, and Literature, for the year 1779* (London: J. Dodsley, 1780), 99–100, ECCO.

134 Antoine Augustin Parmentier, *Manière de faire le pain de pommes de terre, sans mélange de farine* (Paris: Imprimerie Royale, 1779), BnF Gallica; Antoine Augustin Parmentier, *Recherches sur les végétaux nourrissans, qui, dans les temps de disette, peuvent remplacer les aliments ordinaires* (Paris: Imprimerie Royale, 1781), BnF Gallica.

135 Panification refers to bread-making or conversion into bread. It comes from the French, *panifier*, to make into bread. The OED lists this usage in *The Annual Register [...] for the Year 1779* as its first appearance. See OED, s.v. "panification, n."

136 A drachm is "a weight approximately equivalent to that of the Greek coin," or about ⅛ of an ounce in apothecaries' weight or 1/16 of an ounce in avoirdupois weight. Given that Parmentier was an apothecary, it seems likely he is using the apothecaries' weight. The EMMR database does not include any other non-medicinal remedies that use drachm (alternatively spelled dram) as a measurement.

137 Reader, *Potato*, 120–2.

138 Antoine Augustin Parmentier, *Observations on Such Nutritive Vegetables as May be Substituted in the Place of Ordinary Food, in Times of Scarcity. Extracted from the French of M. Parmentier* (London: J. Murray, 1783), 3, 7, ECCO. The French original is slightly different.

139 Louise A. Tilly, "Food Entitlement, Famine, and Conflict," *The Journal of Interdisciplinary History* 14, no. 2 (1983): 333–49.

140 Cynthia A. Bouton, *The Flour War: Gender, Class, and Community in Late Ancien Régime French Society* (University Park, PA: Pennsylvania State University Press, 1993), xvii–xxvi.

141 Rebecca Earle, "Potatoes, Populations, and States," *Early American Studies: An Interdisciplinary Journal* 19, no. 2 (2021): 393–417, https://dx.doi.org/10.1353/eam.2021.0013.

142 Lane Jonah and Véchambre, *Le gout francais*, 40–2.

143 "A Method of Making Leaven," *The Nova Scotia Magazine*, 4 April 1791, Nova Scotia Newspapers on Microfilm, microfilm reel 8063, Nova Scotia Archives.

144 Hannah Glasse, *The Art of Cookery, Made Plain and Easy* (London: the author, 1747), 299–300, ECCO. A nearly identical version was also published as "For Making Bread Without Yeast" in Penelope Bradshaw, *Bradshaw's Valuable Family Jewel*, 10th ed. (London: P. Bradshaw, 1748), sig. C2*r*, ECCO.

145 Leaven refers to a raising agent added to dough. See OED, s.v. "leaven, n."

146 Empting is a "type of yeast deriving from the process of fermentation." It could also refer to another type of rising agent. It may not have been as powerful as the yeast we use today. See OED, s.v. "empting, n."

147 "Some Early 18th and 19th Century Recipes Pasted on Pages of Militia Regulations," Militia Regulations Book, MG 100 vol. 1, no. 5, microfilm reel 786, Nova Scotia Archives.

148 Glasse, *The Art of Cookery*, 309.

149 "To Make Ketchup," 1676–1944, Miller Family Fonds, PANS MG 1, vol. 693, Nova Scotia Archives.

150 Mrs Smith, *The Female Economist: or, A Plain System of Cookery*, 3rd ed. (London: Mathews and Leigh, 1810), 259–60, Google Books.

151 Deborah Irwin, *The Housewife's Guide; or The Economical and Domestic Art of Cookery* (London: W. Mason, [1830?]), 68, Google Books.

152 Kat Eschner, "There's Something Fishy About the Ketchup You Put on Your Burgers," *Smithsonian Magazine*, 5 June 2017, smithsonianmag.com, https://www.smithsonianmag.com/smart-news/ketchup-fishy-origins-180963511/.

153 Richard Bradley, *The Country Housewife and Lady's Director, in the Management of a House, and the Delights and Profits of a Farm*, 3rd ed. (London: Woodman and Lyon, 1728), 140, ECCO.

154 "Pancakes, Wonders, Sauce for Boiled Cod, Catchup," 1786, Commissioner of Public Records, RG 1 vol. 411 no. 10, Nova Scotia Archives, *What's Cooking: Food, Drink, and the Pleasures of Eating in Old Time Nova Scotia*, https://archives.novascotia.ca/cooking/archives/?ID=4.

155 "Catchup, Oysters," 1809, Miller Family Fonds, MG 1, vol. 652, no. 7, Nova Scotia Archives, *What's Cooking: Food, Drink, and the Pleasures of Eating in Old Time Nova Scotia*, https://archives.novascotia.ca/cooking/archives/?ID=76.

156 Bradley, *The Country Housewife* (1728), 143.

157 Richard Bradley, *The Country Housewife and Lady's Director, in Every Month of the Year*, 6th ed. (London: W. Bristow, 1762), 264, ECCO.

158 Penelope Bradshaw and [Edward] Lambart, *Bradshaw's Valuable Family Jewel: or, the Complete House-wife*, 11th ed. (London: P. Bradshaw, 1749), sig. D3*v*, ECCO.

159 Bradley, *The Country Housewife* (1762), 264.

160 Bradley, *The Country Housewife* (1728), 35, 31.

161 Raffald, *The Experienced English Housekeeper*, 13, 72.

162 Raffald, *The Experienced English Housekeeper*, 61–2, 63, 65, 256.

163 Raffald, *The Experienced English Housekeeper*, 124, 114.

164 Sarah Harrison, *The House-Keeper's Pocket-Book: And Compleat Family Cook* (London: T. Worrall, 1733), sig. A1, 49–50, ECCO.

165 Harrison, *The House-Keeper's Pocket-Book*, 49–50.

166 Richard Briggs, *The English Art of Cookery, According to the Present Practice*, 3rd ed. (London: G.G. and J. Robinson, 1794), ECCO.

167 Mrs Nourse, *Modern Practical Cookery, Pastry, Confectionery, Pickling and Preserving* (Montreal: Armour and Ramsay, 1845), 345, Canadiana.

168 An Experienced Lady, *The American Housewife and Kitchen Directory*, 3rd ed. (New York: Dayton and Saxton, 1841), 29, Google Books.

169 Anne Clark, *The Surprise Cook Book: Containing Valuable Recipes in all the Departments, Including Sickroom Cookery* (St Stephen, NB: St Croix Soap Manufacturing Co, [1899?]), 14, 23, 132, 254, Canadiana.

170 "Some Early 18th and 19th Century Recipes Pasted on Pages of Militia Regulations," Militia Regulations Book, MG 100 vol. 1, no. 5, microfilm reel 786, Nova Scotia Archives.

171 [Mrs A.L. Webster], *The Improved Housewife, or Book of Receipts*, 2nd ed. (Hartford: n.p., 1844), 154, Google Books. The book does not name a publisher, but the Library of Congress indicates that it was first copyrighted in 1843. We have not been able to access a first edition of the book to confirm where it was published. Subsequent editions, accessible in Google Books, from 1847 (9th edition) and 1851 (14th edition) were printed in Hartford; a 20th edition was printed in Boston in 1855.

172 Janet Long, "Tomatoes," in *The Cambridge World History of Food*, ed. Kenneth F. Kiple and Kriemhild Coneè Ornelas (Cambridge: Cambridge University Press, 2000), 351–8.

173 Philip Miller, "Lycopersicon," in *The Gardener's Dictionary*, 2nd ed. (London: John and James Rivington, 1733), sig. 5H, ECCO; Philip Miller, "Lycopersicon," in *The Gardener's Dictionary*, 3rd ed. (London: printed for the author, 1737), sig. 5P, ECCO.

174 Véronique Bergougnoux, "The History of Tomato: From Domestication to Biopharming," *Biotechnology Advances* 32 (2014): 171–2.

175 John Abercrombie and Thomas Mawe, "Solanum," in *The Universal Gardener and Botanist: Or, A General Dictionary of Gardening and Botany*, 2nd ed. (London: G.G. and J. Robinson, 1797), sig. 6Q3*v*, ECCO.

176 Long, "Tomatoes," 357; Bergougnoux, "The History," 175.

177 "To Make Mangoes," *Almon Scrapbook*, 1700–1954, Almon Family Fonds, MG 1 vol. 14, microfilm reel 14894, Nova Scotia Archives.

178 See "Harrico of Mutton" in this chapter.

179 *OED Online*, s.v. "mango, n.1 and adj."

180 Harrison, *The House-Keeper's Pocket-Book*, 112–13. Bradley, *The Country Housewife* (1762) includes a similar offering described as "an extraordinary Receipt for Pickling of CUCUMBERS to imitate Mango's" (59) as well as one "To Pickle green MELONS, in Imitation of MANGO" (79).

181 Emily J. Warschefsky and Eric J.B. Von Wettberg, "Populations Genomic Analysis of Mango (*Mangifera indica*) Suggests a Complex History of Domestication," *New Phytologist* 222 (2019): 2024.

182 "Receipt of Our Dear Mary Byles of Granada," *Almon Scrapbook*, 1700–1954, Almon Family Fonds, MG 1 vol. 14, microfilm reel 14894, Nova Scotia Archives.

183 *Almon Scrapbook*, 1700–1954, Almon Family Fonds, MG 1 vol. 14, microfilm reel 14894, Nova Scotia Archives.

184 "*OED Online*, s.v. "plum cake, n."

185 Pearl ash, also known as potash, is potassium carbonate, a compound that produces air bubbles when combined with acidic ingredients. Used from about 1780 for its bubble-producing effects, pearl ash was widely used in cake making before the introduction of baking soda and baking powder and was in 1790, notes Linda Civitello, *Baking Powder Wars: The Cutthroat Food Fight That Revolutionized Cooking* (Chicago: University of Chicago Press, 2017), 20, "[t]he first patent issued in the United States." As Civitello also explains, cake baking was once "even more laborious than making bread," but chemical leaveners would facilitate more spontaneous baking and, because "[c]ake making was not locked into a certain day of the week as bread baking was," they "also moved housewives away from baking in large batches" (12, 26).

186 William Ellis, *The Country Housewife's Family Companion* (London: James Hodges, 1750), 77–8, ECCO.

187 Catharine Brooks, *The Complete English Cook; Or, Prudent Housewife* (London: for the author, 1770), 59, ECCO.

188 Cleland, *A New and Easy*, 156.

189 Mary Kettilby, *A Collection of Above Three Hundred Receipts in Cookery, Physick and Surgery* (London: Richard Wilkin, 1714), 93, ECCO.

190 Kettilby, *A Collection*, 93.

191 Penelope Bradshaw, *The Family Jewel, and Compleat Housewife's Companion: Or, the Whole Art of Cookery Made Plain and Easy* (London: R. Whitworth, 1754), 61 2, ECCO.

192 Bradshaw, *The Family Jewel*, 62.

193 "Approved Receipts," *The Halifax Gazette* 11, no. 231, 21–28 November 1765, Nova Scotia Newspapers on Microfilm, microfilm reel 8152, Nova Scotia Archives.

194 Donald F. Chard, "Bushell, John," in *Dictionary of Canadian Biography*, vol. 3 (Toronto: University of Toronto Press; Quebec: Presses de l'Université Laval, 2003–), http://www.biographi.ca/en/bio/bushell_john_3E.html.

195 Tremaine, *Bibliography*, 3, 602–3.

196 Tremaine, *Bibliography*, 599.

197 Kettilby, *A Collection*, 86–7.

198 Lady Charlotte Campbell Bury, *The Lady's Own Cookery Book, and New Dinner-Table Directory*, 3rd ed. (London: Henry Colburn, 1844), 274, Google Books.

199 Steven Stellingwerf, *The Gingerbread Book* (New York: Rizzoli Publishing, 1991), 8–9.

200 Bethany Aram, "Caribbean Ginger and Atlantic Trade, 1570–1648," *Journal of Global History* 10, no. 3 (2015): 415–16, https://doi.org/10.1017/S1740022815000200.

201 Aram, "Caribbean Ginger," 416, observes *c.*1420 as the approximate date of "[t]he first known recipe for gingerbread."

202 Bradley, *The Country Housewife* (1762), 206.

203 Bradshaw, *The Family Jewel* (1754), 114.

204 Charlotte Cartwright, *The Lady's Best Companion; Or, Complete Treasure for Sex* (Blackburn: Henry M'allum, 1799), 41, ECCO.

205 Bradley, *The Country Housewife* (1762), 250.

206 OED *Online*, s.v. "molasses, n."

207 Diane Tye "'A Poor Man's Meal': Molasses in Atlantic Canada," *Food, Culture & Society* 11, no. 3 (2008): 336–7, https://doi.org/10.2752/175174408X347892.

208 Tye, "A Poor Man's Meal," 337–9.

209 *Almon Scrapbook*, 1700–1954, Almon Family Fonds, MG 1 vol. 14, microfilm reel 14894, Nova Scotia Archives.

210 Benjamin Rumford, "Of Food: Chapter VI, Of Indian Corn," in *Essays, Political, Economical, and Philosophical*, 3rd ed. (Dublin: W. Porter and J. Archer, 1796), 1: 253–64, ECCO.

211 David Knight, "Thompson, Sir Benjamin, Count Rumford in the Nobility of the Holy Roman Empire (1753–1814), Natural Philosopher and Philanthropist," in *Oxford Dictionary of National Biography* (Oxford: Oxford University Press, 2004), online.

212 Rumford, "Of Food," 248, 261.

213 Rumford, "Of Food," 249.

214 Rumford, "Of Food," 253.

215 Rumford, "Of Food," 257

216 Rumford, "Of Food," 258–9.

217 Rumford, "Of Food," 254.

218 Rumford, "Of Food," 265.

219 Rumford, "Of Food," 265.

220 Paul David Nelson, "Pepperrell, Sir William, First Baronet (1696–1759), Army Officer and Merchant," in *Oxford Dictionary of National Biography* (Oxford: Oxford University Press, 2004), online.

221 "The Siege of Louisbourg in 1745," in *The American Historical Register*, ed. Charles H. Browning (Philadelphia: Historical Register Publishing, June 1895), 954,

Google Books; Henry Burrage, "Colonel Nathaniel Sparhawk of Kittery," in *Collections and Proceedings of the Maine Historical Society*, 2nd series (Portland: published by the society, 1898), 9, 261–2, Google Books.

222 C. Thimelthorpe, A *Short Inventory of Certayne Idle Inventions the Fruites of a Close and Secret Garden of Great Ease, and Litle Pleasure* (London: Thomas Marsh, 1581), 22, EEBO. The first reference to the hasty pudding listed in the OED is to 1598 and as an example of "poor means meate" in John Florio's *World of Words*. See OED *Online*, s.v. "hasty pudding, n."

223 Joseph Cooper, *The Art of Cookery Refin'd and Augmented* (London: R. Lowndes, 1654), 142, EEBO.

224 Vester, *A Taste*, 22–6.

225 "History," *The Hasty Pudding Institute of 1770*, https://www.hastypudding.org/history/#hpc-history.

226 J.A. Leo Lemay, "The Contexts and Themes of 'The Hasty-Pudding,'" *Early American Literature* 17, no. 1 (1982): 3–23; Joel Barlow, *The Hasty-Pudding, a Poem, in Three Cantos* ([Fairhaven, VT]: J.P. Spooner, 1796), ECCO.

227 Barlow, *The Hasty-Pudding*, 7.

228 Barlow, *The Hasty-Pudding*, 4.

229 Lemay, "The Contexts," 6, 19.

230 Vester, *A Taste*, 27.

231 "To Make a Rice Pudding," *The Halifax Gazette* 11, no. 231, 28 November 1765, Nova Scotia Newspapers on Microfilm, microfilm reel 8152, Nova Scotia Archives.

232 *Almon Scrapbook*, 1700–1954, Almon Family Fonds, MG 1 vol. 14, microfilm reel 14894, Nova Scotia Archives.

233 See "Harrico of Mutton," in this chapter.

234 *The Complete Family Piece: and, Country Gentleman, and Farmer's, Best Guide* (London: C. Rivington, 1736), sig. A1, 123, ECCO; *The Lady's Companion: or, an Infallible Guide to the Fair Sex*, 4th ed. (London: T. Read, 1743), 2: 62, ECCO.

235 Kettilby, *A Collection*, 53.

236 *The Ladies Cabinet Enlarged and Opened* (London: T.M., 1654), 206–7, EEBO.

237 Peter A. Coclanis, "Distant Thunder: The Creation of a World Market in Rice and the Transformations It Wrought," *American Historical Review* 98, no. 4 (1993): 1050–78.

238 Kenneth Morgan, "The Organization of the Colonial American Rice Trade," *The William and Mary Quarterly*, 3rd series, 52, no. 3 (1995): 433–44.

239 John Marshall, "Directions for Miss McDonald," Macdonald Family (St Peter's) Papers, no. 42, 1–6, Acc. 2664, Prince Edward Island Public Archives.

240 *An Account of Several Work-Houses for Employing and Maintaining the Poor* (London: Joseph Downing, 1725), 67, ECCO; *An Account of the Publick Hospital for the Diseased Poor in the County of York* (York: C. Ward and R. Chandler, 1743), 26–9, ECCO.

241 Juliana Adelman, "Invalid Cookery, Nursing and Domestic Medicine in Ireland," *Journal of the History of Medicine and Allied Sciences* 73, no. 2 (2018): 188–92.

242 Ken Albala, "Food for Healing: Convalescent Cookery in the Early Modern Era," *Studies in History and Philosophy of Science* 43, no. 2 (2012): 323–8.

243 Albala, "Food for Healing," 328.

244 Albala, "Food for Healing," 324.

245 The Manuscript Notebook of Sarah Creighton Wilkins, 1779–1833, MacDonald Family Fonds, MG 1 no. 1, microfilm reel 10618, Nova Scotia Archives.

246 Steven Shapin, "'You Are What You Eat': Historical Change in Ideas About Food and Identity," *Historical Research* 87, no. 237 (2014): 377–92.

247 John Hill, *The Useful Family Herbal. Or, an Account of All Those English Plants, Which Are Remarkable for Their Virtues* (London: W. Johnston, 1754), 264, ECCO.

248 Wendy Wall, "Just a Spoonful of Sugar: Syrup and Domesticity in Early Modern England," *Modern Philology* 104, no. 2 (November 2006): 156, https://doi.org/10.1086/511711.

249 Farley, *The London Art of Cookery*, 439.

250 Glasse, *The Art of Cookery*, 120.

251 Glasse, *The Art of Cookery*, 237.

252 Glasse, *The Art of Cookery*, 120.

253 Both Farley and Glasse are cited in one of the panada recipes in Mary Cole, *The Lady's Complete Guide; or Cookery in All Its Branches* (London: Kearsley, 1788), 457, ECCO. Other panada recipes are almost identical. See Charles Carter, *The London and Country Cook* (London: Charles Hitch, Stephen Austen, and John Hinton, 1749), 323, ECCO; Richard Steele, *The Ladies' Library:or, Encyclopedia of Female Knowledge* (London: J. Ridgway, 1790), 2: 182, ECCO; William Augustus Henderson, *The Housekeeper's Instructor* (London: W. and J. Stratford, [1790?]), 299, ECCO.

254 Hill, *The Useful Family*, 322.

255 Kettilby, *A Collection*, 76–7.

256 *Almon Scrapbook*, 1780–1800, Almon Family Fonds, MG 1 vol. 14, microfilm reel 14894, Nova Scotia Archives.

257 "Efficacy of Blackberry Jelly in Treating Gravel and Stone," *Nova Scotia Packet and General Advertiser* (Shelburne), no. 71, 7 September 1786, Nova Scotia Newspapers on Film, microfilm reel 4823, Nova Scotia Archives; "Efficacy of the Black-Berry Jelly, in Curing the Stone and Gravel," *The Nova Scotia Magazine*, no. 422,

3 December 1790, Nova Scotia Newspapers on Film, microfilm reel 8063, Nova Scotia Archives.

258 "As the Season for Making a Jelly of Black-Berries Is Approaching," *New-York Journal and Patriotic Register* (New York), no. 2074 (3 August 1786), Readex: America's Historical Newspapers.

259 Rev. Dr Mather Byles to his sisters, 1 December 1785, Almon Family Fonds, Series A 1993 35 D, microfilm reel 807, Nova Scotia Archives.

260 Anon., *The Compleat Herbal; Or, Family Physician. Giving an Account of All Such Plants as Are Now Used in the Practice of Physic* (Manchester: G. Swindells, 1787), 107, ECCO; E. Sibly, *Culpeper's English Physician; and Complete Herbal. To Which Are Now First Added, Upwards of One Hundred Additional Herbs* (London: E. Sibly, 1794), 89, ECCO. As Kim E. Hummer, "*Rubus* Pharmacology: Antiquity to the Present," *HortScience Horticultural Science* 45, no. 11 (2010): 1588–9, https://doi.org/10.21273/HORTSCI.45.11.1587, points out, the benefits of blackberry were so well known by 1652 that Culpeper described brambles as a plant that "needeth no description" (Culpeper qtd. in Hummer 1589); it had been recognized by the ancient Greeks and Romans for its usefulness in "preventing stomachaches, stopping excess fluxes of bodily fluids" and treating "droopy eyes, mouth sores, hemorrhoids, and snake-bites."

261 Hummer, "*Rubus*," 1589.

262 Handley Chipman's Notes, 1776, Chipman Family Papers, vol. 2, no. 205, MG vol. 218, microfilm reel 10154, Nova Scotia Archives.

263 James Doyle Davison, *Handley Chipman: King's County Planter* (n.p.: distributed by the author, 1988), 46.

264 "Chipman Family Papers: Planters of Cornwallis," Nova Scotia Archives, https://archives.novascotia.ca/chipman/.

265 "Chipman, Handley," Acadia University Archives, https://archives.acadiau.ca/islandora/object/sketches%3A32.

266 Anon., *The Medical Museum: Or, A Repository of Cases, Experiments, Researches, and Discoveries, Collected at Home and Abroad* (London: W. Richardson and S. Clark, 1764), 3:8, ECCO.

267 Botanist Michel Adanson (1727–1806) was the author of *Histoire naturelle de Senegal* (1757) and *Familles naturelles des plantes* (1763). His work was published in English as *A Voyage to Senegal, the Isle of Goree, and the River Gambia* (London: J. Nourse and W. Johnston, 1759), translated by "an English Gentleman, who resided some Time in that Country" (sig. A1); though Adanson discusses couscous in the book, he does not mention lalo or the baobab.

268 As the instructions go on to explain, this is the West African name for a powder made from the leaves of baobab. See John Rashford, "The Use of Baobab Leaves (*Adansonia digitata* L.) for Food in Africa: A Review," *Economic Botany* 74, no. 4 (2018): 488.

269 Tisane, a nourishing medicinal infusion.

270 Rashford, "Use of Baobab," 488–9. Rashford also explains the tree, native to arid regions of Africa, has been introduced elsewhere but is not widely consumed in the Americas.

271 Christine Buchmann, Sarah Prehsler, Anna Hartl, and Christian R. Vogl, "The Importance of Baobab (*Adansonia digitata* L.) in Rural West African Subsistence – Suggestion of a Cautionary Approach to International Market Export of Baobab Fruits," *Ecology of Food and Nutrition* 49 (2010): 146–9.

272 Bruce J. Hargreaves, "Parallels in Plant Use in Africa and North America," *The Society of Malawi Journal* 34, no. 1 (1981): 56–71.

273 OED *Online*, s.v. "couscous, n."

274 Rashford, "Use of Baobab," 489.

275 Agriculture lecture notes of Dr James Dinwiddie, 1793, item 13, James Dinwiddie Fonds, MS-2-726, Dalhousie University Archives and Special Collections.

276 "Administrative History / Biographical Sketch," 2017, Finding Aid – James Dinwiddie Fonds, MS-2-726, 3, Dalhousie University Archives, https://findingaids.library.dal.ca/downloads/james-dinwiddie-fonds.pdf.

277 Bradley, *The Country Housewife* (1728), 71–93; Robert Brown, *The Compleat Farmer; Or, the Whole Art of Husbandry* (Dublin: James Hoey, 1759), 26, ECCO.

278 Sally McMurry, "Women's Work in Agriculture: Divergent Trends in England and America, 1800 to 1930," *Comparative Studies in Society and History* 34, no. 2 (1992): 252, 254.

279 Sandra Sherman, *Fresh from the Past: Recipes and Revelations from Moll Flanders' Kitchen* (Lanham, MD: Taylor Trade Publishing, 2004), 190.

280 Sherman, *Fresh from the Past*, 257.

281 Brenda Dunn, *A History of Port-Royal / Annapolis Royal, 1605–1800* (Annapolis Royal and Halifax: The Historical Association of Annapolis Royal / Nimbus Publishing, 2004), 3.

282 A.R. MacNeil, "Early American Communities on the Fundy: A Case Study of Annapolis and Amherst Townships, 1767–1827," *Agricultural History* 63, no. 2, (Spring, 1989): 104.

283 J.A. Ruddick, *An Historical and Descriptive Account of the Dairying Industry of Canada* (Ottawa: Dept. of Agriculture, 1911), 10, Canadiana; MacNeil, "Early," 105.

284 Graeme Wynn, "Late Eighteenth-Century Agriculture on the Bay of Fundy Marshlands," *Acadiensis* 8, no. 2 (1979): 89.

285 Richard Blundel and Angela Tregear, "From Artisans to 'Factories': The Interpenetration of Craft and Industry in English Cheese-Making, 1650–1950," *Enterprise & Society* 7, no. 4 (2006): 713.

286 McMurry, "Women's Work," 257.

287 Ruddick, *An Historical*, 23, 26, 35.

288 "Directions for Making Cheese," *The Nova Scotia Magazine*, 1 March 1791, Nova Scotia Newspapers on Microfilm, microfilm reel 8063, Nova Scotia Archives, Early Modern Maritime Recipes, https://emmr.lib.unb.ca/recipes/directions-making-cheese; "Receipt for Making Parmesan Cheese," *The Nova Scotia Magazine*, 5 November 1791, Nova Scotia Newspapers on Microfilm, microfilm reel 8063, Nova Scotia Archives. Also available at Early Modern Maritime Recipes, https://emmr.lib.unb.ca/recipes/receipt-making-parmesan-cheese.

289 "From the Quebec Herald. Directions for Making Cheese," *Gazette of the United States* (Philadelphia) 3, no. 16 (22 June 1791), 61, Readex: America's Historical Newspapers; "From the Quebec Herald. Directions for Making Cheese," *Independent Gazetteer* (Philadelphia) 9, no. 1347 (2 July 1791), [1], Readex; "Directions for Making Cheese," *American Mercury* (Hartford, CT) 7, no. 365 (4 July 1791), [1], Readex; "Miscellany. Directions for Making Cheese," *Newport Herald* (Newport, RI) 5, no. 228 (16 July 1791), [1], Readex; "Directions for Making Cheese," *Vermont Gazette* (Bennington, VT) 9, no. 8 (18 July 1791), [1], Readex; "From the Quebec Herald. Directions for Making Cheese," *Litchfield Monitor* (Litchfield, CT) 6, no. 315 (20 July 1791), [4], Readex; "From the Quebec Herald. Directions for Making Cheese," *City Gazette* (Charleston, SC) 9, no. 1835 (21 July 1791), [2], Readex; "From the Quebec Herald. Directions for Making Cheese," *Independent Chronicle* (Boston) 23, no. 1186 (21 July 1791), [4], Readex; "Directions for Making Cheese," *Thomas's Massachusetts Spy; Or, The Worcester Gazette* (Worcester, MA) 20, no. 955 (21 July 1791), [1], Readex; "Directions for Making Cheese," *Connecticut Journal* (New Haven, CT), no. 1239 (27 July 1791), [1], Readex; 'From the Quebec Herald. Directions for Making Cheese," *The Essex Journal & New-Hampshire Packet* (Newburyport, MA), no. 370 (27 July 1791), [4], Readex; "Directions for Making Cheese," *The New Hampshire Journal: Or, The Farmer's Weekly Museum* (Walpole, NH) 1, no. 1 (11 April 1793), [1], Readex; "From the Nova-Scotia Magazine. Directions for Making Cheese," *Washington Patrol* (Salem, NY) 1, no. 3 (10 June 1795), [4], Readex; "Rural Economy. Directions for Making Cheese," *The Farmers' Register* (Chambersburg, PA) 1, no. 11 (27 June 1798), 46, Readex; "Directions for Making

Cheese," *Newburyport Herald* (Newburyport, MA) 2, no. 63 (4 June 1799), [4], Readex; "Directions for Making Cheese," *Green Mountain Patriot* (Peacham, VT) 2, no. 71 (27 June 1799), [4], Readex.

290 "Directions for Making Cheese," *The Nova Scotia Magazine*.

291 Manuscript Notebook of Dr William James Almon, 1780–1800, Almon Family Fonds, MG 1 vol. 10, microfilm reel 10045, Nova Scotia Archives.

292 Lois K. Kernaghan, "Almon, William James," in *Dictionary of Canadian Biography*, vol. 5 (Toronto: University of Toronto Press; Quebec: Presses de l'Université Laval, 2003–), http://www.biographi.ca/en/bio/almon_william_james_5E.html.

293 Mr Jahrig, "On the Sugar of Milk," *The Literary Magazine and British Review* 8 (May 1792), 328–30, HathiTrust.

294 Mr Jahrig, "Milk: On the Sugar of Milk," in *The New Encyclopaedia; or, Modern Universal Dictionary of Arts and Sciences* (London: C. Cook, 1799), 3: sig. 8A*v*, ECCO.

295 M. Jahrig, "Sur le sucre de lait naturel," in *Observations sur la physique, sur l'histoire naturelle et sur les arts*, ed. M. l'Abbé Rozier, M. J.A. Mongez, and Jean-Claude Delamétherie (Paris: Bureau du Journal de Physique, November 1791), 39: 368–9, BnF Gallica.

296 Lake Baikal is located in southeast Siberia in the republic of Buryatia and Irkutsk. See G. Ivanovich Galazy, "Lake Baikal," *Encyclopedia Britannica*, https://www.britannica.com/place/Lake-Baikal.

297 That the Selenga River flows from Mongolia into Lake Baikal suggests that the author intends Mongolian rather than Mogul (or Mughal). See "Selenga River," *Encyclopedia Britannica*, https://www.britannica.com/place/Selenga-River.

298 A wooden implement specifically designed for stirring chocolate beverages.

299 J.L. Dyvernois, *A Dissertation on the Sugar of Milk*, trans. D. d'E [...] (London: T. James, 1753), sig. A, ECCO.

300 Dyvernois, *A Dissertation*, 2–3.

301 Dyvernois, *A Dissertation*, 5.

302 Dyvernois, *A Dissertation*, 1–21.

303 Manuscript Notebook of Dr William James Almon, 1780–1800, Almon Family Fonds, MG 1 vol. 10, microfilm reel 10045, Nova Scotia Archives.

304 "Means of Lessening the Consumption of Sugar," *The Phoenix; Or, Weekly Miscellany Improved* 3, no. 53 (10 July 1793), 348–9, Google Books.

305 Lorenz Florenz Crell, *Crell's Chemical Journal; Giving an Account of the Latest Discoveries in Chemistry* (London: R. Baldwin, 1793), 1: 202, 242, ECCO. Almon's notebook also includes an entry describing the usefulness of charcoal in cleaning utensils, improving oral hygiene, and purifying water, a discovery credited to

"a gentleman at Petersburg," who is likely Lowitz (Manuscript Notebook of Dr William James Almon, 1780–1800, Almon Family Fonds, MG 1 vol. 10, microfilm reel 10045, Nova Scotia Archives, 262).

306 An historic name for a region of what is now Romania.

307 Manuscript Notebook of Dr William James Almon, 1780–1800, Almon Family Fonds, MG 1 vol. 10, microfilm reel 10045, Nova Scotia Archives, 238.

308 Elizabeth Abbott, *Sugar: A Bittersweet History* (Toronto: Penguin, 2008), 150, 148.

309 *The Royal American Gazette* 11, no. 676 (24 January 1785), 1, Nova Scotia Historical Newspapers, https://archives.novascotia.ca/newspapers/archives/?ID=88.

310 Thomas Jefferson, *Notes on the State of Virginia* (Paris: n.p., 1782), 133–4, ECCO.

311 The anonymous "Essay on Bees, Honey, and Honey-Dews" and Abbé Bouffier's "Observations on the Origin of Honey" were published in *The Nova Scotia Magazine*, 1 December 1789, Nova Scotia Newspapers on Microfilm, microfilm reel 8062, Nova Scotia Archives; "Useful Method of Preserving Bees, Lately Adopted in America," *The Nova Scotia Magazine*, 5 May 1790, Nova Scotia Newspapers on Microfilm, microfilm reel 8062, Nova Scotia Archives.

312 "To the Printer," *Nova Scotia Gazette*, 21 January 1768, Nova Scotia Newspapers on Microfilm, microfilm reel 9466, Nova Scotia Archives.

313 Manuscript Notebook of Dr William James Almon, 1780–1800, Almon Family Fonds, MG 1 vol. 10, microfilm reel 10045, Nova Scotia Archives, 262.

314 See "Thick Ginger Bread" for an account of the importance of molasses in Maritime history and culture.

CHAPTER TWO

1 Anne Marie Lane Jonah and Chantal Véchambre, *Le gout francais au Canada atlantique, 1604–1758: Une histoire gastronomique / French Taste in Atlantic Canada, 1604–1758: A Gastronomic History* (Sydney, NS: Cape Breton University Press, 2012), 158–78.

2 Mr Clifford, "An Approved Method of Making Cider," *The Nova Scotia Magazine*, 4 May 1791, Nova Scotia Newspapers on Microfilm, microfilm reel 8063, Nova Scotia Archives. The recipe is available also at https://emmr.lib.unb.ca/recipes/approved-method-making-cider.

3 The Manuscript Notebook of Sarah Creighton Wilkins, 1779–1833, MacDonald Family Fonds, MG 1 no. 1, microfilm reel 10618, Nova Scotia Archives.

4 Manuscript Notebook of Dr William James Almon, 1780–1800, Almon Family Fonds, MG 1 vol. 10, microfilm reel 10045, Nova Scotia Archives.

5 James Moreira, "The Tradition of Rum: Rum in the Atlantic Provinces," in *Tempered by Rum: Rum in the History of the Maritime Provinces*, ed. James H. Morrison and James Moreira (Porters Lake, NS: Pottersfield Press, 1988), 15–16, 19.

6 Moreira, "The Tradition," 15, 22–3.

7 Emily Burton, "The Alcohol Paradox: Consumption, Regulation, and Public Houses in Three Maritime Colonies of Northeastern British America, 1749–1830" (PhD thesis, Dalhousie University, 2015), 290–8, https://central.bac-lac.gc.ca/.item?id=TC-NSHD-64718&op=pdf&app=Library.

8 Emily Burton, "Rum, Revenue and Roads: The Licensing of Public Houses in Nova Scotia, 1749–1831," *Journal of the Royal Nova Scotia Historical* Society 13 (2010): 83.

9 Burton, "Rum, Revenue and Roads," 83–4.

10 Robert James Merrit, *Imperial Paradoxes: Training the Senses and Tasting the Eighteenth Century* (Montreal and Kingston: McGill-Queen's University Press, 2021), 115.

11 Merrit, *Imperial Paradoxes*, 114–25.

12 Merrit, *Imperial Paradoxes*, 133.

13 Merrit, *Imperial Paradoxes*, 155.

14 Derrek Eberts, "To Brew or Not to Brew: A Brief History of Beer in Canada," *Manitoba History* 54 (2007): 3.

15 James E. McWilliams, "Brewing Beer in Massachusetts Bay, 1640–1690," *The New England Quarterly* 71, no. 4 (1998): 543.

16 Burton, "Rum, Revenue and Roads," 81.

17 William Paine, First Notebook of Medical Memoranda, 1769, Loyalist Collection, MIC–Loyalist FC LFR.P3W5P3, microfilm reel 2, University of New Brunswick.

18 Carol Anne Janzen, "Paine, William," in *Dictionary of Canadian Biography*, vol. 6 (Toronto: University of Toronto Press; Quebec: Presses de l'Université Laval, 2003–), http://www.biographi.ca/en/bio/paine_william_6E.html.

19 C. Stuart Houston, "Scurvy and Canadian Exploration," *Canadian Bulletin of Medical History* 7 (1990): 162.

20 Martin Cornell, "A Short History of Spruce Beer in Britain," *Brewery History* 165 (2016): 7.

21 Charles van Ravenswaay, "America's Age of Wood," *Proceedings of the American Antiquarian Society* 809 (1970): 60.

22 Sylvanus Urban, "Of the Cultivation of Exotics, Particularly of the American Fir Tree," *The Gentleman's Magazine* 26 (London, January 1756), 16, HathiTrust.

23 Manuscript Notebook of Dr William James Almon, 1780–1800, Almon Family Fonds, MG 1 vol. 10, microfilm reel 10045, Nova Scotia Archives.

24 Nancy Jean Turner and Patrick von Aderkas, "Sustained by First Nations: European Newcomers' Use of Indigenous Plant Foods in Temperate North America," *Acta Societatis Botanicorum Poloniae* 81, no. 4 (2012): 302.

25 John Josselyn, *New Englands Rarities* (London: G. Widdowes, 1672), 64, EEBO.

26 Cornell, "A Short History," 6.

27 Philip Miller, *The Gardeners Dictionary*, 2nd ed. (London: C. Rivington, 1733), sig. B*v*, ECCO.

28 Thomas Prior, *An Authentic Narrative of the Success of Tar-Water, In Curing a Great Number and Variety of Distempers* (London: W. Innys, C. Hitch, and M. Cooper, 1746), 33, ECCO.

29 Cornell, "A Short History," 5.

30 Samuel Deane, *The New-England Farmer; Or Georgical Dictionary* (Worcester, MA: Isaiah Thomas, 1790), 23, ECCO.

31 Amelia Simmons, *American Cookery: Or The Art of Dressing Viands, Fish, Poultry and Vegetables* (Hartford: Hudson and Goodwin, 1796), 47, Evans Early American Imprint Collection.

32 Burton, "The Alcohol Paradox," 298.

33 *Almon Scrapbook*, 1700–1954, Almon Family Fonds, MG 1 vol. 14, microfilm reel 14894, Nova Scotia Archives.

34 "A type of yeast deriving from the process of fermentation." See OED *Online*, s.v. "empting, n."

35 *The Lady's Companion: Or, an Infallible Guide to the Fair Sex*, 4th ed. (London: T. Read, 1743), 2: 326–9, ECCO; George Watkins, *The Complete English Brewer; or, the Whole Art and Mystery of Brewing* (London: J. Cooke, [1770?]), ECCO; E. Hughes, *A Treatise on the Brewing of Beer* (Uxbridge: printed for the author, 1796), HathiTrust.

36 McWilliams, "Brewing Beer," 566.

37 T.H. Breen, "An Empire of Goods: The Anglicization of Colonial America, 1690–1776," *Journal of British Studies* 25, no. 4 (1986): 484.

38 William Graham, *The Art of Making Wines from Fruits, Flowers, and Herbs, All the Native Growth of Great Britain* (London: W. Nicoll, 1770), ECCO.

39 Metonicus, *The Nova Scotia Calender, or an Almanack for the Year* [...] 1789 (Halifax: Anthony Henry, 1789), n.p., Nova Scotia Archives; Marie Tremaine, *A Bibliography of Canadian Imprints, 1751–1800* (Toronto: University of Toronto Press, 1999), 292–3, EBSCOhost.

40 Richard Bradley, *The Country Housewife and Lady's Director* (London: D. Browne, 1732), 97, ECCO.

41 Anonymous, *Adam's Luxury, and Eve's Cookery; Or, The Kitchen-Garden Display'd* (London: R. Dodsley, 1744), 174, ECCO.

42 Eliza Smith, *The Compleat Housewife: Or Accomplish'd Gentlewoman's Companion*, 15th ed. (London: R. Ware et al., 1753), 387, ECCO. Smith died in 1732, and her book was first published 1727.

43 *The Royal American Gazette* 11, no. 691 (9 May 1785), 1, Nova Scotia Historical Newspapers, Nova Scotia Archives, https://archives.novascotia.ca/newspapers/archives/?ID=96.

44 Captain W. Moorsom, *Letters from Nova Scotia; Comprising Sketches of a Young Country* (London: Henry Colburn and Richard Bentley, 1830), 58, Google Books.

45 A less refined version of granulated sugar that had been broken off the cone-shaped loaves in which sugar was usually sold.

46 Trueman Family Notebooks, Account books, Diaries, and Artifacts, 1750, Trueman Family Fonds, 1750–1931, Accession 0102, Mount Allison University Archives.

47 "Trueman Family Fonds," *Marshland: Records of Life on the Tantramar: Archival Sources*, Mount Allison University Archives, https://libraryguides.mta.ca/ld.php?content_id=35196877.

48 Elizabeth Moxon, *English Housewifery*, 10th ed. (Leeds: Griffith Wright, 1769), 139–40, ECCO.

49 *The Royal American Gazette* 11, no. 691 (9 May 1785), 1, Nova Scotia Historical Newspapers, Nova Scotia Archives, https://archives.novascotia.ca/newspapers/archives/?ID=96.

50 Richard Bradley, *The Country Housewife, and Lady's Director, for Every Month of the Year* (London: W Bristow, 1762), 322, ECCO.

51 Graham, *Art of Making Wines*, 26.

52 For a summary of the plant's many traditional uses, see Sepide Miraj, Rafieian-Kopaei, and Sara Kiani, "*Melissa officinalis* L: A Review Study with an Antioxidant Prospective," *Journal of Evidence-Based Complementary Alternative Medicine* 22, no. 3 (2017): 385–94, https://doi.org/10.1177/2156587216663433.

53 William Paine Papers, reel 1, MIC–Loyalist FC LFR.P3W5P3, Loyalist Collection, University of New Brunswick.

54 Bradley, *The Country Housewife* (1762), 312.

55 Sarah Harrison, *The House-Keeper's Pocket-Book; and Compleat Family Cook*, 2nd ed. (London: R. Ware, 1739), 196, ECCO.

56 Moxon, *English Housewifery*, supplement 24.

57 "Ginger," *Encyclopedia Britannica*, 20 May 2023, https://www.britannica.com/plant/ginger.

58 "Some Early 18th and 19th Century Recipes Pasted on Pages of Militia Regulations," Militia Regulations Book, MG 100 vol. 1, no. 5, microfilm reel 786, Nova Scotia Archives.

59 Mrs Smith, *The Female Economist*, 3rd ed. (London: Mathews and Leigh, 1810), 288, Google Books.

60 A less refined version equivalent to what is now called *light brown sugar*.

61 The Manuscript Notebook of Sarah Creighton Wilkins, 1779–1833, MacDonald Family Fonds, MG 1 no. 1, microfilm reel 10618, Nova Scotia Archives.

62 John Claudius Loudon, *The Gardener's Magazine* 8 (London: Longman, Rees, et al., 1832), 541–2, Nineteenth Century Collections Online.

63 London, *The Gardener's Magazine*, 542–5.

64 Gina Marzolo, "Gooseberry," *Agricultural Marketing Resource Center*, https://www.agmrc.org/commodities-products/fruits/gooseberry.

65 "History," *Competitive Gooseberry Growing*, https://goosegogs.wordpress.com/history-2/.

66 A berry winemaker in British Columbia's Fraser Valley currently sells gooseberry wine for $65 CAD a bottle. See "Princess Gooseberry Wine," *Canada Berries*, https://canada-berries.com/products/princess-gooseberry-wine-750ml.

67 Mary Cole, *The Lady's Complete Guide; Or, Cookery in All Its Branches*, 3rd ed. (London: G. Kearsley, 1791), 352, ECCO.

68 "An Approved Receipt for Making Gooseberry Wine," *The Farmer's Magazine* (Edinburgh) 9, no. 33 (March 1808), 20, archive.org.

69 Scrapbook containing Trueman Family Papers, 1755–1851, Trueman Family Fonds, Accession 0102, Mount Allison University Archives.

70 "Receipt for Making Currant Wine," *The Nova Scotia Magazine*, 4 March 1791, Nova Scotia Newspapers on Microfilm, microfilm reel 8063, Nova Scotia Archives.

71 Anthony Allaire, Diary and Order Book, 1780–1794, Beverly Robinson Papers, S37A, F19, New Brunswick Museum Archives and Research Library.

72 Ephraim Chambers, *Cyclopædia: or, An Universal Dictionary of Arts and Sciences*, 2nd ed. (London: D. Midwinter, et al., 1738), 2: sig. 13Bb2*v*, ECCO. This same section is also found in Dennis De Coetlogon, *An Universal History of Arts and Sciences* (London: Hart, 1745), 1: 11, ECCO.

73 "A large cask or barrel, usually for liquids, esp. wine, ale, or beer, or for various provisions." See *OED Online*, "tun, n.1."

74 William Paine Papers, reel 1, MIC–Loyalist FC LFR.P3W5P3, Loyalist Collection, University of New Brunswick.

75 A measurement of wine that is equal to "two hogsheads or 63 wine gallons (105 imperial gallons)." See *OED Online*, s.v. "pipe, n.2."

76 *OED Online*, s.v. "raisin, n."

77 "Receipt to Make Raisin Wine," *Nova Scotia Gazette* 2, no. 74, 31 December 1767,

Nova Scotia Newspapers on Microfilm, microfilm reel 9466, Nova Scotia Archives; "A Receipt to Make a Rich Pleasant Wine," *Nova Scotia Gazette* 2, no. 76, 21 January 1768, Nova Scotia Newspapers on Microfilm, microfilm reel 9466, Nova Scotia Archives.

78 Anne Battam, *The Lady's Assistant in the Oeconomy of the Table*, 2nd ed. (London: R. and J. Dodsley, 1759), 192, ECCO.

79 Mary Kettilby, *A Collection of Above Three Hundred Receipts in Cookery, Physic, and Surgery*, 4th ed. (London: printed for the author, 1728), 83, ECCO.

80 Peter Latta, "Eighteenth-Century Immigrants to Nova Scotia: The Yorkshire Settlers," *Material Culture Review* 26 (June 1988), https://journals.lib.unb.ca/index.php/MCR/article/view/17367/22625.

81 Samuel Eliot Morison, "The Commerce of Boston on the Eve of the Revolution," *Proceedings of the American Antiquarian Society* 32 (12 April 1922): 47, Periodicals Archive Online.

82 Carl Robert Keyes, "Raisins," *The Adverts 250 Project*, https://adverts250project.org/tag/raisins/.

83 William Paine Papers, reel 1, MIC-Loyalist FC LFR.P3W5P3, Loyalist Collection, University of New Brunswick.

84 "Receipt to Make Raisin Wine," *Nova Scotia Gazette*.

85 A hogshead is a large cask, historically 63 wine gallons or about 238 litres. See OED *Online*, s.v. "hogshead, n."

86 A hundredweight is "An avoirdupois weight equal to 112 pounds." See OED *Online*, s.v. "hundredweight, n." The recipe is calling for 448 pounds or 203 kilograms of raisins.

87 The neat weight is the clear weight, or the weight free from any reductions, presumably the weight not including that of the barrel or the stalks. See OED *Online*, s.v. "neat, adj. (n.2 and int.) and adv."

88 A bung is a stopper, or more specifically a cork stopper for a cask. See OED *Online*, s.v. "bung, n. 1."

CHAPTER THREE

1 Holly Dickinson, "Women of the Healing Arts: Domestic Medicine in Nova Scotia, 1750–1850" (master's thesis, Dalhousie University, 2021), 48–9, 63–6.

2 Londa Schiebinger, *Secret Cures of Slaves: People, Plants, and Medicine in the Eighteenth-Century Atlantic World* (Stanford, CA: Stanford University Press, 2017), 49.

3 Harold Cook, "Medicine," in *The Cambridge History of Science*, ed. Katharine Park and Lorraine Daston (Cambridge: Cambridge University Press, 2006), 3: 420–1.

4 Drew Lopenzina, *Red Ink: Native Americans Picking Up the Pen in the Colonial Period* (Albany: SUNY Press, 2012), 8.

5 W.H. Mechling, "The Malecite Indians, with Notes on the Micmacs," *Anthropologica* 8 (1959): 244.

6 Robin Wall Kimmerer, *Braiding Sweetgrass: Indigenous Wisdom, Scientific Knowledge and the Teachings of Plants* (Minneapolis: Milkweed Editions, 2013), 48–9.

7 Laurelyn Whitt, *Science, Colonialism, and Indigenous Peoples: The Cultural Politics of Law and Knowledge* (Cambridge: Cambridge University Press, 2009), 1.

8 "A Receipt for the Bite of a Mad Dog," *The Halifax Gazette*, 9 December 1752, Nova Scotia Newspapers on Microfilm, reel 8152, Nova Scotia Archives.

9 "A Receipt for the Bite of a Mad Dog," *The Dublin Journal*, ed. George Faulkner (1 September–5 September 1747), 2, Seventeenth- and Eighteenth-Century Burney Newspapers Collection.

10 "A Receipt for the Bite of a Mad Dog," *The Ladies Magazine or, the Universal Entertainer* 3, no. 23 (30 September–14 October 1752), 362, ECCO.

11 "The bark of a tree or plant." See OED *Online*, s.v. "rind, n.1."

12 John Douglas Blaisdell, "A Frightful – but Not Necessarily Fatal – Madness: Rabies in Eighteenth-Century England and English North America" (PhD diss., Iowa State University, 1995), 9–33.

13 Girolamo Ruscelli, *A Verye Excellent and Profitable Booke Conteining Sixe Hundred Foure Score and Odde Experienced Medicines Apperteyning Unto Phisick and Surgerie* [...], trans. Richard Androse (London: Henry Denham, 1569), 15, EEBO.

14 Daniel Clericus and Jacob Mangetus, "Of the Mad Dog," in *Bibliotheca Anatomica, Medica, Chirurgica, &c.* (London: John Nutt, 1714), 3: 273–5, ECCO.

15 Blaisdell, "A Frightful," 112–41.

16 Mark Harrison, "From Medical Astrology to Medical Astronomy: Sol-Lunar and Planetary Theories of Disease in British Medicine, c. 1700–1850," *The British Journal for the History of Science* 33, no. 1 (2000): 25–48.

17 *The Perfect and Experienced Farrier* (London: T. Fawcet, 1660), 12, EEBO.

18 "A Receipt for the Bite of a Mad Dog," *The Halifax Gazette.*

19 "Ringworms," *The Royal Gazette and the Nova Scotia Advertiser* 1, no. 37, 8 December 1789, Nova Scotia Newspapers on Microfilm, microfilm reel 8162, Nova Scotia Archives.

20 Marie Tremaine, *A Bibliography of Canadian Imprints, 1751–1800* (Toronto: University of Toronto Press, 1999), 600–610, EBSCOhost.

21 Gordon Goodwin and Claire E.J. Herrick, "Jodrell, Sir Paul (1746–1803), physician," in *Oxford Dictionary of National Biography* (Oxford: Oxford University Press, 2004), online.

22 The plural form of the word *animalcule*, which refers to any small animal or an even smaller microscopic organism. See OED *Online*, s.v. "animalcule, n." and "animalcula, n."

23 "A general term for any pustular herpetiform eruption of the skin, as eczema, herpes, impetigo, ringworm, etc." See OED *Online*, s.v. "tetter, n."

24 Amiya Kumar Mukhopadhyay, "A Historical Note on the Evolution of 'Ringworm,'" *Indian Journal of Dermatology, Venereology and Leprology* 85 (2019): 126.

25 Mukhopadhyay, "A Historical Note," 126.

26 Stephen Freeman, *The Ladies' Friend, and Family Physical Library* (London: James Nunn, 1788), 462, ECCO. On "epithem," see OED *Online*, s.v. "epithem, n." On ringworm shrub, see Krishna Rany Das, Arihiro Iwasaki, Kiyotake Suenaga, and Hishasi Kato-Noguchi, "Evaluation of Phytotoxic Potential and Identification of Phytotoxic Substances in *Cassia alata* Linn. Leaves," *Acta Agriculturae Scandinavica, Section B – Soil & Plant Science* 69, no. 6 (2019): n.p., https://doi.org/10.1080/09064710.2019.1603322. They indicate that this plant is *Cassia alata* or *Senna alata,* also known as candlebrush, and that because "The plant has been effectively used to treat ringworm infections [...] it is also known as ringworm shrub."

27 Allan Everett Marble, *Surgeons, Smallpox, and the Poor: A History of Medicine and Social Conditions in Nova Scotia, 1749–1799* (Montreal and Kingston: McGill-Queen's University Press, 1993), 6–7.

28 Andrew J. Ghio, "Particle Exposure and the Historical Loss of Native American Lives to Infections," *American Journal of Respiratory and Critical Care Medicine* 195, no. 12 (2017): 1673.

29 James C. Riley, "Smallpox and American Indians Revisited," *Journal of the History of Medicine and Allied Sciences* 65, no. 4 (2018): 445–9.

30 Russell Thornton, "Health, Disease, and Demography," in *A Companion to American Indian History*, ed. Philip J. Deloria and Neal Salisbury (Oxford: John Wiley & Sons, 2004), 68–73, ProQuest Ebook Central.

31 Daniel Paul, *We Were Not the Savages: A Mi'kmaq Perspective on the Collision Between European and Native American Civilizations* (Halifax: Fernwood Publishing, 2000), 165; C.P. Stacey, "Amherst, Jeffrey, 1st Baron Amherst," in *Dictionary of Canadian Biography*, vol. 4 (Toronto: University of Toronto Press; Quebec: Presses de l'Université Laval, 2003–), http://www.biographi.ca/en/bio/amherst_jeffrey_4E.html.

32 Riley, "Smallpox," 450.

33 William B. Spaulding and Maia Foster-Sanchez, "Smallpox in Canada," *The Canadian Encyclopedia* (Historica Canada, 2006), https://www.thecanadianencyclopedia.ca/en/article/smallpox.

34 Marble, *Surgeons*, 48, 51, 55.

35 Marble, *Surgeons*, 105.

36 Marble, *Surgeons*, 101.

37 Marble, *Surgeons*, 105–6.

38 "Andrew Davison, Thomas Davison and Asa Davison charged with threatening to shoot and kill anyone who tries to remove Andrew Davison, Junior, sick with small pox, from his father's house, Horton," 14 February 1776, Chipman Family Papers – Planters of Cornwallis, MG 1 vol. 183, no. 3, Nova Scotia Archives, https://archives.novascotia.ca/chipman/archives/?ID=643.

39 Marble, *Surgeons*, 112.

40 Spaulding and Foster-Sanchez, "Smallpox," n.p.

41 Marble, *Surgeons*, 8.

42 Zabdiel Boylston, *An Historical Account of the Small-Pox Inoculated in New England* (London: S. Chandler, 1726), 2, ECCO.

43 H. Bazin, *Vaccination: A History from Lady Montagu to Genetic Engineering* (France: J. Libbey Eurotext, 2011), 31, ProQuest Ebook Central.

44 Bazin, *Vaccination*, 3.

45 Benjamin Colman and Daniel Neal, *A Narrative of the Method and Success of Inoculating the Small Pox in New England* (London, 1722), 6.

46 Colman and Neal, *A Narrative*, 8–9.

47 Mather's primary opponent in the pamphlet war was William Douglass, who was "backed by no few of the more outraged of the colony." See John T. Barrett, "The Inoculation Controversy in Puritan New England," *Bulletin of the History of Medicine* 12, no. 2 (1942): 171.

48 Anon., *An Account of the Method and Success of Inoculating the Small-Pox, in Boston in New-England*, (London: J. Peele, 1722), 1, ECCO. Kelly Wisecup posits that the "Knowledge of inoculation was transmitted from Africa to Boston as early as 1706, when Mather's congregation purchased an African slave as a gift," the man he renamed Onesismus. See Kelly Wisecup, "African Medical Knowledge, the Plain Style, and Satire in the 1721 Boston Inoculation Controversy," *Early American Literature* 46, no. 1 (2011): 27.

49 Anon., *An Account of the Method*, 1–2.

50 Anon., *An Account of the Method*, 9.

51 Anon., *An Account of the Method*, 10.

52 Anon., *An Account of the Method*, 18.

53 Marble, *Surgeons*, 8.

54 G. Patrick O'Brien, "'Gilded Misery': The Robie Women in Loyalist Exile and Repatriation, 1775–1790," *Acadiensis* 49, no. 1 (2020): 46.

55 Andrew M. Wehrman, "The Siege of 'Castle Pox': A Medical Revolution in Marblehead, Massachusetts, 1764–1777," *The New England Quarterly* 82, no. 3 (2009): 385.

56 "Small Pocks, 1775–1779," *Colonial North America at Harvard Library*, https://colonialnorthamerica.library.harvard.edu/spotlight/cna/catalog/990127721830203941.

57 Victoria Akerman, "Smallpox and Fear of Inoculation," *Atlantic Loyalist Connections*, https://loyalist.lib.unb.ca/atlantic-loyalist-connections/smallpox-and-fear-inoculation.

58 Marble, *Surgeons*, 112.

59 Head was evidently "known to have been in Halifax as early as 1759 and to have resided, during the period 1765–1805, in various other towns in Nova Scotia" (Marble, *Surgeons*, 49).

60 "Memorial of Michael Head, surgeon, to the Legislature praying compensation for inoculating certain (named poor persons when smallpox threatened several townships)," Commissioner of Public Records, RG 1 vol. 301, no. 19, Nova Scotia Archives, https://archives.novascotia.ca/assembly/archives/?ID=19&Page=200812443.

61 Untitled Diary Entry on Smallpox Inoculation, September 1792, Murray Family Manuscript Diary, MG 1, vol. 728, Nova Scotia Archives. Typescript Transcription, https://emmr.lib.unb.ca/recipes/372.

62 [Mrs M. Guyot], *A Brief History of the Small Pox Epidemic in Montreal* (Place of publication not identified: n.p., 1886), 3, 5, Canadiana.

63 Untitled Diary Entry on Smallpox Inoculation, September 1792, Murray Family Manuscript Diary, MG 1 vol. 728, Nova Scotia Archives. Typescript Transcription, https://emmr.lib.unb.ca/recipes/372.

64 *Nova Scotia Gazette and the Weekly Chronicle*, 5, no. 252, 4 July 1775, Nova Scotia Newspapers on Microfilm, microfilm reel 8156, Nova Scotia Archives.

65 Tremaine, *Bibliography*, 604–5.

66 "Transmitted thro' the Air to a great distance, by means of Steams or Effluvia expiring from the Sick," as in a 1728 example. A 1603 usage describes contagion as "an evil qualitie in a bodie, communicated vnto an other by touch." See OED *Online*, s.v. "contagion, n."

67 An emetic is a medicine that induces vomiting. "Tart Emittick" may refer to tartar-emetic, or potassio-antimonious tartrate, a poison used in eighteenth- and nineteenth-century medicine to induce vomiting. See OED *Online*, s.v. "tartar, n.1" and "emetic, adj. and n."

68 Calomel is mercurous chloride, often used in medicine in the eighteenth and

nineteenth centuries. It takes the form of a white powder. See OED *Online*, s.v. "calomel, n."

69 Jalap is the plant *Exogonium purga* or *Ipomoea purga* native to Mexico from which was derived a purgative drug. See OED *Online*, s.v. "jalap, n."

70 The pustules or skin lesions that form the rash of an infectious disease, like smallpox. See OED *Online*, s.v. "variola, n."

71 Lester D. Stephens, "Of Mercury, Moses, and Medicine: Views of Dr John M.B. Harden," *The Georgia Historical Quarterly* 59, no. 4 (1975): 404.

72 *The Pharmacopoeia of the Royal College of Physicians at Edinburgh* (London: John Nourse, 1748), 37, ECCO.

73 *Pharmacopoeia*, 37.

74 William Nisbet, *The Clinical Guide; Or, a Concise View of the Leading Facts on the History, Nature, and Cure of Diseases* (Edinburgh: J. Watson & Co., 1793), 103, ECCO.

75 Arthur Boylston, "The Origins of Inoculation," *Journal of the Royal Society of Medicine* 105, no. 7 (2012): 311, https://www.ncbi.nlm.nih.gov/pmc/articles/PMC3407399/.

76 Untitled Diary Entry on Smallpox Inoculation, September 1792, Murray Family Manuscript Diary, MG 1, vol. 728, Nova Scotia Archives. Typescript Transcription, https://emmr.lib.unb.ca/recipes/372.

77 Metonicus, "To Preserve the Face From Being Deformed by the Small-Pox," *The Nova Scotia Calender, or an Almanack* (Halifax: Anthony Henry, 1791), n.p.

78 Richard Lower, *Dr. Lowers, and Several Other Eminent Physicians, Receipts Containing the Best and Safest Method for Curing Most Diseases in Humane Bodies* (London: John Nutt, 1700), 46, EEBO; Theophilus Lobb, *The Good Samaritan; or Complete English Physician* (London: J. Cooke, [1761?]), 49, ECCO; Peregrine Montague, *The Family Pocket-book: or, Fountain of True and Useful Knowledge* (London: George Paul, [1762?]), 142, ECCO.

79 "An ointment for the skin or hair." See OED *Online*, s.v. "pomatum, n."

80 A fatty substance in the head of whales and some dolphins. See OED *Online*, s.v. "spermaceti, n."

81 "Fresh, new, or unused bees-wax." See OED *Online*, s.v. "virgin wax, n."

82 A common unit of measurement, one drachm is the equivalent of ⅛ of an ounce in apothecaries' weight (it is 1/16 of an ounce in avoirdupois weigh). See OED *Online*, "drachm, n." The apothecaries' weight is likely being used here.

83 Hannah Woolley, *The Queen-Like Closet; Or, Rich Cabinet Stored with all Manner of Rare Receipts* (London: R. Lowndes, 1670), 30, EEBO.

84 Lady Mary Wortley Montagu, "Saturday. The Small-Pox," *Eighteenth-Century Poetry*

Archive, lines 6–8, 65–6, https://www.eighteenthcenturypoetry.org/works/o5152-w0110.shtml#o5152-w0116.

85 Michael Bennett, "Jenner's Ladies: Women and Vaccination Against Smallpox in Early Nineteenth-Century Britain," *History* 93, no. 4 (2008): 499, 504.

86 Jennifer Evans and Sara Read, *Maladies and Medicine* (Barnsley, Yorkshire: Pen & Sword Books, 2017), 87.

87 Roy Porter and George Sebastien Rousseau, *Gout: The Patrician Malady* (New Haven and London: Yale University Press, 1998), 49.

88 Christopher Rivard, Jeffrey Thomas, Miguel A. Lanaspa, and Richard J. Johnson, "Sack and Sugar, and the Aetiology of Gout in England between 1650 and 1900," *Rheumatology* 52 (2013): 421–6.

89 Katherine Allen, "Recipe Collections and the Realities of Fashionable Diseases in Eighteenth-Century Elite Domestic Medicine," *Literature and Medicine* 35, no. 2 (2017): 344.

90 Porter and Rousseau, *Gout*, 71, 50, 72.

91 Evans and Read, *Maladies*, 84.

92 Martina Scholtens, "The Glorification of Gout in 16th- to 18th-Century Literature," CMAJ / JAMC *Canadian Medical Association Journal* 179, no. 8 (2008): 805.

93 Francis Spilsbury, "Cures Performed by the Antiscorbutic Drops," in *Free Observations on the Scurvy, Gout, Diet, and Remedy*, 4th ed. (London: 1788), 55, 60, ECCO.

94 "For the Gout," *The Nova Scotia Gazette and the Weekly Chronicle* 10, no. 709, 1 November 1780, Nova Scotia Newspapers on Microfilm, microfilm reel 8158, Nova Scotia Archives.

95 W.S.C. Copeman, *A Short History of the Gout and the Rheumatic Diseases* (Berkeley: University of California Press, 1964, 2021), 52.

96 Copeman, *A Short History*, 51.

97 Dutch can refer both to the people of Holland and the Netherlands, as well as, in the sixteenth and seventeenth centuries, to the people of Germany. See OED *Online*, s.v. "Dutch, adj., n.1, and adv."

98 A "kitling" is a kitten or the young of any animal. See OED *Online*, s.v. "kitling, n. and adj."

99 Flay.

100 Used primarily in the sixteenth and seventeenth centuries, "contund" means to pound or bruise. See OED *Online*, s.v. "contund, v."

101 Bacon.

102 Rosin, or resin.

103 Copeman, *A Short History*, 51.

104 Nicholas Culpeper, "A Special Remedy for the Gout," in *Culpeper's School of Physick, or, The Experimental Practice of the Whole Art Wherein Are Contained All Inward Diseases from the Head to the Foot* (London: N. Brook, 1659), 141, EEBO. Culpeper also offers "An Excellent Remedy for the Gout," which instructs the user to instead "Take a Badger, the fattest you can get, kill him, and scald him like a Pig, then make a hole in one of his sides, take out his guts, garbage and all and put into his belly Nettles two handfuls, two ounces of Brimstone, four yolks of Eggs, and four ounces of Turpentine incorporated well together, then sow up his belly close, and roast him, and save the dripping for an excellent remedy for the Gout" (140–1).

105 D.G., *The Harangues or Speeches of Several Famous Mountebanks in Town and Country* (London: T. Warner, 1700), 11, EEBO.

106 D.G., *Harangues*, 11. The book's satiric bent is evident also in blaming the quacks' victims as much as the perpetrators, and it includes chapters titled "The High German Doctor and English Fool," 8, and "The Horse Doctor's Harangue to the Credulous Mob," 13.

107 *The Harangues, or Speeches, of Several Celebrated Quack-Doctors, in Town and Country* (London: J. Robinson, 1750 and London: J. Thomson, 1762), 11, 15, 13, ECCO. The poem also appears in a 1725 version of the book, *The Harangues or Speeches of Several Famous Mountebanks in Town and Country* (London: T. Warner, 1725), ECCO, but does not include the character of a quack, the merry receipts, or the additional three songs.

108 *The Harangues, or Speeches*, 37–41, ECCO.

109 Diary of Henry Nase [typescript], 1776–1794, Nase Family Papers, S116–2, F4, New Brunswick Museum Archives and Research Library.

110 One of the species of veronica. See *OED Online*, s.v. "speedwell, n."

111 Probably winter's bark, an aromatic bark from a South American shrub thought to resemble cinnamon. Sometimes winter's bark was misidentified as the bark of the wild cinnamon tree, *Canella winterana*. See *OED Online*, s.v. "winter's bark, n." For example, Richard Brookes, *The British Dispensatory, Containing a Faithful Translation of the New London Pharmacopoia, Publish'd by the College of Physicians, And enforced by the King and Council* (London: Edward Cave, 1747), 5, ECCO, describes "white Cinnamon" that is only "improperly called winters bark." *The Pharmcopoeia of the Royal College of Physicians at Edinburgh* (London: John Nourse, 1748), 71, ECCO, likewise cautions that winter's bark, "has been for a long time confounded with canella alba." James Alleyne's *A New English Dispensatory* (London: Tho. Astley, 1733), 120, ECCO, also notes that it is "generally confounded with the *Canella alba*."

112 Royal College of Physicians of London, *Pharmacopoia Londinensis: Or, the New London Dispensatory* (London: J. Dawks, 1716), 27, ECCO.

113 William Salmon, *Collectanea Medica, the Country Physician: Or, a Choice Collection of Physick: Fitted for Vulgar Use* (London: John Taylor, 1703), 223, ECCO.

114 John Armstrong, *A Synopsis of the History and Cure of Venereal Diseases* (London: A. Millar, 1737), 487, ECCO.

115 Richard Brookes, *The General Practice of Physic* (London: J. Newbery, 1754), 138, ECCO.

116 Society of Gentlemen, *A New and Complete Dictionary of Arts and Sciences* (London: W. Owen, 1754), 4: 3276, ECCO.

117 *Herman Boerhaave's Materia Medica, or the Druggist's Guide* (London: J. Hodges, 1755), 270, ECCO.

118 Patrick L. Owen and Timothy Johns, "Xanthine Oxidase Inhibitory Activity of Northeastern North American Plant Remedies Used for Gout," *Journal of Ethnopharmacology* 64 (1999): 149, 152. Although they provide references that connect other plants to particular First Nations, for speedwell (*Veronica officinalis*), the article refers to a source that lists only its European medical uses and indicates that it was introduced to North America from Europe and Asia (152).

119 On alder, see John Josselyn, *An Account of Two Voyages to New-England* (London: Giles Widdows, 1674), 70, EEBO, where physician and traveller John Josselyn reported that "an *Indian* bruising of his knee, chew'd the bark of Alder fasting and laid it to, which quickly helped him." According to Virgil J. Vogel, *American Indian Medicine* (Tulsa: University of Oklahoma Press, 2013), 270, alder was also taken internally by the Onondaga as a "remedy for ague and inflammation," by the Penobscots "to stop cramps and wretching," and by the Montagnais to purify the blood and treat cholera. "The Mi'kmaq," according to Laurie Lacey, *Mi'kmaq Medicines* (Halifax: Nimbus, 2012), 22, also "steeped the dried inner bark from alders in water and used it to treat stomach cramps, kidney ailments, fever, and neuralgic pain"; Lacey further recounts hearing of alder bark topically applied "for treating lameness in the body." On angelica, see J.T. Garrett, *The Cherokee Herbal: Native Plant Medicine from the Four Directions* (Bear & Company; Simon & Schuster, 2003), 206.

120 William Lewis, *The New Dispensatory* (London: J. Nourse, 1765), 79, ECCO.

121 *The General Dispensatory, Containing a Translation of the Pharmacopoeias of the Royal Colleges of Physicians of London and Edinburgh* (London: J. Newbery, 1753), 284, ECCO; Evans and Read, *Maladies*, 84.

122 Anon., *A Collection of Receipts in Physic, Being the Entire Practice of a Late Eminent Physician* (London: Lockyer Davis, 1752), 63, ECCO. The author is identified in the book's 1754 edition as "Dr Bloxam."

123 Maryann Napoli, "Honey as Medicine Has a Long History – New Zealand Honey Is Focus of Intensive Research," *HealthFacts* 25, no. 11 (2000): 4.

124 Andrzej K. Kuropatnicki, Malgorzata Losek, and Marek Kucharzewski, "Honey as Medicine: Historical Perspectives," *Journal of Apicultural Research* 57, no. 1 (2018): 117.

125 John Huxham, "Of the Constitution of the Air and Epidemic Diseases," in *The Works of John Huxham* (London: W. Bent, 1788), 1: 170–1, ECCO.

125 Once widely taken internally, antimony is now recognized as a possible carcinogen and a cause of respiratory ailments. See Katherine D. Watson, "Review of R. Ian McCallum, *Antimony in Medical History* (Auckland and Edinburgh: Pentland Press, 1999)," *Medical History* 45, no. 1 (2001): 141.

127 Dr William James Almon, "List of Quack Medicines, Family Nostrums &c.," The Manuscript Notebook of Dr William James Almon, Almon Family Fonds, MG 1, microfilm reel 10045, Nova Scotia Archives.

128 "Advice to the Gouty," *The Royal Gazette* 2, no. 47, 16 February 1790, Nova Scotia Newspapers on Microfilm, microfilm reel 8163, Nova Scotia Archives.

129 "A Hint to Persons Afflicted with the Gout," *The Universal Magazine of Knowledge and Pleasure* 84 (June 1789), 306–7, HathiTrust.

130 "Cloaking or concealing something, disguising or making inconspicuous." See *OED Online*, s.v. "palliation, n."

131 Gouty. See *OED Online*, s.v. "podagrical, adj. and n." and "podagrous, adj."

132 Richard Barnett, "Bitter Medicine: Gout and the Birth of the Cocktail," *The Lancet* 379 (2012): 1384.

133 Steven Shapin, "Trusting George Cheyne: Scientific Expertise, Common Sense, and Moral Authority in Early Eighteenth-Century Dietetic Medicine," *Bulletin of the History of Medicine* 77, no. 2 (2003): 272.

134 Matthew P. Romaniello, "True Rhubarb? Trading Eurasian Botanical and Medical Knowledge in the Eighteenth Century," *Journal of Global History* 11 (2016): 4.

135 Romaniello, "True Rhubarb?," 4.

136 M.R. Lee, J. Hutcheon, E. Dukan, and I. Milne, "Rhubarb (*Rheum* species): The Role of Edinburgh in Its Cultivation and Development," *Journal of the Royal College of Physicians of Edinburgh* 47, no. 1 (March 2017): 108.

137 Lee, Hutcheon, Dukan, and Milne, "Rhubarb," 104.

138 Allen, "Recipe Collections," 344.

139 Evans and Read, *Maladies*, 86.

140 Timothy Bennet, *An Essay on the Gout* (London: Richard Ford, 1734), 17, ECCO.

141 Rivard, Thomas, Lanaspa, and Johnson, "Sack and Sugar," 421.

142 The Latin term *aquae vitae* appeared in the French as *eau-de-vie*, in Gaelic

vernacular as *uisge beatha*, and as *akvavit* in Scandinavia. David Gentilcore, *Food and Health in Early Modern Europe* (London: Bloomsbury, 2016), 157, 169.

143 William Buchan, *Domestic Medicine*, 2nd ed. (London: W. Strahan and T. Cadell; Edinburgh: A Kincaid et al., 1772), 379, ECCO.

144 Richard Kentish, *Advice to Gouty Persons* (London: J. Murray, 1791), 74–5, ECCO.

145 Kentish, *Advice*, 78.

146 J.K. Crellin and Jane Philpott, *Herbal Medicine Past and Present: A Reference Guide to Medicinal Plants* (Durham, NC: Duke University Press, 1990), 302.

147 Mark Harrison, "Scurvy on Sea and Land: Political Economy and Natural History, c. 1780–c. 1850," *Journal for Maritime Research* 15 (2013): 7–12.

148 "An Extract," *The Royal Gazette and Miscellany of the Island of Saint John* 2, no. 32 (30 January 1793).

149 Tremaine, *Bibliography*, 648, 668–9. Tremaine has this newspaper published only in 1791–92, but Heather Boylan, *Checklist and Directory of Prince Edward Island Newspapers 1787–1986* (Charlottetown: Public Archives of Prince Edward Island, 1987), 141, https://www.islandlives.ca/islandora/object/ilives:209752#page/1/mode/2up indicates that it was published 1791–1794[?], a range encompassing the date of this recipe.

150 Boylan, *Checklist and Historical Directory*, 141.

151 Tremaine, *Bibliography*, 668.

152 "A Certain Radical Cure for the Scurvy," *The Weekly Entertainer* 1 (13 March 1783), 304, ECCO.

153 *A New Medical Dictionary* (London: J. Johnson, 1775), sig. Yy, ECCO, identifies this mineral as "calomelas," so named because it becomes black when ground with volatile spirits; calomel is mercury chloride, a powder. See also OED *Online*, s.v. "calomel, n."

154 Molasses.

155 Gilbert Blane, *Observations on the Diseases of Seamen*, 2nd ed. (London: Joseph Cooper, 1789), 506–9, ECCO.

156 John Elliot, *The Medical Pocket-Book*, 10th ed. (Boston: Printed by Joseph Bumstead, 1791), 88, ECCO.

157 I. Barberis, N.L. Bragazzi, L. Galluzzo, and M. Martini, "The History of Tuberculosis: From the First Historical Records to the Isolation of Koch's Bacillus," *Journal of Preventive Medicine and Hygiene* 58, no. 1 (2017): E9–E12. "In 1838–39," the authors note, "up to a third of English tradesmen and employees died of TB," but only "a sixth in the upper class" (E10).

158 Frank M. Snowden, *Epidemics and Society: From the Black Death to the Present* (Yale University Press, 2019), 28.

159 Buchan, *Domestic Medicine*, 218.

160 Edward Strother, *The Family Companion for Health* (London: F. Fayram, 1729), 347, 54, ECCO.

161 Benjamin Marten, *A New Theory of Consumptions: More Especially of a Phthisis, or Consumption of the Lungs* (London: R. Knaplock, 1720), 1, ECCO. More recently, Frances Wilson has noted that London remains "the TB capital of Europe." See "How London Became the Tuberculosis Capital of Europe," *The Guardian*, 26 November 2018, https://www.theguardian.com/cities/2018/nov/26/how-london-became-the-tuberculosis-capital-of-europe. In his treatise, Strother, *Family Companion*, 345, notes that "A Consumption is one of the most frequent Diseases that infests Mankind; and more especially in this our Nation."

162 Stefan Grzybowlski and Edward A. Allen, "Tuberculosis: 2. History of the Disease in Canada," *Canadian Medical Association Journal* 160, no. 7 (1999): 1025–6.

163 Metonicus, "To Make Milk-Water," *The Nova Scotia Calender, or an Almanack* (Halifax: Anthony Henry, 1791), n.p.

164 Richard Lower, *Dr. Lower's, and Several Other Eminent Physicians Receipts*, 2nd ed. (London: John Nutt, 1701), 41, ECCO; Peregrine Montague, *The Family Pocket-book* (London: George Paul, 1762), sig. A2, 141–2, ECCO.

165 John Pechey, *The Compleat Herbal of Physical Plants*, 2nd ed. (London: R. and J. Bonwicke, 1707), 152, ECCO.

166 Buchan, *Domestic Medicine*, 222.

167 Nicholas Culpeper, *The English Physician Enlarged* (London: J. Bruce, et al., 1787), 66, ECCO.

168 Joseph Miller, *Botanicum Officinale; Or a Compendious Herbal* (London: E. Bell, 1722), 208, Wellcome Collection, https://wellcomecollection.org/works/ht72m2ch.

169 Miller, *Botanicum Officinalle*, 40.

170 Muhammad Akram, Rida Zainab, Muhammad Daniyal, Shafqat Rasul, and Naveed Munir, "Phytochemistry and Pharmacology of *Artemisia absinthium Linn*: A Multipurpose Medicinal Plant," *Plant Biotechnology Persa* 5, no. 1 (2023): n.p., http://pbp.medilam.ac.ir/article-1-172-en.html.

171 See, for example, Manisha Nigam, Maria Atanassova, Abhay P. Mishra, Raffaele Pezzani, Hari Prasad Devkota, Sergey Plygun, Bahare Salehi, William N. Setzer, and Javad Sharifi-Rade, "Bioactive Compounds and Health Benefits of *Artemisia*

Species," *Natural Product Communications* 14, no. 7 (2019): n.p., https://doi.org/10.1177/1934578X19850354. For an account of its use in North America, see T.E.C., "Three 18th Century Prescriptions for the Treatment of Worms in Children," *Pediatrics* 61, no. 4 (1978): 579, https://doi.org/10.1542/peds.61.4.579.

172 "An Admirable Receipt for a Consumption," *The Nova Scotia Gazette and the Weekly Chronicle* 4, no. 189, 3 May 1774, Nova Scotia Newspapers on Microfilm, microfilm reel 8155, Nova Scotia Archives.

173 "From the London Chronicle. To the Printer," *Pennsylvania Chronicle* (Philadelphia, PA) 1, no. 14 (27 April 1767), Readex: America's Historical Newspapers.

174 "To the Printer," *The Universal Museum, and Complete Magazine of Knowledge and Pleasure* (London: J. Payne, February 1767), 64, ECCO.

175 "An Admirable Receipt for a Consumption," in *The Royal American Magazine, or Universal Repository of Instruction and Amusement* (Boston: Greenleaf's, 1774), 176, ECCO.

176 In the eighteenth century, a type of wine produced in Malaga (Spain). See *OED Online*, s.v. "mountain, n. and adj."

177 Balsam of Gilead is named in Nathan Bailey, *Dictionarium Domesticum, Being a New and Compleat Houshold Dictionary* (London: C. Hitch et al., 1736), sig. E, ECCO, as "Opobalsamum, or Balm of Mecca, so call'd because it is brought to us from thence." It is described as being of the consistency of syrup, fragrant, and costly, with purposes that include opening lung obstructions, healing erosions, causing expectorations, relieving "inward decay," and treating kidney diseases and those of the urinary tract.

178 From the tolu tree, from South America, used from the late seventeenth century. See *OED Online*, s.v. "tolu, n." John Olgiby, *America: Being the Latest, and Most Accurate Description of the New World* (London: printed by the author, 1671), 402, EEBO, includes tolu as an "excellent Balsam" from "Carthagena" in New Andalusia (likely Cartagena in contemporary Chile): "It is gather'd in a Spoonful of black Wax, stuck under the Hole cut in the Bark of a low Pine-Tree, out of which in hot Weather runs a Golden colour'd Gum, very soveraign, and of an excellent smell."

179 "An aromatic gum resin obtained from trees of the North African genus *Boswellia* (family Burseraceae), [...] formerly used as a medicine but now chiefly as incense." The first reference in the *OED* dates to 1398. See *OED Online*, s.v. "olibanum, n."

180 Grossly, or coarsely. See *OED Online*, s.v. "grossly."

181 A honey produced in southwestern France by bees who are kept in Mediterranean scrub that includes rosemary, thyme, and lavender, dating from the twelfth

century. See "Narbonne Honey," *Cook's Info*, https://www.cooksinfo.com/narbonne-honey.

182 Buchan, *Domestic Medicine*, 234.

183 Buchan, *Domestic Medicine*, 234.

184 Mr Thorley, "Narbonne Honey," c. 1700–1799, Wellcome Collection, https://wellcomecollection.org/works/aap2kxng.

185 Christopher Parsons, "Consuming Canada: *Capillaire du Canada* in the French Atlantic World," in *Drugs on the Page: Pharmacopoeias and Healing Knowledge in the Early Modern Atlantic World*, ed. Matthew James Crawford and Joseph M. Gabriel (Pittsburgh: University of Pittsburgh Press, 2019), 162.

186 Parsons, *Consuming Canada*, 175.

187 "To the Printer," *The Universal Museum*, 64.

188 Pehr Kalm, *Travels into North America; Containing Its Natural History, and a Circumstantial Account of Its Plantations and Agriculture in General*, trans. John Reinold Forster (London: T. Lowndes, 1770), 3: 118–19, ECCO.

189 Cornwallis, King's County Business Papers, Unidentified Account Book, 1732–1803, MG 3 no. 166, microfilm reel 12259, Nova Scotia Archives.

190 Noel Chomel, *Dictionnaire Oeconomique: or, the Family Dictionary*, ed. R. Bradley (Dublin: L. Flinn, 1758), 1: sig. Iii2, ECCO.

191 T.K. Lim, "*Prunus avium*," in *Edible Medicinal and Non-Medicinal Plants* (Springer, Dordrecht, 1988), https://doi.org/10.1007/978-94-007-4053-2_52.

192 Barry Cahill, "New England Planters at the Public Archives of Nova Scotia," Chipman Family Papers: Planters of Cornwallis, *Nova Scotia Archives*, accessed 12 June 2021, https://archives.novascotia.ca/chipman/planters/; abridged and reprinted from Barry Cahill, "New England Planters at the Public Archives of Nova Scotia," in *They Planted Well: New England Planters in Maritime Canada*, ed. Margaret Conrad (Fredericton: Acadiensis, 1988), 120–31.

193 Thor Arnason, Richard J. Hebda, and Timothy Johns, "Use of Plants for Food and Medicine by Native Peoples of Eastern Canada," *Canadian Journal of Botany* 59, no. 11 (1981): 2189–325; Scott Sheu, "Black Cherry," *Foods Indigenous to the Western Hemisphere*, AIHDP: American Indian Health and Diet Project, https://aihd.ku.edu/foods/agave.html.

194 Peter Whitney, *The History of the County of Worcester, in the Commonwealth of Massachusetts* (Worcester, MA: Isaiah Thomas, 1793), 229, ECCO.

195 Anne Jacobson Schutte, "Suffering from the Stone: The Accounts of Michel de Montaigne and Cecilia Ferrazzi," *Bibliothèque d'humanisme et renaissance* 64, no. 1 (2002): 21–2.

196 "Effectual Cure for the Stone," *The Royal Gazette and Nova Scotia Advertiser* 6, no. 261, 15 April 1794, Nova Scotia Newspapers on Microfilm, microfilm reel 8152, Nova Scotia Archives.

197 "Effectual Cure for the Stone," *Columbian Centinel* (Boston, Massachusetts) 20, no. 48 (22 February 1794), 1–2, Readex: America's Historical Newspapers.

198 "From the Columbian Mirror, Effectual Cure for the Stone," *Baltimore Daily Intelligencer* (Baltimore) 1, no. 86 (5 February 1794), 3, Readex: America's Historical Newspapers; "From the Columbian Mirror. Effectual Cure for the Stone. Mr. Price," *Virginia Chronicle* (Norfolk), 4, no. 233 (8 February 1794), 1, Readex; "From the Alexandria Gazette," *New-Jersey Journal* (Elizabethtown, NJ) 11, no. 539 (12 February 1794), 1, Readex; "From the Alexandria Gazette. Effectual Cure for the Stone," *New-York Daily Gazette* (New York), no. 1604 (12 February 1794), 2, Readex; "Miscellany. From the Alexandria Gazette," *Massachusetts Mercury* (Boston) 3, no. 18 (28 February 1794), 4, Readex; "Effectual Cure for the Stone Mr. Printer from Columbian Centinel Mr. Russell," *United States Chronicle* (Providence, RI), 11, no. 529 (27 February 1794), 2, Readex; "From the Alexandria Gazette. Effectual Cure for the Stone," *American Apollo* (Boston, MA) 3, no. 22 (27 February 1794), 1, Readex; "From the Alexandria Gazette. Effectual Cure for the Stone," *Thomas's Massachusetts Spy: Or, The Worcester Gazette* (Worcester, MA) 22, no. 1091 (27 February 1794), 1, Readex; "From the Columbian Mirror, &C. Effectual Cure for the Stone," *Hartford Gazette* (Hartford, CT) 1, no. 12 (20 February 1794), 1, Readex; "From the Columbian Mirror. Effectual Cure for the Stone," *The South Carolina State-Gazette & Timothy & Mason's Daily Advertiser* (Charleston, SC) 55, no. 4348 (28 February 1794), 2, Readex; "From a Late Alexandria Paper. Effectual Cure for the Stone," *Providence Gazette* (Providence, RI) 31, no. 9 (1 March 1794), 2, Readex; "Extracted from a Late Alexandria Paper. Effectual Cure for the Stone," *Connecticut Courant* (Hartford, CT) 29, no. 1519 (3 March 1794), 3, Readex; "From the Centinel," *Eastern Herald* (Portland, ME), 3 March 1794, 4, Readex; "From the Columbian Mirror," *The Essex Journal & New-Hampshire Packet* (Newburyport, MA), no. 507 (5 March 1794), 4, Readex; "Extracted from a Late Alexandria Paper. Effectual Cure for the Stone," *Norwich Packet* (Norwich, CT) 21, no. 1043 (13 March 1794), 4, Readex.

199 "Communicated by a Friend for the Rural Visiter. Effectual Cure for the Stone," *Rural Visiter* (Burlington, NJ) 1, no. 35 (25 March 1811), 188, Readex: America's Historical Newspapers.

200 Benjamin Russell, the founder of the *Columbian Centinel*. See "Columbian Centinel," Directory of U.S. Newspapers in American Libraries, *Library of Congress*, https://www.loc.gov/item/sn83021272/.

201 That is, *The Columbian Mirror and Alexandria Gazette.*

202 A county in Virginia.

203 In what is now West Virginia.

204 A measurement for liquid: in the US, four fluid ounces (.118L) and in Britain, 5 imperial fluid ounces (.142L). See OED *Online*, s.v. "gill, n.2."

205 Member of the Pennsylvania State Assembly, brigadier general of the state's troops in 1776, and member of the Continental Congress. See *Biographical Dictionary of the United States Congress*, s.v. "Roberdeau, Daniel, 1727–1795," https://bioguide.congress.gov/search/bio/R000303.

206 OED *Online*, s.v. "cancer, n. and adj."

207 Buchan, *Domestic Medicine*, 600.

208 See Arnason, Hebda, and Johns, "Use of Plants," 2189–325.

209 Dr William James Almon, The Manuscript Notebook of Dr. William James Almon, Almon Family Fonds, MG 1, microfilm reel 10045, Nova Scotia Archives. We have not been able to access the August 1793 edition of the *Boston Magazine* to confirm the original reference.

210 "Cure for a Cancer," *Windham Herald* (Windham, CT), 6 July 1793, "Windham County Newspapers," Windham County Connecticut CTGenweb Project, accessed 26 November 2020, http://www.ctgenweb.org/county/cowindham/records/newspaper/windhamherald/july1793.html.

211 "About National Gazette," *Chronicling America: Historic American Newspapers*, The Library of Congress, accessed 26 November 2020, https://chroniclingamerica.loc.gov/lccn/sn83025887/.

212 David Hale, *The Columbian Almanac, for the Year of Our Lord 1794* (Philadelphia: Stewart & Cochran, 1793), sig. [F?], ECCO.

213 "From the Maryland Gazette," *Independent Gazetteer* (Philadelphia, PA) 6, no. 526 (18 August 1787), 3, Readex: America's Historical Newspapers; "Charles County, July 2," *Pennsylvania Packet* (Philadelphia, PA), no. 2665 (21 August 1787), 2, Readex; "From the Maryland Gazette, of August 9, 1787," *Boston Gazette* (Boston, MA), no. 1727 (3 September 1787), 1, Readex.

214 "Some Account of the Present State of Nova Scotia," *The Weekly Entertainer; or Agreeable and Instructive Repository* 8 (27 October 1786), 323, ECCO.

215 James Stuart, *A Dissertation on the Salutary Effects of Mercury, in Malignant Fevers* (Philadelphia: Tomas & Samuel F. Bradford, 1798), 35–6, ECCO.

216 Salvator Winter, *A New Dispensatory of Fourty Physicall Receipts* (London: n.p., 1649), 12, EEBO.

217 Mechling, "The Malecite Indians," 259; Vogel, *American Indian*, 201.

218 Garrett, *The Cherokee Herbal*, 86–7.

219 William Paine Papers, Loyalist Collection, MIC Loyalist FC LFR.P3W5P3, University of New Brunswick.

220 Carol Anne Janzen, "Paine, William," in *Dictionary of Canadian Biography*, vol. 6 (Toronto: University of Toronto Press; Quebec: Presses de l'Université Laval, 2003–), http://www.biographi.ca/en/bio/paine_william_6E.html.

221 A syrup made by the concentration of fruit juice. See OED *Online*, s.v. "rob, n.1."

222 *Phytolacca americana* is the native North American plant commonly known as pokeweed. The name poke comes from Algonquin, *pocan*. OED *Online*, s.v. "poke, n.4."

223 OED *Online*, "pokeweed, n."

224 Michael J. Franklin, "Piozzi [née Salusbury; other married name Thrale], Hester Lynch (1741–1821), writer," in *Oxford Dictionary of National Biography* (Oxford: Oxford University Press, 2004), online.

225 Larry W. Mitich, "Common Pokeweed," *Weed Technology* 8, no. 4 (1994): 888.

226 Mitich, "Common Pokeweed," 888.

227 Vogel, *American Indian*, 70.

228 Benjamin Shultz, *An Inaugural Botanico-Medical Dissertation, on the Phytolacca Decandra of Linnaeus* (Philadelphia: Thomas Dobson, 1795), 1–2, Wellcome Collection, https://wellcomecollection.org/works/qskjk5k4/items.

229 Schultz, *An Inaugural Botanico*, 15.

230 Schultz, *An Inaugural Botanico*, 20; Garrett, *The Cherokee Herbal*, notes that the Cherokee made a tea of poke leaves and lemon balm that would "calm the chest when you have a deep cold and cough" (253).

231 Shultz, *An Inaugural Botanico*, 22.

232 Shultz, *An Inaugural Botanico*, 44–51.

233 Metonicus, "The following method of curing cancers," *The Nova Scotia Calender, or an Almanack* [...] (Halifax: Anthony Henry, 1789), n.p.

234 *The Monthly Review, Or Literary Journal* (London), 78 (January–June 1788), 476, HathiTrust; Benjamin Moseley, *A Treatise on Tropical Diseases; and on the Climate of the West-Indies* (London: T. Cadell, 1787), 518–19, ECCO.

235 *The Edinburgh Practice of Physic, Surgery, and Midwifery* (London: G. Kearsley, 1803), 3: 403, Internet Archive.

236 Josiah Richardson, *The New England Farrier, and Family Physician* (Exeter, NH: J. Richardson, 1828), 135, National Library of Medicine Digital Collections.

237 Benjamin Moseley, *Treatise on Tropical Diseases* (London: T. Cadell, 1789), 524, ECCO.

238 Benjamin Moseley, *Treatise on Tropical Diseases*, 2nd ed. (London: T. Cadell, 1792),

518, ECCO. In Moseley's texts, the version of the recipe in the first and second edition is the same.

239 From the fourteenth century, an ointment composed of vegetable juices, but more recently, a lead plaster made with lead oxide, olive oil, and water. See OED *Online*, s.v. "diachylon | diachylum | diaculum, n."

240 Another term for sublimate of mercury.

241 Lester D. Stephens, "Of Mercury, Moses, and Medicine: Views of Dr. John M.B. Harden," *The Georgia Historical Quarterly* 59, no. 4 (1975): 404.

242 "Methods of Treatment to Be Used for the Recovery of Persons Apparently Dead by Drowning," *Nova Scotia Gazette and the Weekly Chronicle*, 7 March 1786, Nova Scotia Newspapers on Microfilm, vol. 16, no. 1039, microfilm reel 8162, Nova Scotia Archives.

243 Tremaine, *Bibliography*, 604.

244 Royal Humane Society, *Reports of the Humane Society Instituted in the Year 1774, for the Recovery of Persons Apparently Drowned* (London: J. Rivington and J. Johnson, 1778), 83–7, ECCO; Royal Humane Society, *Plan and Reports of the Society Instituted at London in the Year MDCCLXXIV. for the Recovery of Persons Apparently Drowned* (London: 1775), 7–10, ECCO.

245 Carolyn D. Williams, "Hawes, William (1736–1808), philanthropist and physician," in *Oxford Dictionary of National Biography* (Oxford: Oxford University Press, 2004), online.

246 L.A.F. Davidson, "Founders and Benefactors of the Royal Humane Society (act. 1774–c. 1808)," in *Oxford Dictionary of National Biography* (Oxford University Press, 2010), online.

247 Davidson, "Founders and Benefactors." Horsfall was elected fellow of the Royal Society on 14 April 1768. See "Horsfall; James (–1785)," Past Fellows, *The Royal Society*, https://catalogues.royalsociety.org/CalmView/Record.aspx?src=CalmView.Persons&id=NA3222&pos=1.

248 *History of The Humane Society of the Commonwealth of Massachusetts* (Boston: T.R. Marvin, 1876), 1–2, National Library of Medicine Digital Collections.

249 The bottom or backside, or literally the anus or rectum. OED *Online*, s.v. "fundament, n."

250 A medicine injected into the rectum, such as an enema or suppository. OED *Online*, s.v. "clyster, n."

251 Spirit of hartshorn is an aqueous solution of ammonia made from harts' horn (the antler of a hart, or male deer). See OED *Online*, s.v. "hartshorn, n."

252 That is, Society for the Recovery of Persons Apparently Drowned.

253 Pertaining to apoplexy, a historical disease characterized by an inability to move and the malfunction of the senses believed to be caused by an effusion of blood into the brain. See OED *Online*, s.v. "apoplexy, n."

254 Craig Spence, *Accidents and Violent Death in Early Modern London: 1650–1750* (Woodbridge: Boydell, 2016), 79.

255 Handley Chipman, "Of Restoring a Drowned Person," Handley Chipman's Notes, vol. 2, Chipman Family Papers, 1760–1899, MG 1 vol. 218, microfilm reel 10514, Nova Scotia Archives.

256 David Hosack, *An Enquiry into the Causes of Suspended Animation from Drowning; with the Means of Restoring Life* (New York: Thomas and James Swords, 1792), III, ECCO.

257 James Howell, "To His Highly Esteemed Friend and Compatriot Judge Rumsey," *Organon Salutis an Instrument to Cleanse the Stomach: As Also Divers New Experiments of the Virtue of Tobacco and Coffee, How Much They Conduce to Preserve Humane Health*, by W.R. (London: R. Hodgkinsonne, 1657), sig. B4, EEBO.

258 William Salmon, *The Family Dictionary* (London: H. Rhodes, 1695), sig. X4*v*, EEBO.

259 Richard Mead, *A Mechanical Account of Poisons, in Several Essays*, 3rd ed. (London: J. Brindley, 1745), 175, ECCO. This essay was first printed in 1702, but in 1745 this reflection was added to the text.

260 Daniel Legare, *An Experimental Inquiry into the Effects of Tobacco Fumes on the System* (Philadelphia: John M. Oswald, 1805), 11–12, National Library of Medicine Digital Collections.

261 *The Annual Register, or a View of the History, Politicks, and Literature, for the Year 1765* (London: J. Dodsley, 1766), 133, ECCO.

262 Paul, *We Were Not the Savages*, 26.

263 Sieur de Dièreville, *Relation of the Voyage to Port Royal in Acadia or New France*, trans. Mrs Clarence Webster, ed. John Clarence Webster (Toronto: Champlain Society, 1933), 180.

264 de Dièreville, *Relation of the Voyage*, 182.

265 P.F.X. de Charlevoix, *History and General Description of New France*, trans. John Gilmary Shea (New York: John Gilmary Shea, 1866), 1: 267, Canadiana; P.F.X. de Charlevoix, *Histoire et Description Generale de la Nouvelle France* (Paris: Ganeau, 1744), 1: 126, Canadiana.

266 Legare, *Experimental Inquiry*, 30.

267 Richard Clarke, "A Receipt for Deafness," Transcript of Register A 1786–1792 kept by Reverend Richard Clarke, Transcripts from Gagetown church records,

1786–1841, Marianne Grey Otty Collection, S119–S119B–1, F106, New Brunswick Museum Archives and Research Library, 13.

268 Emily Cockayne, "Experiences of the Deaf in Early Modern England," *The Historical Journal* 46, no. 3 (2003): 496–7.

269 Pewter.

270 Lennard J. Davis, "Universalizing Marginality: How Europe Became Deaf in the Eighteenth Century," in *The Disability Studies Reader*, ed. Lennard J. Davis (New York: Routledge, 1997), 110–27.

271 Cockayne, "Experiences," 493–6.

272 Thomas Lupton, *A Thousand Notable Things. Containing Modern Curiosities* (London: G. Conyers, 1706), 52–3, 128, ECCO.

273 Penelope Bradshaw and [Edward] Lambart, *Bradshaw's Valuable Family Jewel: or, the Complete House-wife*, 11th ed. (London: P. Bradshaw, 1749), sig. D6, ECCO.

274 *The Complete Family-Piece: and, Country Gentleman, and Farmer's Best Guide*, 3rd ed. (London: C. Rivington, 1741), 72, ECCO.

275 Chomel, *Dictionnaire Oeconomique*, 1: sig. Nnn2*v*.

276 Jonathan Odell, Jonathan Odell Notebook, 1763–1818, Odell Family Fonds, S29B–F28(1), New Brunswick Museum Archives and Research Library.

277 Alfred G. Bailey, "Odell, Jonathan," in *Dictionary of Canadian Biography*, vol. 5 (Toronto: University of Toronto Press; Quebec: Presses de l'Université Laval, 2003–), http://www.biographi.ca/en/bio/odell_jonathan_5E.html.

278 Olive Jones and Allen Vegotsky, "Turlington's Balsam of Life," *Northeast Historical Archaeology* 45 (2016): 1–61.

279 George B. Griffenhagen and James Harvey Young, "Old English Patent Medicines in America," *Pharmacy in History* 34, no. 4 (1992): 217.

280 See for example, William Buchan, *Domestic Medicine, or a Treatise on the Prevention and Cure of Diseases* (Philadelphia: Joseph Cruikshanks, et al., 1784), 485–6, ECCO.

281 "Patent Medicines," *Journal of the Philadelphia College of Pharmacy* 5, no. 4 (1834): 28.

282 Jones and Vegotsky, "Turlington's Balsam," 37.

283 Tolu is a balsam obtained from the bark of the tolu tree. OED *Online*, s.v. "Tolu, n." It is considered to be a mild balsam, used as an expectorant (Jones and Vegotsky, "Turlington's Balsam," 41).

284 Styracin is a crystal obtained from storax and balsam of Peru. OED *Online*, s.v. "styracin, n." Storax and balsam of Peru were components of Turlington's version. Storax was used as an expectorant (Jones and Vegotsky, "Turlington's Balsam," 40).

285 Benzoin is a resin obtained from styrax benzoin, a tree in Sumatra and Java. See

OED *Online*, s.v. "benzoin, n." Gum benzoin was used as an expectorant (Jones and Vegotsky, "Turlington's Balsam," 40).

286 Aloe socotrina was a gum resin obtained from Socotara, an island in the Indian Ocean. Aloe socotrina was used as a purgative (Jones and Vegotsky, "Turlington's Balsam," 40).

287 Myrrh is an aromatic gum resin that comes from the tree of the genus *Commiphora*, found in Africa and the Middle East. OED *Online*, s.v. "myrrh, n.1." It was considered to be heating and used medically to induce sweating and as an expectorant and an antiseptic (Jones and Vegotsky, "Turlington's Balsam," 39).

288 Olibanum is an aromatic gum resin that comes from trees of the genus *Boswellia* found in North Africa. OED *Online*, s.v. "olibanum, n.1." Also called gum juniper, it is aromatic and a diuretic (Jones and Vegotsky, "Turlington's Balsam," 42).

289 Angelica root is the root of the angelica plant, native to northern and eastern Europe OED *Online*, s.v. "angelica, n." It is aromatic and acts as a mild laxative (Jones and Vegotsky, "Turlington's Balsam," 41).

290 aa is an abbreviation for ana, meaning "of each."

291 Spirits of rectified wine were made by distilling wine. It provided a solution in which to mix the other ingredients, while also being healthful in itself as a pain reliever, a stimulant, and a way to stop bleeding (Jones and Vegotsky, "Turlington's Balsam," 42).

292 Robert Turlington, *By Virtue of the King's Patent. Turlington's Balsam of Life Is Prepared and Sold by the Patentee* ([London]: n.p., [1744?]), ECCO.

293 "John Boyd has for sale," *The Port-Roseway Gazetteer and the Shelburne Advertiser* 1, no. 16 (27 January 1785), 3, Nova Scotia Historical Newspapers, online.

294 "Thomas Wallace, from London," *New Brunswick Courier* (Saint John) 22, no. 22 (3 November 1832), 1, New Brunswick Historical Newspapers Project, online.

295 Griffenhagen and Young, "Old English," 199–229.

296 The Manuscript Notebook of Sarah Creighton Wilkins, 1779–1833, MacDonald Family Fonds, MG 1 no. 1, microfilm reel 10618, Nova Scotia Archives.

297 Sarah Harrison, *The House-Keeper's Pocket-Book; and Compleat Family Cook*, 5th ed. (London: R. Ware, 1751), 256–7, ECCO.

298 Unused beeswax, a fine quality of wax. OED *Online*, s.v. "virgin wax, n."

299 Alkanet root, from the plant *Alkanna tinctoria*, is used to make a red dye. The plant is also called dyer's bugloss or orcanet. OED *Online*, s.v. "alkanet, n."

300 A gum resin from the tree *Styrax officinalis*, long used in European medicine. OED *Online*, s.v. "storax, n."

301 Another resinous substance obtained from a tree, *Styrax benzoin*, in Sumatra. OED *Online*, s.v. "benzoin, n."

302 *Beeton's Domestic Recipe Book* (London: Ward, Lock and Co., [1870?]), 69–70, Google Books.

303 See for example, Charles Carter, *The Compleat City and Country Cook: Or, Accomplish'd Housewife*, 2nd ed. (London: A. Bettesworth et al., 1736), 285, ECCO; Eliza Smith, *The Compleat Housewife: Or, Accomplish'd Gentlewoman's Companion*, 14th ed. (London: R. Ware, et al., 1750), 351, ECCO; *The Complete Family-Piece* (1741), 19; *The Whole Duty of a Woman; or an Infallible Guide to the Fair Sex* (London: T. Read, 1737), 689, ECCO; *The Servants' Guide and Family Manual, with New and Improved Receipts*, 2nd ed. (London: J. Limbird, 1831), 104, Nineteenth Century Collections Online.

304 Mary Kettilby, *A Collection of Above Three Hundred Receipts in Cookery, Physick and Surgery*, 2nd ed. (London: Mary Kettilby, 1719), 72, ECCO.

305 Booklet of Remedies in French, Miller Family Fonds, MG 1 vol. 693, Nova Scotia Archives.

306 For more on this recipe collection, see Danielle Arseneau, "Growing Acadian Medicine: From the Acadian Homeland to Nova Scotia Gardens," *Early Modern Maritime Recipes*, 2017. 1–8, https://emmr.lib.unb.ca/sites/default/files/inline-files/Arseneau_AcadianMedicine_0.pdf.

307 "[Latin] UntitledRecipe / To Treat Venereal Warts," *Early Modern Maritime Recipes*, https://emmr.lib.unb.ca/recipes/latin-untitledrecipeto-treat-venereal-warts.

308 "Fonds MG 1 volumes 582–695," Nova Scotia Archives, accessed 17 June 2023, https://memoryns.ca/miller-family-fonds.

309 *Encyclopedie Françoise, Latine et Angloise, ou dictionnaire universel des arts et des sciences* (Lyon: Jean-Marie Bruyset, 1761), 1: 395, ECCO. John Aitken, *Systematic Elements of the Theory and Practice of Surgery* (London: W. Gordon and W. Creech, 1779), 92, ECCO, explains the malady further, establishing it as the Latin "pernio," in French "mules" and "engelure," and in English "chilblain" and "kibe."

310 Hippocrates, *On Ancient Medicine*, trans. Mark Schiefsky (Leiden: Brill, 2005), 97, EBSCOhost.

311 Aitken, *Systemic Elements*, 93.

312 Daniel Turner, *De Morbis Cutaneis. A Treatise of Diseases Incident to the Skin* (London: R. Bonwicke, et al., 1714), 183, ECCO; Daniel Turner, *Traité des maladies de la peau en général*, trans. M.[?] (Paris: Jacques Barois, 1743), 2: 6–7, HathiTrust.

313 "Si le Engelures sont entâmées," *Early Modern Maritime Recipes*, https://emmr.lib.unb.ca/recipes/si-les-engelures-sont-entamees.

314 Turner, *De Morbis*, 189.

315 Turner, *De Morbis*, 190–1; Turner, *Traité*, 8–11.

316 Turner, *Traité*, 11.

317 Galen, "Mixtures," in *Galen: Selected Works*, trans. Peter N. Singer (Oxford: Oxford University Press, 1997), 216, 277.

318 Moyse Charas, *Pharmacopée Royale, Galenique et Chymique* (Paris: Chez l'auteur, 1676), 802, BnF Gallica.

319 Nicholas Lemery, *Pharmacopée Universelle*, 5th ed. (Paris: Saint & Saillant et al., 1764), 2: 1093, BnF Gallica.

320 OED *Online*, s.v. "ammoniac, adj. and n."

321 Jean-François Nicolas, *Nouveau Dictionnaire de Médecine & de Chirurgie* (Paris, 1772), 4: 107, BnF Gallica.

322 *Philosophical Transactions* (London: T.N., 1741), 309, ECCO.

323 "Remede efficace contre les Engelures," *Journal Oeconomique, ou Memoires, Notes et Avis* (Paris: Antoine Boudet, 1758), 28, BnF Gallica.

324 "Reméde contre les Engelures," *Affiches d'Austrasie* 1 (2 Janvier 1766), 21, BnF Gallica.

325 OED *Online*, s.v. "frostbite, n."; *The Weekly Magazine* 1, no. 9 (31 March 1798), 264, Internet Archive.

326 "Cure for frost bites," *American Museum*, no. 6 (1 December 1788), 572, American Antiquarian Society Historical Periodicals Collection.

327 Booklet of Remedies in French, Miller Family Fonds, MG 1 vol. 693, Nova Scotia Archives.

328 Noël Chomel, *Dictionnaire oeconomique: contenant divers moyens d'augmenter et conserver son bien, et même sa santé* (Paris: Le Conte & Montalant, 1709), 107, Université Paris Cité, https://www.biusante.parisdescartes.fr/histoire/medica/resultats/index.php?do=page&cote=01208&p=1135.

329 "Remêde pour l'estomac," *EMMR* database, https://emmr.lib.unb.ca/recipes/remede-pour-lestomac; "Contre la Gravelle," *EMMR* database, https://emmr.lib.unb.ca/recipes/contre-la-gravelle; "Remêde Contre la Goute et le Rumathisme, bien éprouvé," *EMMR* database, https://emmr.lib.unb.ca/recipes/remede-contre-la-goute-et-le-rumathisme-bien-eprouve.

330 Noël Chomel, *Dictionnaire Oeconomique: or, The Family Dictionary* (London: D. Midwinter, 1725), ECCO.

331 Guyac, or guaiacum, is a kind of tree native to the West Indies and warmer parts of the Americas. See OED *Online*, s.v. "guaiacum, n."

332 Sarsaparilla, a species in the order smilacae, is native to the Americas, found from Mexico to Peru; Jamaica sarsaparilla, mentioned below, is *Smilax officinalis*. See OED *Online*, s.v. "sarsaparilla, n."

333 Senna is "a shrub of the genus *Cassia*, native in tropical regions." See OED *Online*, s.v. "senna, n."

334 Jon Arrizabalaga, "Syphilis," in *The Cambridge World History of Human Diseases*, ed. Kenneth F. Kiple (Cambridge: Cambridge University Press, 2008), 1030, Cambridge Histories Online.

335 J. Worth Estes, "The European Reception of the First Drugs from the New World," *Pharmacy in History* 37, no. 1 (1995): 3–4.

336 Estes, "European Reception," 6–7; the actual origins of the disease remain the subject of scholarly debate. See Arrizabalaga, "Syphilis," 1027–9.

337 Nicolas Monardes, *Joyfull Newes out of the Newe Founde Worlde*, trans. John Frampton (London: William Norton, 1577), fol. 10*v* [misnumbered as 12*v*], EEBO.

338 Estes, "European Reception," 7–8.

339 Monardes, *Joyfull*, fol. 15*v*.

340 Anna E. Winterbottom, "Of the China Root: A Case Study of the Early Modern Circulation of *Materia medica*," *Social History of Medicine* 28, no. 1 (2014): 39.

341 Vogel, *American Indian*, 359–61.

342 For more on the early modern European exploitation of Taino knowledge of guaiacum, see Edith Snook, "Grace Mildmay's Recipes and Indigenous Knowledge in the Early Modern Atlantic World," *Atlantic Studies* 19, no. 2 (2022): 229–34.

343 Monardes, *Joyfull*, fol. 9*v*.

344 Monardes, *Joyfull*, fol. 12 [misnumbered as 10].

345 Monardes, *Joyfull*, fol. 16–16*v*, 81–81*v*; Monardes repeats with more details his account of the people living in the region of the Guaiaquil River taking this sarsaparilla juice to sweat and to effect a cure (fol. 80–80*v*). On the name of the people who lived there, see "Manteño-Huancavilca Territories," Native Land Digital, https://native-land.ca/maps/territories/manteno-huancavilca/.

346 Monardes, *Joyfull*, fol. 12*v*, 16–16*v*.

347 Chomel, *Dictionnaire oeconomique* (1725), 2: sig. 6D3*v*.

348 Chomel, *Dictionnaire oeconomique* (1725), 1: sig. E.

349 *The Pharmacopoeia of the United States of America* (Boston: Wells and Lilly, 1820), 115, 213, National Library of Medicine Digital Collection.

CHAPTER FOUR

1 Jason Hall, "Maliseet Cultivation and Climatic Resilience on the Wəlastəkw / St. John River During the Little Ice Age," *Acadiensis* 44, no. 2 (2015): 6.

2 Hall, "Maliseet," 9, 12.

3 Hall, "Maliseet," 5–6.

4 William C. Wicken, *Mi'kmaq Treaties on Trial: History, Land, and Donald Marshall Junior* (Toronto: University of Toronto Press, 2002), 35, Canada Commons.

5 Daniel Paul, *We Were Not the Savages: A Mi'kmaq Perspective on the Collision Between European and Native American Civilizations* (Halifax: Fernwood Publishing, 2000), 51–2.

6 Hall, "Maliseet," 8, 12, 15–16.

7 Andrew Parnaby, "The Cultural Economy of Survival: The Mi'kmaq of Cape Breton in the Mid-19th Century," *Labour / Le Travail* 61 (2008): 75–6.

8 Paul, *We Were Not the Savages*, 239, 273, 332; see also Parnaby, "The Cultural Economy," 72–7.

9 Parnaby, "The Cultural Economy," 78.

10 John Reid, "*Pax Britannica* or *Pax Indigena*? Planter Nova Scotia (1760–1782) and Competing Strategies of Pacification," in *Essays on Northeastern North America, 17th & 18th Centuries*, by John Reid with Emerson W. Baker (Toronto: University of Toronto Press, 2008), 176.

11 Hall, "Maliseet," 23.

12 Jean Daigle, "Acadian Marshland Settlement," in *Historical Atlas of Canada, Volume I: From the Beginning to 1800*, ed. R. Cole Harris (Toronto: University of Toronto Press, 1987), 72, ProQuest Ebook Central.

13 Karl W. Butzer, "French Wetland Agriculture in Atlantic Canada and Its European Roots: Different Avenues to Historical Diffusion," *Annals of the Association of American Geographers* 92, no. 3 (2002): 451–70.

14 Kenneth Donovan, "Imposing Discipline upon Nature: Gardens, Agriculture and Animal Husbandry in Cape Breton, 1713–1758," *Material Culture Review* 64 (Fall 2006): 20–37.

15 Daigle, "Acadian," 75.

16 Graeme Wynn and Debra McNabb, "Pre-Loyalist Nova Scotia," in *Historical Atlas of Canada, Volume I, From the Beginning to 1800*, ed. R. Cole Harris (Toronto: University of Toronto Press, 1987), 94–8, Canada Commons. Illustrating the persistence of settler colonial ideology, this map essay seems not to include Indigenous people in its population counts and represents land not used by settlers as "vacant" (97).

17 Graeme Wynn, "Late Eighteenth-Century Agriculture on the Bay of Fundy Marshlands," *Acadiensis* 8, no. 2 (1979): 80–9.

18 A.R. MacNeil, "Early American Communities on the Fundy: A Case Study of Annapolis and Amherst Townships, 1767–1827," *Agricultural History* 63, no. 2 (1989): 110–11.

19 Reid, "*Pax Britannica*," 171–90.

20 Wicken, *Mi'kmaq Treaties*, 209.

21 Ronald Rees, *Land of the Loyalists: Their Struggle to Shape the Maritimes* (Halifax: Nimbus, 2000), 19.

22 Rees, *Land of the Loyalists*, 38–9.

23 Neil MacKinnon, *This Unfriendly Soil: The Loyalist Experience in Nova Scotia 1783–1791* (Kingston and Montreal: McGill-Queen's University Press, 1986), 101–2.

24 Graeme Wynn and L.D. McCann, "Maritime Canada, Late 18th Century," in *Historical Atlas of Canada: Volume I: From the Beginning to 1800*, ed. R. Cole Harris (Toronto: University of Toronto Press, 1987), 97–8, Canada Commons.

25 Rees, *Land of the Loyalists*, 30–7.

26 Ann Gorman Condon, "1783–1800, Loyalist Arrival, Acadian Return, Imperial Reform," in *The Atlantic Region to Confederation: A History*, ed. Phillip Buckner and John Reid (Toronto: University of Toronto Press, 2017), 141, ProQuest Ebook Central.

27 Mary Fissell and Roger Cooter, "Exploring Natural Knowledge: Science and the Popular," in *The Cambridge History of Science: Eighteenth-Century Science*, ed. Roy Porter (Cambridge: Cambridge University Press, 2008), 4: 139–46.

28 James Fisher, "The Master Should Know More: Book-Farming and the Conflict over Agricultural Knowledge," *Cultural and Social History* 15, no. 3 (2018): 315–31, https://doi.org/10.1080/14780038.2018.1492792.

29 Rees, *Land of the Loyalists*, 31–2.

30 "Remarks on the Manufacturing of Maple Sugar," *The Nova Scotia Magazine* 3 (October 1790), 249–54.

31 *Remarks on the Manufacturing of Maple Sugar; with Directions for Its Further Improvements* (Philadelphia: Johnson, 1790), Google Books; "Remarks on the Manufacturing of Maple Sugar; by a Society of Gentlemen, in Philadelphia," *Universal Asylum, & Columbian Magazine* 5, no. 2 (August 1790), 106–7, American Antiquarian Society Historical Periodicals Collection; "Remarks on the Manufacturing of Maple Sugar; by a Society of Gentlemen, in Philadelphia," *Universal Asylum, & Columbian Magazine* 5, no. 3 (September 1790), 153–6, American Antiquarian Society Historical Periodicals Collection.

32 For more on these instructions, see Edith Snook, "'A New Source of Happiness to Man'? Maple Sugaring and Settler Colonialism in the Early Modern Atlantic World," in *In the Kitchen, 1550–1800: English Cooking at Home and Abroad* (Amsterdam: Amsterdam University Press, 2022), 265–86. For more on Drinker, see David W. Maxey, "The Union Farm: Henry Drinker's Experiment in Deriving Profit from Virtue," *The Pennsylvania Magazine of History of Biography* 47, no. 4 (1983): 607–29.

33 H.A. Schuette and Sybil C. Schuette, "Maple Sugar: A Bibliography of Early Records," *Wisconsin Academy of Sciences, Arts, and Letters* 29 (1935): 209–36.

34 Chrestien LeClercq, *New Relation of Gaspesia: With the Customs and Religion of Gaspesian Indians*, trans. William F. Ganong (Toronto: Champlain Society, 1910), 135–6.

35 Leanne Betasamosake Simpson, *As We Have Always Done: Indigenous Freedom Through Radical Resistance* (Minneapolis: University of Minnesota Press, 2017), 154.

36 Maxey, "The Union Farm," 621–9.

37 Peter Latta, "Eighteenth-Century Settler Immigrants to Nova Scotia: The Yorkshire Settlers," *Material History Bulletin* 28 (1998): 50.

38 "On the Method of Raising Seedling Potatoes," *Weekly Chronicle* 9, no. 461, 28 March 1795, Nova Scotia Newspapers on Microfilm, microfilm reel 8165, Nova Scotia Archives.

39 Marie Tremaine, *A Bibliography of Canadian Imprints, 1751–1800* (Toronto: University of Toronto Press, 1999), 610–11, 617–19, EBSCOhost.

40 Anne Digby, "Hunter, Alexander (1729?–1809), physician," in *Oxford Dictionary of National Biography* (Oxford: Oxford University Press, 2004), online; Alexander Hunter, *Georgical Essays: In Which the Food of Plants Is Particularly Considered*, 2nd ed. (London: T. Durham, 1773), 4: 94–9, ECCO.

41 "On the Method of Raising Seedling Potatoes," *Pennsylvania Packet* (Philadelphia, PA) 2, no. 90, (12 July 1773), Readex: America's Historical Newspapers.

42 The apple of the potato seems to refer to the fruit of the potato plant. See *OED Online*, s.v. "potato, n."

43. Hunter, *Georgical Essays*, 4:97.

44 John Reader, *Potato* (New Haven, CT: Yale University Press, 2009), 3–130.

45 Mary Tolford Wilson, "Americans Learn to Grow the Irish Potato," *New England Quarterly* 32, no. 3 (1959): 333–50.

46 Kenneth Donovan, "Imposing Discipline upon Nature: Gardens, Agriculture, and Animal Husbandry in Cape Breton, 1713–1758," *Material Culture Review* 64 (2006): par. 19.

47 Bill of fare, including list of food supplies, for victualling the Free Blacks on the voyage to Sierra Leone, submitted to the Lieutenant Governor, Commissioner of Public Records – Black Refugees series, RG 1 volume 419, number 18, Nova Scotia Archives, *Looking Back, Moving Forward: Documenting the Heritage of African Nova Scotians*, https://archives.novascotia.ca/african-heritage/archives/?ID=40&Page=201112041.

48 Winslow qtd. in Rees, *Land of the Loyalists*, 59.

49 "Extract from a small French Work," *The Royal Gazette and Miscellany of the Island of Saint John* 1, no. 6 (23 September 1791), University of New Brunswick Microfilms.

50 "Extracts from a Very Valuable French Book," *American Museum, or Universal Magazine* 8, no. 3 (September 1790), 142–3, American Antiquarian Society Historical Periodicals Collection; "Extracts from a Very Valuable French Book," *The Christian's, Scholar's, and Farmer's Magazine* 2, no. 2 (June and July 1790), 247–8, American Antiquarian Society Historical Periodicals Collection; "From a Little French Work," *New-York Daily Gazette* (New York), no. 573 (27 October 1790), 1026, Readex: America's Historical Newspapers; "From a Little French Work," *Pennsylvania Packet* (Philadelphia, PA), no. 3665 (29 October 1790), 3, Readex; "How to Multiply the Increase in Corn," *The Halifax Gazette* 5, no. 214, 1 April 1793, Nova Scotia Newspapers on Microfilm, microfilm reel 8166, Nova Scotia Archives.

51 Pons-Augustin Alletz, *L'Agronome: Dictionnaire portatif du cultivateur*, 2nd ed. (Paris: Chez Nyon, 1764), 1: 128.

52 A. Glenn Crothers, "'The Projecting Spirit': Social, Economic and Cultural Change in Post–Revolutionary Northern Virginia, 1780–1805" (PhD diss., University of Florida, 1997), 388.

53 Potassium nitrate, the chief ingredient in gunpowder. See OED *Online*, s.v. "saltpetre, n." Like the lime in the next method, saltpetre is alkaline. Potassium nitrate is today frequently used as a fertilizer.

54 Although the term *corn* was widely used in England to describe any kind of grain, the context of these instructions likely means to address only the grain we now know exclusively as corn. See OED *Online*, s.v. "corn, n.1."

55 Arturo Warman, *Corn and Capitalism: How a Botanical Bastard Grew to Global Dominance*, trans. Nancy L Westrate (Chapel Hill: University of North Carolina Press, 2003), 13, EBSCOhost.

56 Michael Blake, *Maize for the Gods: Unearthing the 9,000-Year History of Corn* (Oakland: University of California Press, 2015), 17–36.

57 Warman, *Corn and Capitalism*, 151.

58 Kevin James Malachy Leonard, "Mi'kmaq Culture During the Late Woodland and Early Prehistoric Periods" (PhD diss. University of Toronto, 1996), 185.

59 Hall, "Maliseet," 6.

60 Hall, "Maliseet," 16–25.

61 N.E.S. Griffiths, *From Migrant to Acadian: A North American Border People, 1604–1755* (Montreal: McGill-Queen's University Press, 2004), 175, Canadian Electronic Library / desLibris.

62 Justin Niermeier-Dohoney, "'To Multiply Corn Two-Hundred-Fold': The Alchemical Augmentation of Wheat Seeds in Seventeenth-Century English Husbandry," *Nuncius: Journal of the History of Science* 37, no. 2 (2022): 284–314.

63 Niermeier-Dohoney, "To Multiply," 299.

64 Niermeier-Dohoney, "To Multiply," 313.

65 "Letter from Bejamin Marston to Edward Winslow," 3 April 1791, Winslow Papers, vol. 7–85, UNB MG H2, microfilm MIC-Loyalist FC LFR.W5E3P3, University of New Brunswick Archives and Special Collections.

66 Maud Maxwell Vesey, "Benjamin Marston, Loyalist," *The New England Quarterly* 15, no. 4 (1942): 622–51.

67 The city in western England.

68 Christopher Halm, "'Enquiries on *Plaister of Paris*': A Material History of Early Agrochemical Knowledge in the United States of America, 1785–1812," *Annals of Science* 77, no. 2 (2022): 172–5, https://doi.org/10.1080/00033790.2020.1738749.

69 *On the Effects of Gypsum, or Plaster of Paris, as a Manure; Chiefly Extracted from apers and Letters on Agriculture, by the Agricultural Society in Canada* (London: James Phillips, 1791), 4, 7, 18, ECCO.

70 G.C. Adams, *Gypsum and Anhydrite Resources in Nova Scotia* (Halifax: Nova Scotia Department of Natural Resources, 1991).See also "Mining Highlights," *Nova Scotia Canada*, accessed 4 August 2022, https://novascotia.ca/natr/meb/mineral-resources/mining-highlights.asp.

71 "Mr Henry," *The Royal Gazette and the Nova Scotia Advertiser* 3, no. 148, 17 January 1792, Nova Scotia Newspapers on Microfilm, microfilm reel 8163, Nova Scotia Archives.

72 William Lewis, *Experiments and Observations on American Potashes … Made at the Request of the Society for the Encouragement of Arts, Manufactures, and Commerce, in Consequence of an Application from the House of Representatives of Massachusetts Bay* (London: printed by order of the Society, 1767), 6–11, ECCO.

73 Thomas Stephens, *The Method and Plain Process for Making Pot-Ash* (London: R. Griffiths, 1755), 7, ECCO.

74 Species of cardus, beans, centaury, hops, southernwood (artemisia), wormwood, tobacco, dandelions, and sow thistles are all indexed in Marian C. Munro, Ruth E. Newell, and Nicholas M. Hill, *Nova Scotia Plants* (Province of Nova Scotia, 2014), https://ojs.library.dal.ca/NSM/pages/view/Plants.

75 In the eighteenth century, the word *potash* referred to an alkaline substance (potassium carbonate) produced by leaching the ashes of burned plants in pots; today, naturally occurring potash is mined. See OED *Online*, s.v. "potash, n."

76 Alkaline.

77 Having strong acid or alkaline properties. See OED *Online*, s.v. "sharp, adj. and n.1."

78 Tartar is a substance found in the early modern period as a hard crust adhering to the sides of wine casks; it is bitartrate of potash, or acid potassium tartrate. Calx of tartar (below) refers to tartar that has been calcined, or burned. See OED *Online*, s.v. "tartar, n.1." As the recipe explains, the purpose of mixing in this substance is to produce a greater quantity of salt from the ashes.

79 William I. Roberts, III, "American Potash Manufacture Before the American Revolution," *Proceedings of the American Philosophical Society* 116, no. 5 (1972): 383, 386.

80 C.A. Browne, "Historical Notes upon the Domestic Potash Industry in Early Colonial and Later Times," *Journal of Chemical Education* 3, no. 7 (1926): 754.

81 Stephens, *The Method*, 18.

82 Stephens, *The Method*, 18.

83 "A Certain Cure," *The Nova Scotia Magazine* 4, no. 3, March 1791, Nova Scotia Newspapers on Microfilm, microfilm reel 8063, Nova Scotia Archives.

84 Anon., *Dictionarium Rusticum & Urbanicum: Or, A Dictionary of All Sorts of Country Affairs, Handicraft, Trading, and Merchandizing* (London: A. and J. Churchill, 1704), sig. Hh6, ECCO.

85 Anon., *The Complete Grazier: Or, Gentleman and Farmer's Directory*, 4th ed. (London: J. Almon, 1776), 191–2, ECCO.

86 George Winter, *A New and Compendious System of Husbandry: Containing the Mechanical, Chemical, and Philosophical Elements of Agriculture* (Bristol: W. Routh, 1787), 231, ECCO.

87 *The American Magazine, or Universal Magazine* (Philadelphia), 4 (July–December, 1788): 350–1, HathiTrust.

88 *Dictionarium Rusticum*, sig. Hh6; *The Complete Grazier*, 192.

89 "Mr. Fraser's Report of Devon," *The Royal Gazette and the Nova Scotia Advertiser* 6, no. 299 (13 January 1795), Nova Scotia Newspapers on Microfilm, microfilm reel 8165, Nova Scotia Archives.

90 Robert Fraser, *General View of the County of Devon* (London: C. Macrae, 1794), 75, ECCO.

91 "History," *Purebred Sheep Breeders Association of Nova Scotia*, accessed 20 December 2020, https://www.sheepnovascotia.ns.ca/history/.

92 François Castonguay, "Sheep Farming," in *The Canadian Encyclopedia*, Historica Canada, article published 18 April 2013, https://thecanadianencyclopedia.ca/en/article/sheep-farming.

93 OED *Online*, s.v. "wood-evil, n."

94 Naghmeh Dehghani, Mohsen Afsharmanesh, Mohammad Salarmoini, and Hadi Ebrahimnejad, "Characterization of Pennyroyal (*Mentha pulegium*) Essential Oil as an Herbal, Antibacterial, and Antioxidant Substance," *Comparative Clinical Pathology* 27 (2018): 1575–81.

95 Allfred Maroyi, "*Scabiosa columbaria*: A Review of Its Medicinal Uses, Phytochemistry, and Biological Activities," *Asian Journal of Pharmaceutical and Clinical Research* 11 (2019): 10–14.

96 Jinming Peng, Tianyong Hu, Jin Li, Jing Du, Kerui Zhu, Baohui Cheng, and Kakai Li, "Shepherd's Purse Polyphenols Exert Its Anti-Inflammatory and Antioxidative Effects Associated with Suppressing MAPK and NF-KB Pathways and Heme Oxygenase-1 Activation," *Oxidative Medicine and Cellular Longevity* 2019 (2019): 1.

97 William Chapman, Pocket and Account Book, Webster Manuscript Collection / Fort Beauséjour National Park, Accession 7001, Mount Allison University Archives.

98 W.C. Milner, *Records of Chignecto* ([Nova Scotia?]: n.p., [1907?]), 40–2, Canadiana; Howard Trueman, *The Chignecto Isthmus and Its First Settlers* (Toronto: W. Briggs, 1902), 76, 186, Canadiana.

99 Milner, *Records*, 42.

100 Lucille H. Campey, *Planters, Paupers, and Pioneers: English Settlers in Atlantic Canada* (Toronto: Natural Heritage Book, 2010), 19–59.

101 A thick, sticky plaster applied to the body of a horse. See OED *Online*, s.v. "charge, n."

102 Resin.

103 A kind of resin obtained from the spruce-fir tree and sourced from Neufchâtel (now in Switzerland, once in Burgundy, France). See OED *Online*, s.v. "Burgundy, n."

104 Another kind of resin, from the mastic tree, frequently used in medicine, but also in varnish. See OED *Online*, s.v. "mastic, n. and adj."

105 Camphor is a crystalline, transparent substance with a strong smell and bitter taste, often used in medicines. See OED *Online*, s.v. "camphor, n."

106 Another gum or resin, this from the palm tree *Calmus draco*. See OED *Online*, s.v. "dragon's blood, n."

107 A bony growth on the pastern bones, between the fetlock and hoof, of a horse. See OED *Online*, s.v. "ringbone, n."

108 A bony tumour formed on the splint bone and shank of a horse. See OED *Online*, s.v. "spavin, n.1."

109 An oil from sea animals, especially from the blubber of the right whale. See OED *Online*, s.v. "train oil, n."

110 C.A.V. Barker, "History of Veterinary Medicine," in *The Canadian Encyclopedia*, Historica Canada, article published 7 February 2006, https://www.thecanadianencyclopedia.ca/en/article/history-of-veterinary-medicine.

111 Louise Hill Curth, *The Care of Brute Beasts: A Social and Cultural Study of Veterinary Medicine in Early Modern England* (Leiden: Brill, 2010), 57–69, 95–6, EBSCOhost.

112 Curth, *The Care*, 36–40.

113 Curth, *The Care*, 118–41.

114 John Quincy, *Pharmacopoia Officinalis & Extemporanea. Or, a Complete English Dispensatory, in Four Parts*, 12th ed. (London: Thomas Longman, 1742), 97, ECCO.

115 William Merrick, *The Classical Farrier. Exhibiting the Whole Anatomy of That Noble Animal the Horse*, 2nd ed. (London: printed for the author, 1789), 791, ECCO.

116 Merrick, *The Classical Farrier*, 790.

117 Merrick, *The Classical Farrier*, 799.

118 John Reeves, *The Art of Farriery both in Theory and Practice*, 3rd ed. (London: Carnan and Newbery et al., 1771), 349, ECCO.

119 Captain Burdon, et al. *Full Instructions for Country Gentlemen, Farmers, Grasiers, Farriers, Carriers, Sportsmen*, 2nd ed. (London: [s.n.], 1732), 25, ECCO.

120 William Gibson, *A New Treatise on the Diseases of Horses* (London: A. Millar, 1751), 364–71, ECCO.

121 Andrew Wear, *Knowledge and Practice in English Medicine, 1550–1680* (New York: Cambridge University Press, 2000), 266–73, EBSCOhost.

122 Merrick, *Classical Farrier*, 800.

123 Merrick, *Classical Farrier*, 426–7.

124 Erra Pater, *The Book of Knowledge; Treating of the Wisdom of the Ancients* (London: Thomas Norris, 1720), 100, ECCO.

125 F.R., *The Experience'd Farrier, or Farring Completed*, 4th ed. (London: G. Conyers, et al., 1720), 1, ECCO.

CHAPTER FIVE

1 Peter Ennals and Deryck Holdsworth, *Homeplace: The Making of the Canadian Dwelling over Three Centuries* (Toronto: University of Toronto Press, 1998), 5–9, EBSCOhost.

2 Ennals and Holdsworth, *Homeplace*, 32–3.

3 Ennals and Holdsworth, *Homeplace*, 76–81.

4 Mary Byers and Margaret McBurney, *Atlantic Hearth: Early Homes and Families of Nova Scotia* (Toronto: University of Toronto Press, 1994), 175–9. See also "de

Gannes–Cosby house," *Canada's Historic Places*, Parks Canada, https://www.historicplaces.ca/en/rep–reg/place–lieu.aspx?id=7122&pid=0.

5 Byers and McBurney, *Atlantic Hearth*, 179–80. See also "220–224 St. George Street," *Canada's Historic Places*, Parks Canada. https://www.historicplaces.ca/en/rep-reg/place-lieu.aspx?id=2790.

6 Ennals and Holdsworth, *Homeplace*, 63.

7 Ennals and Holdsworth, *Homeplace*, 3.

8 Peter Ward, *A History of Domestic Space: Privacy and the Canadian Home* (Vancouver: UBC Press, 2007), 15, ProQuest Ebook Central.

9 Ronald Rees, *Land of the Loyalists: Their Struggle to Shape the Maritimes* (Halifax: Nimbus, 2000), 19.

10 Rees, *Land of the Loyalists*, 19–42.

11 Ennals and Holdsworth, *Homeplace*, 31.

12 Neil MacKinnon, *This Unfriendly Soil: The Loyalist Experience in Nova Scotia, 1783–1791* (Kingston: McGill-Queen's University Press, 1986), 62–6.

13 Rees, *Land of the Loyalists*, 42–5.

14 Rees, *Land of the Loyalists*, 83–5.

15 Byers and McBurney, *Atlantic Hearth*, 114–17.

16 Ennals and Holdsworth, *Homeplace*, 4.

17 Kenneth Donovan, "Communities and Families: Family Life and Living Conditions in Eighteenth Century Louisbourg," *Material History Bulletin* 15 (1982): 33–47.

18 Richard Henning Field, "Claiming Rank: The Display of Wealth and Status by Eighteenth-Century Lunenburg, Nova Scotia, Merchants," *Material History Review* 35 (1992): 1–7.

19 M.A. MacDonald, "Before the Loyalists: The Material Culture of New Brunswick's Early Settlers," *Material History Bulletin* 28 (1988): 17, 28–31.

20 M. Elaine MacKay, "Three Thousand Stitches: The Development of the Clothing Industry in Nineteenth-Century Halifax," in *Fashion: A Canadian Perspective*, ed. Alexandra Palmer (Toronto: University of Toronto Press, 2004), 166–9; E.M. Razzolini, "Costume Research and Reproduction at Louisbourg," *Material History Bulletin* 14 (1982): 59–65. See also Peter J. Larocque, "'The Work Being Chiefly Performed by Women': Female Workers in the Garment Industry in Saint John, New Brunswick, in 1871," in *Fashion: A Canadian Perspective*, ed. Palmer, 139–65.

21 Razzolini, "Costume Research," 59–65.

22 Gail G. Campbell. *"I Wish to Keep a Record": Nineteenth-Century New Brunswick Women Diarists and Their World* (Toronto: University of Toronto Press, 2016), 211–20.

23 Jane L. Cook, *Coalescence of Styles: The Ethnic Heritage of St John River Valley Regional Furniture, 1763–1851* (Montreal: Acumen Publishing, 2001), 90–3.

24 Cook, *Coalescence*, 59, 66.

25 Bonnie Huskins, "'Shelburnian Manners': Gentility and the Loyalists of Shelburne, Nova Scotia," *Early American Studies: An Interdisciplinary Journal* 13, no. 1 (2015): 151–88.

26 Huskins, "Shelburnian Manners," 169–71.

27 Huskins, "Shelburnian Manners," 158.

28 Huskins, "Shelburnian Manners," 187–8.

29 Anthony Allaire, Diary and Order Book, 1780–1794, Beverly Robinson Papers, S37A, F19, New Brunswick Museum Archives and Research Library.

30 [Frances H. Green], *The Housekeeper's Book* (Philadelphia: William Marshall, 1837), 195, Digital Library for the Decorative Arts and Material Culture, University of Wisconsin-Madison; Marie Martinelo, *The New York Cook Book: A Complete Manual* (New York: Worthington & Col, 1890), 137, Google Books; Fanny Lemira Gilette, *Mrs. Gillette's Cook Book: Fifty Years of Practical Housekeeping* (Akron, OH: The Werner Company, 1899), 502–3, HathiTrust.

31 Lorna Weatherill, *Consumer Behavior and Material Culture in Britain 1660–1770* (Cambridge: Cambridge University Press, 1988), 31.

32 Beth Kowaleski-Wallace, "Women, China, and Consumer Culture in Eighteenth-Century England," *Eighteenth-Century Studies* 29, no. 2 (1995 / 96): 155.

33 Susan Buys and Victoria Oakley, *Conservation and Restoration of Ceramics* (London: Routledge, 2014), 64.

34 The Manuscript Notebook of Sarah Creighton Wilkins, 1779–1833, MacDonald Family Fonds, MG 1 no. 1, microfilm reel 10618, Nova Scotia Archives.

35 Eliza Smith, *The Compleat Housewife: or, Accomplish'd Gentlewoman's Companion*, 10th ed. (London: J. and H. Pemberton, 1741), 346, ECCO.

36 *OED Online*, s.v. "red, adj. and n., and adv."

37 Stanislav Strekopytov, "Corrosive Sublimate and Its Introduction as an Insecticide for Preserving Natural History Specimens in the Eighteenth Century," *Archives of Natural History* 48, no. 1 (2021): 23, https://doi.org/10.3366/anh.2021.0686.

38 William Salmon, *The Family-Dictionary: or, Houshold Companion*, 3rd ed. (London: H. Rhodes, 1705), 111, ECCO.

39 *The Housemaid: Her Duties, and How to Perform Them* (London: Houlston and Sons, n.d.), 44, Nineteenth Century Collections Online.

40 Michael F. Potter, "The History of Bed Bug Management: With Lessons from the Past," *American Entomologist* 57, no. 1 (2011): 14–15.

41 Dawn Day Biehler, *Pests in the City: Flies, Bedbugs, Cockroaches, and Rats* (Seattle: University of Washington Press, 2013), 5, ProQuest Ebook Central.

42 Biehler, *Pests*, 8–9.

43 *The Nova-Scotia Almanack, for Town and Country for the Year of Our Lord 1820* (Halifax: Edmund Ward, [1819?]), n.p., Canadiana; Elizabeth Driver, *Culinary Landmarks: A Bibliography of Canadian Cookbooks, 1825–1949* (Toronto: University of Toronto Press, 2008), 10, identifies this as Nova Scotia's first published recipe collection.

44 The Manuscript Notebook of Sarah Creighton Wilkins, 1779–1833, MacDonald Family Fonds, MG 1 no. 1, microfilm reel 10618, Nova Scotia Archives.

45 *Domestic Management, or the Art of Conducting a Family; with Instructions to Servants in General* (London: H.D. Symonds, [1800?]), 42–3, ECCO.

46 Alkanet root is the root of the plant *Alkanna tinctoria*, which has a black root that is used to make a red dye used in dyeing cloth. *OED Online*, s.v. "alkanet, n."

47 Rose pink is a paint pigment made from brazilwood. See Ralph Mayer, *The Artist's Handbook of Materials and Techniques*, 3rd ed. (New York: Viking Press, 1970), 65.

48 Linseed oil is made by pressing it from the seeds of flax plants; the cold-pressed oil is considered to be superior to that pressed with the aid of steam.

49 *Domestic Management*, 42–3.

50 Temple Henry Croker, Samuel Clark, and Thomas Williams, *The Complete Dictionary of Arts and Science* (London: printed for the authors, 1764), 1: sig. 5X2, Gg, ECCO, lists "rose pink" as one of the red colours used in painting, and the "chief use" of alkanet root as "colouring oils, plaisters, lip-salves, &c. which receive a find deep red from one fortieth their weight of the root."

51 The Manuscript Notebook of Sarah Creighton Wilkins, 1779–1833, MacDonald Family Fonds, MG 1 no. 1, microfilm reel 10618, Nova Scotia Archives.

52 Candles can be made of tallow (from sheep or cow fat) or wax, and tallow candles can be dipped or moulded; dipped candles are ordinary and moulded candles, newly invented in Paris in the eighteenth century, are made with a metal mould. See "Candle," in Ephraim Chambers, *Cyclopædia: or, an Universal Dictionary of Arts and Sciences* (London: James and John Knapton, et al., 1728), 1: 145–6, ECCO.

53 John Townshend, *The Universal Cook; or, Lady's Complete Assistant* (London: S. Bladon, 1773), 304, ECCO.

54 Townshend, *The Universal Cook*, 304; Eliza Fowler Haywood, *A Present for a Servant-Maid. Or, the Sure Means of Gaining Love and Esteem* (Dublin: George Faulkner, 1744), 71, ECCO.

55 *The Complete Man and Maid Servant: Containing, Plain and Easy Instructions for Servants of Both Sexes* (London: J. Cooke, 1764), 40, ECCO.

56 Patricia Malcolmson, *English Laundresses: A Social History, 1850–1930* (Urbana: University of Illinois Press, 1986), xi–xiv, 3–6.

57 Suzanne Morton, "Separate Spheres in a Separate World: African-Nova Scotian Women in late-19th-Century Halifax County," *Acadiensis* 22, no. 2 (1993): 67–71.

58 Kathleen M. Brown, *Foul Bodies: Cleanliness in Early America* (New Haven: Yale University Press, 2009), 109–11.

59 Brown, *Foul Bodies*, 111.

60 The Manuscript Notebook of Sarah Creighton Wilkins, 1779–1833, MacDonald Family Fonds, MG 1 no. 1, microfilm reel 10618, Nova Scotia Archives.

61 Maria Eliza Ketelby Rundell, *A New System of Domestic Cookery, Formed upon Principles of Economy: and Adapted to the Use of Private Families Throughout the United States* (New York: R. McDermut & D.D. Arden, 1814), 291, Nineteenth Century Collections Online.

62 "Boot Polish History," Blanco and Bull, accessed 30 May 2023, https://www.blancoandbull.com/boot-cleaning/boot-polish-history/.

63 John Mason Good, Olinthus Gregory, and Newton Bosworth, *Pantologia: A New Cabinet Cyclopaedia* (London: G. Kearsley et al., 1819), 2: sig. N5, Google Books.

64 Constant de Massoul, *A Treatise on the Art of Painting, and the Composition of Colours* (London: published by the author, 1797), 19–20, ECCO; John Barrow, *Dictionarium Polygraphicum* (London: C. Hitch and C. Davis, 1735), 1: sig. E2*v*, defines black ivory as "ivory burnt" and specifies its use by painters and jewellers.

65 William Paine Papers, Loyalist Collection, MIC-Loyalist FC LFR.P3W5P3, University of New Brunswick.

66 Priscilla Homespun, *The Universal Receipt Book*, 2nd ed. (Philadelphia: Isaac Riley, 1818), 314–15, HathiTrust. The Library of Congress lists an earlier edition in 1814, which attributes authorship to "a society of gentlemen in New York."

67 William Paine Papers, Loyalist Collection, MIC-Loyalist FC LFR.P3W5P3, University of New Brunswick.

68 Translated as "be of good cheer." The word is recorded in the Roger Williams, "A Key into the Language of America," *Collections of the Rhode Island Historical Society* 1 (1827): 160–1, Archive.org, as being used in Wampanoag funerals and ceremonies for the dead.

69 Later known as potassium chlorate, the compound is "a very flammable mixture with combustible materials" that "may be ignited by friction," and is used in making matches, as well as other uses that include disinfectants. See "Compound Summary for CID 6426889, Potassium Chlorate," PubChem, National Center for Biotechnology Information, https://pubchem.ncbi.nlm.nih.gov/compound/

Potassium-Chlorate. The oxymuriate to which Paine's recipe refers is an archaic term for chloride or chlorate. See OED *Online*, s.v. "oxymuriate, n." Potash, which was also used as a generic term for fertilizer, referred to potassium carbonate. See OED *Online*, s.v. "potash, n.1."

70 OED *Online*, s.v. "muriatic acid, n." notes that "The name muriatic acid has been superseded in formal chemical nomenclature by hydrochloric acid, but still persists in commercial and industrial use." The compound has many uses that include "cleaning, pickling, electroplating metals, tanning leather, and refining." See "PubChem Compound Summary for CID 313, Hydrochloric Acid," PubChem, National Library of Medicine, https://pubchem.ncbi.nlm.nih.gov/compound/Hydrochloric-Acid.

71 Roger Williams, "Key into the Language of the Indians of New England," *Collections of the Massachusetts Historical Society, for the Year 1794* (Boston: 1794, rpt. Boston: Munroe & Francis, 1810), 3:237, Internet Archive; Williams, "A Key into the Language of America," 160–1.

72 "Sketch of the Life of Roger Williams," *Collections of the Rhode Island Historical Society* 1 (1827): 9–16, Internet Archive; Francis J. Bremer, "Williams, Roger (c. 1606–1683), religious controversialist and founder of Providence, Rhode Island," in *Oxford Dictionary of National Biography* (Oxford: Oxford University Press, 2004), online.

73 Julie A. Fisher, "Roger Williams and the Indian Business," *New England Quarterly* 94, no. 3 (2021): 355.

74 Roger Williams, *A Key into the Language of America, Or, an Help to the Language of the Natives in That Part of America Called New-England* (London: Gregory Dexter, 1643), EEBO.

75 "Sketch of the Life of Roger Williams," 14.

76 See *Proto-Algonquin Dictionary*, Algonquin Dictionaries Project, https://proto algonquian.atlas-ling.ca; Fisher, "Roger Williams," 356–7.

77 Williams, "Key into the Language," *Collections of the Massachusetts Historical Society, for the Year 1794* (1810), 3: 237.

78 Christine Delucia, "The Terrapolitics in the Dawnland: Relationality, Resistance, and Indigenous Futures in the Native and Colonial Northeast," *New England Quarterly* 92, no. 4 (2019): 572.

79 David J. Silverman, "'We chuse to be bounded': Native American Animal Husbandry in Colonial New England," *William & Mary Quarterly* 60, no. 3 (2003): 511–48.

80 Delucia, "The Terrapolitics," 578.

81 John and William Trueman Notebook, Trueman family notebooks, account books, diaries, and artifacts, 1750, 1771–1883, Trueman Family Fonds, 1750–1931, vol. 1, Accession 0102, Mount Allison University Archives.

82 *Ouse / ous* are alternative spellings of *ooze* but both are specifically used in the context of the tanning process to refer to the liquid produced within the tanning vat in which the hide is being steeped. See OED *Online*, s.v. "ooze, n.2."

83 Peter C. Welsh, "A Craft That Resisted Change: American Tanning Practices to 1850," *Technology and Culture* 4, no. 3 (1963): 299.

84 David L. Salay, "Marching to War: The Production of Leather and Shoes in Revolutionary Pennsylvania," *Pennsylvania History: A Journal of Mid-Atlantic Studies* 60, no. 1 (1993): 60–3.

85 Salay, "Marching," 60–3; Welsh, "A Craft," 305–11.

86 James Fowler, "List of New Brunswick Plants," Report of the Secretary for Agriculture, 50, https://qspace.library.queensu.ca/bitstream/handle/1974/9055/listofnewbrunswi00fowl.pdf?sequence=1.

87 "A Cheap Method," *Nova Scotia Gazette* 2, no. 54, 20 August 1767, Nova Scotia Newspapers on Microfilm, microfilm reel 9466, Nova Scotia Archives.

88 Marie Tremaine, *A Bibliography of Canadian Imprints, 1751–1800* (Toronto: University of Toronto Press, 1999), 601–2.

89 William Smith, *An Historical Account of the Expedition Against the Ohio Indians in the Year 1764* (Philadelphia: n.p.; London: rpt. for T. Jefferies, 1766), 47–8, Wellcome Collection.

90 William Trueman, "How to Make Fat Drying Oyl," John and William Trueman Notebook, https://emmr.lib.unb.ca/recipes/256.

91 Smith, *An Historical Account*, 47.

92 Smith, *An Historical Account*, 47–8.

93 Smith, *An Historical Account*, 38–9.

94 The Manuscript Notebook of Dr William James Almon, Almon Family Fonds, MG 1, microfilm reel 10045, Nova Scotia Archives.

95 "Process for Removing Spots of Grease from Books and Prints," *Philosophical Magazine*, ed. Alexander Tilloch (London: printed for the proprietors, 1798), 2: 30–1, HathiTrust.

96 "Procédé pour enlever les taches du suif de dessus les livres & les estampes, par M. Deschamps le jeune …," *Bibliothèque Physico-Économique* 1 (1791): 1, 381–3, BnF Gallica.

97 "Method of removing Spots of Grease from Books and Prints," *Monthly Magazine, & American Review* 1, no. 3 (June 1799), 236–7, HathiTrust.

98 *The New Family Receipt Book: Containing Seven Hundred Truly Valuable Receipts in Various Branches of Domestic Economy* (London: John Murray, 1810), 246–7, Google Books.

99 "Process for Removing Spots," *Philosophical Magazine*, 30–1.

100 "Method of Removing Spots of Grease from Books and Prints," *Lady's Monthly Museum* 9 (October 1802), 274–5, Internet Archive; "Method of Removing Grease-Spots from Books," *Juvenile Miscellany* 3, no. 3, 3rd series (January and February 1832), 322, Internet Archive.

101 Lois K. Kernaghan, "Almon, William James," in *Dictionary of Canadian Biography*, vol. 5 (Toronto: University of Toronto Press; Quebec: Presses de l'Université Laval, 2003–), http://www.biographi.ca/en/bio/almon_william_james_5E.html.

102 Jonathan Odell, Notebook Containing Poems by Other Writers, Various Recipes and Remedies, c. 1763–1818, Odell Family Fonds, S29B–F28(1), New Brunswick Museum Archives and Research Library.

103 Galls are growths that appear on trees. See OED *Online*, s.v. "gall, n.3."

104 Green copperas is the name for protosulphate of iron, which was used in making ink, dyeing, and tanning. Early modern people also identified blue copperas, of copper, and white copperas, of zinc. See OED *Online*, s.v. "copperas, n."

105 A gum exuded by an acacia tree found in northern Africa; it has been part of English medicine since the medieval period. See OED *Online*, s.v. "gum arabic, n."

106 A crystalline form of alum, a mineral salt. See OED *Online*, s.v. "alum, n.1" and "rock alum, n." Alum has also long been used medicinally.

107 Margaret M. Fagan, "The Uses of Insect Galls," *The American Naturalist* 52, no. 614 (1918): 155–64.

108 Diary of Thomas Wright, 1769–1773, Thomas Wright Fonds, CA PCA Accession 3241, Prince Edward Island Public Archives.

109 H.T. Holman, "Wright, Thomas," in *Dictionary of Canadian Biography*, vol. 5 (Toronto: University of Toronto Press; Quebec: Presses de l'Université Laval, 2003–), http://www.biographi.ca/en/bio/wright_thomas_5E.html; Earle Lockerby, "Thomas Wright and the Holland Survey," *The Island Magazine*, no. 66 (2009): 30–8.

110 Stephen J. Hornsby, *Surveyors of Empire: Samuel Holland, J.F.W. Des Barres, and the Making of The Atlantic Neptune* (Montreal: McGill-Queen's University Press, 2011), 63–4.

111 John Barrow, *Dictionarium Polygraphicum: or, the Whole Body of Arts Regularly Digested* (London: C. Hitch and C. Davis, 1735), 1: sig. L4, ECCO.

112 Godfrey Smith, trans., *The Laboratory, or School of Arts* (London: T. Cox, 1738), 236, ECCO.

113 True lake is transparent, made from a dye and a base such as aluminum hydrate or calcium sulphate, but lake sometimes refers to a red dye or to other less transparent pigments made with dye and other metal compounds. See Rutherford J. Gettens and George L. Stout, *Painting Materials: A Short Encyclopedia* (New York: Dover, 1966), 124.

114 Ochre comes in yellow, red, and brown. It is a pigment made of natural earth colored by iron oxide. See Gettens and Stout, *Painting*, 134.

115 A mineral salt. See note 106 for this chapter.

116 Also called blue bice, blue verditer is a copper carbonate. It was commonly used in medieval painting as a cheaper substitute for azure or ultramarine blues but has fallen out of use. See Gettens and Stout, *Painting*, 98.

117 Massicot is a yellow pigment made by gently roasting white lead. See Gettens and Stout, *Painting*, 129.

118 Also called Chinese Ink, Indian ink is also a long-standing painting material. It is made by burning pine wood or oil in a lamp and then mixing the "lamp black" or soot with fish glue and scent. See Gettens and Stout, *Painting*, 105.

119 Dead colour is the term used to describe the first preparatory layer for painting. See OED *Online*, s.v. "dead colour | dead color, n."

120 Hornsby, *Surveyors*, 55.

121 Hornsby, *Surveyors*, 1–6.

122 *The New London Toilet: or, a Compleat Collection of the Most Simple and Useful Receipts for Preserving and Improving Beauty* (London: Richardson and Urquhart, 1778), 7, ECCO.

123 For more on this, see Kathryn Woods, "The 'Fair Sex': Skin Colour, Gender and Narratives of Embodied Identity in Eighteenth Century British Non Fiction." *Journal for Eighteenth Century Studies* 40 (2017): 49 66, https://doi.org/10.1111/1754-0208.12386.

124 "Method of Making Mortar," *The Nova Scotia Magazine* 4, no. 11, November 1791, 667–8, Nova Scotia Newspapers on Microfilm, microfilm reel 8063, Nova Scotia Archives.

125 *The Annual Register, or a View of the History, Politics, and Literature, for the Year 1771* (London: J. Dodsley, 1772), 121–2, ECCO.

126 Robert Dossie, "Article III. Account of a Method of Making Mortar," in *Memoirs of Agriculture, and Other Oeconomical Arts* (London: J. Nourse, 1768), 2: 20–6, ECCO.

127 Slaked lime is lime that has been hydrated. See OED *Online*, s.v. "slake, v.1" and "unslaked, adj."

128 John P. Speweik, "The History of Masonry Mortar in America, 1720–1995," *Seventh Canadian Masonry Symposium* (McMaster University, 4–7 June 1995,

Canada Masonry Design Centre), 663–4, http://canadamasonrydesigncentre.com/download/7th_symposium/F–6.pdf; Vitruvius Pollio, *The Architecture of M. Vitruvius. Pollio*, trans. W. Newton (London: James Newton, 1791), 1: 28, ECCO.

129 Speweik, "The History of Masonry Mortar," 663–5.

130 Paul B. Jenison, "The Availability of Lime and Masonry Construction in New England: 1630–1733," *Old-Time New England* 67, no. 1–2 (1977): 21–6.

131 Randall F. Miller and Diane N. Buhay, "The Historic Limestone Quarry on Green Head Island in Saint John, New Brunswick, Canada," *Atlantic Geology* 50 (2014): 20–1, 23.

132 *A Chronology of Minerals Development in Canada* (Ottawa: Natural Resources Canada, 2001), 2, https://publications.gc.ca/collections/Collection/M39-78-2001E.pdf.

133 Dossie, "Article III," 2: 21.

134 Dossie, "Article III," 2: 20–6.

135 Dossie, "Article III," 2: 26.

136 Speweik, "The History of Masonry Mortar," 666–7.

137 Handley Chipman's Notes, vol. 2, 1776, Chipman Family Papers, MG vol. 218, microfilm reel 10154, Nova Scotia Archives.

138 "A Method of Making a Very Good Lacque," *Universal Magazine of Knowledge and Pleasure* 33, no. 231 (December 1763): 332–3, HathiTrust.

139 A deposit formed in the process of fermenting grape juice; it adhered to the side of wine casks. See OED *Online*, s.v. "tartar, n.1."

140 A mineral salt. See OED *Online*, s.v. "alum, n.1."

141 A red dye made from the insect *Coccus cacti*, found on a species of cactus that grows in Mexico. See OED *Online*, s.v. "cochineal, n."

142 "A Method," *Universal Magazine*, 332–3.

143 John and William Trueman Notebook, Trueman family notebooks, account books, diaries, and artifacts, 1750, 1771–1883, Trueman Family Fonds, 1750–1931, vol. 1, Accession 0102, Mount Allison University Archives.

144 Amelia Trueman (b.1861) was the great granddaughter of William Trueman and in 1895 married Herbert Harrington of Syndey, NS. See "Amelia P. Trueman," Atlantic Canada Genealogy Project, last modified 12 February 2021, https://www.chignecto.org/getperson.php?personID=I11100&tree=Main.

145 *England's Happiness Improved: Or, an Infallible Way to Get Riches, Encrease Plenty, and Promote Pleasure Containing the Art of Making Wine of English Grapes, and Other Fruit, Equal to That of France and Spain, &c.* (London: Roger Clavill, 1699), 79, EEBO.

146 OED *Online*, s.v. "dragon's blood, n."

147 Probably sandarac, a resin from northern Africa used in the preparation of spirit varnish. See OED *Online*, s.v. "sandarac, n."

148 Likely anatta/annotto/arnotto, a red dye obtained from the shrub (*Bixa orellana*) native to Central America; it imparted a red/orange/gold colour. See OED *Online*, s.v. "annatta | annatto, n."

149 This text is edited for readability.

150 William Salmon's *The Family Dictionary, or, Houshold Companion* (London: s.n., 1695), sig. U3–U3*v*, EEBO, defines the spirit of wine as wine that has been distilled. It is used in medicines, as well as varnish. Double rectified spirit of wine would be distilled twice to obtain a purer alcohol.

151 A resin from northern Africa, especially used in the preparation of varnish. See OED *Online*, s.v. "sandarac, n."

152 A resin in pellet-sized form. See OED *Online*, s.v. "seedlac, n."

153 Theodore Zuk Penn, "Decorative and Protective Finishes, 1750–1850: Materials, Process, and Craft," *Bulletin of the Association for Preservation Technology* 16, no. 1 (1984): 26–7.

154 Private Instructions & Hints, MacDonald Family (St Peter's) Papers, 1784, Acc. 2664, no. 154, Prince Edward Island Public Archives.

155 F.L. Pigot, "MacDonald of Glenaladale, John," in *Dictionary of Canadian Biography*, vol. 5 (Toronto: University of Toronto Press; Quebec: Presses de l'Université Laval, 2003–), http://www.biographi.ca/en/bio/macdonald_of_glenaladale_john_5E.html.

156 For more on Helen MacDonald, see J.M. Bumsted, "MacDonald of Glenaladale, Helen," in *Dictionary of Canadian Biography*, vol. 5 (Toronto: University of Toronto Press; Quebec: Presses de l'Université Laval, 2003–), http://www.biographi.ca/en/bio/macdonald_of_glenaladale_helen_5E.html.

157 Georges Arsenault, *The Island Acadians 1720–1980* (Charlottetown: Ragweed Press, 1989), 20–36.

158 Pliny the Elder, *Natural History*, trans. H. Rackham (Cambridge: Harvard University Press, 1967), 3: 579.

159 Sina Ebnesajjad, *Handbook of Adhesives and Surface Preparation: Technology, Applications and Manufacturing* (Amsterdam: William Andrew, 2011), 137–8, 160.

AFTERWORD

1 Hillary Nunn, *Recipes on the Move in Early Modern England and British North America: Domestic Medicine, Mobility, and Manuscript Culture* (Amsterdam: Amsterdam

University Press, 2025), 1. Nunn's book, which has many shared interests with this one, came out just as we were making the final edits on our book. It is regrettable that these connections could not have been explored more here.

Index

McGill-Queen's Studies in Early Canada / Avant le Canada

Series Editors / Directeurs de la collection : Allan Greer and Carolyn Podruchny

1 A Touch of Fire
Marie-André Duplessis, the Hôtel-Dieu of Quebec, and the Writing of New France
Thomas M. Carr, Jr

2 Entangling the Quebec Act
Transnational Contexts, Meanings, and Legacies in North America and the British Empire
Edited by Ollivier Hubert and François Furstenberg

3 Listening to the Fur Trade
Soundways and Music in the British North American Fur Trade, 1760–1840
Daniel Robert Laxer

4 Heirs of an Ambivalent Empire
French-Indigenous Relations and the Rise of the Métis in the Hudson Bay Watershed
Scott Berthelette

5 The Possession of Barbe Hallay
Diabolical Arts and Daily Life in Early Canada
Mairi Cowan

6 Enthusiasms and Loyalties
The Public History of Private Feelings in the Enlightenment Atlantic
Keith Shepherd Grant

7 Fashioning Acadians
Clothing in the Atlantic World, 1650–1750
Hilary Doda

8 Before Canada
Northern North America in a Connected World
Edited by Allan Greer

9 Regards sur l'âme en Nouvelle-France
Histoire des spiritualités individuelles et collectives en espace colonial
Sous la direction de Joy Palacios et Anne Régent-Susini

10 Workers of War and Empire from New France to British America, 1688–1783
Richard H. Tomczak

11 The Jesuit *Relations*
A Biography
Micah True

12 Canada in the Age of Rum
Allan Greer

13 Early Modern Maritime Recipes
Circulating Knowledge in the Atlantic World
Lyn Bennett and Edith Snook